ON BEING A SUPERPOWER

ON BEING A SUPERPOWER

SUPERPOWER

*And Not Knowing
What to Do About It*

Seymour J. Deitchman

Westview PRESS

A Member of the Perseus Books Group

Copyright © 2000 by Westview Press, A Member of the Perseus Books Group

Published in 2000 in the United States of America by Westview Press, 5500 Central Avenue, Boulder, Colorado 80301-2877, and in the United Kingdom by Westview Press, 12 Hid's Copse Road, Cumnor Hill, Oxford OX2 9JJ

Find us on the World Wide Web at www.westviewpress.com

Library of Congress Cataloging-in-Publication Data
Deitchman, Seymour J.
  On being a superpower : and not knowing what to do about it
/ Seymour J. Deitchman.
    p.   cm.
  Includes bibliographical references and index.
  ISBN 0-8133-6775-1 (hc.)
  1. National security—United States.   2. United States—Military
policy.   3. World politics—1919–   I. Title.
UA23.D4423   2000
355'.033073—dc21   99-39624
                                                                                       CIP

The paper used in this publication meets the requirements of the American National Standard for Permanence of Paper for Printed Library Materials Z39.48-1984.

10   9   8   7   6   5   4   3   2   1

To Trudy
and a half-century of duo-monologues

CONTENTS

PREFACE

If any lesson about the national security of the United States was learned during the Cold War, it is that the defense of the United States must begin at once in our own heads and far from our shores and that the conception of "national security" deals with much more than armed forces. The armed forces are an essential element of national security—they are at its core—but they can count for naught if we don't get the other parts right. Despite that lesson, the United States is going into the next millennium with great confusion about how it has to provide for its security.

We have come out of the Cold War with unparalleled ability to use our economic and military power to influence events and nations almost anywhere in the world. Argument waxes about what we want to do with that power, as well as about what kind of military we need to protect the nation in this new circumstance. We confront a host of resource-demanding social problems and more taxes than we want to pay. Now that the Cold War is over, for what purposes do we need continually modernizing armed forces with the ability to project military power anywhere in the world? How big should those armed forces be, how often do they need new weapons costing billions of dollars, and how much should we pay to equip them and hold them ready for action? Some argue that we need enough armed force to fight two major regional wars simultaneously. Others ask why we need more than a good set of missile defenses and minimal armed forces to guard our borders and give the Qadaffis and Saddam Husseins of the world their comeuppance (preferably by aerial bombing) if they transgress on our welfare. Holders of both points of view argue about whether we should use whatever forces we have in any particular international situation that arises.

The nation is thus far from united about what it will require to defend itself and how it should go about doing so. Before we can think about those questions we must have some view of the world in which the armed forces will be asked to operate. We then need some conception of what we will ask them to do in that world. To understand that, we must have something of a national portrait in mind from which to start. One need not predict events and national responses with great accuracy to explore what the nation may or may not do as time passes. One has only to be guided by past revealed behavior. Although I do not subscribe to fatalistic theories about national behavior driven by "national character," it must certainly be true that as one reads the history of our country and observes our behavior under stress one sees certain responses to the stress of threats to our security and welfare that are more likely to occur than others.

But it is also true that the nation is changing rapidly, in population and in outlook. Also, events never happen cleanly, as one would think about them in the abstract. Although national plans to meet future contingencies are never full of unanticipated, nasty developments that face us with streams of unpleasant choices, the life of a great nation is constantly beset by them. There are always loose ends that turn out to have surprising importance and impact; there are always unanticipated circumstances and conditions and unintended consequences. And these developments almost always take us by surprise, so that our responses are rarely guided by our plans. As in chaos theory, it doesn't take much variation in a culturally conditioned response to some stimulus from overseas to send the aftermath spinning in completely unexpected directions.

As legions of other writers have discovered before me in trying to deal with such circumstances, some phenomena involving people and their possible reactions to each other and to events impinging from outside their ken are more easily conveyed by fiction than by rational discourse. There are times when that is the best way to convey an atmosphere and what has created it, as well as to indicate how it might condition events. In keeping with this notion, I have started this book with two chapters of scenarios. In them, I have tried to describe the kind of world I think we and the other developed countries are creating for ourselves and for the rest of humankind. Then I have put forward some fictional descriptions of how I think the nation might react to events that the world could well present to us for action. I call this part of the book "fantasy," and I present it to challenge your imagination so that you will be more receptive to the remaining musings and propositions for the future that make up the meat of the book.

Many readers may not like the results of these intuitive leaps of imagination. *Surely*, they will think, *our great nation will know better than to get itself into the kinds of scrapes this author describes.* To me, however, it is not at all obvious that the nation will recognize or meet the serious latent and emerging national security problems that will face it in time to deal with them expeditiously and therefore with maximum effectiveness and minimum pain. The reasons for such a conclusion are the purpose of this book and will emerge in due course—painfully slowly, without a doubt.

On a personal note, I have been among the hundreds of writers and analysts who have tried to come to grips with the problems of U.S. national security over the years since World War II, having written several books on national security and the armed forces over some thirty-five years. They are listed in the Bibliography, along with many others that I have found useful in crafting this work and that have helped me think through the problems this work tackles.

This book is a "think-piece" about the future of U.S. national security. To assemble it, I have relied upon the knowledge and insights gained in more than half a century of dealing with the nitty-gritty of national security problems at all levels, from analyzing, designing, and testing parts of military systems to helping guide a major war effort and the policies of an alliance. These experiences lead me to what may be unconventional interpretations of our national security problems and our approaches to them, as well as to what I think are likely reactions to situations I have imagined and to those that one can see coming as surely as one breathes the air of a new day.

I must also note a fundamental difference between this book and most of those that I and others have written about this subject in the past, indeed, between this book and any of the reports any of us "national security experts" have written or worked on for various government advisory committees. The ultimate outcome of most of that other work has been prescriptive: The tone is, "This is what I or our group of authors, who have studied the problem very carefully and thoroughly, have found, and this is what I or we think ought to be done." This book, by contrast, is descriptive: It concentrates less (but not negligibly) on what I think *ought* to be done and more (but not exclusively) on what I think *is likely to be* done by our nation in furtherance of its national security. It also explains why. That's the story I have to tell.

Finally, some acknowledgments are in order. To single out any specific ones among all the colleagues I have interacted with over the years, in this country and in others, to accumulate the knowledge and the understanding on which this book is built would slight all of those not mentioned. I hope many if not all of them will read the book and see in it the outcomes of the hours of discussion, argument, and analysis that we undertook together about a near infinity of subjects. None of my own thoughts and beliefs about these subjects could have been developed without the sharpening and leavening effects of their inputs. Wherever you all are as you read this, and as you recognize parts of yourself in it, I also recognize and am happy to acknowledge my indebtedness to each and every one of you. And I am also happy to take ultimate and final responsibility for all opinions, rationales, and correct or incorrect statements of fact included here.

In the same vein, no book of this kind can be considered complete unless it has been read and criticized by critical minds whose ideas about the world and about my subjects may often differ from mine. I am especially grateful to my friends, Lee Hunt and Vice Admiral William Moran (USN, retired), for having made that essential contribution. Their reactions helped me sort through some of my own confusions, and they have made it a much better book than it would have been otherwise.

Finally, some parts of the book have borrowed from material I wrote for inclusion in a report of the Naval Studies Board of the National Research Council.[1] These include much of the discussion of the state of the world in Chapter 3, discussion of some of the vulnerabilities of the new armed forces in Chapter 6, and discussion of the counterstrategies those in the world who are hostile to us may use to defeat our own national security strategy in Chapter 7. Although only some of the material is used verbatim, I borrowed from it heavily before enlarging on the ideas it conveys, and I am grateful to the National Academy Press for permission to do so.

This book was completed and entered the publication process before the crisis on East Timor blew up. Comparisons with Kosovo have been drawn in discussions about possible U.S. participation in the United Nations peacekeeping force for East Timor. The discussion in Chapter 7, of strategic conditions affecting possible U.S. intervention in world events that involve our interests to greater or lesser extent, should help interpret the difference between the two cases. Both involve important humanitarian concerns. Kosovo is embedded within areas of vital U.S. interest in Europe and engages our interests directly through NATO. East Timor is thousands of miles from such areas in the Pacific and touches on our strategic interests less directly, through relations among the United States, its Pacific allies, and Indonesia. It should not be surprising that the balance among contending claims on our conscience and our resources is struck differently in the two cases. There will be more crises of this kind, with still other outcomes, as you will see on reading further.

—*S. J. Deitchman*

---

[1]"Technology for the United States Navy and Marine Corps, 2000–2035: Becoming a 21st-Century Force," Volume 1, Overview, Washington, D.C., National Academy Press, 1997.

PART ONE
FANTASY

I

SCENARIOS

History is mostly guessing; the rest is prejudice.

—*Will and Ariel Durant*

Much of the pain of conflict between nations comes from misperception based on preconception. It is hard to think outside the box, so to speak, of our set ideas about the world. That can have disastrous consequences, as many examples in twentieth-century history, both here and elsewhere, will attest.

The purpose of Chapters 1 and 2 is to come to grips with what I will call the "scenario paradox." In the Pentagon, planning for national security starts with scenarios of possible wars for which our military must prepare. It is part of our folklore that the military always prepares for the last war. That isn't true today. As we will see in Chapters 6 and 7, the armed forces are ahead of the game in preparing for the kinds of conflict that the world of the twenty-first century may offer. However, the scenarios on which defense planning is based do indeed tend to be replays of the last wars, with a strong added flavor of "if we had it to do now, this is how we would do it."

The reasons for this paradox are many, but they are rooted mainly in the tendency of a large bureaucracy to arrive at the least common denominator of opinion to which all the subordinate participating agencies can agree. There is also concern that if the planning scenarios become too imaginative they will also become highly speculative; it is hard for a government to commit billions of dollars to highly speculative ventures. Also, the foreign policy agencies of the bureaucracy tend to be afraid to think officially about the more offbeat and unpleasant kinds of developments for fear that the divulgence of the products of their thinking might bring about the unpleasantness they fear.[1] So we settle for that least common denominator in our planning activities. The risks in doing that are that we will not be prepared to deal with real events when they happen. The only way to defend against those risks is to build armed forces that are adaptable and versatile enough to meet the real events. To do that, however, we have to understand what those events might be, and to do *that* we have to stretch our imaginations. My observation after decades in the defense planning business is that the bureaucracy doesn't do that very well.

Thus, Chapters 1 and 2 try to set the stage for serious discussion of all the factors that may affect our national security by reviewing some of the kinds of troubles the country might face. These can come about because we have unwise policies. They can also surface when other countries see opportunities for adventures beyond their borders that they think will be unopposed and leave them better off than before. We saw such behavior in the preludes to the Japanese attacks on Southeast Asia and the United States during World War II, as well as in Saddam Hussein's 1990 attack on Kuwait before the Gulf War. Countries can also simply feel frustrated at an inability to fulfill some great national imperative and therefore reach for an opportunity to do so when they think the time and circumstances are right, like Russia trying to dominate Afghanistan as a step toward building access to the Indian Ocean and the ambitions of mainland China to bring an errant Taiwan into the fold.

These kinds of brawls may emerge from purely national ambitions on the part of the aggressing countries. It is also fashionable for political opposition in the United States to seek someone in this country to blame for their occurrence. Still, without casting any blame, it must be obvious that it takes two to make a bargain, two to develop an opportunity for conflict. In 1941, Japan thought that we were preoccupied with Germany at the same time that we were starting to threaten their own security and military ambitions in China with our embargoes on oil and the like. Their rulers saw both an opportunity and a need to capture resources to support their ambitions in China and elsewhere. In 1979 Russia thought they saw an opportunity to establish control of the Afghan government; they evidently thought we wouldn't be able to do anything much if they invaded a landlocked country on their border in Central Asia. In 1990 Saddam Hussein had reason to believe that we wouldn't oppose his invasion of Kuwait. Our actions in allowing him to threaten the freedom of the seas in the Persian Gulf when Iraqi forces attacked "large naval targets"—tankers—

---

[1]As one example, I was in the position, in the 1960s, of offering Defense Department cooperation and funding to the State Department to start looking ahead into the problems that the developing rebellions against Portuguese colonial rule in Angola and Mozambique would pose for us and to start thinking about how we would deal with such problems. The reaction by the State Department was that if it even became known that we were studying that problem, that would be an international disaster. Those at State preferred to wing it.

during Saddam's war with Iran, and the ambiguity of the message on Kuwait delivered by the Bush administration, could have reinforced him in such beliefs. China has given every indication that they believe we do not take the depth of their feeling about Taiwan seriously enough. Indeed, the chorus of the remaining exponents of the post–World War II "China lobby" about recognizing and protecting an independent Taiwan must give them reason to think so.

We can bring home the implications of such unintended interactions by thinking about some scenarios—visualizations of events that *could* occur—describing how the interactions may develop, say, a decade or two from now. In these scenarios, we will set the stage for conflict and describe its early stages; however, like playwrights who are better at setting up the situation in the first act than they are at resolving it in the third, we won't really be able to bring the conflicts to a satisfying close. That step will be left as an exercise for the reader, because when you learn how the situation develops you will arrive at your own preferred way of resolving it. And who knows how it would be resolved in real life; these are, after all, "only" mind games.

Scenarios are used all the time by military and Defense Department planners to test ideas about force requirements and the shape and equipment of military organizations. The scenarios used for such purposes tend to be "neat" and encapsulated, expressing closed situations particular to the conflict being explored in order to make them easier to work through. The problem is that actual events are never so well behaved; real-world scenarios tend to be messy and contain many loose strands that nobody knows how to tie together. We saw this in Korea, in Vietnam, in the aftermath of the Gulf War, in Somalia, Bosnia, and Kosovo. Here we will try to invent a few of the messy scenarios. However, be alert to the possibility that the "realistic" scenarios presented in Chapters 1 and 2 may appear passé or even ridiculously wrong by the time you read this. Their only purpose is to alert you to the *kinds* of events that can happen unexpectedly to a country not on the alert for the unexpected, especially the kinds of things that can go wrong because of what *others* do (not usually accounted for in our planning scenarios). Afterward, I will try to show that even if they are far wide of the mark they can be used to reinforce some important points about planning for U.S. national security.

THE STATE OF THE WORLD

In the real world, conflicts don't just appear full-blown. They start from some state of the world that sets them up and makes their occurrence more or less likely. For this purpose, we'll therefore postulate that today's geopolitical situation continues, with some adverse changes for U.S. security, into the 2010–2020 decade. That may not remain true next week, let alone by the time you read this, but it gives some starting conditions for portraying the conflict scenarios. In fact the scenarios wouldn't change much if the state of the world predicted below is off the mark.

What will the United States be like then? We'll describe it in great detail later. For the time being, let's imagine it is much as we see it today: with a strong economy containing weak elements, such as trade deficits scattered around the world; with a population turning inward to their own pursuits and not much interested in the rest of the world except for direct threats to our trade, our resources, our self-image, or to the homelands of one of our major ethnic minorities, disconnected from world events, perhaps, except for some events they can identify with personally, such as the death of Princess Diana; with politics that is faction-ridden with many modern issues that are difficult to face, such as monopoly control of communications, control of exotic emissions into the environment, and the medical care and dying of an aging population. As it stands today, national decisionmaking remains difficult in the absence of some urgent drivers that focus the national mind. Perhaps the scenarios we are about to describe will do that.

We have our first female president. To everyone's wonder, and to the disappointment of some, her administration and actions in office are not much different from those of her male predecessors. Actions and reactions are driven as much by needs and events as by personalities, and, as we learned from Golda Meir, Indira Ghandi, and Margaret Thatcher, any woman tough enough to fight her way to the top in national politics will not behave, just because of her gender, too differently from any man.

On the international scene, we postulate that NATO still exists. It has been enlarged to include Central Europe and Sweden, but not as much as many would-be entrants had hoped. It has also bifurcated into distinct North American and European branches, with loosened political and military ties both within the European branch and across the Atlantic. The UN has been gradually weakened by a succession of post–Cold War crises. That, plus what we find to be a distinctly anti-American bias in its outlook, has essentially removed the UN from our horizon as a first resort when new crises arise. Thus, the United States is much more prone to take unilateral military actions in pursuit of its own interests than it was during the Cold War. The Yugoslavia issues are subject to severe periodic flare-ups that cause arguments within NATO and continuing tensions between the United States and Russia. Russia quietly supports the Greater Serbia idea, because if that were established it would give them a friendly country providing secure access to the Mediterranean from overland, but they back away from it whenever NATO challenges them strongly. Instead, an atmosphere of hostility on the Russian side and of resentment on the American side has grown.

Russia remains essentially separated from the rest of Europe, as it has been throughout its history. It remains ineffectual. It still tries to struggle out of its economic collapse and reestablish relations with the former Soviet countries, with indifferent success in a system that mixes persisting communist command economy ideas with a market economy that is dominated by robber barons. The Anti-Ballistic Missile (ABM) Treaty and Strategic Arms Reduction Treaties (START) are essentially dormant in the political dynamics of the time. Neither the United States nor Russia have wished to make the expenditures to change the strategic offense or defense weapons situation by very much, but the United States keeps trying to break out of the ABM Treaty by building a comprehensive national missile defense. The continuing technological difficulties in making such a system work have foiled success, however.

The U.S. nonproliferation regime for weapons of mass destruction is faltering. Full nonproliferation treaty implementation is still held up by Israel and the Arab states, as well as by India and Pakistan. Following the 1998 Indian and Pakistani nuclear weapon tests, some additional countries—Iraq, Iran, and North Korea among them—are believed to have acquired nuclear weapons, although they haven't tested any. Chemical and biological weapons are believed to be held by all the latter countries, as well as by Algeria, Libya, and others. Chemical and biological weapons are available to terrorist groups, but nuclear weapons are still not out on the economy.

Relations with Japan have been reinforced by the United States in an effort to sustain Japan's orientation away from acquisition of nuclear weapons. The relationship continues to be stressed periodically by economic disputes; we still have bases there, though much reduced. The Koreas are not unified; North Korea has held on to life, whereas South Korea has recovered from the near economic collapse of the mid-1990s and is continuing its economic development, with some ups and downs. Military tensions on the peninsula have continued but have not led to more than occasional incidents. A U.S. Army division, shrunken in size as U.S. defense budgets have declined, is still deployed north of Seoul, and a tactical fighter wing is deployed at airfields in central South Korea.

China's industrial economy is fully modern, supported by an archaic agricultural base that is just now starting to modernize. As a whole, the Pacific Rim economies, recovered from the economic trauma of the 1990s and with some safeguards in place against similar collapses (but with other possibilities making the rest of the world nervous), are booming again. In combination the Pacific Rim countries, including Japan and China, are outstripping the United States and Europe economically, and they are beginning to show a level of integration that transcends national boundaries. China's economy is now leveling off to modest growth, and Japan and China are economic rivals for access to and control of the remainder of the Pacific Rim economies.

Turkey's resentment at lack of U.S. support in its arguments with Europe and with Greece over Cyprus, and Turkey's vicious response to the perpetual Kurdish war of independence, have cooled U.S.-Turkey relations. Governments in most of North Africa and the Middle East are generally hostile to the West, under the influence of their more radical elements. Israel is hanging on in a loose, tacit alliance with Jordan. The Palestinians have declared victory by saying they have a state, but Israel has effectively kept the state from coalescing, with continuing costs in casualties for both sides. Iran keeps stirring the conflict by arming Hezbollah and Hamas; the conflict suits its design to spread through and eventually dominate the Middle East. Turkey is nominally still in NATO and loosely tied to the European Union, but not as a full member. The United States is essentially out of Turkey militarily, Iraq is back in charge of its whole country, and the only U.S. footholds in the Middle East are on the Arabian Peninsula, under political conditions like today's, and in the Israel-Jordan complex, which doesn't help much strategically. Iraq has rebuilt its armed forces.

The United States is much more dependent on Middle East oil, but Europe is now benefiting from a modernizing Caspian supply source. Japan still depends heavily on the Middle East for oil. Oil exports from that area are starting to level off; the world economy is looking to Russian oil and China's new fields in the Spratlys and on the mainland to fill the gap. However, China is hoarding its new oil for internal use and is competing with the West for Central Asia's oil. The United States still has a modest military presence in Saudi Arabia (tactical fighter squadrons at two bases, and a small Army reception force) and a naval presence in Bahrain and Abu Dhabi. The House of Saud still rules Saudi Arabia, nervously looking north.

U.S. trade with Latin America burgeoned after the creation of the Western Hemisphere Common Market. In the Caribbean, Castro has gone, but a communist military dictatorship has succeeded him, so that U.S. relationships with Cuba have not changed appreciably. Internal politics still keep the United States at odds with the world about trade with Cuba, despite a body of U.S. opinion saying the regime would collapse if the United States would simply turn loose the trade demons. Panama has taken over the Panama Canal, operating it successfully with contracted U.S. help. In the past few years, a combination of uneventful and successful operation of the canal by the Canal Company that was constituted in 1999 upon the U.S. withdrawal from Panama, questioning by Congress about the value and cost of the remnant U.S. military presence there, and increasing coolness toward it by the current Panamanian government has led to the withdrawal of U.S. troops that had remained to help protect the canal. The drug cartels based in Colombia continue to operate, and the United States continues to struggle with them.

Haiti has again gone off the world screen, whereas Africa south of the Sahara continues in world and U.S. headlines but does not affect world politics or the world economy appreciably beyond its current effects in the resource markets and the continuing demands for humanitarian help. The world has tired of intervening in intertribal quarrels, and after several severe flare-ups with many deaths such quarrels have subsided as the parties have exhausted themselves.

Also stressing the world, mainly in countries in Europe and Africa but occasionally the United States itself, are periodic flows of refugees from the incessant conflicts in Africa and along the European periphery. These are not so easily ignored, and the United States as well as the countries directly affected are continually asked for humanitarian assistance. Repatriating refugees remains an essentially unsolved problem, however, and the inability to do so creates continuing conflicts within host countries.

Advanced armaments have spread worldwide. In particular, Russia has tried to rebuild its forces after the Chechnya disaster, with uncertain success. China has completely modernized its forces with Russian aircraft and armor, advanced air defenses, modern submarines, and extensive tactical missile holdings. It has a large naval force capable of making amphibious landings supported by land-based aviation, cruisers, and destroyers, as well as the beginnings of a carrier force based on copies of purchased Russian carriers and related aviation technology. China's successful poaching of U.S. warhead technology allowed it to accelerate its quest for nuclear parity with the United States. Iran has built modern theater ballistic missile and air defense forces, and has purchased several old Backfire bombers with complements of stand-off supersonic antiship missiles from the Russians. It has several modern conventional submarines and fast patrol boats with advanced antiship cruise missiles, and it has displayed a space launch capability; otherwise Iran remains much as it is today. Clandestinely supported terrorism is still Iran's favored strategic weapon system, but this has become buried more deeply as Iran has tried to open more to the rest of the world. Japan has kept up in military and space technology but keeps small forces; it exercises sovereignty-related activity over waters to about 1,000 miles out from its shores while relying on the United States for protection of its line of oil supplies and its overall security vis-à-vis China and Russia. The Republic of Korea's (ROK) relationship to all the others is much as it is today, with allowance for an appropriate level of force modernization. They have a modern army and air force and air defenses, but we have kept them from building a ballistic missile force.

The entire world has a modern computer- and space-based information and communications infrastructure. This is simply the culmination of today's trends; more so than any other development, it serves to tie together the world's economies and cultures. A most worrisome parallel development is the availability, to nations and cyberterrorists alike, of information warfare capabilities permitting attacks against heavily computerized financial, transportation, and social support systems. An unwelcome by-product is the ability of lawless groups like the world's Mafias and the drug cartels to use the information infrastructure both to further and to mask their activities while the encryption genie, gradually emerging from the bottle the United States vainly tried to keep it in, makes it increasingly harder to track them or to anticipate where their attentions will turn next.

Although there have been many skirmishes, such as the punishing U.S. attack on Iraq at the end of 1998 and the NATO attack on Serbia intended to change the latter's Kosovo policy, there has been no major war involving the industrial powers (at least at the level of the Gulf War or the Korean War of the 1950s). Consequently, the U.S. defense budget by 2015 has been allowed to decline to less than $200 billion— the equivalent of about $130 billion today, even at today's low rates of inflation. That represents roughly half the defense budget at the turn of the century. We have spent all new procurement money on a few favorite tactical aircraft programs of the Services, while the number of Army divisions, Air Force tactical aircraft squadrons, Navy carrier battle groups, and Marine divisions has shrunk by about a third. Despite valiant efforts on the part of Service leaders, training and readiness have declined to the point where only a few units are ready for fast response to crises that need military input.

With this background, we can now think about some unpleasant possible developments in international conflicts on the world scene. Think about these scenarios unfolding in phases, with timing uncertain except for the overall duration that such events are estimated to require for their full development.

A FAR EAST SCENARIO

This scenario takes place over a six-week period.

Phase 1: Preliminaries

Taiwan has built strong trade relations with the rest of the world while it exists in a shadowy state: not recognized as a nation yet an economic power to be reckoned with. It balks under increasing mainland interventions in its internal politics and relations with other nations, and in desperation declares its independence. China declares that unacceptable and peremptorily orders Taiwan to retract, on pain of dire consequences. China initiates a partial mobilization, especially massing forces along the coast facing Taiwan, and it warns other nations to keep out of this internal Chinese quarrel.

U.S. trade with Taiwan has been building, and there have been many cultural exchanges and cross-visits among politicians of both countries. China has repeatedly

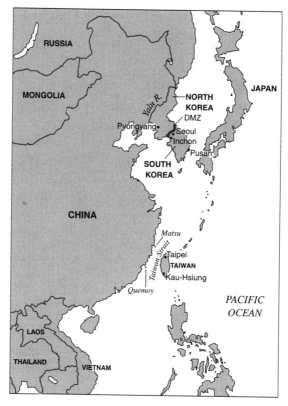

Far East

objected to the political exchanges even while benefiting from the reinvestment of Taiwanese profits from the U.S. trade. The dance of strained and relaxed relations between China and the United States has, as a consequence, continued indefinitely, always fueled by the desire to sustain now-extensive economic relationships. But U.S. conservatives, who insist on protecting Taiwan from outright Chinese attack, have made common cause with liberals who are still concerned about China's refusal to accept American ideals of human rights and democracy.

The two groups form a powerful political bloc that indicates to the president that they will not countenance a Chinese conquest of Taiwan. Under pressure from both political directions, the president and Congress declare that Taiwan is a friendly democratic country to which we extend U.S. protection. If the Taiwanese freely express their wish to become an integral part of China under direct Chinese government control, we will respect that, but we will protect them against forcible reunification with the mainland. To back up this promise, the president orders reinforcements to the U.S. 7th Fleet and orders the fleet to cover the Taiwan Strait to help the island's overmatched forces stop a Chinese invasion.

Phase 2: The United States Gets Into the Fight

China begins by attacking Quemoy and Matsu and launching conventionally armed ballistic missiles with runway-breaking submunitions against airfields to immobilize the Taiwanese air force; it starts loading the invasion force. Quemoy and Matsu are two small islands just off the Chinese coast in the Taiwan Strait. They figured strongly in an earlier standoff over a possible Chinese invasion of Taiwan, when President Dwight Eisenhower was under pressure, which he resisted, to retaliate against bombardment of the islands by the Chinese army after the communist conquest of mainland China. One result of that contretemps, however, was a pledge to protect Taiwan from invasion by the Communist Chinese. That set-to went no further. Since that time, the islands have been fortified by the Taiwanese armed forces, and the mainland Chinese cannot afford to leave them as a potential source of attack in the rear of their invasion force. They also don't want to risk counterattack by the fairly powerful, U.S.-supported Taiwanese air force.

The Chinese missiles do enough damage to close the airfields, despite the American antimissile defenses with the fleet; as always, no system works quite as well in battle as it did on the test range. Simultaneously with these attacks, China again warns the United States to keep out of the quarrel, and it warns Japan it will not be considered a neutral if the United States uses Japanese bases to intervene. The Japanese quietly inform the United States that they have no desire to get into this quarrel and that they would prefer we use other bases for what is obviously planned as a military intervention in the growing crisis. The United States must therefore mount its response from its bases in Korea and Guam, meaning a longer logistic support line to be protected, which in turn would result in longer response times and fewer forces on the spot.

While all this is developing, Taiwan's civilian information infrastructure begins to display erratic behavior: Banks are finding files erased or distorted, broadcasts are being jammed, computerized shipping manifestos and airline reservation files are disappearing, and individual Taiwanese in all walks of life are finding it difficult to conduct their usual business activities on the worldwide web. Worse still, their military command, control, and communications (C3) system begins to fall apart under information warfare attack that exploits obvious vulnerabilities. They are finding it difficult to sustain uninterrupted communications among ground, naval, and air defense units. Overseas connections, including those to U.S. military forces, become erratic. It is therefore difficult to coordinate U.S. policy with Taiwanese military and civilian activities. Even U.S. communications with its representatives on the island are becoming difficult to sustain, from a combination of jamming and interruption by spurious messages.

In the face of these attacks, the president sends a team of "information warriors" to help fight off China's information warfare attacks. They will have to fly to the fleet and land from there by helicopter, however, the airfields being at least temporarily unusable. She further beefs up the forces en route to Taiwan, borrowing heavily from those in and around Korea and in the Arabian Sea. She orders the fleet to provide air cover to Taiwan and to stop any attempted invasion of the main island by interdicting Chinese amphibious forces after they launch their attack. On advice of her Pacific commander, however, she orders U.S. forces to stay out of the Quemoy-Matsu fight, because that is a sideshow that will draw off forces needed for the main engagement. That is immediately branded a needless and politically unacceptable tactical retreat by the conservatives who have been pushing for intervention. Worse still, in their view, she issues specific orders, leaked instantly to the media, that there will be no physical attacks on or tactical overflights of the Chinese mainland.

There is ample precedent for this order in President Truman's refusal to let General Douglas MacArthur widen the Korean War by attacking China across the Yalu River, which forms the Korean border with China. In the current case, the president also has to consider that China now possesses nuclear weapons and the missiles to deliver them against the U.S. mainland in retaliation for an attack on mainland China. The Joint Chiefs of Staff (JCS) are convinced that the Chinese will stand down if their invasion force is disrupted and severely damaged by conventional air attacks before it embarks; they advise the president to tough it out. Although they give her their considered opinion that China won't risk massive nuclear retaliation by attacking the U.S. mainland, they cannot guarantee that. The president, supported by her civilian national security advisers and her Cabinet, is beginning to realize that the Chinese determination to hold Taiwan surpasses rational balancing of alternatives; it is at the level of religion. She concludes that saving Taiwan is not worth the risk of a nuclear attack on even one U.S. city and so she issues her order, which will not be rescinded through the entire engagement. (She knows that this may cost her reelection to the presidency, downstream, but that is set aside as something she will deal with later, after the specific events off the Chinese coast are played out.)

Phase 3: It Gets Worse

The North Korean military has been restless under restraints that leader Kim Jong Il has put in place regarding an attack on the South. They are still smarting under the humiliation of having the South and the U.S. imperialists bail their country out of near-famine, and they have not fully accepted Kim as the absolute ruler his father, Kim Il Sung, was. Moreover, the agreements to build new nuclear reactors for them have not yet been fully implemented, and as far as they can see, they probably never will be. They have managed to move ahead with their nuclear weapon program despite inspections and the self-imposed constraints the civilians accepted against their advice. They have been spoiling for a fight, and they see this as a good time to further their ends, since the United States is occupied with China and has even been drawing naval forces away from Korea.

Sporadic fighting flares up along and on the South's side of the DMZ, the demilitarized zone between the two Koreas, as accusations fly back and forth. The North infiltrates commandos through tunnels, which they have driven under the DMZ over the decades, to disrupt the South and prepare the way for invasion.

The Republic of Korea, confident and powerful, views the armed forces of the North as a hollow force, larger than the South's but ill-trained and ill-fed. It decides that now is as good a time as any to unify Korea on its own terms and end the dangers from the North once and for all. The ROK initiates an attack north on both ends of the DMZ. On the western end, they pass through U.S. forces, who are caught in the flow. Although the U.S. and South Korean forces are still technically part of the UN Command remaining from Korean War days, no other countries are represented any longer. It is essentially a U.S. show. With China able to exercise a veto over any action by the UN Security Council, the president decides to keep the UN out of the fight rather than risk adverse rulings that opponents of the war at home can seize upon for political reasons.

The U.S. forces avoid joining the South Korean attack while awaiting orders from Washington, but they make defensive preparations against the possibility of a North Korean counterattack against them. North Korea launches conventional ballistic missile attacks on South Korean cities and the airfields that would support air operations against the North's forces, and they warn Japan that they will use those missiles to attack U.S. bases there if the United States joins the ROK attack. They hint broadly, in their strident propaganda broadcasts, that they have nuclear warheads for their missiles and are not afraid to use them if driven to it.

The president tries to get the ROK to call off the attack, but no response is forthcoming. She doesn't want two wars on her hands (under tough budget constraints, the United States had long since abandoned the strategy of preparing enough armed forces to fight two major regional wars simultaneously) and concludes that the ROK is the aggressor this time. She orders U.S. forces to disengage and to move south from the battle front. She orders the evacuation of U.S. forces from the peninsula but sustains their authority for defending themselves if attacked—by anyone! Many members of Congress are furious over this, considering that the North Korean forays across the border were the beginning of aggression and viewing the ordered withdrawal as a betrayal of our alliance. Others support it, however, so that Congress dissolves into a well of acrimony, without effect on the developing conflict.

Phase 4: The Tar Baby

China mines Taipei, Tainan, and Kau-Hsiung, the three major harbors of Taiwan island, and launches its invasion force. U.S. naval aviation engages that force, with the loss of several aircraft but imposing substantial losses of embarked Chinese ground troops. Japan opts out and publicly asks the United States not to use bases there for these fights. No other Pacific Rim nation offers to get involved; the UN is at an impasse, since either China or the United States will veto the other's competing resolutions calling for cessation of hostilities under terms favorable to its side.

Meantime, ROK forces break through and start their march north to Pyongyang. China threatens to join in the missile attack on the ROK if they don't desist. A Chinese submarine lands a torpedo on one of the U.S. carriers that has been leading the attack on the invasion force; there are many casualties, and the carrier develops a serious list. It is damaged enough to be unable to launch aircraft, although it is in no danger of sinking. The carrier retires from action, taking with it a large fraction of the aircraft that were attacking the invasion force.

There are still no secure land bases from which the U.S. Air Force can launch its tactical aviation, although the bomber force has been contributing to the fight from bases in the United States, Guam, and Diego Garcia. However, the finely tuned targeting system that helps the bombers attack the moving amphibious targets is disrupted by Chinese electronic warfare, which reduces the bombers' effectiveness markedly. Then, a lucky shot at extreme range by an SA-10 SAM that was sold to the Chinese by the Russians downs a U.S. JSTARS E-8 radar plane (the Joint Surveillance and Target Attack Radar System) that was watching movement of the invasion forces on land from over the Taiwan Strait and helping with the targeting when those forces embarked and went to sea. Unable to anticipate the movement of invasion forces over the Taiwan Strait far enough in advance for their several-hour strike flights, and with disrupted communications making the transmittal of targeting information by the Navy unreliable when they reach the Taiwan area, the bombers are forced to stand down, further reducing the attack on the invaders.

Meantime, Chinese and North Korean agitation foments riots against U.S. forces in South Korea; they are attacked by civilians for not supporting the ROK's war against the North and for running away, and they are attacked by students with communist sympathies for being there in the first place. The combination of civil disorder and roads clogged with South Korean army units moving north interferes with the U.S. force movement south to Pusan for evacuation. They reach Pusan in small units a few at a time, stretching out the loading time for evacuation and making them targets for North Korean and Chinese missiles in their encampment areas. There is a huge irony in their preparing to evacuate Korea through Pusan: The Pusan perimeter was the site of the final and successful stand of the U.S. Army in 1950, before it broke out to pursue the North Korean invaders after MacArthur's brilliant flanking landing at Inchon.

The president orders all available naval forces to resist the Chinese attack. She sends Army combat engineers and advanced Patriot air and missile defense units to Taiwan to repair and keep the airfields open; they, too, will have to be landed from Navy amphibious ships and move overland to their work and combat positions, since none of the airfields is usable as yet. She orders the U.S. Air Force Combat Command to deploy to Taiwan whenever runway and defense conditions permit. Despite the precarious state of the anti-invasion effort, she refuses to lift her orders against striking the mainland. She seeks Japanese permission to use our bases there to land the forces evacuated from Korea, giving assurances that the bases will not be used for counterattacks, but China and North Korea scare the Japanese off again. The Joint Chiefs decide to send the evacuated forces to Australia (they have permission) and Guam. The president denies their request to send Army combat troops into Taiwan, but she orders the Navy to clear mines from the harbors and to build and protect a temporary logistic port and airfield on Taiwan's east coast, the opposite coast of the island from the invasion.

The Marines make a landing at the point designated for the port and set up a perimeter to protect the Sea-Bees (Navy Construction Battalions) that will start the building. Missile defense is to be provided by the fleet. The United States marshals surface and air reserve lift forces to assist and tries to charter additional sealift, but with no good multinational coalition in place that proves hard to do. All available U.S. Navy combat aircraft (there are now three carriers in the area) are fully engaged in opposing several Chinese attempts to establish beachheads on Taiwan's western coast, providing air cover to the Taiwanese ground forces. Army and national intelligence agency units are desperately trying to reestablish the combined U.S.-Taiwan command, control, and communications system in the face of the Chinese counter-C3 campaign. One of the carriers is detailed to cover the evacuation from Pusan, further weakening the resistance to the invasion. That has now established several footholds, and it is clear that although determined resistance can slow them there will be no stopping the invasion forces from moving across the island unless their base of support on the mainland can be put under heavy attack.

At this point, the domestic scene in the United States is one of turmoil and recrimination. The president issues an order declaring a national emergency and orders national guard troops to active duty. She orders Army units to be ready to move. She prepares orders imposing price ceilings to prevent profiteering, and she thinks about a general mobilization.

Then, she sits back and contemplates her position. She is on the path to committing the nation to a major war with China. For China, this is a deeply felt quarrel with an errant province that has avoided Chinese control for more than a century. For the United States, it is peripheral to U.S. interests except on a critical matter of principle. All her instincts, and much of her military advice, tell her there is no winning that war in fighting on the Chinese mainland. She has the option of attacking the Chinese mainland base of the invasion from the air, which could escalate to destroying part or all of China with a nuclear missile attack, thereby risking a rain of destruction on the United States. Would China back down in the face of that threat? Current indications are not encouraging.

The carefully constructed commercial and other civil engagements with China, which indeed have been gradually moving China toward a more democratic government, as well as our relations with Japan and Korea, are in a shambles. Yet to back down now, when a carefully nurtured, friendly democracy on Taiwan is in deep trouble, would indicate to the world that the United States either could not or would not defend its friends in a crisis of survival. Yet the purity of this mandate is tainted by the complicated and confusing action in Korea and all the arguments over that predicament. The clamors both for and against widening the war are reaching a crescendo pitch at home.

With no satisfactory chance for a "win" in sight short of a national commitment to all-out war with China—and that one highly problematic—she convenes the National Security Council to consider whether to follow that commitment to its logical conclusion or whether some means can be devised to cut our losses. As part of that, she must assess the short- and long-term prospects for picking up the pieces afterward. . . .

A MIDDLE EAST SCENARIO

This scenario takes place over a thirty-day period.

Phase 1: A Long-Term Strategy Under Fire

Since the Roosevelt administration in World War II, even earlier, the United States has maintained friendly relations with the Saudi royal house on the Arabian Penin-

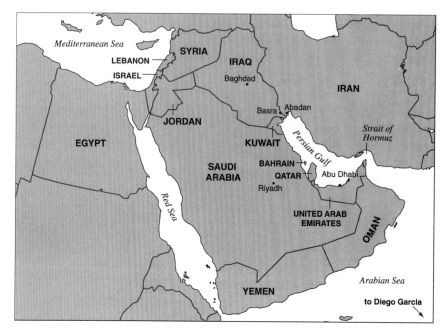

Middle East

sula. But they, as the keepers of Mecca, the holiest shrine of Islam, and the other countries (Bahrain, Qatar, and the United Arab Emirates) on the southern shore of the Persian Gulf (or the Arabian Gulf, as it has started to be called in this country since the Gulf War of 1991) have been under repeated attack by Islamist forces that have swept all of North Africa and the rest of the Middle East. Especially, Saudi support given to the United States in the ongoing conflict with Iraq has angered the more radical fundamentalists. The Saudi rulers have staved off attacks by governing in something close to a strictly Islamist fashion, but this has not fully satisfied the opposition. The United States has additional major sources of oil, in Nigeria, Venezuela, and Mexico, but we guard the Saudi oil fields as a key source. They provide oil to us and Japan and act as a reserve for us and our allies.

Now, the fundamentalists stage a half-successful coup against the House of Saud. The Saudi military splits, one faction supporting the coup, the other opposing it. They fight, inconclusively. The rebels insist that the United States depart Saudi soil; the loyalists don't dare to call publicly for U.S. help, but privately they ask the United States to stay. Iran weighs in on the side of the rebels, offers them help, and inveighs against the U.S. presence in "their" Gulf. Iraq again acts threateningly toward Kuwait and the southern shore of the gulf beyond, and they advise

Iran to stay out of their sphere. Sporadic fires are started by rebel saboteurs in the Saudi oil fields, and pipeline flows to ports on the gulf are shut off intermittently. Europe tries to calm the rising tension, warning the United States not to count on European help in any military intervention. Japan pleads for calm and privately expresses concern about interruption of its oil supply. Both Europe and Japan declare that their use of Saudi and United Arab Emirate oil is purely commercial and does not depend on political support of either faction; they can come to terms with any regime that appears. Indeed, secretly, they are already seeking deals with the rebels.

The president orders the strengthening of U.S. forces in the area; she sends a squadron of Air Force F-22s, two squadrons of strike fighters, and a brigade of the 82nd Airborne Division to bases in the Saudi interior. She orders one more Army brigade from the United States to land there, with heavy weapons units—tanks, artillery, and antiaircraft protection—that can be transported by air, to reinforce the 82nd Airborne. Finally, she gives her area commander, the Commander in Chief (CINC) of the U.S. Central Command, the freedom to take whatever measures are needed to protect the arrivals and their access to the sea and to guard against interruption of the oil flow from the region. The Navy builds up a strike force of two carriers and two guided-missile cruisers in the Arabian Sea, with several destroyers and two attack submarines in support. The naval force includes a Marine Amphibious Ready Group, which has three amphibious warfare carriers, several supporting ships, and a brigade-sized Marine Expeditionary Force afloat, at a high state of readiness. The president also secretly orders preparation of plans to evacuate all U.S. forces from the Arabian Peninsula. Thus, both the intervention and the disengagement options are being held open.

Phase 2: Digging Deeper

The Saudi internal conflict continues unresolved, accompanied by several attempted terrorist-style attacks against the U.S. presence in Saudi Arabia and naval bases in Bahrain and Abu Dhabi. With good intelligence, aided by the Saudi military loyalists, all these attacks are deflected with relatively minor damage. Iraq builds up forces along the Kuwaiti border and also along its border with Iran from Baghdad to Basra, and Iran counters with a buildup of its own, facing them and threatening Iraq's northern oil fields. Iran mines the Strait of Hormuz at the entrance to the gulf, as well as the United Arab Emirate and Bahraini ports. Building up forces along the shores of the strait, Iran declares it closed. It has left a channel through the minefield, which it will disclose if the United States acts to evacuate forces from the Arabian Peninsula and leave Islam to resolve its own affairs.

The United States at this point is divided. One side calls for building up our other oil and energy alternatives, with a policy of U.S. noninvolvement in highly incendiary Middle East affairs; the other side calls for preserving the world's oil supply and freedom of the seas on principle. Congress decides (by a narrow majority that could easily shift) that prospective U.S. casualties are not a price worth paying for oil, especially if the Saudis don't want us there and our allies won't support us in military action. With a sense-of-the-Congress resolution, it signals its refusal to support military action in the Persian Gulf area if that would mean intervening in a civil war.

The president is on the verge of ordering evacuation of all U.S. forces from the area, but she hesitates. There are matters of important principle involved here, and her military advisers, supported by many in Congress and the public, indicate that if the United States backs down in the face of military pressure much of our strategy of nearly three centuries' standing—to support freedom of the seas and trade—will go down the drain. They also argue that U.S. credibility as a guarantor of the peace and guardian of our own and allied vital interests will suffer irreparable damage, effectively taking the United States out of its major role in world affairs. It is up to the United States, they argue, to exercise leadership in the face of the allies' willingness to sacrifice principle for uncertain economic gains. If we follow them, we will have allowed the fundamentalist regimes to call the tune on energy prices and therefore the welfare of all our economies.

China is standing on the sidelines for this game. Through the years they have secured their oil supply from fields in Central Asia, and they don't need to become involved here. Indeed, should the United States, Europe, and Japan lose—by miscalculating the monetary and political prices the fundamentalists would charge for oil they came to control or by becoming embroiled in a Middle East war—China could benefit greatly, both strategically and economically. The United States quietly starts economic moves in world oil markets to secure alternative U.S. supplies, and Congress debates whether to start an alternative fuels program. Still the president hesitates: She is keeping all options open while preparing to defend our interests with military force as soon as she hears her key constituencies articulate a clear definition of what they think those interests really are.

Thus, the U.S. force buildup continues. The president orders the Navy to clear the strait and the Emirate and Bahrain harbors of mines, these being matters of freedom of the seas, and she publicly gives her area CINC permission to attack the Iranian side of the strait if Iran opens fire first on the minesweeping forces. Naval plans include a Marine landing on that shore to ensure destruction of gunboat and destroyer harbors and missile emplacements that would threaten minesweeping and shipping in the strait, if necessary. The president opens negotiations with Europe,

Japan, and Russia about strategy to follow in the area to allow the Saudis to settle their own affairs, keep intervention out, and ensure continuing flows of essential oil or arrange alternatives. The United States undertakes a strong information campaign to support this strategy and also to help Saudi loyalists prevail. World oil prices have soared, bringing the economies of Europe and Japan to the brink of major recession and threatening to drag the United States down with them. The president opens the Strategic Petroleum Reserve for limited domestic addition to disrupted supplies. Congress continues to debate the desirable extent of U.S. involvement and energy alternatives, yet nothing is decided. The president is coming under increasing criticism for that, but neither the media nor Congress nor the opinion polls show any clear popular direction for decision. It is up to the president to take the initiative, but she still hesitates, and events will decide for her.

Phase 3: Our Allies Drop Out

With help from Iran, the Saudi rebellion moves in favor of the rebels. The unrest spills over into Bahrain, Qatar, and the Emirates, where mobs surround U.S. installations and hamper their free operation. Local forces cannot control them, and U.S. attempts to disperse the mobs and defend U.S. citizens are hampered by the agitators' tactics of putting women and children in the forefront of their attacks, so that any movement by the defenders appears to attack the women and children.

Iran and Iraq square off over border clashes and start conventional missile exchanges on their major cities while ground forces prepare for battle. Neither country feels strong enough to take the initiative of a preemptive ground campaign, however. Thus engaged, Iraq doesn't yet invade Kuwait, either. A Navy Arleigh Burke–class guided missile destroyer on tanker escort duty is hit by a large mine and is sunk with the loss of more than fifty crewmembers. Under cover of the resulting furor in the United States, minesweeping forces in the strait are then engaged by Iranian fast patrol boats using the latest, hard-to-countermeasure version of the French Exocet missile; despite the protection of the minesweepers by carrier aviation one mine hunter is lost. U.S. Navy carrier strike aircraft and Air Force attack airplanes from Arabia attack the Iranian boat bases and missile sites on the northern side of the strait. The Saudi rebels keep up a running series of nuisance attacks on the air bases used by the U.S. Air Force, exacting small casualties and some aircraft damage that are played up by the media. Iranian radio and television broadcasts keep up a drumbeat to the effect that the U.S. military has no business being in the area, noting that U.S. actions are endangering the world's oil supply, which doesn't need a U.S. military presence to sustain flow to the rest of the world. (In fact, they bugle the embarrassing fact, which raises another uproar in Congress and the media, that, through all these events, the United States has been buying its oil after it is delivered to secondary ports outside the gulf.) Europe reiterates its lack of support for U.S. military intervention, whereas Japan just lays low.

While the United States is preoccupied with its actions around the Strait of Hormuz, Iraq attacks at Abadan, Iran's oil port at the head of the gulf, also along the Iranian passageway to the gulf; this area was the focus of the Iran-Iraq War of the 1980s as well. The United States desists from a response, just warning Iraq that they will be attacked if they turn on Kuwait itself. Russia secretly starts to support Iran with intelligence and promises of weapon replacement. Turkey denies U.S. requests for access to airfields from which the northern reaches of both Iran and Iraq can be attacked.

Congress now changes its stand and supports the president in intervention. The president orders the Marine brigade that had been embarked in the Arabian Sea to land on the ground in Saudi Arabia, as soon as the Navy has opened the strait, and she openly declares U.S. support of the loyalists, indicating that we will withdraw our military units from the area as soon as the internal Saudi quarrel is settled. An urgent military campaign is undertaken to open and assure freedom of passage through the Strait of Hormuz. This will involve securing both shores to as much depth as necessary. U.S. Army forces also move to guard against an Iraqi attack into Kuwait. U.S. reinforcements are ordered to the area. Saudi and Emirate air and ground forces are also involved.

Marine units that have landed on the Iranian shore of the strait are attacked, but they manage to set up some roadblocks against meager Iranian forces coming to reinforce the Iranian units along the shore (Iran is keeping most of its army facing Iraq along its western border). The Marines start to move inland while bringing fleet fire against sites that were hidden from the aerial reconnaissance that was finding targets for our tactical strike aircraft.

Phase 4: Full-Scale War

There is now full-scale warfare between Iran and Iraq, under cover of which Iraq has turned on Kuwait, to capture it for its own purposes. An Iranian submarine—one of several that Iran had purchased from Russia and that have been held in some contempt by the U.S. Navy as being relatively ineffective and not well trained—sinks a Military Prepositioning Ship in the Arabian Sea, not only causing the loss of equipment needed to support the army reinforcements but also creating many U.S. casualties. To add insult to injury, it escapes from Navy antisubmarine warfare forces. The U.S. media have a field day of recrimination and Monday-morning quarterbacking, and Congress plans hearings. There are dark mutterings about impeaching the president for not having ensured the readiness of our military units, as well as calls for the Secretary of Defense to resign.

At the same time, U.S. intervention in the internal Saudi fight has become a cause célèbre in the Islamic world, leading France and Russia to condemn it, each for its own reasons. This simply assures that the United States will not be able to form a broad coalition to support any action. Iran and Iraq, while fighting each other, both attack Israel with long-range missiles having conventional warheads. This is strictly an ideological move to taunt the United States and to emphasize our alien presence in the Middle East, but the United States now has the problem of keeping Israel from joining the war and perversely helping the Saudi rebels' cause by doing so. At the same time, both Iran and Iraq brandish their reputed nuclear weapon holdings against American forces in the Gulf and against Israel, and Iraq reminds the world that they have had a long-standing biological warfare program.

Japan and the United States form an economic alliance to assure alternative oil supplies for both until the conflict is over. Russia openly supports Iran and warns all sides against using nuclear weapons. Syria tries to lay low but is under pressure from both Iran and Iraq to join one of them. The Syrians try to play both sides, not very successfully; they feel that at all costs they must not appear to be allied with the United States, even tacitly. The United States warns Syria to stay out of the fight but requests military passage across Syria to Iraq. Syria, between regimes, welcomes the opportunity to retain at least the appearance of neutrality and will not allow the use of Syrian soil for transit by U.S. forces.

All African countries and those in Southern and Central Europe, including France, deny the United States overflight rights to support operations in Saudi Arabia or Israel and Jordan. This means that either the United States must provide fighter escorts, at great cost in combat aircraft, tankers, and diversion from the real objective, or take roundabout routes that greatly extend the flight time and reduce the amount of supplies that can be delivered. Some of each is done, establishing supply lines around South Africa and across the Pacific to Diego Garcia and northwest to Arabia from there while logistic aircraft fly through the middle of the Mediterranean with fighter escort from the Sixth Fleet units that have not been ordered to the Arabian Sea. But this interference with direct supply routes limits the size of the military forces the United States can bring to the area.

The United States is now trying to bring reinforcements through the conflict at the Strait of Hormuz toward Kuwait, where the 82nd Airborne and the Marines are barely holding off the Iraqi attack. The reinforcement move is a dangerous operation, risking many casualties en route before the troops even get into the fight in any strategically and tactically important way. To cover the move and create a diversion, U.S. Navy attack aircraft and Air Force bombers are allowed to strike strategic and tactical targets in Iraq, as well as those in Iran that threaten U.S. positions and access to the nations on the southern shore of the gulf, with the constraint that holy Islamic sites in Iran and Baghdad may not be hurt.

The United States can't keep Israel from responding to the attacks on its territory with commando and air force actions deep into both Iraq and Iran, many of which are repelled with heavy Israeli casualties. In a secret communication to the United States, Israel threatens the use of nuclear weapons if attacks on it do not stop. The United States therefore starts integrating its military action with the Israelis so that it may exercise restraint against Israeli nuclear use. But the secret collaboration leaks out, leading to a storm of Islamist clamor along the lines of "we knew it all the time" and "now they show their true colors." The Saudi government is now not certain that it wants the help it is getting, although it knows it may lose everything without it.

The United States undertakes a damage-limiting information warfare campaign. That consists of broadcasts in and from the area giving the U.S. side of events, together with secret electronic warfare operations to disable and disarm both Iraqi and Iranian military command and control. The U.S. media, especially CNN, which still has reporters and camera personnel in Iran and Iraq, keep up a drumbeat of criticism, showing how the U.S. government is playing down its desperate condition in the developing conflict, telegraphing force movements, and protesting against jamming of broadcasts from the war fronts and what they call "disinformation" being handed out by U.S. military public affairs officers.

In a move to improve the supply situation, the United States undertakes negotiations with Jordan to be able to use Aqaba as an alternative port of entry into the area. Jordan is now faced with the need for an open break with its Arab and Iranian neighbors; it could say no to the United States, but it will be attacked by the neighbors anyway for its earlier collaboration with Israel. And if it grants the Aqaba request, Jordan will become a war zone as the United States fights its way into Iraq across the Jordanian border. Jordan is thus condemned to probable destruction unless the United States wins the war.

The United States is now involved in a messy, multisided, large-scale internal and external war on the Arabian Peninsula and on both shores of the Arabian Gulf, without its European allies, with only minimal economic support from Japan, and with Russia hostile—not directly involved but egging the Arab and Iranian belligerents on and supporting them with weapons and supplies. Clearly, Russia as well as China will be a major beneficiary of this war, however it turns out, unless the United States wins a clean victory, which Russia judges to be unlikely.

SCENARIOS 25

However, the American president has just called for a general mobilization, and Congress is responding positively. The United States also makes a policy announcement to the world, invoking the potential use of its strategic nuclear deterrent against any who may attack the United States or its forces and allies with nuclear, chemical, or biological weapons. The media debate publicly among themselves whether to support the president. They also can't decide whether to exercise some restraint against telling all their observations of force movements and giving the inside dope on war plans that they have gleaned from discussions in the Pentagon, the State Department, and the White House. They face what to them is a critical issue in weighing the safety of our forces against the public's right to know what is really going on in this conflict that affects it vitally. . . .

A CARIBBEAN SCENARIO

This scenario unfolds over a thirty-day period.

Phase 1: The Cartels Take Charge

The CIA obtains incontrovertible evidence, picked up and spread by the media, that Colombian drug cartels have formed an alliance that has taken over and is running the Panama Canal, behind the cover of a thoroughly corrupted Panamanian government and Canal Company. They are, by very subtle means, using their hold on the canal to collect hundreds of millions of dollars per year in extortionate transit fees, set well beyond the amounts needed to recoup operating costs and make reasonable profits. They also use vessel passages as a means to worldwide distribution of drugs. Vessel inspectors and pilots, including many Americans, easily double as the smugglers who stash the drug shipments aboard. On learning of the CIA report, the media and then Congress start questioning how the administration could have been so lacking in vigilance as to allow the Canal Company's fees to grow so large without being questioned.

The U.S. initiates extended probes to track the money flows and the movements of ships and related activities correlated with drug operations in various countries. The president forms a combined departmental Defense-State-CIA-Justice task force under presidential command (chaired as an alternate by the staff director of the National Security Council) to devise plans to stop the cartels. She orders plans prepared to retake the canal and drive the cartels off, once and for all. All of this (except the money-tracking) is done in a glare of publicity designed to frighten away the cartels and warn off supporting governments.

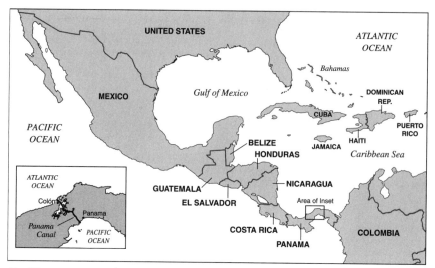

Carribbean

Phase 2: Heating Up

Cuba's military government, which has been profiting as a link in the drug distribution chain, warns against open U.S. intervention in Panama and quickly sends Special Forces to help the "local authorities" prepare to fend off a prospective U.S. invasion. Word is sent out that a U.S. invasion will trigger destruction of the canal, indeed that explosive charges in critical locations on the locks are already set. The rest of the world rationalizes that running a legitimate business will cause the cartels to reform and go straight and that, therefore, the United States should take no deliberate action.

The U.S. news media and the president's political opponents clamor for restraining actions against Cuba, challenging the president to root out the cartels. The message resonates in Congress. The president stalls while she looks at the military resources available. With potential hot spots in the Far East and the Middle East, major ready forces are spread thin, committed to guarding those areas; she is reluctant to risk giving our opponents there an opportunity to create mischief without a quick response capability on the spot. There is also the perennial concern about stirring up the anti-intervention sentiments in Latin America, with whom we have extensive trade that might be jeopardized. The CIA indicates that the training and capability of the Cuban special forces is low and that the cartels constitute little more than an armed "mob" akin to the U.S. Mafia. With the concurrence of the JCS, she decides that with such a low quality of opposition in Panama she can use light but capable forces to secure that area. She orders the Special Operations Command, controlling the integrated and well-trained descendants of the famed Green Berets, Navy SEALs, and Special Air Warriors, to regain control of the canal.

The Special Forces are landed by helicopter in the former Canal Zone at Panama City from a Navy amphibious ship, and they immediately move out to secure the local radio and television stations, the presidential residence, and several transportation centers scattered about the city. They will have air and logistic support from the amphibious fleet off the Pacific shore, and there is a Marine company aboard to reinforce the Special Forces if necessary. There is a small amount of gunfire, but not enough to stop the rapid accomplishment of the Special Forces mission.

Things are looking good. The president orders the State Department to prepare the way for a new and friendly government to take charge. She also authorizes a major information campaign to bring the Latin American governments to accept American intervention because this is an unusual and dangerous situation for them, as well as to persuade our allies overseas that any U.S. action will be in their interest as well. A meeting of the UN Security Council is called, and the United States introduces a resolution backing the actions already taken. That bogs down in squabbling over whether the United States had the right to take the action unilaterally.

Phase 3: Action at Last

Cuba is defiant and hurriedly sends two army battalions to the Atlantic shore of the former Canal Zone to shore up the cartels' defenses (they are not referred to as drug cartels, of course, but as the legitimate government of a sovereign Panama) and to drive the Americans out. They have achieved surprise, and the U.S. Navy has not been ordered to stop them before they land. The Cuban troops commandeer civilian transport and start to move toward the other end of the canal over the only road across the isthmus. That road parallels the canal, but it is masked by vegetation, so that the exact location of the Cubans is hard to discern from the air (there had been many proposals to develop foliage-penetrating sensors through the years, but they fell by the wayside in the incessant budget crunches). The U.S. military commander in the amphibious force offshore is reluctant to bomb them without better information, for fear of hitting the canal (again, acquisition of precision munitions had been allowed to lag, and most of those available were being reserved for the Far East and Middle East theaters).

In Panama City the hostile penetration of canal and Panamanian infrastructure is much deeper than had been realized, and the cartels bring out many "troops" armed with assault guns and some heavy weapons, including antitank grenade launchers and shoulder-fired antiaircraft missiles that can double as assault weapons against buildings. The Special Forces have followed a strategy that would allow them to control the city completely in the presence of light opposition, but as the opposition builds they find themselves in several traps. The amphibious force offshore cannot provide air support without endangering many civilians; the force commander's request to take that risk is denied in Washington, on the personal intervention of the president herself.

She cannot afford the negative media attention that many civilian casualties would bring while the U.S. resolution is before the UN Security Council. A few European and Asian governments are questioning the validity of the information about the cartels that led to the action in the first place, and several Latin American governments are already condemning the U.S. intervention. Also, some antiwar factions in Congress are beginning to take up the cry. Extensive civilian casualties would be the last straw and would defeat the U.S. information campaign against the cartels and Cuba.

The U.S. commander tries to use armed helicopters that can focus their fire much more precisely than attack aircraft, but they are defeated with the loss of two machines by the cartels' grenade launchers and missiles, in a virtual replay of the 1992 engagement with Mohammed Farah Aideed's forces in Mogadishu. Many of the Cuban troops arrive much sooner than anyone predicted was possible, and several pitched battles ensue outside the buildings and areas occupied by the Special Forces. The Special Forces are forced to retreat with some casualties and much fanfare by the Cubans. The Marine company is landed in a large, open area on the edge of the city and helps the Special Forces retreat for cover into the jungle areas north of the city boundary. It intends to ferry them out of Panama in shifts but is forced to depart quickly as the Cuban and cartel forces realize what has happened and start to focus on them.

Other countries, fearful of losing the canal, urge U.S. restraint. Shipping is backing up at both entrances to the canal, and economic penalties from the delay of their containers in the world's "just-in-time" economy are already starting to be felt. While this action is taking place, there is an outbreak of a highly virulent strain of psittacosis (colloquially known as "parrot fever") in South Florida that results in several deaths among older people. The first reaction of the government is that it originated in a large, illegal shipment of tropical birds. But the media speculate that it has been caused by a terrorist biological warfare attack under Cuban aegis. Various purported terrorist cells call the media to "confirm" that speculation. Truth is hard to find.

The president decides she can't wait for the UN decision process to work. She had hoped to have Security Council blessing for actions that might severely affect the international community, but there is no longer any time for that. She orders the Navy to establish a full blockade of Cuba to prevent support or reinforcement of Cuban forces in Panama and belatedly orders a carrier battle group and Marine Amphibious Ready Group with a battalion-sized Marine Expeditionary Force embarked to sail for Panama from the Arabian Sea. Their orders are to defeat the Cuban forces already ashore in Panama, link up with the Special Forces remaining on the isthmus, and complete the mission that the latter had been sent to accomplish. It will take them two weeks to arrive in the Caribbean. A brigade of the 82nd Airborne at Fort Bragg, North Carolina, is alerted to be ready for action, but in the absence of a good landing plan in the confused situation she keeps them on hold. The entire operation will come under the command of the CINC for the Latin American and Caribbean theater, but he is not certain what forces will actually be at his disposal.

Looking ahead, the president also orders the Navy to set up an inspection system to stop and search ships coming out of the canal passage (at either end) for drugs. She heightens Navy and Air Force surveillance of the air routes to the United States from northern Latin America, and she also takes immediate action to interdict worldwide money flows from and to the cartels. The rest of the world protests strongly about arbitrary U.S. search and seizure on the high seas and what they claim will be the illegal penetration of international banking systems, some of which has already been detected despite the banks' security and privacy protections. The president remains defiant as she tries to offset the drumbeat of criticism of her tardy action that has led to "a humiliating military defeat at the hands of a fourth-rate power supporting a bunch of gangsters," as the critics put it.

The president, realizing that she will now face a longer operation that may well lead to Congress invoking the War Powers Act, asks Congress to grant her the power to "do what is necessary." She notes how that could include actions the rest of the world might deem illegal under international law. Congress, thoroughly angry at her poor handling of the crisis, agrees to her request, but not without couching their agreement in language criticizing her handling of the affair thus far. The president also orders the Center for Disease Control in Atlanta and the U.S. Public Health Service to get to the bottom of the psittacosis issue. Finally, she issues presidential orders calling a state of national emergency, so that she can invoke the necessary civil restraints to protect the building invasion force from media prying and so that she can impose controls against price-gouging that is beginning to appear.

Phase 4: Catching Up—A Piecemeal Strategy

Cuban forces in Panama discover the minibase that the escaping U.S. Special Operations Force has established in anticipation of renewed offensive action, in a heavily forested area near Panama's Pacific coastline, outside the former Canal Zone. They attack it. The Special Operations Force is surrounded and cannot break out. In anticipation of U.S. rescue action, canal entry facilities at both ends of the canal are sabotaged by the Cubans. Thus, the canal and the Special Forces are now besieged and held hostage by Cuba and the cartels; Cuba and Panama are blockaded by the United States. Economic penalties in the rest of the world are building. Cuba further threatens to use "any weapons" (read: biological and chemical) to oust the U.S. forces from Panama or to destroy them.

With the reinforcements from the Arabian Sea still many days away, the president belatedly orders the JCS to take any necessary military action to rescue the Special Forces team, capture and reopen the canal without further damage taking place, drive the Cuban forces out of Panama or destroy them, and establish an effective civilian government in Panama. She also orders a joint agency operation (Justice, the CIA, Defense, and State), supposedly "covert" but immediately leaked and trumpeted by the media, to take the drug cartels out of operation once and for all. That could include any action deemed necessary against the cartel bases and their sources of drugs, including the use of sea, air, and ground-raiding forces if local governments do not cooperate, but it does not include the establishment of a permanent U.S. presence anywhere. The president also forbids direct military action against the Cuban mainland, including action by irregular Cuban groups from the United States, although sea and air action to sustain the blockade and defend U.S. forces transiting to Panama is permitted. Cuba is to be starved out, not attacked on the ground. . . .

LESSONS

These three scenarios—Far East, Middle East, Caribbean—represent examples of the kind of trouble this country could face if it takes its security for granted and skimps on the resources to ensure its ability to guard its vital interests and those of its allies. But there is much more to these illustrations than that.

The scenarios show that the unexpected can easily happen in world affairs affecting our national security. Indeed, history says that it usually happens; the Kosovo example is simply a very recent example. But the standard conflict scenarios used to plan military strategy and to set requirements for armed forces and their equipment don't deal with the unexpected. And when Congress is presented with a military budget and descriptions of the armed forces, its members want to know who the enemy is—who are the forces being designed to fight? That determines both the size of the forces needed and how much sophisticated, advanced technology must be built into them, and that, in turn, helps determine the necessary budget. If there isn't some kind of planning scenario, then any such long-range planning will be based on sand, subject to being wafted here and there by the political winds and the desire to use military-oriented resources for many purposes other than to create effective fighting forces. However, such certainty is difficult to achieve, since we must plan for military systems, for force organizations to use the systems most effectively, and for the force dispositions (which require bases), years and even decades in advance of their actual appearance in operations. By then the planning scenarios will have been overtaken by events in today's increasingly confused and fast-changing world scene—in many respects just like the scenarios outlined above.

The only way around this problem is to assume that any action our military forces will get into will not follow the planning scenarios that led to their creation. That means we have to build forces that are flexible and adaptable, forces that have the best capability for moving and fighting that we can provide them, regardless of theater and enemy. The scenarios are useful simply to test our ideas on how they may have to operate: how far to deploy, how fast, against what kinds of possible opponents who may have what kind of equipment, weapons, and tactics. Beyond that, although we will have some idea of who our potential military antagonists will be (analyzed in Chapter 3), we simply won't know precisely *where* or *who* until the time comes for the use of the forces. At that point, it will be too late to change them very much to meet the unexpected. We had better suit them to meet the unknown well in advance, regardless of the budget level allocated to them. Of course, there is a level of budget below which it will be impossible to do that, just as there is a budget level above which we would be creating forces that are larger and more complex than will ever be needed.

Unfortunately, budgeters don't take kindly to planning in an environment of uncertainty. Indeed, Congress has never been willing to appropriate money to meet uncertain or indefinable military contingencies. There may be some justification for that, since there is always competition for funds and more places to put them than there are funds available. As a consequence, however, the tendency in American military budget planning since the end of the Cold War has been to try to lower both thresholds—the minimum practical budget and the maximum sensible budget—under the pressure of other social and civil program necessities that are more apparent and less uncertain.

So, the feat to be accomplished is to plan and build armed forces with the requisite flexibility, adaptability, and capability to meet the unexpected and the unknown while catering to the innate tendencies of the bodies that must designate and appropriate the money. Since the Cold War ended, the only time we have achieved that was during the Gulf War, and then it was more by accident than by design. By great fortune we were able to turn the armed forces that were built to meet the Soviet Union against the lesser opponent and defeat him. Since then, we have been struggling with the problem, in such debates as the number of carriers the Navy should have, whether we should buy more B-2 bombers, when we should deploy a national missile defense, or whether we can close more bases, while a realistic view of today's armed forces tells us that we could not, now, repeat the Gulf War performance. (This is not the place to argue those or other issues of the kind; we must simply note that if we are fortunate the process of mobilizing large naval, air, and ground forces for a major military operation will not be put to the test again very soon.)

There is more. These illustrations bring out the complexity of the world in which armed forces will be used. Indeed, even these complex scenarios don't emphasize the need for the armed forces to participate in peacekeeping missions like Bosnia, or humanitarian missions to protect and assist refugees in time of war, as with the Kurds in northern Iraq after the Gulf War and again when Serbia forced most of the ethnic Albanian population out of Kosovo. Short of an all-out war like World War II among the industrial powers, which seems highly improbable in this age of intercontinental missiles and weapons of mass destruction, no use of military force that we can anticipate in the future can be expected to be cleanly or purely military. The use takes place within a political, social, and economic background involving many players. They all have different outlooks founded in their cultures and in their geographic and economic positions in the increasingly integrated and complex world civilization that we see evolving day by day. A president and a country who plan to meet contingencies ad hoc, in a reactive mode—an approach that these scenarios illuminate—will not remain supreme for very long in such a world, regardless of the strength of the armed forces that can be brought to bear. The armed forces' effectiveness in protecting and furthering the nation's security interests will depend at least as much on the decisionmaking that employs them as on their inherent capability.

Like chess players, we must try to see many moves ahead, or we shall never control our interactions with the world to our maximum benefit, regardless of the raw military power we can bring to bear in any immediate situation. And the factors that determine the moves will involve domestic and international economic, political, demographic, and many human elements. They will include both hostile and humanitarian aspects that cut across national boundaries. Little of this mix usually enters explicitly into our national security thinking and planning. But in fact, those factors have to be taken into account if we are ever to get out of the reactive mode. Then, the armed forces have to be planned to fit into the broader pattern. First, however, we have to decide what we want our armed forces to accomplish in this complicated world. Do we really want to build armed forces that only fight other organized armed forces, as many congressional critics of military use in quasi-peacetime missions insist, or do we want them to do whatever is necessary to protect and further the nation's interests?

As Sun-tzu, the fourth-century B.C. Chinese military philosopher, said in *The Art of War*, in words that are as relevant today as they were when first written, "To win one hundred victories in one hundred battles is not the acme of skill. To subdue the enemy without fighting is the acme of skill." However, we still plan our national security strategy and our use of armed forces according to the more recent, nineteenth-century thinking of Carl von Clausewitz about conflict among the European nation-states: "War . . . is an act of violence intended to compel our opponent to fulfill our will." In his concept, the planned use of military force in war is an essential element in advancing the national welfare, instead of an element in protecting it while we advance it in other ways. If our public, whose views are reflected in congressional action, foresees little or no need for military action or even decides that such action is undesirable to achieve our post–Cold War foreign policy objectives, then they may, mistakenly, feel comfortable allowing the armed forces to languish. However, seeking Sun-tzu's objective does not argue against the need for armed forces. Effective armed forces—that are recognized by the world as effective—are an essential element of the ability to accomplish that objective.

What would we do in each of the above scenarios if we were to treat them in the Sun-tzu mode? In each case, we would have had to recognize the motivations and likely responses of the players as seen from inside their cultures and histories. And we would have had to consciously recognize our own, so that we would not be driven by unconscious cultural biases. We would have had to start building policies that create or preserve friendly, or at least respectful, relationships with the nations involved that would forestall U.S. military action because each party recognizes when and why we would be pressed to take such action and wishes to avoid it.

In the Far East scenario, we would have to recognize and defer to the depth of feeling in China about the Taiwan issue and undertake diplomacy that would encourage a China-Taiwan rapprochement. The Koreas would also require delicate handling, to ensure that we could inhibit the North's urge to create strike capabilities founded on nuclear weapons while encouraging some kind of modus vivendi that could range from a comfortable coexistence of two viable countries to unification under terms both could accept.

In the Middle East scenario, we would have to pursue combined military, diplomatic, and economic policies in the Persian Gulf region that would discourage any country from even thinking about mining the international waters of the strait or the gulf. And we would have to develop (at least in the private counsels of our government, if any such remain) a dispassionate view of the prospects for the Saudi royal house and develop intelligence that could track when it might be in trouble in the evolution of the Middle East governments toward religious nationalism. Then, if we foresaw that the Saudis were in trouble, we would have to decide which side we would be on, or how to maintain a neutral stance that would not turn both sides against us. Such a policy would have to be undergirded by some conception of how we might come to terms with militant Islam without war or the embarrassing predicaments that accompanied the Iranian revolution in the late 1980s.

Finally, in the Caribbean scenario, we would not only have to get a better handle on how to deal with the growing power of the drug cartels than we have now but also develop diplomatic and economic policies toward Cuba that would preclude the possibility that Castro could be followed by an equally repressive and hostile regime.

None of these precautionary, deflective, and preemptive strategies would or will be easy to implement. Indeed, we have been trying to work on all of them with uncertain success, bedeviled by the intractability of the problems, the recalcitrance of the players, and our internal divisions about how to meet both. But we must note that in all cases we would have to build and sustain armed forces of appropriate size and capability to meet contingencies of the kind described—well trained, ready to act, and publicly exercised often enough to demonstrate their capability. As we will see in later chapters, this will be more expensive than we like to contemplate now, but we would have to recognize, as the scenarios illustrate, whether they mirror real-world events or not, that saving this money now could exact a much higher price—in national treasure, lives, and U.S. national position in the world—later.

These policy changes might involve some unpleasant or controversial choices on our part, such as we are making in China today with regard to our view of their human rights record, or as we made in Korea with regard to the North's nuclear program. Later chapters will review some of these problems in more detail. The issue to emphasize here is that we must avoid letting our internal politics and our own cultural values—our ideologies, if one will—color our thinking about where our interests lie. And surely it must be obvious that without credible military capability to back up any policies we adopt none of the policies might make much difference in a world where military force is likely to be used by others.

Can this country make the transition from thinking like Clausewitz to thinking like Sun-tzu? In today's world, will we even survive as a country, as we know it now, through the next century? That seems a strange question to be asking at a time when the United States is deeply conscious of its strength, with the world's strongest economy and armed forces. But there's always more below the surface. Let's look at the question in the next chapter.

2

THE EVAPORATION
OF THE U.S.A.

If you don't know where you are going, you will probably end up somewhere else.

—*Laurence J. Peter*

WHERE THE WORLD HAS GONE

Now let's pick up from the world of the previous chapter, which was much like the one we know today, and look at a very different world that could grow out of it. Bear with me as I try to stretch your thinking into the realm of the improbable—yet all too possible—for reasons that you will see founded in American life today.

The year is almost 2100. What has the world become? In some ways, it looks very much like the world of 2000. In other ways, however, it is nowhere near recognizable, although we should have seen its new configuration coming in the patterns and events of our own time. The world in 2100 is a strange amalgam of the consequences of broad integration of economies on a global scale, political fragmentation in a new "tribalism" that emerged from the ethnic conflicts that erupted as the Cold War ended, and a two-tiered social uniformity strongly shaped by the international communications organizations who control the news and entertainment media.

The global transfers of currencies and resources that the information revolution facilitated have led to a broadly integrated global economy that is controlled mainly by international corporations and traders rather than by national entities. Worldwide services like banking and creation of computer software are distributed in any countries having the requisite intellectual capital among their educated citizens, and manufacturing continues to chase the lowest possible wages within any trainable population. The economic rules by which this system operates have been crafted through a series of market crises to incorporate safeguards against collapses of the kind that hit the United States in 1929 and the Pacific Rim in 1997. With the help of the ubiquitous computer, purchasing power is carefully monitored, and production is adjusted to ensure that demand, inventories, and deliveries of goods and services rarely, if ever, get out of kilter.

One such adjustment has been made to ensure that the labor force in any developed country is gainfully employed. Whenever and wherever a labor surplus threatens to create a recession, the length of the workday and workweek are adjusted to keep people occupied and earning money. This was found to be a much more satisfactory system, both economically and spiritually, than the one of rigid work schedules and a labor force of fluctuating size that required welfare payments in times of reduced production. The change in philosophy was enabled by worldwide stabilization in birthrates as national economies developed and were incorporated into the world economic system in a sort of bootstrap operation. Slack time in the workforce is taken up by the products of the entertainment media—sports, music, theater, news, travel, drugs—all conveyed and supported by television, global personal and public communications and transportation, and locally organized activities. The prices and scope of the activity are adjusted locally to account for the length of the workweek and consequent fluctuations in earning power.

Resource exchanges have been mediated by this global economic machinery. Economically based resource conservation and management are exercised by the global economy in the interest of preserving stable markets, through evolving engineering practices enabled by advancing technology. The changes in those practices are as profound as those that led from the use of wood and masonry in primary structures to the use of steel, and from steel to reinforced concrete and plastics. Waste management is now controlled on a global scale by the global economy, since there was no longer much room or tolerance for the industrial waste products generated by twentieth-century inefficiencies. By and large, the production of waste per unit of economic output and per unit of population has been reduced by process changes that made primary production more efficient, with consequently much reduced waste output. Similarly, there was belated recognition that irreversible trends of climate change had indeed been set in motion during the periods of industrialization and large population growth from the eighteenth to the twenty-first centuries. The trends were now being reflected in sea-level changes, major shifts in crop productivity, and desertification in formerly green regions like the Amazon Basin. These changes have led the world economy to incorporate control of greenhouse emissions into the atmosphere in the production process changes, as well as to moderate the use of lumber in housing construction. Paper is now produced exclusively from farmed trees; its use has been markedly reduced by the prevalence of electronic media, and much of it is recycled. Food production has stabilized with the world population. Synthetic foods, with carefully controlled nutrition characteristics and made from hydrocarbons, algae, cellulose, and food materials previously discarded as waste, make up shortages wherever natural food production falls behind population growth. In fact, some of the synthetics are so tasty and satisfying that the upper classes are starting to adopt them as foods of preference.

As part of all these industrial advances, and because world oil production leveled off and began to decline around 2025, nuclear power now furnishes a large fraction of world energy for all uses. (Although it was found possible to control a fusion reaction in multibillion-dollar laboratory experiments, the engineering problems of making economically viable reactors for general use were not solved before research was cut off in favor of advanced nuclear power plant production.) Much of the world's freshwater now comes from nuclear-powered desalinization plants dotted around most coastal regions of the world and feeding a huge network of pipelines. This solution was forced both by water scarcity in arid regions with growing populations (like Southern California and defoliated Brazil), as well as by groundwater contamination and exhaustion that the growing populations engendered.

These advances, and improvement in the health and survivability of a population that now regularly lives into its nineties in the most developed countries, have been the products of the scientific research enterprise during the hundred years from roughly 1950 to 2050, an enterprise that is now essentially moribund. In the typical fashion of large bureaucratic organizations, innovation was managed in the world economy in the interest of controlling and advancing a steady flow of near-term income. Industrial research was focused on the process changes that led to better control of resources and to more personal income for current consumption. The growth of population and the national needs to provide for the health, education, welfare, and survival of that population, as well as the population's demands for money to satisfy their consumption of goods and entertainment, led to gradual shrinkage of the parts of national budgets devoted to basic research in science and technology, so that as we approach the end of the twenty-first century the industrial research is almost all that remains. Innovative small organizations have all but disappeared, gobbled up almost as soon as they have appeared in what authors Robert Frank and Philip Cook in 1995 called the "winner-take-all" economy that the many elements of the world industrial organization have enforced. The last remaining vestige of government-supported scientific research worldwide was in health care. That gradually wound down with the knowledge that emerged from bioengineering and the Human Genome Project, about how better to control the onset of cancer, to reduce the incidence of genetics-based diseases, and to prevent such virus-based diseases as the common cold and AIDS. Health care reached a generally accepted plateau in the most advanced countries that others, in the less developed countries, are still striving to achieve.

Concurrently with this economic evolution, people have had more time to think about their origins in the dim recesses of history. They seek to be anchored in tradition. They want to feel that in a world where they have little control over their economic fate they know where they came from, that there are others like themselves, and that all of those selves who are alike and share ancient cultural traditions can enjoy each others' company and support each other against the great, uncontrollable "outside." The Western ideas of self-determination encouraged this leaning, since few countries succeeded in forcing those who wanted to preserve their ethnic identity to assimilate into a broader cultural mass. Unconsciously, the world absorbed and applied the lesson that was taught to the Russians in Chechnya and to the United States in the Balkans in the 1990s.

The news and entertainment media (now inextricably interwoven), in their quest for the most profitable programming, encouraged the trend by targeting their documentary and dramatic programs and their news presentations to meet the interests of specific ethnic groups. There was soccer in Argentina, basketball in North America, Mozart in Vienna, and extensive local programming in diverse languages of the resident ethnic groups worldwide. The media also adopted organized religion as an important programming source, so that they became the means for bringing the solace of religion to the various ethnic groups. Each group could have its own variant in its own language, within the broad outlines of the major religions into which the world had divided by the Middle Ages.

This did not mean that national borders disappeared, nor did the result come about without extensive trauma and bloodshed during the early years of the twenty-first century. The system of national borders that was established during the wars of the nineteenth and twentieth centuries proved quite durable, since any attempt to change the borders by force was fiercely resisted by nations and alliances that had a stake in their continued existence. The world soon tired of the incessant bloodshed involved in illustrating that tendency, time after time. However, borders proved completely porous to the flow of ideas and refugees from the violence attending the ethnic agglomeration of peoples.

Thus, in a series of Rwandas, Bosnias, and Kosovos of varying intensity all over the world, ethnic groups came together within the nation-states, excluding others from the areas in which they lived. For example, Ireland remained Ireland, with a Protestant enclave carved out of Ulster and some of the Irish Republic, and Barcelona became the capital of a Basque ministate within the borders of Spain and

France. Some Turks joined together in an enclave in eastern Germany, but most of those whose parents had migrated there to seek work after the twentieth-century wars found they would rather return to their land of origin. The Kurds were allowed to live in a culturally based state of sorts carved out of Turkey, Iraq, Iran, and parts of the Caucasus republics, provided they did not proclaim it a unified political entity. The Sinhalese majority in Sri Lanka finally tired of the bloodshed on its relatively small island and acceded to partition of the island into Sinhalese and Tamil ministates. Chinese minorities were forced out of many of the Southeast Asian countries, to the detriment of those countries' economies. It took decades for the countries to recover from the paroxysm of riots, killing, and starvation that accompanied this massive population shift. Ironically, the economies recovered when international control was established within a Chinese, Japanese, Korean, Southeast Asian, and Australian common market. (Yes, even though it retained much of its European-derived culture, Australia couldn't resist joining the economic powerhouse created when the other economies of the Far East joined together.) That common market left many of the same Chinese families that had been expelled from Indonesia and Malaysia in control of the Southeast Asian economies from financial redoubts like Singapore, Sydney, Taipei, Shanghai, and Hong Kong.

The new global economic flexibility facilitated the integration of these peoples moving from one place to another, since it alleviated the competition for jobs that accompanied population movements under the earlier system of national economies. In a broad swath along the southern Mediterranean shore and into Central Asia, some form of Islam prevailed within all the national borders. The infinite variations in local belief and culture, if shown in various colors on a map, would have made it look like a crazy quilt. Even the Israelis, Palestinians, and Lebanese Christians found enclaves where they could live within informal borders that did not all look like the states they had tried to carve out for themselves. In Africa divisions were perhaps easiest to establish, since overt tribalism remained rampant throughout the century, even as many of the states modernized and joined the world economy.

Such a pattern was repeated across the world over the century—again, not without enormous trauma to individual groups. The world rests now, as we approach the end of the twenty-first century, partly exhausted and partly pacified. The economic order imposed by the international economic system has largely eliminated the causes of economically based conflict among nations, and a certain uniformity of culture has been induced within the ethnic groups by both the output of the economic system and the flow of products from the entertainment system. So, for example, people all over the world sit down to eat in fast-food restaurants in much the same way, although their food and its mode of preparation may differ among, say, Germany, North Africa, and China. American rock music took the world by storm in the years ending the twentieth century and beginning the twenty-first, but during the twenty-first century it has taken on the flavors of the many groups that adopted it and changed it to suit their own folk heritages. The drivers are ubiquitous television, laser discs, and a continually evolving drug culture that drives many of the entertainers and their adherents. All of this exposes every person of one culture to the sounds, looks, and habits of every other culture and induces copying from one to another in fads that flit over the globe like the shadows of clouds on a meadow—and sometimes stay.

The ethnic groups largely govern themselves within the broad framework of nation-states and international collaborations like the European Union, the Western Hemisphere Free Trade Zone, and the Far Eastern Common Market. The national and international presidents, ministers, parliaments, and governing bodies see to it that the relationships among groups, among countries, and among corporations do not erupt in extended and economically costly conflict. If we looked at a political map of the world of 2100, we would see a pattern of nation-states reminiscent of the one we know now. There would be differences—for example, the Russian Far East separated from European Russia and became an independent country, whereas the bits of the Russian Federation in Siberia and the remnants of the Soviet Union in Central Asia became a group of politically independent countries largely along ethnic lines. If the map were colored according to economic unions, we would see only a few broad areas of color: the European Union; the economically linked Confederation of Independent States that evolved from the remnants of the Soviet Union; and the other common markets. And we have already seen the confused picture that would make up the map according to ethnic groups.

This is not a Utopia by any means. The hunt for cheap manufacturing labor, together with the spread of higher education for those who staff the economic system and the service industries, has created a two-tier society. Almost all have some education; the upper tier has more. Almost all participate in the entertainments offered for the hours away from work; the upper tier enjoys more of it and does it very differently. Almost all are able to travel and see some of the world; the lower tier's world is much circumscribed, in distance and comforts. The knowledge the members of each group bring to their work, their activities, and the worlds they see are very different, conditioned by the rewards that the populations at each level can reap from their employment. And large groups of the poor remain, in every society, everywhere.

The division of the world population of more than 10 billion people is, perhaps, 80 percent in the lower tier and 20 percent in the upper tier. The broad middle classes of twentieth-century European and American societies have been absorbed into these two groups, which are not by any means uniform in their structure even though the average makeup of the individual groups differs significantly from one to the other. The 2 billion people in the upper economic level—a huge population by any standard—constitute an aristocracy of the educated and affluent. Although many of them preserve the languages of their ethnic origins to use among themselves, English is their lingua franca, the language of the world economy in all its parts (even France had to succumb to this inexorable pressure). Across national boundaries, they enjoy more expensive entertainment, more computing, communications, and work-lightening machines, more travel and more luxuries. Within all countries, their cultural commonality leads them into the realms of government, able to deal with each other comfortably to get the international relations right that support and facilitate the broad economic order of the world. Of course, the recruits who flow continually into the governing ranks of the economy itself also are drawn from the top levels of this group, constituting a meritocracy of the most affluent.

The lower economic level strives to break into the upper level, and a few succeed, largely coming from an intermediate group that provides advanced (as distinct from menial) services for the upper tier. But social mobility has passed its heyday of the mid–twentieth century. Class distinctions are once again following the examples of the nineteenth-century British governing hierarchy and the ancient Indian caste system. Mostly, the members of the lower tier have to work to eat and to enjoy the mass entertainments brought to them for their leisure time. Work and pursuit of leisure interests allow them little time to strive for more, but they are not so dissatisfied as to rebel en masse. Education systems worldwide reinforce the division between these two classes of the population.

Think about this world as an updated, transformed edition of the one described in George Orwell's 1949 novel, *1984*. There, the world population was governed by Big Brother, a governing entity whom we never saw but who controlled everyone's life through a system of surveillance and coercion, like that used by the Nazis and the Soviet internal security apparatus. It was a repressive, gloomy, and frightening world. At the end of the twenty-first century the world does not look nearly so dark. Big Brother is the world economy, a diffuse entity that no one objects to very strongly because it brings physical sustenance and a measure of intellectual comfort, suited as necessary to peoples' economic circumstances. With advances in health care that can control population size, disease, and many aspects of personality starting at the molecular and genetic levels, and the ubiquitous entertainment media with something for everyone, the surface gloss on the world is much like the biotechnology-driven, pleasure-oriented, socially regimented society described by Aldous Huxley in his 1932 novel, *Brave New World*. In the aftermath of the bloody sorting out of ethnic and religious differences that has characterized much of twenty-first-century history, few things now stir deep passions, and all over the crowded world people live for the moment.

THE EVOLUTION OF USCAN

How and where does the United States fit into all this? It does—yet it doesn't. As the twenty-first century draws to a close, the United States of America (U.S.A.) isn't there anymore. Although there is still a country, and many of the same 380 million people, they aren't *that* country. Here is how it came about. (Before going on with the story, I should remind you that although it may take only a few pages to describe a very complex history, the actual unfolding of that history can take a very long time and be accompanied by much political and human distress. In this case, the events I am about to describe extended over some fifty years during the middle of the twenty-first century.)

The transformation didn't begin in the United States at all. It began with the separation of Quebec from Canada. I have to spend some time telling you about Canada, because events there profoundly affected what happened in the United States later, and you have to understand their derivation.

After decades of agitation for their own country based on their own culture, the Parti Quebecois, which had become the repository of separatist feeling, managed a popular vote in the province that called for separation from the Canada of tradition. Parti leaders were clever enough to call for the plebiscite just after one of the worst insults that could have been visited upon the French-speaking population of Quebec. The governing Conservative Party in Ottawa had gradually become aware of the extent to which Canada had become, like the United States a century earlier, a nation of immigrants. There were a surprising number of Hispanic immigrants from Mexico, following the trade routes opened by the North American Free Trade Agreement (NAFTA); refugees from the Balkan and Kurdish wars; Koreans seeking the better life; and Chinese running from the paroxysms of racial cleansing in Southeast Asia to join the already large Chinese populations in Canada's major cities. Even the Inuit from the north, as they became educated and decided to move south to participate in the general economy, joined the gradually growing "foreign" population. Unlike the previous generations of immigrants in both countries, who learned English and sought assimilation into the general culture that they had found, the new immigrants were inspired by the world trend toward aggregation of ethnic groups into closed and self-contained communities.

The national parliament viewed with concern the results of a recent census showing the distribution of these large population groupings across the formerly English-speaking provinces. They were unable, for both cultural and economic reasons, to come to terms with demands for services in local languages. So they passed a resolution declining further accommodation to those demands and requiring all of

Canada's public business, including that in the provinces, to be conducted in English. All the provincial governments, except that in Quebec, followed suit.

And that's when the Ottawa government lost its cool. Officials feared that with the population of Quebec continuing to demand and to have bilingual government services, based on long precedent, the enforcement of the new law in the remaining provinces would be impossible. So they ordered the dismantling of the bilingual federal infrastructure that had been built in Quebec over more than a century of conciliating the French-speakers. It was a stupid move, of course, but their patience just snapped, their common sense along with it. Followed to its logical conclusion, this order required removing all French legends from signs on all roads and from inside and out of government buildings and all tourist attractions, removing French from all government forms and licenses, and raising arguments about whether and how to deal with removal of French from the public schools. Altogether, it was a task so great that the magnitude and cost of it were beyond contemplation. And that was the question on which the government fell short. The leaders of the separatist party seized the opportunity while the French population was still reeling from the prospect and pushed a ballot proposal through to success.

After the euphoria in Quebec Province and the consternation in the rest of Canada subsided, both sides now had to come to terms with the consequences of the action. There was significant movement of English-speakers in Quebec to the remaining provinces, mainly neighboring Ontario, which was already burdened with social and economic problems in dealing with the large immigrant population there. The population movement cascaded, as successive groups moved farther west in a search for living space. But the westward migration collided with the movement of population east from British Columbia and the Pacific Coast attending the flood of refugees from the upheavals in Southeast Asia. Great burdens were thus put on Canada's provincial governments to provide relocation services, to expand and change school systems, and to rebuild and maintain infrastructure like roads as well as market access. Worse, the police function had to be built up strongly to control the clashes among the moving population groups. Canada, which throughout the twentieth century had viewed itself as a more enlightened and hospitable home for productive peoples displaced by world turmoil than the United States, now found itself dealing with the consequences of ethnic hatreds, cultural clashes, rising crime, and demands for multilingual services more intense than had been faced with Quebec because there were more claimants on the privileges.

Quebec was not having an easy go of it either. The Quebecois, upon approving separation, had assumed that they were only separating socially and that their economic links with the rest of Canada would continue undisturbed. That didn't

Alaska
(U.S.)

CANADA

UNITED STATES

*ATLANTIC
OCEAN*

PUERTO
RICO

MEXICO   *Gulf of Mexico*

*PACIFIC
OCEAN*

CUBA

North America 2000

Evolution of USCAN

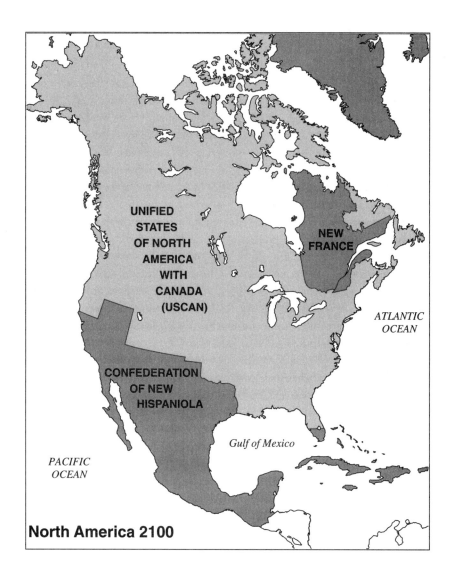

North America 2100

happen. In their political zeal to preserve their identity as New France within the New World (which, actually, was no longer so "new"), they had failed to consider the consequences of carving a new foreign country from within an old, established land. That land, extending west and south from New France, simply turned away. And rather than dealing with it—through a language barrier, after all, that had been at the root of much of the trouble the country was now facing—the rest of Canada built up even more so the already numerous links south to the United States—by land, through the Great Lakes, and along the Pacific Coast—all at the expense of any links to Quebec. Through the newly enhanced economic pathways that their immigrant population had brought, Canadians also reached farther south through the United States to Latin America and westward to the Pacific Rim and China.

Quebec found it hard to stay afloat economically. New France was never economically as strong as it should have been—indeed, that was one of the issues that pushed Quebecois toward their declaration of independence, since they had felt discriminated against by Canada's English-oriented national government. Finding themselves weakened even further by the trends they had set in motion themselves, they now reached south to the eastern United States for more trade, as well as east across the Atlantic to France for both spiritual comfort and economic support. The view south was not encouraging, because Quebec had little to offer except tourism and natural resources that could be exported only at the expense of their own economic potential. American investment for industrial purposes leaned more to the English-speaking parts of Canada, and Quebec was not wealthy enough on its own to build the level and kind of industry that would attract substantial world investment. France tried to welcome Quebecois into the French social community, but both parties soon found that their common language did not bespeak a common culture after all, so that there was less to talk about after the common-law marriage than either party had thought beforehand that there would be. By now France was tightly bound to the European Union and its common currency, the euro, so that it couldn't independently offer the Quebecois as much economic sustenance as either had hoped for when they looked forward so much to their spiritual union.

Thus, the upshot of the impulsive political moves on both sides was a rather small, French-speaking orphan set adrift and a large, nominally English-speaking motherland turning its attention to other parts of the world, especially the United States. Yet Canada faced increasing internal turmoil, spawned partly by the separation and partly by its initially open attitude toward immigration from elsewhere in the conflict-driven world. All this was going on while the United States was facing similar problems of its own, which we must now chronicle.

The main thread of the U.S. story begins in California, as had so many other momentous happenings in American social history. For many years, California's many political and ethnic groups had been at odds. The conflicts were taking place against the backdrop of a growing population and an unexpectedly struggling economy. The state was taking longer than expected to recover from the loss of defense business at the end of the Cold War, and the global economy was increasingly competing with the twin mainstays of the California economy: food and high-technology products.

A growing Hispanic population, largely but not exclusively from Mexico, and a growing Asian population of mixed Chinese, Japanese, Korean, and Southeast Asian derivation, had been in recurrent social conflict with California's Caucasians over control of the economic pie. (The African-American population in California gradually became the smallest of the major minority groups; while fighting continuously to improve their condition, they did not play a major role in the events to be described. Their own struggles added to the attending turmoil, however.)[1] Hispanics, mostly from peasant families who had moved to California during the second half of the twentieth century to seek a better life, made up a large proportion of the laboring class—those who did the fieldwork that produced and harvested the California fruits and produce; those who did the clerking for services others enjoyed; those who did the construction for others to live in, work in, and ride on. They struggled to advance in life, realizing belatedly that they had better send their children to universities in droves so that they could advance into the more affluent parts of the workforce. (Up until the end of the twentieth century, Hispanic registrations in colleges and universities in the California higher education system had been among the lowest of any major group.)

During this same time Asians, coming from a tradition that for millennia had extolled study and hard work, pushed into the upper reaches of the educated and affluent classes, achieving a much higher than proportional representation in the high-tech industries of the state. The non-Hispanic white population saw such developments as threatening its chances to advance economically, even as whites succumbed more so than the others to the blandishments of the worldwide entertainment industry that occupied their time and drained their ambition. What remained for whites was resentment and a struggle to enhance their position by using a political system in which they retained much residual control to exclude others from the full advantages of their growing majority positions. Adding chaos to this struggle were the sporadic and often violent efforts of the black community to break out of their own economic straitjacket, meeting frustration at almost every turn.

---

[1]All the population figures used in this scenario are based on the Bureau of the Census "preferred series" projection by state for the year 2025. Figures on economic output are my extrapolations from data in successive years of the U.S. Statistical Abstract.

None of these interactions took place among totally unified and homogeneous population segments, of course. Different factions within each group had different ideas about how they were or were not being hurt, about what achievements they should aspire to, and about tactics and strategy. And many individuals did very well for themselves under the existing conditions, so that groups were not unanimous in pushing for change. Indeed, those who had made it resisted change to the status quo, feeling unconsciously if not explicitly that any variation from current conditions would only serve to threaten their comfortable lifestyles and great economic accomplishments to date. So the communities were not all unified, and the political struggles took place in all manner of forums, from fights within, to popular ballot proposals invariably followed by court battles, to strikes, to contests in the legislature, to occasional campaigns of "nonviolent" protest in which one party or another would turn violent. The struggles continued without any conclusive resolutions, with one or another population segment gaining the upper hand on one occasion, only to lose it on another.

With all this turmoil, the sunny California of Hollywood legend and chamber-of-commerce PR was not very sunny inside, and it was ripe for a unifying event to make some of the forces for change coalesce. That came to a head as a result of the struggle of the Spanish-speaking population for recognition of their bilingual ambitions—but not at all in the direction they would have planned it to happen.

The Spanish-speaking community in the United States occupied a unique place in the history of U.S. immigration, more so than any other immigrant community. Many of the latter, especially during the great immigration waves from Central Europe during the late nineteenth and early twentieth centuries, had come to the United States seeking the ideal of the American dream. Although the individual immigrants might have been pushed by circumstances into working in the sweatshops of New York's clothing industry, or the Chicago slaughterhouses, or the Buffalo steel mills, they aspired to a better life for their children. The original immigrants set up communities that preserved much of the language and culture they had brought to these shores. Yet their children went to English-language public and parochial schools, where they were indoctrinated into American culture. Then both parents and children moved out into that culture and the broad manufacturing and service economy that they, themselves, were helping to build. In the process they reshaped the culture to their liking in the areas where they were concentrated. Later waves of immigration, such as those escaping Hitler's and Stalin's excesses during the middle of the twentieth century, were not as large as the earlier ones. Those arrivals joined an economy that was already in place and, after World War II, booming thanks to postwar expansion.

The Spanish-speaking immigrants of the second half of the twentieth century, wherever they settled in the United States, also joined an existing and powerful economy, but their situation was different from that of the earlier immigrants. Whether they were running away from the Central American wars or the poverty of their homelands, these Hispanics came to an even more fully developed America that needed their services in the lower-level jobs that the existing population didn't really want, for whatever reasons. Some of them were migrant workers who worked in the fields or small shops for part of the year and sent money back, then decided to stay and try, with more or less success, to bring their families to America. Others entered the country legally or illegally, then couldn't find work, so they subsisted on welfare. Thus, with dreams of rapid advancement held in abeyance by economic circumstances, and being a diverse group living in barrio-ghettos and forming a very large society held together by a common language, they were slower than the other waves of immigrants to enter the mainstream and its education systems. In fact, Hispanics were numerous enough in the areas where they settled to form a mainstream of their own. That included demands to teach their children in their native language, because they felt that the burden of learning a new language—which was not used in the home—on top of other educational demands unfamiliar to much of their culture, would be too much for their children and would hold back their advancement even more. They strove to establish Spanish-speaking communities within the country they had come to, communities that would be nourished by the wealth of that great surrounding milieu.

Thus, for the first time in U.S. history was born the great debate over bilingualism that paralleled the one in Canada. That unresolved debate was at the heart of the events that followed the Quebec secession.

The Hispanic community in Southern California took great encouragement from that Quebecois secession and its aftermath—but drew the wrong lesson from it. Hispanics looked at their situation in relation to the rest of the state. They represented 40 percent of the California population, the largest single ethnic group. They provided most of the essential underpinning to the state's economy, from growing food to filling the service slots in many industries, from tourism to communications. Leaders arose who persuaded them that they were now in a position to resolve the bilingualism issues once and for all in their favor. The threat of secession would be a club they could hold over the heads of the Anglo community to get them to accede to their demands for a bilingual state. So they pressed for legislation that would fully establish California as a bilingual state, with Spanish as well as English on signs throughout the infrastructure, bilingual education in local communities that wanted it, and Spanish as well as English on all official forms, tax returns, and the like.

Other groups in the state viewed this campaign with alarm, as it threatened to ratify their own minority status in the state, which they preferred not to come to terms
with directly. Non-Hispanic whites and blacks joined forces in opposing it. There
were clashes of gangs on the fringes of the black ghettos and Hispanic barrios,
whereas the more affluent white communities took to their gated subdivisions, calling on the news media and lobbyists to press their case. The Asian communities,
strangely, held back. They were in many ways sympathetic to the Hispanics. They
also lived in ghettos of sorts, largely through choice but also enforced by social pressure from whites and blacks to steer clear. In their own communities some of the
older people spoke the Old Country languages regularly. But their children had ac-
climated rapidly and were fully Anglicized. There was a large cultural distance between the Asian and Hispanic communities because of their very different cultural
traditions and relative economic statuses. Asians harbored no drive for bilingualism
in public affairs based on their own languages. They gave more attention to the economic costs and simple nuisance value that the proposed changeover would impose
on them and other non-Hispanic Californians. The mixture of histories and attitudes in the Asian communities led to rather neutral reactions to the bilingual state
proposal; they could tolerate the change, but certainly they were not going to push
for it.

But Asian communities, representing the third largest group in the state with
nearly 20 percent of the population, held the balance of power in California politics. And that came into play when the Anglo community, in its panic over the
prospect of losing what it viewed as a fundamental element of identity, made a mistake analogous to the one made by the Canadian parliament. Without counting the
votes, so to speak, the most conservative political groups initiated a popular ballot
proposal to counter the move in the legislature for a bilingual state. Proposition
670 began thus: "Whereas, California is a state founded in Christendom and dedicated to preservation of our European heritage. . . . " That was enough to push the
Asian communities into an alliance with Hispanics. The proposition was roundly
defeated, and then the law establishing a bilingual state was passed by a modest majority in the legislature.

That might have ended it, but non-Hispanic whites and blacks did not accept the
result gracefully. Harassment and clashes on many levels continued. Hispanics
fought back, as did Asians when they were attacked, and the central-southern region
of the state—roughly from San Francisco south—was riven by rioting and vandal-
ism. Thus began a sustained period of civic turmoil that hurt the state's economy
and its relationships with the rest of the country. The California governor called out
the National Guard, but its makeup reflected that of the state, and many units refused to exercise force to put down aggressive acts by their own ethnic groups. The

U.S. president then sent the U.S. Army to intervene to establish public order. A state of martial law seemed on the horizon.

Tempers on all sides were hot by now, so that the federal intervention did not sit well anywhere. Whites were grateful, thinking it would settle things in their favor. But Hispanics accused the president and the Army of siding with the others. Asians didn't want to get involved, yet the turmoil was clearly impacting their lives, and they didn't like that. So when some Hispanic firebrand raised the secessionist cry, Asians were ready to go along just to quiet the frenzy. They added the refinement that it was mainly the southern half of the state that should secede and form its own country, since that was where most of the gross domestic product (GDP) of the state was generated. They noted that the state's GDP before the rioting was more than $1 trillion, even with the economic problems that had in some ways fed the time of troubles. It was the largest of any state in the United States, larger indeed than most any country except the most industrially advanced ones. They could take care of themselves.

Thus, in one of those unexpected groundswells of public emotion that sweep populations at one time or another, the Hispanic-Asian majority pushed through the ballot proposition promulgating Articles of Secession of the Independent Country of Southern California, which transformed the California territory below the 39th parallel—three-fourths of the state—into a sovereign nation. The air and army National Guard units that were mainly made up of Hispanics and Asians rapidly coalesced into what they called the armed forces of the new country, pledging to defend it against all comers, be they from inside California's borders or from without.

The other groups sought U.S. help in rejecting the secession. That sent the rest of the United States into its own kind of agitation. Some patriots reminded the country of the Civil War that had once been fought to preserve the Union and asked whether this new challenge to American unity could go unopposed. But a century of preaching self-determination for populations worldwide, not to mention the indoctrination of generations of school children with the same idea, were more telling than patriotic exhortations. This was reinforced by the fragmentation of American politics into many groups of political, economic, and ethnic special interests, including Hispanic groups in other states such as Texas, New York, and Illinois, as well as militantly antiwar groups in many parts of the country. So any response to the California secession was stalled.

Popular reaction devolved into a succession of local imbroglios that the police had to pacify. Congress couldn't agree on what should be done. The U.S. president, believing that the economic links between California and the rest of the nation would dominate the relationship in any case, decided that the issue wouldn't be worth shedding blood over even if the country could agree to do that. Indeed, the dislocations attending the disruption of the economic links with California would be so severe that the already agitated state of the country could only degenerate into chaos. As the arguments and inaction continued, acceptance and recognition of Southern California as a sovereign nation-state gradually became the de facto reality.

Thus it turned out that in the new national and world conditions the United States would not fight another Civil War to hold itself together.

This was not lost on other states. First to react was Texas. It, too, had a very large Hispanic minority—10 million out of 27 million, or nearly 40 percent of the population. Although there wasn't the large Asian minority to join the Hispanic coalition, as in California, local conditions made for unexpected alliances. In particular, Texas politics and economics had long followed their own directions, dictated in large measure by increasing links across the border with the growing economic driver that Mexico had become. This independence in outlook was built on a tradition of thinking about Texas as nearly a nation in its own right, dating from the days of its fight for independence from Mexico, continuing through its evolution through cattle baronies that recognized no national master, and then into a modern economic and technological powerhouse that recognized no superior in achievement. From Texas, the United States was coming to be viewed even by non-Hispanic Texans as increasingly alien to Texas's ideals of patriotism and conservative cultural cohesion. Thus, when the Hispanic element in Texas politics started to agitate to follow California into independence, there was a surprisingly sympathetic response by a large majority of the state's population and leadership, across all parts of the political, economic, and social spectrum. Political separation—secession—followed soon thereafter.

Texas and California moved early to increase the economic links between themselves and also with Mexico. To do this they needed easy transit across Arizona and New Mexico. As independent countries, they had to establish immigration and customs checkpoints on their borders, as did the United States. There was a complex evolution of designated crossings and closings at roads and railroads that moved across the borders, and it became clear to all parties that some other arrangement would be necessary. The three nations agreed to confer, and a long-running conference was set up in neutral ground, in Vancouver, British Columbia.

Many other consequences of the secessions were making themselves felt at the same time, however. First was a migration of the disaffected population from California, which tended to drive much of the rest. The opponents of secession recognized that they were now strongly in the minority. Some of them, including the remnants of militias that had flourished in the state during earlier years, tried to organize to fight, but the newly energized National Guard forces quickly put down those rebellions. Some among the losing groups decided that they could live with the new conditions, whereas others decided to try their luck elsewhere. The easiest access to "elsewhere" was through Nevada, Arizona, and New Mexico. Nevada welcomed the new immigrants and tried to integrate them into its entertainment industries, which functioned as totally artificial environments in any case. Arizona and New Mexico reacted negatively. They had experienced a long period of building communities for older Americans who retired there, spent their money there, but created few industries that would contribute to long-term growth. The tourism-oriented industries they did encourage depleted the states' natural environments, degrading the attractions that had brought the growth in the first place. The states were saturated, and they had been striving to develop internally while not encouraging migration from outside. So they closed their borders with the two new countries and tried to turn their attentions inward. It didn't work.

First, because of the low carrying capacities of their environments, their populations were quite small. Again, they had large Hispanic minorities (a third in Arizona, and nearly half of New Mexico's population), who were sympathetic to the Southern California and Texas secessions. To these were added influential minorities of Native Americans. The latter had improved their economic conditions enormously, through combinations of tourist entertainment such as gambling and other services offered on reservations. They viewed the potential immigration of disaffected California groups as threatening their economic and social lives in many respects. Finally, non-Hispanic whites in Arizona and New Mexico judged that the prospective large influxes of immigrants would lead to development that would destroy the fragile balance that had been achieved with their desert surroundings—and their treasured desert lifestyle with it. Thus, no one in the two states favored the immigration, but they found that they did not have the resources to stem it. They received little help from the United States, where the secession battles were still being fought in retrospective recrimination.

New Mexico and Arizona therefore turned to Texas and California for help. Given the need for transit routes for California and Texas goods, the two pairs of states needed one another. While the peace talks between the United States and the new independents were convening in Vancouver, a secret conclave of representatives from the new republics of Southern California and Texas and the states of New Mexico and Arizona got together in Santa Fe to decide how the border, migration, and transit issues would be resolved. That conference followed one lead and then another to their logical conclusions, emerging with plans for a new country that included the four states and was called, provisionally, the United States of the Southwest (US/SW).

Thus, the Vancouver conference, originally convened to adjudicate relationships among the independent California and Texas republics and the truncated U.S.A., now had to deal with the same issues for which it had been convened originally—but in a totally new situation. The United States, minus four of its constituent states, was now negotiating with a major country, nearly 700,000 square miles in extent, having a combined population of 85 million people and an annual economic output of more than $1.5 trillion. Before the negotiations establishing the customs and immigration rules, the extradition agreements, and the trade agreements joining the two countries within the NAFTA umbrella were completed, Nevada took another look at the economic opportunities and decided to join the new country. Then, the southern counties of Florida began agitating for secession so that they, too, could join the new country.

Even though all the issues between the truncated U.S.A. and the new US/SW were resolved over a period of three years at the Vancouver conference, this did not end the story. Canada was watching all the furor with interest, as the U.S.A. was becoming very important to them. After the separation of Quebec and the intensified southern orientation of the remaining Canadian economy, the remnant Canada found that it looked more like the U.S.A. than it ever had before. It was a nation of immigrants, with many divisions among various groups. There was conflict among them, following the American and global trends toward ethnically based nationalism. Even as economic integration proceeded on its own schedule and logic, internal social cohesion was being lost, and the social costs of ethnic division—conflict, crime, an inability to agree on government social and education policies—had grown to match those being experienced south of the border.

At the same time, the U.S.A. was developing an unexpected dependency on the Great Plains provinces of Canada to the north. The gradual warming of the North American climate, along with that of the rest of the globe, had brought a shift of the rainfall patterns of the Great Plains, so that the southern reaches of the highly productive wheat and corn belts had almost imperceptibly lost much of their agricultural productive capacity. As this was happening, the Great Plains provinces had expanded their grain-growing areas. They brought the forests of the Northwest Territories into the lumbering mainstream and used the cleared land to grow wheat; their southern reaches picked up the corn production that had faltered south of the border. The result of this evolution was that the once-superabundant U.S. grain production declined, and the U.S.A. became dependent on Canada for much of its staple food. Thus, as the two countries eyed one another across their common border, they found that they had built a tightly integrated economic union while growing socially and culturally indistinguishable.

From this realization it was but a short step to the inevitable action—a joining of the two large countries into a single political entity. The time taken to accomplish that was longer than might have been expected. It was spent mainly in reconciling the Canadian (parliamentary) and American (republican) forms of government and their apparatuses and in deciding what to call the new entity; the economic integration was already in place. In the end, the federal government was constituted according to a synthesis of the European Union and NATO models.

Each country would elect its legislative and executive government officials according to its constitutional processes. A central bureaucracy was established with an administrative chairman appointed by the president of the U.S.A. and the prime minister of Canada. The three would meet to make executive decisions that affected the entire confederation, whereas the nationally elected executives and legislatures would govern on matters affecting their constituencies alone. (As it would turn out, there would be fewer of the latter than matters affecting both together, at least vis-à-vis the outside world, but the process would evolve to suit the conditions.) The legislatures would have to approve executive actions like budgets and treaties, and they would appoint joint committees to work out and resolve differences on those matters. There would be merged cabinet departments of Defense, Finance, Energy, and Foreign Affairs, again with parallel committees to plan budgets and joint activities and to resolve differences when necessary. The secret foreign intelligence services of the two countries would be merged. The remaining departments were found peculiar to the former national entities and would continue undisturbed for each.

Criminal law was left to continue as it had in the former national entities. The judicial appointment processes and the courts of each country would continue in their original molds, with the supreme courts of the two meeting in joint session to adjudicate matters affecting both. The Joint Supreme Court thus constituted would have to work out constitutional differences to the satisfaction of both national legislatures, but there was much respect for its potential ability to do so. The states, provinces, and their political subdivisions would continue to govern themselves as they had from the beginnings of the respective countries. The entire apparatus was clumsy and slow to make decisions, but in the world that was evolving around it, where the international economy was more and more governing economic affairs and where military strife was subsiding after years of bloodshed within and between nations, the slower decision time didn't matter all that much.

As for naming the new entity, all sorts of possibilities were examined and discarded. Neither country wanted to have "confederation" in the name, although in actuality that was what the newly constituted nation was. The term had unhappy connotations in the remote history of both countries. Canada insisted its name be preserved, and the United States after nearly three hundred years of using the initials "U.S.A." did not want to give up that unique symbol. They finally settled on the rather clumsy Unified States of North America with Canada (or USCAN, pronounced "*you* scan").

By agreement, it was all put up for a referendum to the peoples of both countries, with a year of electioneering spearheaded by the countries' leaders. There were fierce arguments for and against, with both sides predicting gloom and doom from the unknown consequences of the merger or the failure to undertake it. There were predictions of a much rosier world to emerge from the combined natural and human resources of the two countries. There were protests against giving up long traditions on which history and legend were based. In the end, the people of both countries saw the inevitability of merger in the way the national social and economic characteristics and the mutual dependencies were converging; both were shaken by the prospects of national disintegration conveyed by the secession of major segments of what had been considered immutable unions; and they decided by a large margin that they had better join forces before the fragmenting went any further.

And so ended the illustrious histories of the United States of America and Canada, to be supplanted by the beginning and continuing history of the new entity, USCAN. But even that wasn't all. Time was marching on in the southern reaches of the former U.S.A. as well.

As we have seen, the first consequence of the secessions from both the U.S.A. and Canada was migration. People who felt they would be hurt by the new situation, or who didn't want to be in what they viewed as the newly alien environment that the splits had created, picked up and went to the remaining area that they thought would best suit their lifestyles and their social needs. They had problems getting settled as they clashed with and displaced local populations in turn, but in the expanding and increasingly controlled world economy they eventually found places because the economy followed labor markets for production and creation of services. Movement of an educated and productive populace that could also support the ubiquitous entertainment industry caused movement of facilities for goods and services that the migrants could produce.

In Canada, and then in the U.S.A., the migrations pushed people who were running away into conflict with people who had to accommodate to the new arrivals, like it or not. It was different along the southern border with Mexico. As was found in the union to the north, economics drives everything, especially when a majority of the people have a common language and cultural bond as well. In this case, the US/SW—the nation that had formed from the seceded states—became, at first, a magnet for migration from Mexico. The riches of California and Texas were legendary, and the borders were no longer guarded by the U.S. Immigration and Naturalization Service—the hated INS.

Or so many would-be migrants from Mexico thought. But the economies of the two main constituent states, Texas and Southern California, of the new nation had been fairly delicately balanced when they had seceded, and it was more difficult for them to absorb migrants from the south. The environmental constraints on immigration to the other states that made up the US/SW still applied. So the capacity of the new nation to absorb immigrants was rather limited. At the same time, there was less push for migrants to leave from the economy of Mexico, which had developed much more fully under the advantages of NAFTA and the spreading world economy than it had been when NAFTA started decades ago. In addition, the government had become more democratic and had gotten a better handle on drug corruption than had existed in those days—or, perhaps, the growing world of entertainment had made the drug culture more acceptable and had helped to exert more control over its nastier side effects.

Regardless of the reasons, Mexico was now less of a place to leave than it had been when the Hispanic communities of California and Texas were in their formative stages. The combination of reduced incentives to leave Mexico with US/SW resistance to easy absorption of immigrants led to a rapid tailing-off of the northward migration from Mexico. However, enough of it was consummated, in reunification of families that had split even a generation or more ago as "pioneers" moved from Mexico and Central America, as well as in additional entrepreneurial activities, for a solid majority of the population of the new US/SW to have become Hispanic a couple of decades after the nation was formed.

It was only a matter of time, and not so much time at that, before the language and cultural commonality across the US/SW-Mexican border led to talk of political unity as well. Political change without passion and upset is rare, however, and it did not occur in this case, either. On the one side were the irridentists who reminded everyone that the land they occupied had been pried loose from Mexico in a war of conquest two hundred years ago. On the other were the descendants of the mavericks who had fought for the independence of Texas and precipitated the war that had separated the others, and they were joined by the descendants of the oil and cattle barons who had moved in to establish the Texas of fact and legend. Again, the large Asian communities of California remained neutral. They had developed strong ties with sister communities along the U.S. West Coast and up into Canada, and they didn't care that much which government they lived under as long as it didn't turn repressive. But for the others, the arguments bid fair to lead to a civil war, which would have torn the new country apart faster than it had formed and destroyed much of the economy that had made the union so attractive in the first place.

But then wiser heads prevailed. The media, the universities, the technologically oriented communities that had been assembled under NASA, the Cold War defense industries and the former U.S. National Laboratories in New Mexico, the bankers, and all those who were in a position to take a wider worldview insisted that the combative nonsense stop and the main parties to the dispute—the Hispanic and the "ancestral Texan" communities—join in a conference to work out the differences. The advantages of closer economic cooperation, the evil consequences of the open warfare that was being increasingly advocated, and the reasons for the depth of cultural feeling on both sides were all laid out for everyone to see. It became easier to find a way through the mess. What emerged was something very like the merger of nations just then going on to the north—but with some significant differences.

It was decided not to merge the governments but to ally them closely in an economic and cultural confederation with open borders. The very term "confederation" did not have the same unhappy connotations here that it had in the United States and Canada. It was less than a political union but more than a customs union. Economic transfers would flow across the borders as though the border did not exist. Cultural exchanges and travel for any temporary purpose would be unrestricted. Resettlement would be discouraged but could take place on application to both governments and demonstration that there were valid economic accommodations on both sides of the border—the places left behind would not suffer, and those adopted could receive the newcomers profitably. This could be accepted as almost the equivalent of movement among the states of each country by its own citizens, because it was essentially self-regulating. In the current state of the world economy, no one would move to a place where there was no work, when economic and social conditions were almost the same in both the origin and destination country.

And thus was formed the Confederation of Mexico and the United States of the Southwest. But they, too, needed a name that people could hang on to. As in the case of USCAN, this became a great issue, involving pride of descent, tradition, and self-image. The settling argument this time was that the Spanish community had given up the union with Mexico that they really wanted, so the "traditional Americans" had to yield on the name to recognize the Spanish heritage of the majority of the federation's population. The result was the Confederation of New Hispaniola.

The appearance of that entity was exciting to the inhabitants of South Florida, as well as those of Puerto Rico and Cuba. The last was by now no longer under dictatorial rule but simply existed under the sometimes almost benevolent guidance of various economic interests; it had no strong government. The two island-states successively petitioned to join the confederation and were accepted after the usual few years of argument. The unintended consequence of that was to set off another wave of migration from the northern states of USCAN, especially New York and Illinois, that had large Hispanic populations. But there, again, the migrations petered out for reasons similar to those that led to the ending of the migration from Mexico, reinforced now by the social pressure from the would-be migrants' cultural confreres in the new countries.

And so we see how the geopolitical map of North America can change in a century or less. Improbable, you say? Well, look at how much it changed between 1750 and 1850, when the American colonies and then the United States and its European founders, and even major parts of the United States and Canada, were separated by weeks or months of travel needed to communicate and send goods and armies from one part to another. Then let's look at what's going on around us, in the United States and the world, when those times have been reduced to minutes, hours, and days at most. That's what we will be doing in the second part of this book.

PART TWO

REALITY: THE BACKGROUND TO NATIONAL SECURITY

3

WHERE DOES THE WORLD SEEM TO BE GOING?

History is the ship carrying living memories to the future.

—*Stephen Spender*

HOMOGENIZING THE WORLD

Chapters 1 and 2 took a fanciful yet plausible look into the world's future to support some mind-stretching speculations about what might befall our nation in the coming century. But that look was based on some authentic facts and trends, and so it can't be dismissed out of hand as fantasy. Now it is time to look at those and additional facts and trends more seriously and to assess their significance for the security of our nation. The particular concerns are the gradual movement of technology and national economies and cultures into entities that often grow beyond national control. We can understand our security only in terms of their impact on our own country.

The reader of this book does not need still another statistics-filled treatise on the globalization of the world's economy, technology and culture. The current buzzword, "globalization" represents the culmination of a trend that started during the Middle Ages. It is worth reviewing some of its manifestations briefly, touching areas that affect peoples' personal lives. It should be possible to extend from that into some thoughts on how it might affect our nation.

Several books taken together—in particular, *The Rise of the West* (1963), by University of Chicago historian William McNeill, *Technology in World Civilization* (1990), by MIT physicist-historian Arnold Pacey, and *Guns, Germs, and Steel* (1997), by UCLA physiologist-biologist Jared Diamond—are instructive on the subject of how the world reached its current state. They describe from many points of view how the peculiar economic, social, and military circumstances in Europe from roughly 1300 to 1500 initiated an aggressive expansion of Western civilization. Using technology built from Europe's indigenous heritage, together with some key technological inputs from the Middle East and Asia that Europeans adopted and extended, that expansion washed over the world in waves that have continued through the twentieth century. As it enters the twenty-first century, the Western world is feeling the backwash from those waves, especially from the Far East—Japan, China, other countries along the Pacific Rim—but also from India. With the amalgam of values from their own and Western civilizations, and their adoption of Western technology and economic theory and behavior, those nations have now joined Europe and North America in what is truly becoming a fairly uniform world culture—but one with some very important variations driven by persistence of ancient values.

Early notice of the implications of the backwash came to the West with the Russo-Japanese war of 1904–1905, which the Japanese won. The West gave little attention to the long-term nature of the implications arising from that obscure conflict. However, it certainly took notice after the Japanese use of Western technology enabled their expansion over all of Southeast Asia after they defeated the Western powers' "impregnable" fortresses located in Singapore and Pearl Harbor. The period following Japan's defeat in World War II saw the extension into Japan of American and European social and government concepts, in addition to still-advancing technology. In their own adaptations that would challenge the source, the Japanese have implemented, by economic investment and the spread of manufacturing technology and trade, much of the dream of a Greater East Asia Co-Prosperity Sphere that they could not achieve by warfare.[1]

The post–World War II period also saw the spread of one of Western society's less successful ideas, one that nevertheless took more than a half-century to (nearly) run its course, inflicting much pain on humanity in the process. That was, of course, the Marxist philosophy that responded to the European industrial abuses of the mid-

---

[1]The country where they could not succeed even in the economic area, however, was China; the war-engendered antagonisms have run too deep, and China will likely arise by its own efforts to challenge Japan economically as severely as Japan has challenged the United States. China is, of course, another whole story, one that we will revisit shortly in a different context.

nineteenth century. It was defeated, as much as by any other cause, by the same combination of Western philosophical concepts and late-twentieth-century technological advances that transformed Japan and created today's international economy.

Whether transfiguring technology was a consequence or a driver in the spread of Western civilization may be subject to argument, since it is well recognized that technology alone does not shape human affairs. However, I argue here that the combination of social organization that led to the growth of corporate economies (whether state-run or privately run, beginning with the early European expansion), together with the advances in technology that induced their evolution and growth, have contributed in many ways to the economic power of nations, especially that of the United States, Western Europe, and Japan.

One can identify the technological advances that appear to lie at the root of progress in a particular direction. Three identifiable advances have changed the world since World War II: modern air transportation, which can move goods and people around half the world in less than a day; communications, which can move ideas, images, purchase orders, and ownership of enormous economic assets around the world in seconds or minutes; and computers, which enable coordinated control of such assets and the people and machines that create them, from many widely dispersed locations around the world. Of course, there are many other companion advances, but these three epitomize the consolidation of capability that has brought the world together as in no other time in human history.

These developments opened the world to a flood of goods and ideas that led to an economic and political evolution with which the dictatorships of the proletariat could not compete using their antiquated methods of physically enforced, centralized control of human activities. Even the few remaining authoritarian regimes find themselves faltering before the twin assaults of free-wheeling world economic expansion and the communication of Western ideas about life, liberty, and the pursuit of happiness that seem to go with it. China, for example, is rapidly freeing up its economy while trying to maintain close central control of social and civic life. It is widely anticipated (and feared by current Chinese rulers) that in the long run China's social control will be transformed by the impact of economic development.

Perhaps for the time being the populations of North America, Europe, Japan, Australia, New Zealand, and a few other enclaves scattered around the globe benefit most fully in their personal standards of living from the advances in global communications. Gradually, the rest of the world is feeling the benefits as well (more or less rapidly, depending on how the 1990s Asian economic depression resolves itself in various countries). Some of the rest-of-the-world governments may not initially view the trends as beneficial, but they will be overwhelmed by the flood. As even China has recognized, they must transform themselves in some way or die. And other less developed countries are being caught in the swell. Thus, we are <u>living through the approach to a world civilization, or as close to one as humanity</u> may ever come.

It is always easier to reconstruct how something happened than to see it coming. We could argue that the spread of European colonial economies marked early beginnings of today's worldwide economies. Certainly, the British and the East Indians were closely intertwined and mutually interdependent. But that linkage, and others like it, might be attributed to trade alone. True economic integration and cultural melding take much longer, especially in view of the slow movement of goods and services over distances during the colonial period.

The pace of global economic integration picked up at the beginning of the twentieth century. Perhaps the oil companies, beginning late in the nineteenth century, were the harbingers of the modern international corporate economy. Trade, banking, and some industrial investment could move early across international boundaries. In industry, steel and railroads were for a long time indicators of economic development. Their development in one country after another was helped by extension of processes and finances across the oceans. After World War I there was much public concern about the impact of arms companies' international ties on the pursuit of warfare between nations. The automobile industry was also one in which ideas and manufactures moved across national boundaries early in the twentieth century. But the great modern expansion of international business penetrated the public consciousness during the 1950s and 1960s with the Japanese capture of the market for consumer electronics, beginning with small transistor radios. Obviously, too, the worldwide reach of wireless and transoceanic cable communications opened the way for internationalization of communications companies like ITT, a trend accelerated by the inherent global reach of the new satellite communications technology. By the 1960s it was becoming clear that international corporations were assuming a degree of autonomy that, it was feared, might be able to challenge governments.

This fear was articulated in 1968 when Jean Jacques Servan-Schreiber, former prime minister of France, published the book *The American Challenge*. In it he postulated that the greatest challenge to European autonomy came not from some foreign army but from American-led international corporations that would dominate Europe's economy without answering to any European government. He was wrong about the specifics if not the nature of the general phenomenon, as it turns out, because penetration of U.S. companies by foreign (European and Japanese) corporations in the ensuing decades came to be viewed in this country as posing just as much of a challenge to U.S. security as Servan-Schreiber feared we would pose to that of Europe.

The American public became aware of that threat from our flank, so to speak, when U.S. corporations, at least in the automotive industry, were brought up short by the Japanese gauntlet flung down during the 1970s oil crises. It just happened that the Japanese had the small, efficient, inexpensive cars that the United States needed at the time, which helped the Japanese penetrate U.S. automobile markets massively. The U.S. automobile industry had loomed so large in both U.S. and world markets that the entire world economic balance was then tilted strongly away from the United States. And the worries were increased by the propensity of foreign money to seek out and buy U.S. companies and properties when the deficit in the U.S. economy drove up interest and other rates of return and encouraged overseas investors to gobble up American assets.

More profoundly, however, the U.S. and Japanese economies were caught at different phases of advance along a typical logistic curve, so called because of the mathematical equation that describes it. Economies, like many other human and natural phenomena, follow a development curve shaped roughly like a flattened S: They start out slowly, with a gradual buildup; they rise steeply for some indefinite period; then they gradually flatten out and stabilize at some higher level, until something starts renewed growth from the new base. The movement along the logistic curve is not always smooth, but many data from different fields of endeavor and different parts of nature show it to be almost inexorable over the long run.[2]

Viewed from this point of view, it turned out that the Japanese economy, after starting from near-total destruction at the end of World War II, had entered a phase of rapid growth (the steep part of the logistic curve) during the 1970s, at a time when the U.S. trajectory was leveling off due to older technology that had matured before and during the war. Japan's position in the sequence enabled it to renew its manufacturing technology to achieve a new level of economic benefit, whereas the United States, rather than paying special attention to innovative modernization, was recovering the investments that had been made using older technology to meet the postwar demand for goods. Europeans were also rebuilding from a standing start under the Marshall Plan and subsequently, but much of their growth was channeled into building the welfare states that characterize Western Europe today.

The Japanese, focused on overseas resources and a strategy of growth through expansion of exports, were thus uniquely positioned relative to the other industrialized economies to create new manufacturing concepts and technology. They invented "lean" manufacturing that could substitute robotics, computers, and new organizational concepts for old-fashioned production lines to tailor products ad hoc to many variations in demand for specific characteristics. They also pioneered economics-driven advances in product reliability. As Akio Morita, longtime chairman of Sony

---

[2]See, for example, *Little Science, Big Science*, by Derek J. de Solla Price (New York: Columbia University Press, 1963).

Corporation (1976–1994), commented in a 1970s speech, Sony could not afford to keep the 7,000-mile supply line between manufacturing plants in Japan and major markets in the West full of spare parts under the older quality-control concepts that U.S. manufacturers still followed. Those concepts accepted sampling and replacement of significant numbers of failures as the preferred economic solution to quality control, rather than investment in ensuring fewer failures in the first place.

It took U.S. and European companies the best part of two decades to catch up with the Japanese innovations. In the process the manufacture of automobiles took another great step into the realm of international basing. As happens in any area where economic and trade policies interact, cars were manufactured in countries where labor was cheaper and then shipped for sale elsewhere. As a way to learn how to build small, efficient cars, American companies made agreements with Japanese companies to build cars of Japanese design in the United States. Then, under the spur of trade restrictions on imports and associated U.S. legal requirements for certain fractions of automobile parts to be of U.S. manufacture, the Japanese set up manufacturing plants in the United States to build the cars that became best-sellers here. They were followed by BMW and Mercedes-Benz from Europe. Thus, the internationalization of the automotive industry was accelerated even by the attempts to restrict that movement.

But automobiles were far from the only products that expanded into international production. There were many parallel advances in internationalization of manufactures, in areas as disparate as electronics, airplanes, clothing, and chemicals. Basically, the manufactures were chasing cheap, trainable labor, although the skill levels demanded were obviously different across product lines. Whatever the reasons, and wherever the impetus began, we now see a world in which electronic equipment is manufactured throughout the Pacific Rim—Taiwan, Singapore, Korea, Malaysia— as well as in the United States, Europe, and Japan. Commercial (airline-oriented) airplane manufacture, led by Boeing in the United States and by the French-led European consortium Airbus, is distributed worldwide, with Japan, China, other countries along the Pacific Rim, Canada, and European countries such as Spain and Italy all making sections of airplanes that are assembled in the United States and Europe. (This is an expansion of the pattern that developed initially within the United States and Europe, where parts of aircraft are manufactured by various subcontractors and assembled in home plants.) Canada, France, Brazil, and Israel have, in the meantime, become centers for the production of smaller airplanes for use by corporations and feeder airlines.

The dispersal of aircraft manufacturing was led by the demand for a piece of the economic action in exchange for purchasing the companies' aircraft for national airlines, agencies, and corporations, but it has also conveyed mutual economic benefits in other directions. For example, very early in the 1960s, Lockheed found it useful to involve a large group of English aerodynamics and structures engineers in the design of the C-5A military transport airplane, using international communications to receive and incorporate the results of their work into the airplane design being integrated in the United States; they represented a pool of available talent that would otherwise have been idle, and they helped meet a demanding design schedule. Russia, during the Cold War and since, has been helping India build an aircraft industry. The United States, Europe, and Russia are currently suppliers of military aircraft to the world, but manufacturing capabilities are spreading. We can confidently predict that within a half-century or so several Asian nations—China, Japan, and India, at least—will also be suppliers if the demand persists. Similar manufacturing and operating capabilities for space systems have been spreading, so that now launches of commercial satellites, made in any of a half-dozen countries, can be purchased from the United States, Western Europe (through the French-led Ariane consortium), Russia, and China. Japan will soon join this group.

Moving now to other areas of manufacture, we find that it is rare in the United States to buy clothing manufactured here. That was a result of the search for cheap labor in combination with cheap air transportation: garments might be designed in the United States or Europe, cut in Mexico, stitched together in China, and shipped back to the United States for sale at prices cheaper than it would cost to manufacture them totally in the United States. This may be viewed as a way in which U.S. jobs have been exported overseas, but cheap air transportation has its blessings, as well. For example, during the North American winter we can enjoy summer fruit grown in South America, and the movement and distribution of such delicacies creates other jobs to replace the manufacturing jobs lost.

This, indeed, is only one manifestation of the evolution of the U.S. economy from a manufacturing to a service economy. Other areas where service jobs have grown to replace manufacturing jobs lost have included finance, insurance, health care, management support such as strategic and financial planning, review, and problem-solving (all under the rubric of consulting), as well as facilities operations and management, in addition to all the different leisure industries of entertainment, travel, and sports equipment. In the long run there has been a net growth of jobs to match the growth in population, even as manufacturing jobs are lost. In these new areas, especially, computers and worldwide communications and ease of travel have enabled the spread of investment, focused use of distributed talent, and the movement of enormous sums of money in various commodity and currency exchange markets around the world.

Compared with the speed of changes in basic technology and the induced social patterns during most of human history, these radical changes in the world economy have taken place at lightning speed. Most such changes in the past took place over generations and centuries. Beginning with the rapid industrialization of Europe and the United States in the nineteenth century, they began to take place from one generation to the next. Now, with the 50–100 percent increase in the human life span (at least in the developed countries) since the beginning of the twentieth century and the concurrently reduced time for advances in technology, they happen within an individual's lifetime. Consequently, they have been accompanied by great social dislocation in a single generation, with much political conflict as well. Thus, for example, the spread of air-conditioning after World War II facilitated economic changes attending the search for cheaper, nonunion labor and thereby induced population movements that changed the American Southeast. The more recent spread of computers affected jobs and employment for huge parts of the population. In both cases, an older generation either had to adapt, which it did not always do satisfactorily, or else be replaced by a new generation trained to the new conditions.

Viewed in retrospect, however, these developments have an inexorable quality, because they are driven by strong economic and social forces that appear not to be stoppable by any single national or organizational entity; if resistance slows them in one area, they break out in another. As Russian and Chinese demand for U.S. rock music, U.S. imports of Asian-made clothing, and the manufacture of foreign-made automobiles in the United States illustrate, there is no locally based way to stop human ingenuity from finding the most economical and customer-satisfying way to circumvent any political barrier to economic and technological advance—and to social evolution as well. It's much like water finding a way to run downhill.

The growth of the international economy thus represents a strong trend that we in the United States can influence but cannot control. It is one that will affect our national security profoundly. Moreover, it is not only that these trends will affect our physical and economic well-being; they will affect us because our attitudes and awareness have not caught up with current reality. As a consequence of that lag, our own inappropriate behavior in response to external forces may harm us as much as any of the forces themselves.

What *does* the growth of the world economic system mean to America? It means that we have less control over our destiny than many of our leaders think we have or than we think we ought to have. Thus, when our politicians call for unilateral U.S. action in some international crisis, they are causing a dissonance with the international system that is likely to come back to bite us. There are huge concentrations of economic power, information power, and government policy influence in corporate entities of worldwide scope in all vital areas, from agriculture, energy, and transportation to information, banking, communications, and health care. First, these power centers act to influence U.S. policy in directions favorable to themselves. We see signs of this in the intense corporate lobbying that attends most legislative debates, as well as in the controversies surrounding campaign financing, which has come to involve not only major U.S. corporate interests but those from overseas as well. Second, if a policy position challenges the viability of the economic entities, we stand to suffer nationally.

We've seen hints of how such interactions can work during the 1996 set-to with China over its perception that we were supporting Taiwan's probe for independence, as well as in the ongoing arguments about the interaction of our position on human rights and our trade relations with China. Looming large in the background was the big and growing amount of U.S. trade with China, including a special and highly visible big-ticket item: Chinese purchases of Boeing aircraft. Aircraft and aircraft parts, along with computers, machinery, and automotive products, represent a large fraction of total U.S. exports, and the Chinese reminded us of their importance to us by ordering a number of transports from Boeing's rival, Airbus Industries, at the height of the crisis. Another example is contained in the U.S.-imposed embargo on trade with Iran, which has reinforced general French resistance—said to be based on principle—to U.S. foreign policy actions, ongoing or proposed, a resistance that has appeared in many areas from Iraq to the Balkans.

French policy is driven in large measure by economic as well as nationalistic issues, manifested in part in the Middle East by competition between international oil companies based in France and those based in the United States. Any negative impact of our conflict with France over the embargo on trade with Iran and Iraq that affects Middle East oil availability may impact Japan's security, since more than half of Japan's oil comes from the Middle East. That is a matter of concern to the United States because if Japan considers its national security sufficiently threatened it could decide to increase greatly its military forces and in the process to develop nuclear weapons. That would change the power balance around the world, and it would affect our own security profoundly. A security shock to the world triggered by precipitate U.S. policy actions could also stimulate a flight from the dollar (to the euro, for example) by the international traders who can shift tens of billions of dollars overnight. Such massive shifts could devastate the U.S. economy, causing job losses and economic distress around the country, if not the world.

These are, of course, "could-be" speculations. They are mentioned to illustrate that we are no longer in the position where we can act on our own in matters affecting other countries or major economic groupings—and what matters on the international scene don't affect them?—without thinking about wider ramifications rooted in the interlocked international "system." Such concerns do not mean that we should be frozen in our tracks when the need for strong action looms. They do mean that we had better be aware, while deciding what action to take, that many other affected nations, and economic interests that we don't wholly own but that can affect us seriously, may be involved in our decisions.

Awareness of the potential ramifications of our actions may often modulate our responses in international crises, because if we don't account for such factors the reactions of other major "players" affected could undo or distort what we are trying to accomplish. For example, during the December 1998 crisis over weapon inspections that led the U.S. and Great Britain to undertake a punishing set of air attacks against Iraq, Russia threatened to resume full trade with the latter. That would make our position in maintaining sanctions as a means of pressuring Iraq to give up its major weapons programs untenable. Depending on the situation, such perverse effects hurt us more than our direct actions help us. The voices that cry "do thus-and-such; never mind what 'they' think; we should not let 'them' decide our foreign policy" are voices that are stuck in the past.

Others who have not caught up with current conditions are those who would deny American contributions to shoring up international companies' or other countries' economies when they stumble—an argument that heated up during the 1998 Asian financial crisis. They are the same hard-line free-marketers who would have denied bailouts to Lockheed and Chrysler when they were in trouble during the 1970s and 1980s and to Mexico during its 1997 financial crisis—cases where the financial help averted worse disasters that would have harmed our own economy severely if left to run their course. In the end, for example, the Lockheed and Chrysler bailouts led to industrial success that created many jobs and was very beneficial for our economy.

All these go-it-alone voices who profess to have the American taxpayer's interests at heart fail to recognize the complex feedback loops in modern economic enterprises, which have moved from local to national to international in their scope and reach during the past half-century. Those feedbacks can affect the American taxpayer in the long run far more than any immediate savings generated by unilaterally oriented responses to problems overseas. It may be desirable to pay the economic penalties at times, in the interest of higher matters of principle. If the proponents of unilateralism said, instead, "Let's do thus-and-so, and we are willing to accept the possible consequences," they would be recognizing current realities. Few in Congress talk that way in the American political system, whereas the president has to act in the knowledge of the national and international ramifications of any U.S. foreign policy action.

Another implication of the globalization of economic power and the accompanying shifts of political power are that decision time on the international scene has become painfully slow. As long as aggressors can complete their actions before a coalition to oppose them can be built, there is a good chance their actions will succeed.

Such time is extended by the effect of parallel tensions between international and national politics in other countries with whom we may have to make common cause. They, too, feel the internal tension between the new sources of power and persistent nationalistic or xenophobic attitudes among their people and government representatives. And the ability to build coalitions is made even more difficult and time-consuming by the growth of extranational modes of conflict, such as terrorism and information warfare (which we will examine later), because nations are unable to agree on the nature and scope of the attacks. By the time all these things are worked out among several countries to craft a unified action plan, there is a good chance that the results of any aggression will have been consolidated. Undoing them will then cause much more pain and take much more effort, as we saw in the events leading up to the Gulf War, NATO's entry into Bosnia, as well as that in Kosovo.

From all this we can see that from our point of view a major perverse effect of the homogenization of the world's economies and cultures is the added complexity it introduces into planning and action to protect U.S. national security. Most of the effects that we must be concerned about, sketched out in the previous paragraphs, represent an intensification of patterns in international interactions that have existed for decades, even centuries. Indeed, Sun-tzu's fourth-century B.C. work *The Art of War*, mentioned in the Chapter 1, contains a section on fighting coalitions. A primary dictum of coalition-fighting is to try to split the coalition by playing on the disparate interests of its members. What is different today is, first, the impact of technology that helps information travel rapidly and widely at the same time that it makes the information easy to distort, and second, the far greater role of international economic connections that condition national thinking about international issues. We have seen all these factors operate in Saddam Hussein's increasingly successful attempts to split the coalition of European and Arabic states that we are trying to hold together to contain his regime.

These modern developments bring many more voices into the policymaking picture, adding uncertainty of outcome to slower decisionmaking at the same time that modern modes of aggression heighten the importance of focus and speed in containing the aggression. In addition, with the spread of advanced military technology to many nations, both friendly and hostile, we would have to spend much more to gain and sustain a decisive military technological advantage over the countries that would do mischief to us and our interests, just at the time when we have wanted to reallocate resources that we thought were freed by the end of the Cold War.

The disconnects, if we can call them that, between traditional attitudes and modern realities have been at the heart of the abandonment of the bipartisan approach to U.S. foreign policy that Senator Arthur Vandenberg helped craft in the days immediately after World War II. Thus, the scene is set for internal conflict about foreign policy issues, not the least effects of which are to let the world think this nation cannot act and to encourage transgressors against peaceful intercourse among nations and peoples—transgressors such as Iraq in Kuwait, Serbia in Bosnia and Kosovo, as well as Iran and Libya in their support of international terrorists—to think we will not respond to their transgressions. Such is the stuff that wars are made of.

We in the United States have not yet figured out how to take account of the new kind of world that has grown up around us almost without our realizing it. We must think up new ways to act decisively to further our interests in international affairs rather than trashing those interests with "oldthink"-based actions that have unintended adverse consequences. Can we, or will we, do it as we march boldly into the next millennium? That is anybody's guess at this point.

NEW REGIONAL POWERS WITHIN OLD GEOPOLITICAL CONTEXTS

We could be lulled by the persistence of old national boundaries into thinking that interactions among nations across those boundaries will continue much as they have in the past. Nothing could be farther from the truth. History shows us that nations change and their situations relative to each other change. We will find that the spread of European and American civilization to the rest of the world carries with it not only reverberations of Western technology and forms of government but also the beginnings of a new world power structure that, by its very existence, will diminish our own power relative to the world at large. At the same time, friction along the boundaries between adjacent power centers will mean that, although we might work hard at trying to achieve or encourage fully stable and peaceful relationships among the various power centers, we cannot necessarily count on them as we move farther into post–Cold War times. Bear with me while I take you on a quick and somewhat unconventional tour of the post–Cold War world. The purpose of this tour is not to predict what problems may arise, or to predict how they will or must be worked out, or to prescribe actions to solve problems we see right now. It is simply to point up where the persistent and almost intractable hot spots will be and to indicate something of their nature.

William McNeill, cited above, describes a rough balance among the four major civilizations of the Eurasian landmass—Western, Middle Eastern, Indian, and Chinese—during the two millennia from 500 B.C. to 1500 A.D. (Africa south of the Sahara, the Americas, and Australia did not figure much in this balance, for reasons ably illuminated by Jared Diamond, also cited above.) In McNeill's sense, "balance" does not mean that there was not incessant competition and conflict within and among these broad cultural groupings; it means, rather, that no one of them was able to dominate the others completely. That changed with the "rise of the West," to use his term, in the years since about 1500 A.D., when the European powers spread their influence and hegemony around the world. Now that the Western expansion has run its course and the West is feeling the reflected effects of that expansion in the growing strength of other parts of the world that were affected, we seem to be coming into a period of balance not wholly unlike that of the earlier millennia (before 1500)—but on a global rather than a continental scale.

With due allowance for the tendency to homogenize cultures and technology that characterizes the modern world, many of the fundamental cultural traits of the four progenitors of the modern world's culture have been remarkably persistent. Any world-traveled observer waking up today from a Rip van Winkle–like sleep that began, say, in 1492, would (after overcoming bewilderment at the achievements of modern technology) still have no difficulty knowing whether she or he is in a European-, Middle Eastern–, Indian-, or Far Eastern–derived cultural milieu. The geographic domains of the different cultures would be vastly different, however, and there would be some significant divisions within them. If the observer rolled over and went back to sleep for another half-century or so before reawakening, the world would likely appear to have a number of regional power centers and a different pattern of working out conflicts among them.

In the American-European complex, there would be a core with two major outlying branches. The core would constitute what we might now call the North Atlantic grouping, in which the major industrialized states of Western and Central Europe, together with the United States and Canada, have formed a broad industrial and political alliance (enlarging upon the NATO military alliance) to preserve their economic, cultural, and political interrelationships. Like families everywhere, they quarrel a lot and have differences over how to deal with the major and minor regional powers of the other three cultural groupings, but they have come to an understanding that the traditional means of settling quarrels among themselves—organized warfare—is no longer viable. It has been rendered obsolete by the power and destructiveness of the weapons modern technology has helped create. Thus, for all their quarreling, they form a large, rather unified economic and social organization that dominates the North Atlantic region.

Basically, the persisting and slowly evolving NATO alliance is holding the core together, and one of its core members, the United States, is the glue that keeps the alliance from flying apart. The fact that they no longer war among themselves does not bespeak the end of the value of military power, however, especially in dealing with the other regional groupings outside the North Atlantic alliance's cultural and historic milieus. Alone among the North Atlantic allies, the United States is able to project military power around the world, and that capability is made available to the others in the tacit coalitions that they form, as well as to the formal NATO Alliance when it agrees to act as a unit. Even if it is not always practical to use such power in warfare, for the same reasons that the European states recognize the futility of set-tling their affairs by warfare in the old historic modes, the possibility or risk of war-fare is useful in establishing relationships among nations and in guarding against marked changes in the boundaries of the regional power centers. And such power is especially useful in modulating the behavior of smaller nations—by warfare or the threat of it—along the boundaries of the major power centers when those smaller nations threaten the stability and security of the larger core.

We should not be smug in the assumption that the core will always remain cultur-ally and economically unified and internationally cooperative. The growth of a Eu-ropean economy with its own currency—a powerful unifying factor—could lead eventually to some form of the political unity that Frenchman Jean Monnet visual-ized in 1950 when he proposed what has now grown into the European Union. That would transform Western Europe as a whole into a "nation" of some kind that would be about the size of the United States in population and economic power (and in military power, if it wished to develop that way). The NATO alliance could remain a part of this new Europe, but it would be only a part. That alliance itself will in-evitably change as international conditions and relationships change elsewhere. It has yet to fully settle on a replacement satisfactory to all the members for the initial cohering impulse to protect Western Europe from Soviet aggression. There is move-ment toward a more robust European pillar to the alliance, which will have its own military arm and the ability to take independent military action. Friendship could easily turn to rivalry, and rivalry to conflict—not necessarily military conflict—as di-verse interests that are even now becoming divisive, such as competition for Middle East energy resources, differences over how to deal with the Balkans, Turkey, Iraq, and Iran in the long term, and influence with emerging African economies, emerge and clash.

Alternatively, any movement toward a European nation integrating the states of the current European Union could founder on the economic stasis that appears to have set in. This could be induced in part by the welfare-state protections against the kind of economic turmoil that beset the transformation of U.S. industry in the 1980s and 1990s. The global economy's competition could cause schisms through the different reactions of British and German industry, largely privately owned, and French industry, heavily state-owned, that accentuate any centrifugal tendencies in the European Union. Or the United States could simply tire of the continual bicker-ing with its European allies over international economic and political issues and per-petual conflict in the Balkans—if such conflict is not dampened in the reconstruc-tion aftermath of Kosovo—and drift away to pursue other affairs in the Pacific and

Latin America. Were this sort of demise of NATO coherence to happen, it could be quite possible that the European Union would dissolve back into a weak and fractious group of states going their separate ways—one that, though it might avoid open warfare and have a strong economy based on the European common market, would remain politically and militarily weak as a group.

Even now, tensions among France, Britain, Germany, and the United States over many economic and political issues could furnish excuses for such fragmentation if we and they let it happen. NATO is at a crossroads, groping for the formulation of a new mission and perhaps a new identity. The idea has been put forward that NATO must see to the *security* of Europe, rather than simply its defense. Such security could involve military operations out of area—outside the traditional NATO territorial defense boundaries—and also outside the traditional definitions of what constitutes defense against a threat to any nation's security. Indeed, we have seen that trend implemented with the entry into the conflicts attending the breakup of Yugoslavia, although U.S. leadership is still sought. Also, in addition to the movement toward an independent European military arm, Germany has raised the issue of changing NATO's nuclear deterrence policy, and there have been serious disagreements between France and the United States about Balkan and Middle East policy. Inability to find an acceptable common ground in this welter of issues could send the whole structure tumbling. Or the alliance could come together through the need to face the crucial issues of conflict and reconstruction in the former Yugoslavia, which, by entailing the risk and periodic occurrence of outright warfare, could override many of the others.

No one has yet proposed a credible alternative policy other than hanging on, meeting issues in context of real events as they arise, and waiting for a trigger that leads to a whole new view. It is agreed that the United States must remain engaged with Europe; only when we move does that alliance seem to move, even in matters as serious as the genocide in the former Yugoslavia. Together with our relationship with Japan (on which more later), it gives us a sort of anchor to provide for some underlying stability in relationships with much of the industrialized world. But it has been feared that opening a discussion on what NATO is all about, or should be all about, in a world where Article V of the North Atlantic Treaty—which states that an attack on one nation in the alliance is an attack on all—has little meaning in the absence of a massive, Sovietlike threat, would start the unraveling of the alliance. The conflicts in Yugoslavia add another set of potentially destabilizing forces and interfere with the enfolding of Russia into the Western community of nations.

Clearly, there is work to do. As in all marriages, both we and the Europeans, whatever form their nationalities evolve into, will have to work at staying together as a viable economic and political alliance regardless of various disagreements. With due allowance for all the frightening possibilities sketched out in the last few paragraphs, it may be safe to project that, in the manner of marriages, we and our allies will do the necessary work. The realization of the consequences to all the members if any one of the untoward outcomes actually happens will probably be enough to halt centrifugal tendencies at the brink and to hold both the communities and the alliance together for the foreseeable future.

The most important outlier of the North Atlantic grouping is Russia. Russia at the turn of the century is essentially a land in chaos. Its economy is in shreds, it cannot collect taxes to support the activities of a state, its armed forces are in a poor to nonexistent state of training and equipment and are not being paid, and there is essentially no national government whose writ goes beyond Moscow, perhaps not even that far. It is descending into a realm of barter and crime reminiscent of the European landscape in the Dark Ages. The Russian Federation could break apart altogether in a welter of local wars. For the moment, however, let's think about Russia as a viable political and economic entity, which we should assume it will be sooner or later.

Russia has always been somewhere between a European and an Asian power. If it can pull itself out of its current economic and political chaos, over the next decades it may firmly adopt some form of Western economy and culture. That may mean it will be at odds within itself over the differences between its Oriental and Occidental parts, and some part of Far East Russia, splitting in eastern Siberia and looking to its Mongol and Oriental heritage, might well go its separate way. But Russia's interest also turns south, looking for warm-water access and the influence needed to accommodate, along its long southern border, with the Muslim Middle East regional power that we will look at shortly. As part of this, and also for historic reasons that made Ukraine a source of food, energy, and other resources for Russia, the current uneasy independence with economic relationships between the two could later turn either into an alliance or into conflict.

Since the North Atlantic grouping also has an interest in the Balkans and the Middle East, its interests and Russia's tend to clash in those regions. In the Balkans, Russia has, from long historical perspective, supported the Serbian urge toward consolidation of its hold on the entire region that formerly constituted the Yugoslav Federation. Also, given Russia's twentieth-century history and the outlook on human suffering that the experience has generated, at least in government circles that make policy, they are less concerned about the loss of life and ethnic cleansing by the Serbs in the Balkan Peninsula (as well as other groups when they get the chance) than they are about supporting the geopolitical aspirations of fellow Slavs and coreligionists. Culturally and economically, the peninsula is peripheral to NATO Europe's concerns. However, it is a source of challenge to Western moral conscience conditioned by the Holocaust of World War II and the roles played by the Nazi-controlled countries. And as long as Serbia tries to extend its dominion over the entire region by cruel military means and Russia supports that urge, it will be difficult for Russia and the West to have a true rapprochement. Also, by virtue of the religious overtones coincident with the ethnic conflicts in the region, this stand-off also involves Greek and Turkish interests in the outcomes of events in the Balkan Peninsula.

It thus appears that this region—the eastern Mediterranean—will be a continuing source of instability and political, if not military, conflict in the relationships be-tween European nations and Russia. The West will be caught in an unending effort to contain the conflicts that Serbia and the other peoples of the region may generate. It will live in fear of the conflicts spreading to inflame the ancient Greek-Turkish an-tagonisms; that fear will keep the United States and the West engaged in the Balkans indefinitely. And that engagement may well sustain a constant barrier to enfolding Russia into the Western community. Also, as far as the United States is concerned, the barrier will be aggravated by policy differences within the Western alliance and with Russia over Middle East policy.

The most likely outcome of Russian policy with respect to Muslim countries would be Russian formation of alliances of convenience and necessity that support the major powers of the region—Iran and Iraq—in their differences with the West. France aspires to major influence with those countries as well. This is both for eco-nomic reasons (in which Germany joins) and to satisfy the need to maintain friendly relations with the Middle East as one element in guarding its southern flank from in-cursions by Algerian terrorists and refugees. Thus, the French and the Russians seem to be forming another alliance of convenience that, by engaging the United States in disagreements over Iraq and Iran, disturbs the unity of purpose of the North Atlantic grouping. The most effective way for the United States to keep the other countries' relationships with Iran from interfering excessively with its own position in the Mid-dle East would be for it to bring relationships with Iran into something approaching mutual tolerance and respect, if not friendship—not easy to do in view of past and current political circumstances.

There are other Russian quarrels with the North Atlantic alliance. Russia, even though guardedly friendly to the United States and its allies, has had continuing in-ternal arguments about whether that relationship is in Russia's long-term interest. The arguments initially revolved around the admission of Central European coun-tries to NATO. To Russia this looks threatening, no matter how kind a face is put on it. In fact it looks like the victorious alliance pushing its boundary farther east after a bloodless victory in a fifty-year conflict, eating up the land buffer that has protected Russia in the traditional counterinvasion sense of trading land for time. That habit of thinking is obsolete in the modern world yet hard to shed. Russia has warned against the inclusion of the Baltic republics—Lithuania, Latvia, and Estonia—in NATO following the inclusion of Poland, Hungary, and the Czech Republic. If that happens, Russia would again feel beset by enemies and cut off from its access to the sea, and that feeling will likely explode in hostility.

The reaction would be even more violent should Ukraine, traditionally viewed by Russians as essentially a part of their country, become more closely allied with NATO, a connection that the Ukrainians, who do not accept the Russian view of their relationship, seek. The Russian perception of threat from NATO can only be augmented by its reaction to NATO's military operations against ethnic cleansing in the former Yugoslavia; indeed, some conservative Russian politicians immediately emphasized the revival of the so-called NATO threat to Russia. If Russia needed another reason to hold back from an unreserved commitment to friendship with the West, Kosovo is it. And that will be augmented if the United States takes unilateral action that in effect abrogates the ABM Treaty—an issue that we will discuss in detail later.

Taken together with the instabilities engendered by Russia's economic collapse in the struggle to change from a command to a free-market economy and the attending hardships on the population, the tensions in the above areas could well lead to a resurgence of Russian nationalism and xenophobia. That would certainly lead to a resumption of hostile confrontation with the United States and its NATO allies if the alliance holds together. The rise of a leader who preys on the current chaos and resentments could easily bring this about. This would not be the first time in recent world history that a Machiavellian leader would use foreign rivalries and adventures to unify a country or to establish the authority to bring internal order out of chaos, as the histories of Napoleon, Bismarck, Hitler, and Stalin attest.

Perhaps with enough time and a run of good fortune and solicitude about its concerns by the rest of Europe and America, as well as some sort of subsidence of overt conflicts in the Balkans, Russia could eventually grow into a friendly regional power or return to world-power status. Regardless of what the future holds, Russia's size and residual stores of nuclear weapons and delivery systems make it a force to be reckoned with, even today. Another source of concern over Russia's volatility is the risk that its nuclear and other weapons design capabilities will be leaked to hostile countries. (We will take note of this risk in later discussion of threats to our security that cross national boundaries.) This could be one of the greatest dangers facing our nation and the world for the first decade or two of the twenty-first century. The perverse upshot of all these developments is that as long as the Cold War's hostile, two-sided, NATO–Warsaw Pact standoff continued it gave a certain stability to the international relationships in the European and North Atlantic regions of the world, whereas now that the hostility has subsided significantly the relations among nations within the region have entered a time of potentially dangerous instability.

The other noncentral branch of Europe-derived civilization, much changed from its original Iberian character by centuries of relative isolation, is Latin America. For five centuries Latin America was peripheral to European and North American interests, except as a location for refuge and economic exploitation. That is changing rapidly. Economic development in Mexico, Brazil, Argentina, and along the Pacific Coast and northern coast of South America bids fair to make the Latin American region an important economic power in the coming decades. Certainly, it will influence economic and cultural affairs in the United States and Europe in the decades to come. Although the region is not usually viewed as a major power center comparable with the others, that could change as the region's economies strengthen.

Although we may not like to recognize it as such, the northwest Andean region already has a major impact on North America, Europe, and Russia through the drug trade. Rail as we will against it, it constitutes a major component of the total world economy and influences that economy and the constituent societies by drawing off substantial disposable income and in many other ways that we need not recount here. We will examine the region's role as a power center in that context later.

The Middle East grouping includes the countries on the great arc reaching from Algeria along the southern and eastern Mediterranean through Asia Minor into Afghanistan. It extends westward from Algeria to Mauritania on the Atlantic Coast of northern Africa and eastward from Iran and Afghanistan into Pakistan. Characterized by the dominance of the Muslim religion, it has the unity of culture and outlook that came with the Arab-driven Islamic expansion during the seventh and eighth centuries. That expansion reached north into Turkey and Central Asia and included Kazakhstan and the republics along Russia's southern border, stretching from the mountains and deserts of China's Xinjiang Province to the Black Sea, with Christian Armenia tucked in among them.

Like the West, although the Middle East grouping has a certain unity within itself, there are also many divisions within it that create uncertainty and instability in world relationships. Baghdad, at the core of modern Iraq, has a long history as an Islamic center regardless of the shape of the national boundaries that enfold it. There will be continued attempts by Baghdad to sustain the drive toward regional dominance that was thwarted by the Gulf War. It will be opposed by Iran, which is proud of its own long history—going back to the ancient Persian empires—and aspires to regional dominance itself. Iran's reach is longer still. The warlike activity of religious fundamentalists in countries from Algeria to Afghanistan, encouraged and in some cases actively aided by Iran, signals an underlying hostility to the United States and its interests that may be hard to counter in the long run. The "Great Satan" (the derogatory term for America) is not only a power that toyed with Iran's sovereignty by helping to set up the shah's government; it represents all the evils that Christianity and secular godlessness can visit upon the devout Islamic world. Governments in the area that are friendly to the United States, such as that of Egypt, find themselves under terrorist attack by these forces.

Iran is building up its conventional armed forces and reportedly is seeking the ability to field nuclear weapons and the missiles that would carry them as far as Europe and, ultimately, the United States. It is also reaching out to other Muslim countries along Russia's southern boundary from the Caucasus to Kazakhstan as a means of reinforcing its regional influence. Given Iran's huge oil resources, the fact that Iran is at the nexus of Middle Eastern and Central Asian oil flows to the West and Japan, and that it strongly influences the ideology and activity of the destabilizing Islamic ferment, Iran will be one of the dominant regional powers within the Middle East complex. Moreover, its position along Russia's southern border conditions Russian attitudes toward the United States. One of the first U.S.-Soviet confrontations of the Cold War arose when Stalin sent troops into northwestern Iran and President Harry Truman threatened military action against the move.

Thus, Iran lies at the center of a major Middle East geopolitical power flux that will influence our own and our allies' security profoundly. There have been some tentative overtures by Iran toward a friendlier relationship with the United States, to which the United States is responding positively but cautiously. Relations between Iran and the European countries are relatively good. Nevertheless, in the long run the conflicts in the Middle East between religious fundamentalism, which has at its heart religious control of the state, and the Western outlook, which has at its heart independence of the state from religious control, will make for uneasy relationships along the boundary between the two regional groupings. Although the popularly elected president of Iran is the one making overtures to the rest of the world, we must note that the more hostile Ayatollas control the armed forces. Therefore, they control the ultimate tools of conflict, which are growing in power and reach. Moreover, tensions within the region will spill over to generate instability and tensions within the North Atlantic grouping.

The best known such focus of conflict and instability is the perennial Israeli conflict with the Arabs, which one could argue is viewed by Arabs as a modern version of the recurring European invasion of the region dating from the days of the Crusades. Another is the conflict generated by the attempts of militant Islamic fundamentalists to impose their views on countries that don't want them imposed. A third, less expected source of instability is Turkey.

With a Western-type government since the Ataturk Revolution in the 1920s, Turkey—part of it in Europe, part in Asia—has aspired to join Europe, an aspiration that is continually rebuffed by the European Union. This action is viewed by the Turks as religious discrimination. There have also been continuing tensions between Turkey and Greece over Cyprus, and a continuing fear in the West that although both are members of NATO they will go to war with each other over the splits in Cyprus and the Balkans, as well as over sovereignty claims for islands in the Aegean Sea. On its other boundary, Turkey is constantly in fear of being diminished by the possible formation of a separate Kurdish state breaking away from Russia, Turkey, Iran, and Iraq. There are tensions between Turkey and Iraq over Turkish development of water resources in the Tigris and Euphrates Rivers flowing south from Turkey, unhappiness on the part of the Arab states and Iran with Turkey's military cooperation with Israel, and concern within Russia about Turkey reaching northeastward to form an association with Kazakhstan. That would put the resulting alliance, if such an alliance emerges from the overtures, astride much of the oil supply and its pipeline transport that the Western industrialized countries and China view as an important new source. Although Turkey is not in the forefront of our attention, it is clearly in a geopolitical position where events there can affect us profoundly in the long run. And if that weren't enough, its potential reactions to Serb persecution of Muslim populations in the former Yugoslavia make Turkey a shadow in the background that helps drive all of our policy in the Balkans.

From all this, it is clear that the Middle East presents two kinds of threat to the North Atlantic alliance. The first is that Middle East tensions will erupt into open conflict between the Middle East and the North Atlantic grouping (as they have in many terrorist attacks across Europe and the United States, for example). The second is that these tensions will generate conflicts between, for example, Southeastern European states and others either within or outside the North Atlantic alliance over Middle East relations. As part of this instability, conflicts involving Turkey could break up the North Atlantic alliance.

Such conflicts are reflected in the different approaches of the United States, France, and Russia to the Middle East, arising from the different interests each has in the region and in the tension generated among them as a result of those different outlooks. These strains are, of course, exacerbated by, even rooted in, the competition for Middle Eastern oil resources, which still represent the world's largest reservoir of that precious energy source. It can safely be argued that if there were no oil in the Middle East the tensions over access to the region would be much reduced. (Tensions could still arise over access to transportation routes and over religious issues, but modern transportation technology has made that a lesser concern than during the heyday of the British Empire; the West, at least, is less inclined to let religion rule its policies than it has been in the past.) But the need for oil to fuel industry and development in still other regions, including South Asia when that region advances enough industrially, and China, which has already started to reach for the oil, will amplify the effects of Middle East instabilities on U.S. relationships with the rest of the world.

There are even more sources of stress for Europe and North America that are based on Middle East concerns. For example, the essentially religion-derived conflicts in the Balkans involve the United States, Europe, Turkey, Iran, and Russia, all on different sides of the issues; as we have noted, those conflicts also heighten the risks that the building of a friendly relationship between the United States and Russia will be disrupted. It is clear from all this that the interactions between the two major cultural regions will keep the world stirred up for an indefinite time and that the other major regions will increasingly be affected by, and will affect, those interactions over time. The new period of "balance" among regional power centers that seems to be emerging from the Cold War—the one that President George Bush heralded in 1991 as a "new world order"—will clearly not be a tranquil one, for that reason alone.

Events in South Asia east of the Arab and Persian worlds would seem to be relatively isolated phenomena on the world scene, not affecting the North Atlantic, Russia, or the Middle East very strongly. But that view, too, is deceiving. Through the past two millennia or more, India has had a profound influence on world development, spreading its culture to Africa and Southeast Asia, to China in the form of Buddhism, and to Europe in many artifacts and aspects of life that the British brought home after conquering the subcontinent. In modern times, Indian emigrants make up an important part of the intellectual scientific community of the world. Invasions from Central Asia brought Islam to the northern part of India early in the millennium just ending and set the stage for conflict that continues to this day.

Aside from the turbulence among different religious and cultural groups within modern India, the Pakistani-Indian conflict over Kashmir continues. It could result in another war in the area, with the clear possibility that such a war could become nuclear and therefore damaging to other parts of the world. Although the United States wishes to promote democracy around the world as a step toward protecting its own security, our relations with the world's largest democracy, governing a nation of about a billion people, have been prickly since Indian independence from Britain and occasionally tense, subject to Indian resentment over purported U.S. slights and U.S. resentment over Indian friendliness to the Soviet Union. U.S. relations with

both India and Pakistan have been injured by interactions over the acquisition of nuclear weapons by both nations. In any case, it will be difficult for the United States
to maintain truly friendly relations with both nations simultaneously until the conflict between them is resolved.

India is slowly building its industrial strength. It has strong land forces and is expanding its navy. It has a force of missiles, easily tipped with nuclear warheads and
able to reach most of China and much of Southeast Asia and South Asia. At one
time, it expressed outrage that the United States 7th Fleet was operating in the Indian Ocean. Whether such attitudes continue will depend on many unpredictable
events of communication, miscommunication, and perception of real or imagined
slights, threats, or assists to regional interests on both sides. Aside from the obvious
dangers to the world of an India-Pakistani war that could go nuclear, the eventual
presence of a major industrial power in the Indian Ocean will have a profound effect
on the global power balance. That will, in turn, affect the United States in either a
friendly, trade, and cultural-exchange sort of way, or a in a quasi-hostile way that impacts our ability to look after our interests in the Middle East.

In the Far East, China is emerging as a major economic power while its government remains authoritarian and cautiously rigid in the face of imminent change
under the leadership generation that followed the communist revolutionaries. China
will have to change under the pressures of modernizing its economy and the impetus
that a modern, computerized economy gives to the spread of ideas about government. But we should not be surprised if that change goes in directions that may conflict with the ideas about democracy that we are pressing China to adopt.

Chinese culture has been developing and profoundly influencing the world for
7,000 years.[3] A unified Chinese state or closely tied group of states has controlled
much of the territory China occupies today roughly since Roman times. Although
Chinese culture embodies the Confucian idea of learning and an examination-
mediated meritocracy to lead local and state affairs, there is nothing in Chinese culture, as there was in English and European cultures, that would lead to a democracy
of the Western kind. Unlike many of the other cultures of the East, Chinese culture
has been strong enough to resist total absorption of Western ideas as they spread
around the world. Despite Western military meddling in its recent evolution, China
was never conquered and colonized as much of the rest of the world was. So we

---

[3]For those able to travel there, one of the best places to get a visual sense of the sweep and unity of this
culture is in the Far Eastern collection of Chinese art and artifacts in the Royal Ontario Museum,
Toronto, Canada. The display is chronological and is well accompanied by maps and narrative that give a
quick overview of the spread of Chinese civilization since the earliest times.

should expect that the Chinese cultural and governmental adaptation to spreading Western technology and its economic and social impacts will not follow the pattern we are preaching—in particular, the idea of free political thought that leads instead of follows central authority. Chinese governing authorities will likely be forced by the decentralized nature of modern technology and communications to tolerate some of the Western notions about free expression of ideas, but they will work out the need for governance suited to their role in the modern, computer-based economy in their own way, based on their own very strong traditions.

We must remain aware that along with its economic expansion, China is giving increased attention to modernizing and expanding its military forces. Those forces have also inserted themselves into the fabric of civilian Chinese society by assuming a major role in the growing civilian economy. China is also asserting and extending its claims on regional power, in avowed reaction to more than a century and a half of Western exploitation of its weakness attending the failing Qing (or Manchu) Dynasty and successive revolutionary struggles. It is brutally converting Tibet into a Chinese province with a majority Chinese population; it has moved to occupy the Spratly Islands in the South China Sea far beyond its territorial waters; it has reoccupied the remaining European enclaves of Hong Kong and Macao; it is increasing pressure on the world to recognize its claims on Taiwan as an errant Chinese province with which the world must have no independent diplomatic contact; and it has signaled its interest in controlling the seas to significant distances (e.g., 2,500 kilometers) from its coast. And as we were reminded by a Chinese spokesman during the Taiwan crisis of 1996, China has the ability to launch nuclear-armed intercontinental ballistic missiles against the United States.

Looking landward, China has taken steps to ease tensions along its borders with Russia and India. At the same time, it has taken a totally independent approach to foreign policy that has, on balance, been inimical to declared U.S. interests. Although China has helped contain North Korea, it has sold surface-to-surface missiles to Pakistan, Iran, and Saudi Arabia, and it has been suspected of giving assistance to Pakistan and Iran in the development of nuclear weapons. Despite lip service, China has de facto disregarded international norms for the protection of intellectual property that contributes to the growth of the Chinese economy. And it has displayed staunch resistance to U.S.-declared interest in encouraging the growth of democracy and respect for human rights in national and international affairs. Although China continues to pledge cooperation in halting the spread of nuclear and chemical weapons and delivery systems, the recurring need to remind the Chinese government of that pledge signals that it will keep trying to evade the constraints, retreating when discovered. At least, China's cooperation in these areas cannot be taken for granted. Chinese behavior in these matters would be consistent with China's geopolitical imperatives. It is to China's advantage not to have a nuclear-armed North Korea on its doorstep, but it is also to its advantage to stir things up in the Middle East so that we are occupied with concerns there and therefore less inclined to interfere in affairs in China or its immediate geographic vicinity.

In its economic expansion, China has succeeded in attracting Western capital to build indigenous high-technology industries in areas such as automobiles and aviation rather than simply importing finished products from the West. Our total trade with China is roughly twice as large as our trade with France, in dollar terms, but France imports about 30 percent more from the United States than China does. That is, China is exploiting the U.S. market more than it is letting the United States exploit the Chinese market. However, as shown by the continuing competition among major European and American corporations in these and other areas, a potential market of more than 1.25 billion people has Western industry falling all over itself to help China build up its industrial economy, whereas China exploits the help to make itself, ultimately, another fully viable competitor. Meantime, it exports the cheap products of low-technology industry, such as textiles, to the West to finance its growth, in the same pattern that Japan followed to its current economic power.

If China follows the pattern of development of Europe, the United States, and Japan, and barring untoward outcomes from the economic slowdown affecting the Pacific Rim in general, its large expansion at average rates between 5 percent and 10 percent per year could continue for another twenty or more years before it levels off to much lower growth rates along the logistic curve (described earlier), as the economic growths of the United States, Western Europe, and Japan have done. By that time, China might have a gross domestic product (GDP) above $10–12 trillion, exceeding any of the others. (According to data from the Organization for Economic Cooperation and Development, China's GDP in constant 1990 international dollars—dollars adjusted for relative purchasing power—had already surpassed Japan's by 1990.)[4]

All of these developments signal that, barring some major collapse arising out of political battles or other unforeseen events, or stunted growth brought about by overly restricted exchange of ideas that may have political implications and that choke off economic expansion in the process, China will be a major force to be dealt with in the coming years and decades. We have it partly within our power to turn

---

[4]These projections are based on data given in an OECD paper entitled "Chinese Economic Performance in the Long Run," by Angus Maddison. The inferences about future Chinese economic performance are my own, based on the data in Maddison's report and his projections to 2015. Maddison projects that China's GDP in international dollars will essentially equal that of the United States by 2015, whereas its per capita GDP will still be only about a fifth as much. There will clearly be much room for further growth in the Chinese economy.

this major force into one that may be either friendly or hostile to us. If we fail to respect and adapt our policies to China's strong feeling about Taiwan, and if we keep insisting that China must follow our Western traditions of governance instead of waiting patiently until it works out its own within a reasonable, humane framework, we will be helping to build a conflict that will be detrimental to our own well-being as a nation.

But it is probable that, regardless of anything the United States does to help or hinder it, China will develop into a major independent economic and military power both able and eager to project force well beyond its borders, unlike the way it turned back from that course in the fifteenth century.[5] Chinese territorial imperatives and need for resources, driven by today's global perspective, could look very different to China in the twenty-first century than they appeared during that earlier period. This more global view could lead China to attempt a major regional expansion. If that happens, Chinese interests and our own, which are intimately tied to the interests of others around the Pacific Rim, will clash. If events unfold that way, then China could become the "peer competitor" that replaces the Soviet Union as our rival for global power, despite any efforts on our part to develop friendly relations with China—an eventuality about which many of our military leaders express both anticipation and apprehension.

The other countries in the Pacific Rim will also loom large in future U.S. economic welfare and national security. The Republic of Korea remains a close U.S. ally and a potential flash point until there is some resolution of the deteriorating position in North Korea and some move toward peaceful reunification on the peninsula. Reunification would present the United States with a wholly different situation from today's, one that would affect the U.S. security position in the western Pacific profoundly. Surely, the North would not agree to unification of the two Koreas without a U.S. troop withdrawal. That would face us with a bittersweet development. The reason our forces are in Korea is to help guard against invasion from the North. That threat would evaporate with unification, so that there would be no further reason for us to have military forces in the country. That would be one more longtime military obligation we can stop worrying about!

But wait. Our withdrawal from Korea would move our military position much farther back from China's doorstep. That is a good reason for China's encouragement

---

[5]Arnold Pacey describes how the confluence of a series of unhappy interactions with the outside world and the completion of the Grand Canal between North and South China, which enabled grain shipments that did not require coastal sailing, led the Ming Dynasty rulers to turn inward. They decided not to build a navy and not to trade overseas. They had the resources they needed, right at home.

for North Korea to avoid giving us reasons to sustain our presence in the area. But a decline in U.S. military presence in the Far East will reduce our ability to encourage some kind of satisfactory rapprochement between China and Taiwan, and it will affect our relationship with Japan.

Japan, observing developments in China and Russia, has sought an extension of ongoing mutual security agreements with the United States, despite continuing tensions over trade and the U.S. military presence on Japanese soil. One of the reasons we are in Japan is to sustain our ability to protect Korea, among other interests in the western Pacific. If and when that need no longer exists, then we and Japan would have to ask ourselves what our presence in Japan is for. That would raise the need to think about whether China is really an antagonist requiring confrontation or containment by a military alliance. We and the Japanese (and others?) would have to decide whether we want to extend our current loose security agreement into a formal alliance. If that were done, it could lead to amendment of the Japanese constitution, which restricts the Japanese military to self-defense of the islands, and a subsequent significant expansion of Japanese military power. A militarily strong Japan would be more likely to go its own way. But if Japan remained allied with us, that might have the benefit of persuading Japan to continue to eschew nuclear weapons, thereby helping the United States support one of its vital interests: the inhibition of nuclear weapons proliferation.

The net result of all that soul-searching would likely lead in one of two directions: either a further U.S. withdrawal from the Far East, or an open admission of the need of a U.S. military presence in Japan to contain possible Chinese expansion. The Chinese would react strongly to the latter, as they have reacted strongly to the containment suggestion as applied to them in the past. We would then have created one of those situations where antagonism between the United States and China could grow as a self-fulfilling prophesy. As a third alternative, we could just leave things alone and not ask the tricky questions that would bring these unhappy possibilities to a head. This would follow the dictum "let sleeping dogs lie." But if we did that, there would be agitation in this country asking why we have to keep military forces in the Far East now that peace had broken out, when we could reduce the defense budget by the amount they cost and make the money available to meet other needs. And the agitation against the disruptive effects of the U.S. presence would continue in Japan, since a good case for that presence would be harder to make. So we can see that none of the choices for our presence in the Far East after Korean unification (or a Korean peace treaty, even without unification) would be very palatable.

Growing economic power centers in Southeast Asia, such as Malaysia, Thailand, and the other Southeast Asian states, keep a wary eye on China and Japan. As this is written, they are far more concerned with their internal economic affairs, but that will change. They remain friendly to the United States, and, together with Japan and the Republic of Korea, they have encouraged a countervailing U.S. presence in East Asia. They would like us to stay in Japan; that's a good place from which, from their point of view, we can act to contain both China and Japan. They will be quick to note if the United States weakens its security commitment to the area, which a withdrawal from Korea and Japan could signal, and their history suggests that they would then shift orientation away from the United States accordingly.

Thus, once we start down the slippery slope of a military withdrawal from the Far East, we might end by building the outer limits of our Pacific military position at Guam and Pearl Harbor. That would seriously degrade the global reach of our military power. Our ability to use the military instrument in support of diplomacy and economic interests by friendly engagement, or combat when necessary, would be much diminished; response time with substantial force would increase, and the other states in the area would have made other arrangements to guard their security without our help. Cascading all these possible political and military developments together, it is easy to see that, although we have a very strong position in the Far East now, that could either turn very weak or face us with Cold War II, as a result of events over which we might have little control.

Finally, we have to think about how Africa south of the Sahara might affect our security in the future. The area is not developed nearly as much, economically and in many respects politically, as the other areas we have been scanning. How far the current movements toward development in countries from South Africa to Somalia and Sierra Leone will proceed and succeed is very uncertain. But the southern half of Africa has powerful symbolic importance to the United States; it is a source of important mineral wealth to us and much of the rest of the world; and in its ethnic travails its people exert a strong humanitarian pull on the Western world, including the United States. As it develops economically, it will be added to the other centers of commerce, investment, and cultural exchange that the complex U.S. economy and cultural heritage reach out to. However it develops, Africa south of the Sahara will remain an area that we cannot ignore, one that may periodically require military action to protect our own and allied interests or simply to alleviate the effects of mass tragedies such as happened in Somalia and Rwanda. The chief significance for our security will be the impact on our attention and our financial and military resources, in relation to other claims on both.

As if "all the above" weren't enough, there are additional parts of the future geopolitical environment that are affecting us profoundly and that will do so even more in the future. One comes from organizations, sinister in character, that can carry as much weight as countries, or more, without being formally constituted or recognized as national bodies. Another comes from the impact on our popular perceptions when other cultures do not adhere to the Western heritage of chivalrous behavior in conflict and warfare. All that is what we have to look at next.

BEYOND NATIONAL BOUNDARIES

We talked earlier of the logistic curve in the growth of national economies—the curve that starts out slowly, rises steeply, and then levels off at some equilibrium point. Population dynamics seem to follow such a curve within a country or region of the world. The slow start occurs when rather primitive people live in a subsistence economy, in balance with the productivity of their environment, its food resources, diseases, and dangers. As they gain a measure of control over that environment—by inventing or adopting agriculture, for example—their population rises steeply in a kind of bootstrap cycle, driven in part by the need for offspring to replace losses due to war and disease. This has been the usual pattern until the modern age. Then, when longevity has caught up with productivity and war losses have been made up or warfare has declined, population growth in the regions that have reached that happy state has leveled off and even declined.

Different parts of the world are at different stages along this curve. In our modern world civilization with its rapid communications, longevity has increased faster than the economic and cultural changes that would bring birthrates into balance with declining death rates, so that population growth in developing areas has been very large. The advanced industrial nations have essentially reached equilibrium; population in some is even declining. Other countries with very large populations, such as China and India, are striving mightily and with partial success to control their population growth. One could project that at some point, if all the world could reach the stage of advanced industrial development, world population growth would level off to the replacement level, at roughly 10–15 billion people (10 billion is the current projection, revised downward in 1998)—two or three times as many people as there are in the world now. But that is a big "if," with many possible, obvious glitches along the way.

The impact of population growth in reducing the chance for a stable and peaceful world is difficult to overstate. It will affect the world by competition for resources such as freshwater, arable land, fuels for energy, materials and minerals for building and manufacturing, and a clean air and water environment. The competition will exacerbate conflicts inspired by tribalism and religion that tended to be suppressed for a brief century and a half in human history, during the height of British and French Empires and then the Cold War. The industrially developed countries will get into these quarrels because, although they may have decided that warfare is not a good way to settle their own affairs in this age of mass destructiveness, they will be part of the competition for resources that lie in great part in the less developed parts of the world. They will be influenced to participate by their own ethnic and religious histories and outlooks. And they will be affected by the flows of refugees from the ethnic and religious quarrels in the developing parts of the world. Indeed, the refugee problem can demand enormous resources, and it can be highly destabilizing by inducing injustices and causing political conflict. For illustration, we have only to examine our own political conflicts over both legal and illegal refugees from the Central American wars and economic disasters. And the armed forces do get involved, as they did over Haiti and, at times, over Cuba.

Developed countries may believe they have moved beyond tribalism, but they cannot escape the ethnic and tribal backgrounds from which they evolved to their current states of advanced culture over the past few thousand years. We see this in all kinds of exclusionary behaviors by the countries of Europe and Japan in limiting immigration, attempting to segregate the immigrants, forcing them to conform to local customs and remain subservient to the original population. The United States is, perhaps, less rigid about it than the others because its population is an amalgam of peoples and religions from many parts of the world, but even here we have much evidence of ethnic and religious orientation in our local politics, immigration policies, and foreign policy. We got into the Northern Ireland conflict in a big way, for example, although the conflicts in Rwanda, Kashmir, Sri Lanka, and East Timor have been much more deadly in human terms. In many cases—Nazi Germany, Yugoslavia, Rwanda—tribalism has led to attempts to exterminate whole populations. In other cases—again Nazi Germany, Algeria, Iran and Iraq, Israel and the Arabs, and the fragmenting Yugoslavia—religious issues have stimulated the fights. Indeed, the effects of tribalism and religion are difficult to separate.

Tribal associations and religion have been at once the greatest solace and the worst curse of humankind. They give humans, deeply conscious of their isolation in a coldly neutral or hostile universe, an anchor for their emotions and beliefs, structure for their lives, companionship, and a psychic place to call home. Religion gives an explanation of the unknown and hope for life after death, and the tribe or ethnic group provides comfort from fear of the unknown and from the tragedy of losses caused by war and natural disasters. Together, these two primal forces build a community, and humanity is a communal animal. At the same time, tribalism and religion have led to prejudice, intolerance, discrimination, torture, killing, and genocide, more so than any other force in the history of humanity. Even in the competition for resources, tribalism and religion give the rationale for rapacious behavior of nations or religious and ethnic groups within and across national boundaries.

Tribalism, religion, and competition for resources are not phenomena that respect national boundaries. National boundaries have evolved over history from the interactions among peoples and their conquests. But ethnic groups live across national boundaries, resources are distributed regionally according to natural phenomena that occurred long before humanity even existed, and religion, especially the proselytizing religions, make it a matter of doctrine and practice to cross national boundaries. And so the intertwined quarrels among religious and ethnic groups and the competition for resources know no borders and will manifest themselves in various ways in both the industrially developed and the developing parts of the world. Without the perverse discipline of two globally powerful alliances facing each other and attempting to gather in all neutral parties, and until a new such discipline may arise—if it will—the sometimes violent differences that transcend nations will dominate our international security landscape. And those differences will be dealt with according to the strengths of the proponents and opponents of any thrust for dominance in a particular conflict.

Terrorism has grown as a means for the weak to challenge the strong, as well as a means to pursue national objectives by violence without resorting to organized warfare. Local piracy and banditry have existed as long as there has been trade over the oceans or over long land routes through isolated or hostile territory. Exploding bombs to do damage and thereby get attention is not a new phenomenon, either, as Joseph Conrad's 1907 novel, *The Secret Agent*, reminds us. These kinds of activities were spread, and tended to merge into concerted campaigns with national support, by the turbulent evolution of twentieth-century geopolitics. The very advances in transportation and communication that have enabled the growth of global corporate reach have also enabled the spread of these kinds of warfare and criminal activity that do not have to stop at national boundaries.

Terrorism was used by the early Bolsheviks to spread their revolution overseas without explicitly implicating Russia as the perpetrator. Then, terrorism (along with guerrilla warfare) became a major component of the struggles, from the end of World War II through the 1970s or so, to overthrow the pre–World War II colonial empires. Spreading from the Indochinese and Algerian wars against the French, it became a key weapon in the Middle East wars against Israel and its supporters. Following that, terrorism, with variations such as kidnapping of U.S., British, and French citizens, gradually became associated with the spread of Islamism attending the Libyan and Iranian Revolutions and the drive to erase the Western presence in the Islamic world. The use of this weapon as a means of strategic conflict is illustrated by the bombings of the Marine barracks in Beirut, the Khobar barracks in Saudi Arabia, and the U.S. embassies in Kenya and Tanzania, as well as the avowed aim of terrorist leader Osama bin Laden to drive American influence and presence from the Islamic world. Meantime, terrorism was used as a regular weapon in the perpetual Irish religious conflicts and rebellion against British rule, in the Basque push for a state separate from Spain, in Cuba's quest for influence and perhaps hegemony in Central America, and in all of Latin America's guerrilla wars. We saw in the Oklahoma City bombing that terrorism becomes attractive to homegrown rebels who wish to challenge the movement of the United States into closer collaboration with the international community or simply to resist the trend toward tolerance among diverse cultural and racial groups. This was not very different from the homegrown terrorist activity that led the Aum Shinrikyo Society to release nerve gas in the Tokyo subway system and to plan to use biological warfare as well.

Although terrorists articulate many reasons for their attacks, two common threads run through them. The first is simply the attempt to force away a presence viewed as an "occupier." This explains the attacks on Americans and on Israelis, and it also, by indirection, explains attacks in third countries aimed at hurting the citizens and interests of those, such as America and Israel, viewed as enemies. But another very important philosophical reason for terrorism, especially domestic terrorism within countries (at least, for the terrorists who are not hate-mongers who kill out of simple hostility) is the belief that if they disrupt established society enough, and force the governing authorities to become repressive enough, the "people," whose interests they are fighting for, will rise up and establish a more just regime. From their points of view, they can see that they are succeeding. One has only to examine the increasing restriction of access and guarding of entryways to government buildings in Washington, D.C., or the growth of airport security and baggage inspection systems worldwide, to believe that the terrorists are making their point, for either reason.

Partly, the growth of the terrorist tactic through the century has a copycat flavor. Application in one area by one group encourages others to follow, for their own purposes. And the materials are readily available. But there have been hints that the connections among the different terrorist groups may be more organized and more purposeful than that. In 1981 the late Claire Sterling showed, in her book *The Terror Network*, that the various terrorist groups were loosely tied together by a network of training camps scattered in the Soviet Union and the Middle East, as well as by money flows, partly oil-financed, through various banks in Europe, the Middle East, the Bahamas, and other locations. There was a hint of KGB support for the activities. They wouldn't have had to do much more than start them through clients such as Libya and Syria, feed in some seed money and weapons shipments, then do some mild steering and training from the background.

If this was the situation in the 1980s, although the sources of support may have shifted with the demise of the Soviet Union, the ability to orchestrate worldwide campaigns has intensified since then, with improved international communications and organizational capabilities afforded by satellites and computers. This has been suggested by the recent trials of the New York World Trade Center terrorists, whose chief architect was caught planning a series of airliner bombings from the Philippines and who was convicted in part by the information on computer floppy disks that were found in his quarters after he moved to Pakistan, where he was arrested. The same bin Laden mentioned above is believed to be a new source of anti-American terrorist support worldwide; he operates out of a remote base in Afghanistan, using all these modern aids to command and control.

It wouldn't really matter whether the terrorism was state-sponsored or the work of some freelance group with an agenda to push. Even in the latter case, some form of training and an operating base are required. This must be provided within a state, somehow. The state may be unknowing or unable to act at some stage of terrorist plotting, as Germany and Italy were at the times of the Baader-Meinhof Gang and the Red Brigades, and as we were in the face of the Unabomber and the Oklahoma City bombing plot. The state may be passive, as France was in allowing Iranian and other revolutionary groups to live and plot among themselves in Paris during the 1960s. Or the state may be helpless because it is under attack, as Peru was when the Shining Path guerrillas were at the height of their campaign and as Colombia is today. Finally, the state may be active in promoting terrorism by training and supporting terrorists, as Libya, Iran, Syria, Sudan, Cuba, and other states have been. (The examples given are by no means exhaustive.) And with whatever support in operations and sustenance the state provides or fails to provide deliberately, the technology within the state, in the form of computers, communications, transportation, arms and explosives (whether freely provided or illicitly obtained), and food, clothing, and shelter, will be available to the terrorists.

One of the worst terrorist threats hanging over the world like a hidden sword of Damocles is the potential for leakage of Russian nuclear weapons or nuclear weapon capability to the world's malevolent forces. There have been recurrent reports about the sorry state of Russian security control over nuclear warheads in storage. Not only are the weapons poorly guarded; the responsible security troops have not been paid regularly. They could easily be prey for large blandishments. Whether any weapons or nuclear materials can be stolen or secreted out of storage and into the hands of a terrorist organization such as Osama bin Laden or someone who will replace him remains problematical. Russia is a huge country, and the weapons storage sites are deep within it. Shortly after the breakup of the Soviet Union there were several arrests in Western Europe of smugglers who had enriched uranium to sell, but no reports of Uranium-235 or plutonium. Such reports have dried up, but that doesn't mean the threat is gone or even that no nuclear material has been smuggled out of Russia successfully. It just means we haven't heard about any.

Of even greater concern is the possibility that one or more of so-called rogue states, such as Libya, Iraq, and North Korea, will simply hire Russian experts desperate to support themselves and their families. Such states may have little scruple about using nuclear weapons if they have them; they would certainly not hesitate to use them for nuclear blackmail. In this regard, whether the "terrorists" are states or individuals having state support matters little. The effect on the world can be catastrophic. Again, there have been no reports of such assistance to the rogues (except for reports of missile technology assistance to North Korea, which would give them a weapon-delivery capability if and when they acquire or develop warheads). Indeed, a January 8, 1999, report in the journal *Science* quotes many Russian scientists as saying they would not yield to blandishments from such sources. But, they add, they can't speak for everyone, so their assurances do not mean that the help is not being given. Can it be kept secret? We have but to note reports about the observations of the Iraqi nuclear weapons program under International Atomic Energy Commission aegis after the Gulf War. They showed that our intelligence had not found a large part of the Iraqi weapons program. We can also note our uncertainty about the suspected North Korean program to realize that the leakage can be taking place right under our noses without our knowledge. And on the boundary of legitimacy, there are concerns that poverty-stricken Russian scientists may be helping Iran to acquire nuclear capability that can lead to weapons, under the cover of agreed peaceful nuclear power reactor transfers. And we know that Iran is close to or already has a long-range missile capability.

The possibility that nuclear weapons and missiles to deliver them will spread as a result of the Russian state's deprivation and loss of discipline simply adds to the potential for havoc that economic and political chaos in Russia could visit upon the world scene before they are resolved (and perhaps afterward, if they are not resolved in favorable directions). And their help is not the only means by which nuclear weapons will spread, as indicated by the cases of India and Pakistan. Like all technologies in world history, such as gunpowder and steam propulsion, it is only a matter of time before nuclear weapons capability is available to any country and group in the world who wants to spend the effort and resources to acquire them. Sooner or later, we shall have to come to grips with the issue of how to deal with this kind of situation. Although we talk about "weapons of mass destruction" as a single category, nuclear weapons are in a class by themselves in instantaneous and widespread destructiveness. And they may be held not only by nations but also by terrorists, whether nationally sponsored or freelance.

How to fight the terrorists? Conceptually, we know how to do it. In many ways, terrorist war, whatever the weapons used, is like guerrilla war. A relatively small number of disaffected individuals form a secret organization. They gain outside support, in the forms of money and the supplies and arms of their trade. They live largely off the economy they are planning to attack. They operate in secret, isolated cells, with transitory headquarters and changing names, to make themselves hard to trace. They keep themselves fragmented so that one cell, if broken, cannot betray others. They attack vulnerable targets with surprise and disappear into the figurative woodwork; the targets are usually but not necessary civilian, to make the pain on the "enemy" society greater. After an "operation," they must have publicity for what they have done, else it loses much of its point.

The basic principles of fighting against guerrilla war apply here, as well. One has to protect the population; one wants to go after the terrorists themselves; and one wants to eliminate the causes or perceived injustices that motivate them. In these directions in the terrorist context, there are some obvious things to be done. A measure of protection comes from building passive protection into terrorist targets, in the form of precautions against penetration (such as the metal detectors used by all airports today). Gaining good intelligence allows active protection of targets by posting guards and arresting individuals who are known to be plotting a terrorist act. Moving against the terrorists also involves good intelligence and the ability to gather information that will enable prosecution through the legal system. And then we must attack their bases of support, as we did after the bombings in East Africa.

But all these defensive and offensive steps are much more difficult to apply against small cells of terrorists than they are even in guerrilla war. Guerrillas are intent on changing the government of a country; to that extent, at least, it is known where they are and where they must focus their efforts. Unless they are focused on a compact target, as with the Irish Republican Army in Northern Ireland and the Basque terrorists of Spain, terrorists have the entire world at their disposal—especially if they are attacking the United States, its citizens, and its economic or other interests. Since terrorists operate without strong central command, in small groups that aren't even known to each other, and they have all the world's transportation and communications resources open to them, as well as thousands of targets available with which they can make their points, the world provides an almost infinite haystack in which just a few needles must be located and tracked. This requires the cooperation of governments with which we may or may not have good relations.

As we have already noted, passive protection of all possible targets imposes expenses on society that can become too high to be acceptable; then, risks are taken, and sometimes the gamble fails, as when the budgets were not appropriated to build protection into the African embassies. Also, it will often be found that legal moves against them will be blocked by the countries that support them, as Libya did for a decade in the case of the Libyan terrorists accused of masterminding the Pan-Am 103 bombing. Or else physical attacks against them might be inconclusive even when circumstances allow such attacks, as in the case of the attacks against Libya in 1986 and those against Osama bin Laden's bases in Sudan and Afghanistan in 1998.

The attacks may delay future terrorist activity, but they cannot stop it. And in our own country, we cannot move against terrorists without firm evidence of their work, which usually means after their deeds are done, as in Oklahoma City. We have been fortunate in some cases, as with the New York World Trade Center and the embassies in East Africa, to have had the needed kind of cooperation to arrest, prosecute, and punish at least some of the terrorists. But in most cases, they go free.

It also seems that whereas guerrillas' motivations can be changed by changes in government (as happened, for example, in Central America) it is much more difficult to change the motivations of terrorists. Living in isolation as they do, and consumed by hatred of their targets, they tend to be individuals who have been brought up to thrive on violence and who are willing to devote their lives to even a single operation that will hurt the objects of their hatred. The Palestinian suicide bombers who attack Israel are a good example. Perhaps the best that can be achieved against such individuals is to negate their ability to do harm, through attrition and reducing the ability of outside governments to support them. Thus, by military or other means, the approach to neutralizing terrorists, or at least the variety who are organized in favor of a cause, is to deny them sources of support in the global economy—not easy!

Terrorists are not the only ones who can use modern technology to consolidate, coordinate, and magnify the horror of their activities. Every society has had an underworld that organizes criminals and crime to make them more effective and to increase the take for the strong ones who survive the organizing. The criminal activity includes, as we know, control of prostitution, robbery, protection rackets, gambling, loan-sharking, running black markets and smuggling, and much else, with killing along the way as necessary for the benefit of the moneymaking enterprise. Now, with modern technology, the organized criminal groups have it in their power to spread their activities across national boundaries and sometimes to dominate countries and aspects of world commerce. And this is indeed happening.

We read often about so-called white slavery rings in which young girls are kidnapped or purchased in one country and put to work in houses of prostitution in another. Traffic in smuggling immigrants fleeing one country into another (sometimes to work in virtual slavery in such installations as clothing sweatshops) periodically breaks into the news; specifically, smuggling of Chinese or Cubans into the United States is of direct interest at home. Protection rackets can command a share of major elements of a country's economy, as has been reported from Japan, and thereby affect prices and trade worldwide. In Colombia, drug organizations exercise a large measure of control over the country's governance and its economy, and reports of endemic corruption in Mexico indicate that the same is true there. There have been many news stories about the alacrity with which several organized crime groups moved to gain control over large sections of the former Soviet economy as it was being dismantled and privatized. And, of course, the powerful influence of the classic Mafia in Italy periodically breaks into the news with stories of corruption and control that reach up to the prime minister's office and sometimes the minister himself. All of this does not yet mention the impact of organized crime in the United States, where large elements of the legitimate economy—especially transportation and gambling—have been, at a minimum, influenced by assorted racketeers and where all the other organized crime activities continue to flourish despite the most valiant law enforcement efforts.

The most powerful of these activities thrives in today's world by using modern communications, transportation, weaponry, and especially the computerized world banking system. The banking system makes it possible to move around and to hide large amounts of money in a short time, so that the top-level beneficiaries and managers of the criminal activity cannot easily be traced; even if they can be found out and tracked, they cannot easily be apprehended. In addition, since transportation and communications allow rapid transfer of people, goods, and money on a worldwide scale, it could be only a matter of time until the criminal enterprises join forces across national boundaries. This appears to be happening.

In her book *Thieves' World*, written in 1994 shortly before her death from cancer, Claire Sterling describes (again by integrating information widely scattered in the public record) how the major Mafias are coordinating their activities with each other, carving up territories, and sharing the spoils. The five major groups she describes include the Sicilian and derivative American Mafias, the Turkish arms and drug dealers, the several Russian Mafias, the Hong Kong–based Chinese Triads, and the Japanese Yakuza. All these groups have started to spread their wings into other countries; for example, the Triads have been found operating in Europe and the United States, and the Russian Mafias have established a flourishing branch in New York and perhaps elsewhere in the United States, not to mention many parts of Europe. The reason these organizations have started to join forces is to avoid open warfare where their territories overlap. Thus, they make agreements to respect territories and to share markets. As an example, Sterling describes one agreement between the Sicilian Mafia and the Colombian drug cartels, in which the cartels are given access to cocaine markets in Europe using the Mafia supply chain, whereas the Mafia gives them part of the heroin trade into the United States in return for use of the cartels' supply chain to the United States.

In the end, the joining of Mafias at their edges means criminal control of a huge portion of the world economy. Overall estimates are difficult to make, but just examining the worldwide bits and pieces can lead to numbers approaching a significant fraction of that economy. For example, Sterling quotes an estimate of $300 billion per year for the drug trade involved in the agreement just described (in 1993 dollars, equivalent to nearly $400 billion today). One could imagine that with the shares they skim off the Yakuza might have some influence over, say, 20 percent of the Japanese economy, or another $600 billion. It would be possible to add up all such estimates to indicate that the Mafias among themselves may control several trillions of dollars. That is enough to carry much influence around the world, none of it good. And we can take note of the chilling possibility that with such resources the Mafias of the world could join with the terrorists to gain access to nuclear, chemical, and biological weapons for nefarious purposes that suit them jointly.

We in the United States spend a significant—and difficult to count—amount of our gross national product (GNP) fighting the international criminals' activities, if we include the FBI and Drug Enforcement Agency, the parts of the Treasury that worry about smuggling and tax evasion, the parts of the Immigration and Naturalization Service that worry about illegal and smuggled immigration, sections of state and local police forces, and the parts of the armed forces detailed to monitor and interdict drug traffic. As we try to use modern technology to help with the task of fighting the criminal enterprise, the same tools become useful to the criminals. For example, advanced cryptographic capability is rapidly becoming available to the world, and the United States has essentially lost its fight to keep private cryptographic keys available to law enforcement agencies. This will make surveillance of the criminal activity, and interdiction of the money flows, more difficult. How will we know when the criminal activity starts to influence our government and the daily lives of ordinary citizens?

So now we have terrorists and organized criminal enterprises that can and do make war on the United States. That isn't the end of it. We mentioned piracy as a lead-in to this discussion. We are all familiar with tales of piracy from the old sailing days, but in fact it may not be as commonly known that it lingers on in Southeast Asian waters. This could perhaps be considered a localized phenomenon (albeit with modern ships and weaponry), simply an extension of the captures and boardings of an earlier time. But now it can be extended into enterprises ashore that have international scope. With the use of computers, a new brand of pirate can hijack a large enough fraction of a bank's total assets to put it out of business, as happened to Barings, Britain's oldest commercial bank, in Singapore in 1995.

In that case the criminal was caught. But now comes cyberwar, to use a modern phrase. Computerized banking systems and other systems used to control major functions of society, like power and transportation grids and air-traffic control systems, are subject to penetration not only by individuals or groups seeking private gain but also by governments having malevolent purposes. How would you like your bank to tell you all its resources were drained during the night by an unknown source; or that its computerized records had been scrambled so badly that it would take some weeks to sort them out; or that a source of random errors would make all statements and records unreliable for some indefinite period? Why blow up electric transmission towers when a software fix can put a quarter of the country's electricity out of action for days? Or if a computer system cannot be penetrated, an information terrorist backed by the resources of a hostile nation can jam communications or navigation satellites to cause breakdowns in the systems they serve. Think about the impact of a single satellite that failed in 1998 and put most of the nation's pagers out of action for many hours. And what would have happened if the failure had been induced deliberately and the orbital standby satellite had been purposefully put out of action at the same time? And if it came to open warfare with a country that had a few nuclear weapons and didn't want to bring down a rain of counterweapons on itself by exploding one on our territory, that country would have only to explode a weapon or two at the right altitude in space to effectively destroy a significant fraction of our satellite communications and other support capability by means of the electromagnetic pulse (EMP) attending the explosion.

Articles in defense-oriented trade journals have been describing the growing possibilities of modern information warfare since the Gulf War, and many articles in policy-oriented journals have been sounding the alarm. It has been broadcast further by futurist books such as those written by Alvin and Heidi Toffler (e.g., *War and Anti-War*). The Gulf War brought into public view the increasing dependence of the armed forces on computerized information flows and satellite-based communications, navigation, and intelligence systems, and subsequent events and writings have extended our appreciation of this dependence to the civilian domain.

But it is fair to say that this country, and perhaps most of the industrialized world, does not yet either fully comprehend or take with enough seriousness the threat to our organized way of life that penetration or destruction of our computer-dependent systems can pose. Steps are being taken, by private banking and financial systems, to ensure the security of their transactions. There are recurring news stories about groups of hackers being apprehended in the process of penetrating private as well as government systems. There is coming to be a realization that the merging of computer databases about individuals' lifestyles and private affairs for commercial purposes can also provide information useful for nefarious purposes. A degree of hardness against EMP is beginning to be built into our essential space systems. Thus, awareness is growing.

But look at the dilatory pace at which national agencies and the Congress addressed the year 2000 problem, in which many time-linked computer programs based on older computer languages and algorithms that were expected to be replaced by now, but weren't, have been expected to crash in confusion as the two-digit year they depend on changes from *99* to *00*. One had only to observe the reluctance to spend the money it will really cost to solve that problem to realize that it took a long time to comprehended fully the implications of our new dependence on computers to develop, store, and transfer the information needed for management of our economic and civic lives and to control many of our most crucial infrastructure functions in transportation, communication, court processes, and most other activities vital to our modern society. In another area, the reluctance on the part of the civilian world, here and overseas, to allow law enforcement agencies under proper judicial supervision access to encryption keys, which may be vital to anticipating and deflecting dire terrorist and criminal threats to public safety and welfare, suggests how poorly appreciated is the potential of the power to do harm that the new information technology can have in the wrong hands. Of course, the power to do harm can reside with the law enforcement agencies, too. It is a matter of balancing risks. The law enforcement agencies *may* do harm; they have to be watched. The criminals and terrorists *intend* to do harm; they are hard to stop, and totally denying relevant tools to the law enforcement agencies makes it harder. The balance of risks clearly must be reassessed, but we do not yet appear to have fully come to grips with the issue.

The threats to our security come not only from the direct danger to the survival and functioning of our modern systems for acquiring, manipulating, and moving information. Modern information technology also indirectly influences our outlook on foreign affairs and our willingness to expend effort, resources, and lives in defense of our vital interests. War now takes place not only in the locales where actual conflict wells up but also on TV screens worldwide.

Here, we encounter the impact of a clash between our chivalry-centered, European-derived culture and cultures in the rest of the world that are based on different value systems and views about human life. The combination of a barbarian mentality with modern weaponry can bring about frightful results. In the rest of the world they play by different rules, and in doing so they contribute to rendering us impotent in foreign policy in many ways. Refugee streams are created purposefully to destroy segments of a society and to place a burden on adjacent societies (see Bosnia and Kosovo). Males who may join military forces are rounded up and killed arbitrarily (see also Yugoslavia). Women and children do not come first for protection. Rather, they are used as human shields for armed bands or armed forces (Somalia, Rwanda, Kosovo), or they are made to suffer visibly to weaken the resolve of those who have more humanitarian instincts (Bosnia, Kosovo, Iraq). Factories to make chemical and biological weapons are masked in civilian plants that make pharmaceuticals or baby food and that are embedded in population centers for the same reasons (Sudan and Iraq). Civilian opposition populations are starved to bring about surrender (Nigeria and Sudan). Prisoners are not treated humanely; they are tortured for confession of evil intent, to be used in propaganda, and abused until they die (Korea and Vietnam). Dead foes are not given decent burial; their bodies are dragged through the streets as trophies of victory (Somalia). In Vietnam, women and children were first-line participants in the war, whereas we castigated ourselves for firing on women and children (that we were doing so was pointed out to me, accusingly, by a congressional investigating committee in 1965). The flower of a country's growing boys is marched across a field of battle as human minesweepers (Iran). Environmental destruction on a colossal scale is acceptable if it will make an opponent's life more difficult, as was the case when Iraq set all the Kuwaiti oil wells on fire during the Gulf War. Germs and chemicals have been and will be used in warfare unless deterred by the threat of great counterdestruction. While *we* extol a fair fight, others' ideas of winning include treachery, kicking a foe when he is down, setting mines and booby traps without regard to whether they may hurt civilians or soldiers (Vietnam, Afghanistan, Bosnia), kidnapping or killing civilians in attempts to bring governments to heel (throughout North Africa, the Middle East, and Latin America), and using any conceivable weapon to hurt the other side.

And all this is brought to us on our TV screens. But as Peter Braestrup points out in his book *Big Story*, about the 1968 Tet Offensive in Vietnam, the picture we see is distorted by the access allowed to TV reporters and cameramen as a result of the exigencies of battle and the willingness of the opposing sides. And it is also distorted by the reporters' mind-sets about the events they are covering. Thus, we could see the little girl running away from the burning napalm in Vietnam, but we couldn't see the Vietcong soldiers shooting at the aircraft from the village temple to draw the fire to the village. We could see the U.S. Marines setting fire to a village after coming under fire from the village, but we didn't see the Vietcong goon squads disemboweling a village chief in front of his family because he represented the other side. We could see the Saigon police chief summarily executing a prisoner, but we didn't see the North Vietnamese systematically torturing the American pilots they captured. We could see the effect of a U.S. bomb on a command bunker in Baghdad where civilians had been taken to hide, but we couldn't see the atrocities visited on the people of Kuwait by Baghdad's invading army. We could see the privations of the people of Baghdad under the heel of their iron dictator who induced those privations in his continuing quest for power, but we couldn't see the ruthlessness with which he stamped out potential opposition to that absolute power in the rest of his country. We devise a policy to contain Serbia that, allowing for the fears expressed by the media, the pundits, and members of Congress, precludes getting into the quagmire of a ground war in the Balkans. But as soon as the TV images of the ethnic cleansing of Kosovo appear, the media, the pundits, and members of Congress start demanding that we do just that.

Our population's horror in viewing what it does see is intensified by the general bent of our news media to show pain, suffering, and destruction, with their accompanying powerful visuals, to the exclusion of bringing us the contextual material that would allow us to put what we see in perspective or to inform us very much about the surrounding circumstances and deeper meanings of what they are reporting. It is as though during our own Revolutionary War we had been exposed continually to the plight of the Tories who were made to flee to Canada and the suffering of our own troops at Valley Forge without any indication of the larger context for those events or what was happening elsewhere in the country.

The views of conflict and war that are brought to us through these distorted lenses play on the humanitarian instincts that are a trademark of the American ethos to enhance the U.S. population's revulsion against American involvement in armed conflicts. Opponents who have different values understand how to take advantage of that outlook to roll back our influence and render our military power impotent. Think about how the outcome of the Vietnam War was driven in part by the reporting on protest movements at home (which were coordinated with worldwide protest movements whose organization remains obscure to this day); about our failure to reach closure in the Gulf War because our key leaders, President Bush among them, were concerned about how the destruction of the retreating Iraqi army would be portrayed in our media; about our abashed withdrawal from Somalia after the humiliating defeat of an elite company of U.S. Army Rangers; and about how calls to go into Kosovo with ground forces began as soon as the TV pictures of the streams of refugees from Serb ethnic cleansing there began to dispel previously expressed concerns about getting into a Balkan quagmire. Can it be doubted that many of the problems whose aftermath we are grappling with today were set up for us on American TV screens?

Of course, outcomes of that kind occurred before the age of television. Ghandi, for example, couldn't have used his nonviolent passive resistance tactic against Stalin; it depended for its success on the British humanitarian instinct, whereas a cruel dictator would simply have bundled the protesters off to the desert after executing their leader. But television is more immediate and more graphic; whereas print media and newsreel film took a while to penetrate, TV packs an instant wallop. When shown to a populace unused to the pain and suffering of warfare, one wrapped up in its day-to-day affairs and reluctant to lose its loved ones in support of visions they are shown and disapprove of heartily, it can be decisive in shaping public opinion.

Wars can now be triggered, promoted, and abandoned by the agency of America's TV broadcasts. What is shown has no relationship to geopolitics and to which countries are involved. Television images transcend national boundaries in a big way. And the fact that they can do so means that the so-called transnational threats to our security come from inside as well as outside America.

This review of the international situation conveys a sense of prediction, and prediction of international security relations in today's volatile world is indeed a risky business. It doesn't matter, however, whether the predictions prove to be right or wrong in any particular area of the world. Some of the predictions will come to pass, in the sense forecast or in some related way, and other relationships, currently unforeseen, will arise. The key point is that the trends portrayed bespeak an unstable and chaotic international political and military environment. And there is almost no part of the world where we can just say, "Let's ignore that. It won't affect us." We will be affected by our relationships with our North Atlantic allies and our interactions with all the major regional powers emerging or already in place. We will be affected by the frictions along the boundaries of cultural influence of those powers. We will be affected by countries with whom the other regional powers have important connections, even when our own connections with them are indirect. And we will be affected by the hostile or impersonal "powers" that operate across national boundaries.

Thus, what we have looked at that is happening in the world around us will certainly affect our national security. It could in the long run affect the survival of our nation, as we shall see in Chapter 7, which discusses our post–Cold War national strategy. But these events and their consequences are not independent of what is happening within our borders that affects how we view the external events and how we react to them. Now it is time to look at this "inside" story.

4

WHERE DOES THE NATION SEEM TO BE GOING?

History is the product of vast, amorphous and indecipherable social movements.

—Count Leo Tolstoy

There is nothing I am going to describe about our country that you don't know or that hasn't already been written and talked about by those whose specialties make them much more knowledgeable than I am in each area we have to touch on. But it is rarely viewed in the aggregate. To bring out the full, integrated impact of today's trends in America—demographic, social, economic, political, lifestyle—we need to touch on all these areas to greater or lesser extent, so that we can create an integrated description of where the nation seems to be going. The purpose is not to create a learned treatise, brief or lengthy, in any one of the areas but rather to get the big picture. National security can't be discussed in the absence of that overview. (However, it is important for you, the innocent reader, to note that the slant I put on it is the one I want to lead you up to my particular take on our national security future. There are many aspects to America's internal life that are important to the nation's welfare but that are not of first importance to our future national security that I have not touched on to create this national portrait.)

Let's take the long view of progress. Look at where our country was during the Gay Nineties before the turn of the nineteenth to the twentieth centuries. Then look at the achievements that have brought us to the 1990s and the year 2000. From the basis of that comparison, our opening to the future looks boundless. The rest of the industrialized world more or less tracks along with us.

We have come in that time from a world characterized by the hand-cranked telephone, long-distance communication via telegraph, the beginnings of electric lighting, horse-drawn carriages with the motorized carriage as an interesting novelty, rail and steamship transportation, and patent medicine for our ills. Men and women talked in guarded and oblique terms about matters of sex and family, and Victorian values governed social behavior. The United States was just becoming an economic powerhouse, on a par with Britain and Germany, on the world scene.

We have arrived at the computer-driven information age, in which instant communications and data tie the world economy into a single, seamless stream of goods and services. We have personal transportation that wafts us hundreds of miles in a day. We fly overnight between the continents, talk to business and personal partners around the world from a small handset, build buildings over a quarter-mile high, draw power from the atom when we can overcome our fears about its misuse, and manipulate genes to guard and improve our health. We have sent people to the moon. We fight wars at long range from air and space using weapons having precision and power that was unimaginable a century ago—precision to destroy a selected building from thousands of miles away, power that in the extreme of its use can wipe out civilization and perhaps humankind as well. Lifestyles are looser, talk between the sexes about any subject is frank, and a major issue for public argument is whether family life exists at all.

In the coming century, the world will exist in an electronically driven "infosphere" that is as pervasive as the atmosphere and that will affect all human activity in ways we cannot fully predict. We might anticipate the advent of almost limitless energy from fusion power. We may move people in space beyond the earth's and the moon's orbits to reach and explore Mars. We will certainly know how to change the genetic makeup of populations to avoid disease rather than cure it; we may be able to induce the body to grow replacement parts for some that are worn out. Somewhere in the world, someone having a different ethical outlook from ours will likely clone humans who have characteristics they find desirable—a major step toward the manufactured social order depicted in Aldous Huxley's *Brave New World*—and we may even create life in the laboratory if we can resolve the attending ethical issues. We may fight wars with information and lasers rather than with guns and explosives.

The scope of the twentieth century's scientific and technological advances, and their future prospects, are so broad and so varied that their nature and reach are impossible to capture in a few sentences. Yet we must ask ourselves whether all the potential achievements we can foresee will in fact be realized. The reason is that we cannot look at the advance of technology and the economic activity it spurs without thinking about what novelist Graham Greene calls the "human factor."

We have to understand what it is that Americans bring to their quest for security in an uncertain world. Each nation brings something different to such a quest—different outlooks, different techniques, different ways of perceiving and reacting to internal stresses and external events—all born out of its unique historic experiences.

The second half of the twentieth century saw, along with enormous technological and economic change, a social and political revolution of huge proportions in the United States. That revolution built on attitudes inherited from the pioneer days of earlier centuries to give a peculiarly American flavor to the trend of events and governance within the country. Just as a recipe with many ingredients may turn out to have tastes that are surprising to the chef, that peculiarly American flavor, surprising in many of its aspects, will affect what we make of the technological and economic advances we see as possible. Though they may be possible, when tempered by the social climate that has grown and continues to evolve those advances may or may not turn out to be probable. In this chapter we explore the nature of the trends under way. Chapter 5 examines some of the puzzles the trends pose for those who would help the country determine its directions—or even just to fathom what those directions might be. Then we can get on with the core issues of national security in their appropriate context.

THE TWENTIETH-CENTURY
AMERICAN SOCIAL REVOLUTION

The time of social turbulence that is easiest to recall as we approach the end of the century is the 1960s and the Vietnam War protests. It appeared that the youth of the country had cast off all traces of the discipline that had guided their activity before that: the dress codes; the fairly uniform school curricula that were based on attitudes, beliefs, and a degree of regimentation carried over from the previous century; the restraints on sexual behavior; the respect for laws and regulations imposed by adults, at least to the point where banishment to the principal's office was not a punishment most students would willingly sign up for.[1] The expectation that students would spend part of every weekday evening doing homework went away, and parental par-

---

[1] That seems so innocent these days when many urban schools have metal detectors at their entrances, guards in their halls, and teachers who live in fear of an attack by their pupils, doesn't it?

ticipation to the extent of insisting that their children strive for good grades and abide by school rules of conduct seemed to have lost effect. Hippies living in communes and chanting "No, no, we won't go!" and groups of students taking over university presidents' and faculty offices and trashing records became the symbols of the rebellion. But in fact by the time it was over the general population had, all unknowingly, adopted many hippie habits in dress, behavior, and outlook. This was because the war protests merely accelerated a vast social transformation that was in the making anyway.

It really started in the wake of World War I, with the Roaring Twenties that saw radical changes in attitude and behavior not much different from those of the sixties. The twenties saw prohibition, bootleggers and gangsters, speakeasies, flappers, and the blossoming of the automobile as a means of transport and recreation. Freud's ideas about human psychology were becoming current, and Dewey's theories promoting progressive education that worried about students' mental and emotional health along with their lessons were making inroads into the rigidly curriculum-based educational philosophies of the previous century. But then the Great Depression of the 1930s intervened.

People had to turn their attention to keeping alive. College students found themselves fortunate to take jobs that had nothing to do with their education, such as driving elevators[2] or selling used clothing; those who could make a good impression, through dress and respectful attitude, succeeded better than those who were openly rebellious. The government-funded Works Progress Administration (WPA) tried to give people the dignity of work, albeit for very low pay. The government-funded activities included everything from digging ditches, to interminably calculating twelve-place tables of logarithms by hand, to putting on plays and painting pictures, all at the expense of becoming the butt of opponents' jokes about leaning on shovels all day. Women worked if and as necessary to help support their families.

With it all, however, much of the change in social institutions, appearances, and mores that took place in the 1920s remained. The changes continued while World War II pulled the country out of the depths of the Depression—and subsequently. The war helped lay the foundation for what followed. During the war, men's lives were disrupted by military service while women worked to maintain their households and to sustain war industries in the presence of manpower shortages. By the end of the war, as historian Doris Kearns Goodwin points out in her 1994 book, *No*

---

[2]Elevators needed human operators on manual start, stop, and door controls in those days. Push-button controls came a couple of decades later.

Ordinary Time, a broad middle class had been created by earnings in factories producing war materiel. A pattern of migration to where jobs were had evolved, changing the previous pattern of stable households and communities. Much more of the population moved into the cities. And the pattern of women working outside the home changed the roles of the sexes in family life and in society for 10–20 percent of the nation, sending the divorce rate soaring. The relationships among ethnic groups and among the races were also put on a new course. People from all the groups who had worked together and had fought together could develop a new view of each others' worth as people and companions, in and out of the workplace and the battlefield. It was spotty, but it was a start. The seeds of the later civil rights movement germinated here. African Americans who had experienced these changes were expected by the white majority to go back to the old ways after the war. The social pressure built by that expectation in the conditions of a new social environment would have to explode some day, as it did in the 1950s and 1960s.

Immediately after the war there was a period of catching up, of reestablishing households, of acquiring the goods whose production and use had been deferred by the war. Men went to school to learn trades and professions under the government-funded GI Bill of Rights,[3] passed in 1944 and designed to compensate them for the risk of death and the disruption of their lives they had suffered during the war. Money was made available under the GI Bill to purchase housing that industry hurried to furnish. Jobs were created by the demand for goods, and the country bootstrapped itself up the economic ladder to finish building a vast and reasonably comfortable middle class—three-quarters of our population, more or less, depending on how "middle class" is defined. That middle class moved into mass-produced suburbs that worried philosophers for their uniformity and the material-acquisition attitudes they seemed either to generate or to symbolize.

The general freeing-up of constraints on behavior and attitudes was also moving slowly ahead during the 1950s. Catching up with war-delayed progress gave way to a different way of life, spurred by suburban development, automobile travel, the radicalism of abstract expressionism in the art world, and the beginnings of the TV-driven revolution in the way the media drove popular awareness and attitudes. At the same time, the onset of the Cold War, war in Korea, and publicly expressed fears of the "bomb" as the Soviet Union exploded its own nuclear weapons led to anxieties about war and peace that were reflected in the excesses of the McCarthy era in Con-

---

[3]For those too young to remember, the acronym "GI" stood for *g*overnment *i*ssue, which characterized everything about a soldier from his skivvies to his food, shelter, weapons, and rules of behavior while in uniform.

gress and the growth, amid contention and controversy, of foreign aid and counter-Soviet alliances.

Thus, the country was ripe for a blowup in social attitudes and behavior as it entered the 1960s. Then, the social revolution that had begun in the twenties was reinvigorated by the onset of the civil rights movement. It was vastly accelerated after the United States became deeply involved in Vietnam and began to draft young men into the armed forces to fight there. It was shaped by the confluence of the civil rights movement, the war protests, and the women's movement, the effects being exacerbated by the war-induced inflation of the 1970s. Its most prominent outward manifestations may be the attending revolution in sexual mores and the relaxing of constraints on manners and language. It might be symbolized by the abolition of the Hayes Office that had censored earthy language and explicit displays of sexual behavior in motion pictures. That also led to the different treatment of women and the use of street language in Hollywood's films and television and, subsequently, in most casual gatherings of people. Different attitudes toward marriage and divorce followed, reducing the previous stigma of divorce as women asserted their greater independence and equal status with men before the law. Many marriages that had struggled with indifferent and abusive relationships under the old mores now came apart, and the divorce rate soared while single parenthood became as much a norm as the two-parent family. Open companion living relationships between couples, as trial marriage or as protection against the trauma of failed marriage and divorce, also became current.[4]

The freeing of school curricula, program requirements, and dress codes from the rigidities of the pre–World War II period, and their broad nationwide variability, are another effect, not as commonly recognized as being part of the same family of events. However, they flow logically from the evolution of more permissive theories of child-rearing and from the new psychological outlooks based on Freud and Dewey. These effects are reinforced by the sheer necessity to leave children on their own for more time while two parents work full-time outside the home, as well as by the alternative social models presented on a medium (television) becoming an ubiquitous if unintended educator with no social controls. They are confirmed by the inability of the public school systems to assume very effectively the role of teacher and enforcer of moral values that society has tried to thrust upon them.

---

[4]By contrast, in the early 1940s one of the twentieth century's great philosophers, Bertrand Russell, was disinvited from teaching a course on the history of Western philosophy at the City College of New York because the press publicized the fact that he had at one time advocated trial marriage between sexually maturing couples. It was feared that he would give American youth the wrong ideas about sex and marriage.

In fact it is difficult to describe in a short space the pervasiveness of the changes in attitude and behavior that came front and center during the postwar decades.[5] To understand fully the depth of the change, we must look rather more deeply into causes. This is difficult to do in a short space, and I must reiterate that this work is not intended to be a treatise on this subject, however important it is. But we should note some straws in the winds of change that drove the change to where it has arrived today.

Although the boost to the social revolution in the aftermath of World War II came in part from the life-altering experiences of those who went to fight, there was also a high impact on those who stayed at home because they had much greater responsibility thrust on them by the circumstances of the war. Not only were theories of child-raising growing more permissive; they were forced to become so because during the war the many working women didn't have the time to watch their children closely enough to enforce strict standards of behavior. Nor was there the male-oriented disciplinary role that characterized the earlier family (at least in myth if not always in practice). Between the theory and the practice, the belief in the woodshed gradually evaporated. Then the children, growing up in a time of great economic expansion, without the pressures of the Great Depression that kept their parents' noses to the grindstone, became used to getting much of what they wanted in the way of material goods and allowed behavior, just for the asking. This was not calculated to instill discipline. And the schools were reflecting the effects of this change, even as the new generation of children was growing up, because their teachers were early members of the new generation as well. We should not forget that younger faculty members were part of the 1960s student protests.

The general change of attitude came to full fruition during the Vietnam War protests, which started in the universities. Students' antiwar and antidraft concerns and fears were joined with a more general rebellion against often arbitrary and condescending faculty and school administration attitudes and rigidities. The rebellion led to a general casting-off of respect for existing regulations and a search for new and more accommodating levels of behavioral restraint, or lack of it. All students were not participants in this rebellion, of course, just as whole populations are rarely active participants in antigovernment rebellions, but all were profoundly affected by it.

---

[5]On a personal and somewhat superficial but profoundly symbolic level, my wife and I often contrast the conditions in her women's dormitory at the University of Wisconsin with the situation faced by our daughter, who went into a coed dormitory at Colorado State University nearly thirty years later. At Wisconsin, the house mother enforced a strict discipline for hours of return from dates and forbade blue jeans—"if you wear blue jeans, you will act like blue jeans." At Colorado State, there was no house mother and no dress code; our daughter was strictly on her own and fully responsible for her own behavior in all respects.

The GI Bill greatly expanded the colleges, and large numbers of the women who had worked during the war and the men who had benefited from the GI Bill wanted their children to have a college education, too. Once the women had that, they wanted to use it by working at something productive before taking time to have families and children. Thus, the beloved but increasingly mythical family, with a father as the breadwinner and a mother as the homemaker, and children happily going to school to prepare for the same lifestyle, had in fact gone out of style in large part as a result of the very activities—defending U.S. interests around the world—that those who are trying to recapture the past now extol.

Once women were working for their own satisfaction, they could also help with the family finances. When the Vietnam-spurred inflation started to take a bite, it then became a ratchet instead of a chance to make a few extra dollars and experience "fulfillment." So what started out as a movement to emancipate women (at least, the women of the burgeoning middle class) from the drudgery of keeping the household then enslaved them to the necessity to add to the family earnings. Although this was happening, changes in attitudes about men's and women's roles lagged so that women did not become entirely free from the household chores in any case. The heroic supermom who holds down two jobs as wage-earner/careerist and as household manager has become a new, postrevolutionary American icon.[6]

Along with that change, the rearing of children had to change as well. For many of the families with working mothers—well more than half of the families in modern America—childhood has become in large measure a time of day care, latchkey kids, TV as baby-sitter, daytime nannies, and children let free from the discipline of family responsibility. This has joined the permissiveness that was growing in the education system to lead to a general release from discipline in the society. The effects of this release were exacerbated by the multiple protest movements of the sixties.

All this describes what happened to what one might call the "majority community": white, middle-class America. But the black community that makes up an important and influential 15 percent or so of our population also contributed strongly to the social revolution. Colored troops and Negro factory workers (to use the terminology of the time) had earned some hard-won freedom and thought they had done a pretty good job in World War II (in fact they did), a feeling reinforced by their per-

---

[6]According to the U.S. Statistical Abstract, just under 32 percent of married women with "husbands present" were in the civilian labor force in 1960. By 1996 that had grown to just more than 61 percent, and the trend is still up. The participation rate for single women and women who are divorced, widowed, or separated has also been increasing. Over the same time period, it moved from 59 to 67 percent for the former, from 41 to 48 percent for the latter.

formance in Korea. But then they were expected to settle back into the repressed environment whence they had come. And in the postwar era, when liberal American attitudes toward nonwhite peoples around the world were evolving in a time of positive feeling toward the United Nations, it seemed wrong to much of the U.S. population to let the Ku Klux Klan–type society that they perceived in much of the South to continue. On top of that, President Harry Truman set an example by outlawing Jim Crow segregation policies in the armed forces, so that white and black troops would serve in units together.

Thus, the time and attitudes ripened for the rebellions in the South against enforced segregation and inferior status of the black population, rebellions that were powerfully reinforced by liberal opinion and assistance from the North. And finally, the poor black community in the South found jobs being eliminated as the South's agricultural economy was being mechanized at a high rate, and blacks saw the prosperity of northern cities growing, so they undertook a massive migration there. Expectations weren't necessarily fulfilled for all of them, but they were for many of them, as indicated by the steadily growing black middle class, and it was the seeking rather than the finding that counted in changing the face of America.

With the crowding of the cities and the migration of middle-class white families to the suburbs the city cores were gradually abandoned, and they rotted along with the residual, largely black populations within them that hadn't been able to take advantage of the growing prosperity of the expanding metropolitan areas. The schools were not able to adapt well to the new populations. They were further disrupted by court-ordered busing of children to different parts of the cities, a scheme designed to even out the inequities and disparities in schooling that were based on race and income disparities between the white and black populations. Of course, busing for desegregation purposes was only part of the reason for busing. School districts everywhere consolidated for economic reasons, so that most children could no longer simply walk to a neighborhood or nearby rural school. As a result, children spent more time on buses going to more efficient central schools, and transportation schedules, delays, and anomalies (such as "snow days" when the buses couldn't run) came by drift of events to affect the timing and scope of education more than any rational planning would have allowed them to.

Although illegal substance abuse as we currently define it has been with the country since early in the twentieth century, its profound impact and side effects were given big boosts by the aftermath of the Eighteenth Amendment to the U.S. Constitution and by the Vietnam War. Prohibition gave us organized crime on a large scale. The Vietnam period, which saw increased drug use by some of the war protesters at home and the ready availability of drugs in Southeast Asia, gave us a much expanded drug culture that has helped the spread and operation of organized crime on a worldwide scale. These effects have reflected back into how we live. The organized criminal activity and its products, together with the economic inequities and racial conflicts attending the evolution of the cities, have spawned an expansion of individual criminal activity that affects us in ways we can hardly count. Living space and its configurations and the attitudes of the more affluent populations are determined in part by the avoidance of crime. Police attention and municipal budgets are driven by levels of criminal activity. Our society sets limits on how much it wants to spend for police protection. When criminal activity increases, the attention of the police we are willing to pay for turns to dealing with that and away from maintenance of general order within the system of laws, in such matters as traffic enforcement, for example. Put together with the growth of problems among people that may be attributed to simple increases in population density, those neglected areas tend to become major irritants. This is perhaps one of the causes of the decline of civility in day-to-day interactions among citizens that our media have increasingly decried.

Finally, in this brief review of the evolution of a society over a century, we must note some accompanying profound changes in the work ethic. As in all the other areas, there are great variations within a population as large as ours, so we must deal with averages and perceptions. It appears that we came out of the nineteenth century with a Puritan work ethic that honored hard work, perseverance, and service. This was at least in part enforced by economic necessity; one worked hard at the job one had over the hours that were demanded as a matter of subsistence. One tried to serve one's superiors or customers well because otherwise one would be fired or the customers would go elsewhere. During the Great Depression one had to work at whatever job one could find, or one would become a "bum on the Bowery"—a favorite Hollywood-inspired metaphor of the day, based on the imagery of one of New York City's worst slums, wherever in the country one might be.

But that changed with the expansion of the economy, with the enlargement of the welfare state, with the consolidation of neighborhood businesses into large-scale retail enterprises, and with the changes of values attending new waves of migration within and into the United States. In many instances, quality of service has deteriorated as people's jobs have become more specialized and less inspiring. In many areas, there is less feeling of personal responsibility for a job well done, less pride in one's work, less feeling of loyalty to one's firm and those it serves. The age of restructuring and consolidation of firms to achieve competitive efficiency and economies of scale had the unfortunate side effect of illustrating that there is usually no loyalty down in a large organization, even while loyalty up is expected.

The effects of such a realization would be predictable. Store clerks who did not know the merchandise because they had no hand in ordering or displaying it could not be as responsive to customers' needs. Workers lost in large organizations performing relatively minor jobs could become more concerned with what would be going on off the job, after hours, than with what was happening on the job itself. Immigrants in service jobs who might be unused to the work world of the urban, schedule-driven United States could not give the kind or level of service many of their clients demanded without extensive indoctrination and training that was often not forthcoming. People with responsible jobs, who did the jobs well, could nevertheless wish to use their leisure time taking advantage of the recreational opportunities their higher incomes could afford. Leisure-time industry, from Disneyland to recreational vehicles to hotels and restaurants, grew at a rapid pace.

Again, we must reiterate that this does not describe an entire national population, within which will be found variations from the driven, type A executive to the conscientious office worker and sales clerk to the classic slacker and the welfare queen of modern mythology. But the general drift has been from "nose to the grindstone" to "I've got lots of other things to do with my life than give it all to this job." The outcome of this drift in terms of performance of the nation as a whole is probably not very significant, as attested by the power and vitality of modern America's society and economy. But we are talking about attitudes, and attitudes affect behavior over the long run.

It becomes clear from all these very imperfect and incomplete historical notes that in the aggregate we have seen, in the evolution of American society from the end of World War I to the end of the twentieth century, movement toward looser clothing, looser sex, looser language, a looser work ethic, looser discipline in education and everyday living, and, as we shall see shortly, a looser view of community responsibility. This is the social orientation with which Americans must face the growing and unfamiliar security challenges of a world without the Cold War focusing our attention on the subject. America has always risen to challenges to its security and integrity, in one way or another. The important thing to keep in mind is that the nation that enters the twenty-first century is not the same nation that met the challenges of German, Japanese, and Soviet imperialism. But some important underlying characteristics remain, and that's what we look at next.

ATTITUDES
Fundamental Outlooks and Their Genesis

The population of a country as large and diverse as the United States will not always respond predictably to specified stimuli according to someone's perception of its "national character." Especially in the United States, with its mix of people from all over the world that is unique in history, the different cultural backgrounds that those people bring to any national problem make for a degree of unpredictability that would be difficult to overcome.

And yet . . . and yet, if we search through history, we find that individual countries, including ours, do often display typical responses to particular stresses and that those typical responses may vary from one country to the next. Some countries may be belligerent, some passive; some may attack their neighbors to right real or imagined wrongs or to gain strategic advantages or simple loot, whereas others may wish simply to be left alone. All such traits emerge from millennia-long histories that are reflected in national cultures of populations whose origins may, in the dim recesses of the past, have emerged from a nomadic, sedentary, militant, passive, rural, urbanized, or some other background representing a complex mix of these derivations. As Jared Diamond points out in his 1997 book, *Germs, Guns, and Steel,* such backgrounds may have been driven by geography, climate, and the accidents of where in the continental vastnesses of the world the people and their civilizations happened to have originated.

How, then, could we talk about the typical responses of the American people, who represent an amalgam of a large number of the cultural backgrounds of the rest of the world? Surely, that mixture will make American reactions to the stresses of the modern world even more difficult to predict than the reactions of any other, more homogeneous people. Indeed, a lesson drawn from Chapter 2 is that the nation whose security we are concerned about today is not the nation that met the Cold War threat half a century ago.

There are unifying factors, however, that have influenced the successive masses of immigrants and newly empowered internal migrants who have contributed to the composition and activities of our population. The cultures of the new immigrants and the migrating populations—for example, African Americans moving from southern farms to northern cities, or Hispanic refugees from the Central American wars—have continually merged into the resulting patterns because, apparently, they are satisfying to the primal human urge to be as free of externally imposed constraints as possible. We must understand the resulting attitudes if we are to assess what the country is *likely* to do in furtherance of its interests in the complex world of the twenty-first century, as distinct from thinking about what it *ought* to do.

Two influences in our history make themselves felt in particular. One is the impact of the frontier, which made the world appear limitless and invited the taking of its bounty by those bold and strong enough to go and get it. The other is the U.S. Constitution, which limits government power, assures people that they will be free of arbitrary and oppressive coercion and compulsion to conform to rules of religion, taxation, or class division by a government they had no hand in creating, and assures them that they can change their government when it displeases them.

These influences interact to make up what might indeed be called an "American personality" that successive waves of immigrants have come to adopt over time and that creates attitudes that affect how America responds to stimuli from any part of the world. Even though the freedom of the frontier was concentrated in the rural, forested, or open vastnesses of the North American continent, the freedom to move ahead to further one's own fortunes that characterized the movement into those spaces became part of the American psyche. The attitudes were translated back into the existing and urbanizing America by all sorts of media: the motion pictures that emerged from Hollywood just as the frontier was disappearing into the sunset; the continuation on radio and television of stories about Dodge City, ranching, oil and lumber empires, cattle drives, the Lone Ranger, and on and on. The universal appeal—worldwide as well as nationwide—of the freedom of the wide open spaces is attested by the earlier popularity of the author Zane Gray, which preceded the popularity of the Western in cinema, the *Dallas* TV series, and the image of the Marlboro Man, among many others.

The constitutionally guaranteed freedoms from overly oppressive government that accompanied the expansion of opportunity on the frontier and in the urban world have acted to assure people that when they have seen and seized an opportunity to get ahead they have some reasonable protection against regimentation by the heavy restraining hand of government or by the tight reins of existing economic power—sometimes more, sometimes less, as the political winds and the reactions to some entrepreneurs' occasionally rapacious behavior ebb and flow. Whether or not they can build great economic power on their own, they can be free to pursue their own interests without undue restraint. The Constitution guarantees that whenever there is a risk of government taking away the fruits of a person's labor, or blocking the development of those fruits, the representatives of the population can act to pull the government up short. This doesn't mean unlimited freedom to plunder. Legal processes like antitrust laws do work, sometimes after too long a time, to stop unlimited and harmful exploitation of freedoms and protections. But the contest between constraint against illegality and unfair advantage, on the one hand, and undue restraint of opportunity to prosper on the other have been and are a continuing feature of American governance to an extent unmatched anywhere else in the world.

What attitudes have these historical factors engendered in the outlooks America brings to consideration of its national security? Some are entirely predictable, and like all side effects some are surprising and disturbing.

"What's There Is Mine"

The most obvious effect of the frontier mentality is the "taking" attitude. Resources, whether land, water, or air or what grows in, on, under, or over them are considered to be infinite, and if "I" can somehow gain control over them "you" can't interfere with "my" taking of them. The inevitable procession into the "tragedy of the commons," an idea put forward in 1968 by Garrett Hardin to describe the situation that emerges if every taker decides to use a common resource at will, is little comprehended, and regulation to avoid it is stoutly opposed by those with an interest in exploiting resources. The notion that the resources may be limited and their taking of them by "you" may harm "me" or give "you" the ability to limit "my" freedom to enjoy their benefits is resisted and has to be imposed from outside. This imposition is invariably accompanied by much political furor as the right level of constraint is sought by trial and error in the courts and in the halls of the Capitol.

The attitude carries over into issues of accommodation with other countries in areas where interests overlap. It affected the U.S. position on the law of the sea, for example, in terms of exploiting ocean-floor resources, and it has affected negotiating positions on environmental matters. It could become vital in a future in which contention for scarce resources becomes more the rule than it is today. It appears now in arguments about whether and how much the federal government ought to charge for grazing and logging rights on federal lands. It shows in pressures to make available for commercial exploitation bandwidth in the radio spectrum that might be needed for military communications and electronic warfare, thus affecting national security directly.

"You Can't Limit Me"

The taking attitude extends beyond resources to matters of freedom to act in society that are guaranteed by the Constitution. It is accepted that government at any level cannot limit the right of individuals to assemble and express themselves for any frivolous or serious purpose, as long as the assemblages do not act to threaten law, order, or the existence of the government. It is also accepted in consequence that anyone has great freedom to say anything one wants to say on any subject, even if what is said has harmful effects on others. This carries over into use of the radio spectrum and all other communications media, and in recent court decisions it appears to be applied to physical acts, like burning the flag, which is interpreted as speech because it expresses an idea. Again, the net effect is to convey a feeling of freedom to do what one wants and to resist constraints applied in the interest of maintaining order and discipline in society. The problem with constraints applied by government, as we have come to realize, is that they are never subtle, and they have a great tendency to grow beyond their intended scope and effect. This is another aspect of the contending forces described above.

"And I Want It Now"

Beyond fractious political processes, there are other side effects in the frontier-driven, constitutionally guaranteed exercise of individual freedom that condition our approach to national problems. One consequence is a short-term outlook that inhibits the nation's staying power in matters that require patience and stamina. Why stick with something that isn't working or try to make it work better if there will be something different just beyond the next (literal or figurative) mountain and we have only to go after it? If we decide to do something it must be implemented with little delay, and it must pay off *now* or the argument is made that it is a failure and it should be abandoned.

If the president asks for an investment policy and it is granted by Congress, it is deemed a failure if it doesn't pay off before the next fiscal year. If we change something in the education system, the test scores have to show immediate improvement or else we conclude it didn't work and clamor for the next scheme. If we call a meeting to negotiate something on the international scene, it is dubbed a failure if a treaty doesn't emerge after a day or two of negotiations. In the war in Vietnam, which our policy said it was vital to win on behalf of the free world, we gave up more than once in keeping military pressure on Hanoi just as it was being severely hurt by the pressure, so that it had the opportunity to recover. And we cut off aid to the South Vietnamese government just as the South Vietnamese army, under our "Vietnamization" policy, was beginning to show the ability to hold off North Vietnamese divisions with our air support.[7] When Mikhail Gorbachev announced perestroika, a plan to restructure the Soviet economy that would have to take a generation of changing attitudes among a people steeped in communist totalitarianism, our news media were calling it a failure because it didn't show dramatic results in six months. The 1999 NATO air campaign to reduce and contain Serbia's aggression against ethnic Albanians in Kosovo, which had been intended and announced as requiring weeks or months, was proclaimed a failure in the media after less than a week. The problem with such conclusions by the media is that Congress is often influenced to act on them. These few

---

[7] These judgments are based on the history by William S. Turley in *The Second Indochina War* (Boulder: Westview Press, 1986). Professor Turley had postwar access to records of both sides.

random examples show that short-termness in either domestic or foreign policy can have serious effects on our domestic welfare and our world position.

Many reinforcements of the short-term outlook are inherent in our system. Government drives in that direction: A president must show results in two years; he or she starts running for the second term early in the third year of the first term; under the Twenty-second Amendment to the constitution he or she becomes a lame duck, unable to exercise effective power, early in the second term. Congressmen are elected every two years; they need accomplishments to take back to the voters to increase their chances for reelection. The conduct of the economy drives in that direction: Stock prices, and therefore the welfare of corporations and the riches of individuals, are determined by quarterly showings of profit and loss. New chief executive officers of corporations in trouble are expected by the all-powerful stockbrokers and money managers to turn them around in a year or they are considered failures who will be overwhelmed by the competition. Business and public developments like stadiums, shopping centers, and highways are always controversial, and if they are not well along or completed quickly within the terms of office of the elected officials who sanctioned and supported them they may be opposed and languish or be modified, delayed, or even halted. The media look for rapid results because gradual evolution does not command headlines, and reporters who told about the beginning of something want to be able to report on (and judge) the ending of it before they are scooped, go on to the next major assignment or job, or lose interest because it is moving too slowly and there is nothing dramatic to report.

The problem with a short-term outlook, of course, is that in our complex technological society it takes increasingly greater time to get things done (e.g., to implement major programs, to bring about and measure the effects of significant change, or to design and acquire the fruits of a major engineering enterprise or scientific advance). This is a consequence of both the time it takes to bring complicated systems on line and the decision time needed to explore and either reassure people about or contain potential unforeseen side effects. Thus, for example, we are almost always under pressure to underestimate the cost and difficulty of implementing new systems, such as the international space station, and especially software-dependent systems like the Washington, D.C., subway system fare cards and Denver's new airport baggage handling system. Then we clamor that they are taking too long, and in the process we often delay them further and run their cost up higher. Or else we never let them happen, as has been the case with the increasingly urgent need to make permanent nuclear waste disposal facilities. In some cases this may work very much to our detriment, as we have given up (at least, for a long "temporary" interval) on using atmospherically clean nuclear power and cut back on research to find ways to generate power from nuclear fusion.

"And Who Are You to Tell Me . . . "

The frontier heritage and constitutional restraints on government clearly lead to (or may even have emerged from) an irreverence for and an antagonism toward authority. The irreverence is reflected in the unwillingness to accept "authority" as the final arbiter of behavior or disputes or even of what is fact. We regard sports and entertainment figures with more respect than we regard our government leaders, people with extensive education are considered eggheads, and those with wealth are often reminded that their wealth alone does not earn them respect (although it certainly helps). The antagonism toward authority is expressed in the adversarial system of resolving disputes. Carried to extremes in today's world, it now places the nation in some danger of denying the value of all knowledge in making decisions vital to its future.

There is a reason our society is so litigious. It emerges from the notion that anyone who can persuade his or her peers, by whatever means, of the "rightness" of a case should win the argument and carry the day. "Winning" is determined by getting enough votes, whether from a jury or the electorate. That is considered fair, and it encourages argument about but not necessarily light on issues that are becoming increasingly complex in our technology-based civilization. Indeed, the importance and quality of technical expertise in helping to resolve arguments become lost in such an environment. Each side of a dispute tries to turn one side or another of the inevitable factual uncertainty about complex scientific and technical matters to its own advantage in attempting to sway the opinions of those who must vote on an issue—jurors and the public at large. They do this by presenting only one side of an issue, using selected facts and arguments that support their case, and denigrating the facts and arguments that support the opposing case. Although this approach may have the benefit of forcing the sides to confirm the reliability of their facts and reinforce the rigor of their arguments, it can serve only to confuse most of the population who are asked to judge and who have no expertise to detect and evaluate distortions of technical fact or warped judgments based on such distortions.

And, of course, we extend these aspects of the adversarial process to all our activities, including the making of laws and the conduct of foreign policy. We saw it in operation in laws that affect not only U.S. trade with countries with whom we have quarrels, such as Iran and Cuba, but in our extension of constraints to companies in other countries who have different ideas about those quarrels. In the long run, this kind of self-centered and arbitrary action can make it more difficult for us to make coalitions in areas where truly vital interests may be at stake.

"Not with My Money"

The unwillingness to accept the idea of limits on resources and the consequent need for restraints on their exploitation, together with a general hostility to the taxing powers of government, combine to make for a reluctance to pay, or even to recognize, the true cost of anything the government or private enterprise may undertake to build or operate. The most flagrant examples occur in the areas of environmental pollution control and transportation, where the producers of by-products that are costly to deal with, whether toxic substance emission or highway deterioration or traffic congestion, continually resist incorporating the damage control or avoidance expense into their processes and shift them to the public instead. Governments must then pay to fix the problems, but they must raise tax money to do so. This is often resisted, with the result that the final payer is the individual member of the public, and that payment is usually indirect, in inconvenience, time lost, reduced safety, and the like. Elsewhere, the resistance to taxation per se is manifest in a trend toward various kinds of user fees imposed by governments at various levels to disguise the fact of taxation or to shift the burden elsewhere (to transient businesspeople or tourists, for example).[8]

This reluctance to pay for what we need and even to raise the money to do so is not unique to Americans, of course, but we Americans have a larger say over matters of cost allocation and taxation in our governmental system than most other peoples, even democratically governed peoples, may have. This may apply to things like environmental management, provision of transportation infrastructure, the management of the armed forces, and provision of electric power to households and industry. It results in massive cost-shifting from parts of the economy and society where the costs are obvious and therefore can be resisted to parts of society where they are harder to detect and therefore harder to allocate consciously. For example, power lines remain exposed to damage from storms and falling trees because power companies do not want their rates to reflect the costs of avoidance, such as burying power lines and trimming trees. And the populace may well resist higher rates. But the costs paid by those who lose power, in disrupted work, spoiled food, untreated medical emergencies, and so forth do not get reckoned in the balance sheet. The inconvenienced parts of society then, without realizing it, pay the indirect "taxes" that the initial protesters have shirked. This appears to be the most obvious effect of the re-

---

[8]Adding substantial taxes to car rentals, a commodity mostly used by travelers, has become a way to pay for local needs in several cities and is a prime example of this practice.

luctance to pay true costs. It can be argued, in contrast, that since the public is the ultimate beneficiary of the process that produces the waste there is justice in allocating the cost to individual members of the public, even when the cost cannot be fully expressed quantitatively. The tug-of-war over this problem is a continuing feature of the American scene, often vocalized.

The attitude carries over into foreign policy and defense policy. Although the nation was willing to follow the idea of helping Europe get back on its feet after World War II, and to extend aid to Greece and Turkey at the beginning of the Cold War, our population gradually balked at foreign aid. The reluctance to spend money to help foreigners even when it helped our own purposes often made it difficult to fulfill promises made in the name of security assistance, and it sometimes reached perverse conclusions. For example, Congress refused to appropriate money to build bomb-resistant, reinforced concrete shelters for our combat aircraft based in Germany, even though such passive protection of our aircraft was essential for their survival in case of a Warsaw Pact attack. Congress would rather enforce the view that "we won't pour concrete on German air bases; that's their job," even though our own Air Force's survival, and ultimately that of our nation, was at stake.

"Who Are We Gonna Fight?"

We have also had difficulty in getting out of the Cold War mentality in which we must have an identifiable enemy with whom to come to grips. This need lies behind some of the hostility to China that we see in much of our public discourse, and it is reflected in books that worry about the "coming war" with China, with Japan, or with other nations. If we don't immediately see an enemy, then consciously or unconsciously we work to contrive one. We don't take the trouble to distinguish between true enmity and differences arising from different cultures and clashing interests, differences that should be subject to reconciliation. We want to decide who are friends and who are enemies first. Then we go about resolving differences in ways that either resolve conflicts or that enhance hostility.

Thus, for example, we have more trade overall with China than with France. Our attitudes about the economic impact of accommodation or conflict on trade might logically be expected to be more favorable to China than to France, or at least about the same for the two, if trade were a determining factor in the relationships between the United States and the other countries. Yet our attitudes toward the two countries are divergent. We are willing to compromise with France on French agricultural subsidies that distort world markets and compete unfairly with our own overseas agricultural sales. We collaborate with France in many areas of defense technology, through NATO institutions and bilaterally. A scandal about French industrial espionage subsides quickly. We essentially ignore the fact that France is a key supplier of advanced antiship missiles to avowedly hostile nations—missiles that would be used mainly against our Navy. In contrast, large and important political factions in the United States forsake few opportunities to characterize dealings with China as abandoning our values for mere mercantilism. They raise a furor about technical information that may have leaked to China in the process of using Chinese launch vehicles for civilian satellite launches even though they earlier blessed the commercial advantages such cooperation would give to American industry. Revelations of possible Chinese espionage heighten tensions between the United States and China. Many groups trying to influence our China policy consistently act as though they would rather impose sanctions than talk about reconciling differences.

This emotional approach to foreign policy conditions much of the commentary on foreign policy in the popular media; it arises in Congress when we review the need for defense budgets of a certain size; it makes for difficulty in comprehending the idea that we must be prepared for many kinds of military contingencies, the origin and advent of which we cannot forecast and easily describe. This need for a worthy enemy we can point to in justifying military action also underlies much of our aversion to costs and casualties expended in support of mere interests. "Interests" alone do not present us with an enemy we can tangle with; they require only vigilance, as well as actions that entail expense and sometimes military casualties. Such expenditures in support of interests are not as easy to justify as actions to foil an enemy. The implicit or explicit expression that this or that interest isn't worth one dollar of American treasure, or one young American's life, has become common since the Cold War, in relation to Somalia, Haiti, Bosnia, Kosovo, and other areas where there may be national interests to defend that are less than vital.

These observations do not at all suggest that there would be virtue in casually squandering treasure and lives on furthering interests overseas on the mere chance that they may later be found to affect us in important ways. The problem with the transmitted attitude of uncertainty in the absence of a defined superenemy is the potential encouragement of adventurism based on miscalculation by those who find it in their own interest to diminish ours, as happened when Saddam Hussein invaded Kuwait in 1990. This is not a new problem in history, ours or any other nation's. But it arises in more intense form for us just at the point when increasing instability in world affairs makes it desirable for us to convey steadfastness and sturdiness of will rather than reluctance to become engaged and capriciousness in the final decisions.

The unrequited desire to know who our enemy is also combines with our reluctance to pay the true cost of many public policies to constrain spending on the military budget. As we shall see later, many required expenditures related to personnel, to the integration of more complex forces in an environment of more complex need, and for steps to make the armed forces more robust against some of the vulnerabilities being built into them by their adoption of modern technology and its organizational concomitants would significantly increase defense expenditures. The general public, and its representatives in government, are reluctant to spend more for defense at a time when they thought the end of the Cold War should reduce such expenditures. Their priorities are now going in different directions. The lack of an identified enemy essentially denies them a rationale to think and act against their impulses at such a time. By the time such an enemy appears, partly as a result of the public policy the need for such an enemy encourages, partly from simple clashes of interests with major powers developing around the world, the cost to catch up will prove to be much higher than the cost to keep up would have been.

"I Know!"

Another attitude that conditions our relationship with the world is the unbounded certainty we have in the rightness of our views. Not surprisingly for a nation that has the world's third largest population, the world's largest economy, and a relatively short history during three-quarters of which we were insulated from the rest of the world by the oceans, we have trouble recognizing any other country's outlook. Our public knows little of other nations' histories that would condition their outlooks, and we believe that our point of view should prevail in all international councils. And we are quick to judgment about others. Much of this attitude is reflected in the series of laws that require the executive branch to publish annual reports about how all countries in the world (except our own) treat human rights, fight or support terrorism, cooperate in fighting the drug cartels, and deal with other subjects like the exercise of religious freedom.

These reports are undoubtedly a good thing in bringing to our own people's and the world's attention that there are wrongs to be righted and in tracking the status of the efforts to do so. They also help to inform debate in this country about foreign policy, which is indeed their intent. But the reports, and our insistence that our views on almost any issue must be accepted by the rest of the world, also convey a certain hubris. They bring down on us the world's opprobrium for our arrogance, and they make it difficult for us to conduct the kind of quiet diplomacy that might sometimes do more than public condemnation to right the wrongs we despise.

"The People's Right to Know"

The idea that secrecy in international affairs amounts to perfidy is deeply ingrained on our laws and our psyche—and for good reasons. Open covenants openly arrived at allow the people of a democracy to decide issues of war and peace for themselves, rather than having the outcomes thrust upon them without their knowledge and against their will.

But there are times when one wants to keep discussions and some activities among nations and within nations quiet. In a bargaining situation, to arrive at any international agreement there must be give-and-take. "Give" means giving up something that someone on one's own side wants, and "take" means that the other side has to do the same. Without such exchanges, agreements cannot be reached, unless by diktat from a position of extreme military strength, and not many such situations will obtain without engendering hostility and subsequent conflict. If the result of the bargaining is shown to the affected populations after all the exchanges have been agreed to, then they can judge the gains and losses, and accept or reject them, as a whole. But if bargaining positions are broadcast in advance, then all factions for or against will marshal their forces to influence the outcome, and after the free-for-all the negotiators will be hard put to step down from positions they may have floated as starting points for the give-and-take inherent in negotiations.

This reasoning applies to all bargaining situations, whether internal to the country, as in labor negotiations and the planning of a new road, or in the country's relations with other nations. In addition, there may be actions a government wants to take quietly that run counter to its publicly stated positions—covert operations, for example, to help change a recognized government with whom we are in conflict and to protect one with whom we are having public differences. Finally, in some kinds of activity, such as intelligence-gathering, one wants to give away neither one's sources nor one's methods, for then the gathering of the intelligence can be easily foiled or, even worse, deceived.

From all this it must be accepted that there are times when government must have secrets. But one of the results of the concatenation of the Bay of Pigs debacle, of the furor over the government's conduct of the Vietnam War, of Watergate, and of the concurrent political and social revolution in which "citizen power" was the most extolled virtue, was the breakdown of the ability to keep official secrets in the United States in almost any circumstances. Congress demanded more visibility into the activities and decision processes of the defense establishment and the CIA. The system of classification in national security matters came under attack, and the courts' support for release of the Pentagon Papers, which described in detail the arguments and decision processes that had led to the unpopular Vietnam War and its conduct, started a media and congressional attack, not only on the classification system but also on government secrecy in general.

This culminated in the Freedom of Information Act of 1966, which allowed any citizen to sue for release of information deemed germane to the public's right to know about things that would affect it. The attack was intensified by the events that led to President Richard Nixon's resignation. The reaction to secrecy attending the bombing of North Vietnamese supply routes through Cambodia, and the emulation of CIA dirty tricks in the search for evidence of who had released the Pentagon Papers and in the Nixon reelection campaign, swamped resistance to changing the old system. Essentially, the stresses of the Vietnam War blew the government's cover and made it impossible to keep official secrets—"good" ones or "bad" ones alike—for very long. If there was any doubt, President Ronald Reagan's Iran-Contra affair, in which the proceeds of secret arms sales to Iran were used to finance counterrevolutionary forces in Nicaragua against the will of Congress, rammed it home.

The current pattern of the Congress-media axis was refined and flourished. In that pattern, reporters smoke out a story, usually based on something that the government has tried to keep secret for either legitimate or nefarious reasons. Congress then calls for and has an investigation, making for more media headlines and stories. The two reinforce each other until a story has run its course or leads to an even hotter one. The art of the leak, to drive policy or to foil it, has been perfected along the way. Ability to keep a secret is no longer one of the great virtues; the admirable quality now seems to be to know how to release private or classified information for best effect without getting caught.[9]

All this has made it more difficult for malfeasance involving the public trust to succeed for any significant time. That is the benefit. But the government's ability to keep its activities quiet when that is necessary and beneficial to formulation and conduct of foreign policy has been a critical loss in the process. It must now be assumed that any activity or negotiation the government may undertake will become public knowledge, usually prematurely and in harmful ways. The change in our ethical outlook about keeping secrets is perhaps best illustrated by the oxymoron of public calls by individuals in Congress and the media for covert operations to overthrow Iraqi dictator Saddam Hussein.

---

[9]I was first exposed to extended action by the Congress-media axis during the 1960s, in a dispute about Defense Department support of research in the social sciences. The action of the axis was illustrated most starkly in the matter of President Clinton's impeachment. One couldn't help noticing that when Congress was in recess from mid-November 1998 to its post-Thanksgiving special session, the impeachment stories left the front pages of the *Washington Post* and the opening bulletins of the network news broadcasts. Congress had the ball at that time, and the media had to wait while they wound up for the pitch. Earlier, the media had been largely responsible for breaking the stories that led through special counsel Kenneth Starr to the impeachment hearings in the first place. When Congress returned, the front page coverage was renewed.

The sequence of events that strongly modified the government's ability to keep secrets when it is necessary to do so also led to a backlash against secrecy in the conduct of our national political affairs. This has been most strongly felt in the nominating process for the presidency. In the years before the mid-1960s there were a few primaries, but the nomination decisions were mainly made behind closed doors—the famous, or infamous, smoke-filled rooms—before and during the national political nominating conventions. After the turmoil of the sixties both political parties moved toward the use of primary elections as the main nomination vehicle.

The unintended effect of this change has been what amounts to a two-year presidential election campaign, effectively reducing to two years the useful time during which a president can carry out the duties of his office relatively unfettered by having to run for the office. (One has to assume such an outcome was unintended, for what politician in his right mind would want to foist such a system on the country deliberately—unless, perhaps, it was part of a plot by local politicians to reduce still further the power of the presidency. In our time of seeing conspiracies in any coincidence of events, someone might almost believe that.) In the nomination process, for good or ill, the experience and wisdom of the much-maligned party chiefs in selecting the nominee have been relegated to a minor role. The long presidential campaign intensifies the need and demand for money, distorting and corrupting the political process at least as much, in its own way, as the previous system was believed to have been corrupted by the sway of the party bosses. The resulting and persistent media saturation is very likely a contributor to the declining voter turnouts that the same media decry.

"I Don't Believe It"

A concomitant of the "people's right to know" is the media need to bring it to the people's attention forcefully—more forcefully than the other guy can, so you can sell more newspapers, get more advertisers to pay for airtime, and generally gain fame and fortune. This competition, together with exploitation of the general distrust of government engendered by the Vietnam-era arguments and Watergate, has led to a generally revisionist approach to all news reporting on the part of the news media. Nothing is what it seems; whatever you propose, here's what's wrong with it; if it failed, you're lying about why. Stories of malfeasance gain priority and notoriety over stories reporting the facts of any event. Such professional skepticism has been at the root of many fictional stories purported to be fact, such as the 1996 story about the CIA introducing crack cocaine into California as a way of financing its Nicaragua counterinsurgency efforts, and the 1998 story that the United States used chemical weapons to kill American defectors in Laos during the Vietnam War. The revisionist attitudes of the media are reflected in public attitudes toward government and policy matters. They are yet another turnoff, making it more difficult to persuade the general population of the necessity and rightness of foreign policy and military actions necessary to support national security.

"You Go Your Way, I'll Go Mine"

Despite all the negatives on national attitudes in the preceding comments, there is a positive side to the national outlook they describe. One of the beneficial effects of the way the U.S. population has agglomerated through the centuries is an attitude of tolerance for diverse beliefs and customs that is probably unique in the history of nations and the world. This may seem a strange observation in this time of conflict over affirmative action, immigration, and exclusionary politics. But all things of this kind are relative.

The country has come a long way in its accommodation to having a diverse citizenry since the times when we pushed the Indians out of their ancestral homelands and resisted the idea of considering former slaves to be human beings deserving equal treatment with white citizens. People in this country have always segregated themselves into neighborhoods and activity centers with their country mates, whether Irish, or Greek, or Italian, or Polish, or Mexican, or Chinese, or white, or black, or WASP, or Jewish, or any of the other groups that make up our population—not to mention de facto segregation by socioeconomic status. There are often conflicts along the boundaries of these neighborhoods. And outside those conflicts we have, at times of stress, treated minorities badly, as when we discriminated against people of German descent and sent citizens of Japanese descent to internment camps during World War II. Yet with it all, in the second half of the twentieth century we accommodated to the idea that people of many derivations and cultures live here and that even though any group of us may not understand or like all of them we cannot for long discriminate strongly against them in things that matter. The politics of accommodating the views and needs of the different groups is an important driver of our political system. Indeed, the impulse to recognize and respect others' viewpoints and cultural heritages within our country have led to the often exaggerated deference to those things that make up what we call "political correctness" today.

We don't go to war with each other over our beliefs and ancestry the way the Serbs have done. We don't, for long, sustain laws that permanently exclude a segment of our population from the benefits of citizenry and from the opportunity to prosper in our economy, as many European and Asian countries do. We don't, for long, allow members of our media to attack one group of citizens consistently or incite riot against them without giving that group recourse elsewhere in the media and in the courts. We recognize that all these groups will have an influence on our elections and our government, and they are courted in our electoral process. Shopping areas and marketing are established to cater to various groups. Diverse churches and other places of worship flourish, mainly without interference. And in the common places where people of various derivations mix, such as national parks, it is difficult to say where any visitor has come from or what ancestral group may be represented. Thus, over a 400-year history a nation of immigrants has learned to accommodate, tolerate, work with, and befriend fellow-citizens who may have different origins. Rarely in the 7,000 years of advanced civilizations has this ever happened.

There are two flies in this ointment, however. The first is that our belief in the rightness of our views tends to make this tolerance stop at water's edge. Although we are willing to live within the rules of social discourse that have evolved from tolerance, one aspect is that individual groups in the entire population don't take the trouble to learn much about the others. Ignorance and prejudice continue; they simply aren't acted upon, and "others" are tolerated and ignored as long as they don't interfere with each other. It's a big country, and there is room for everybody (until that changes). The obverse side of this coin is that since the tolerance is not curiosity or knowledge or empathy driven we needn't go out of our way to comprehend and be tolerant of overseas groups that we don't have to live with. Together with our attitudes about the rightness of our own views, this extends into questioning why we have to intervene on behalf of the overseas groups if they are beset in ways that have implications for our own security—as in the former Yugoslavia, for example. And there we have some of the roots of national isolationism.

"Here, Let Me Help"

There is also a streak of generosity that may be another product of the frontier mentality, built when people lived in relative isolation and could turn only to neighbors in time of trouble. This is manifested whenever there is a natural disaster in our own country and neighbors, outsiders, and the government pitch in with rescue and assistance. Indeed, the very existence of the Red Cross and other relief organizations attests to it. It has been applied in our dealings with the world over the past half-century, in ways that range from the immediate offers of aid and the dispatch of military forces in the wake of a natural disaster to the entire foreign-aid concept that began with the Marshall Plan and extended throughout the Cold War. It spawned the Peace Corps, the intent being to provide technical assistance to people in developing nations without attaching the negative implications of security assistance.

Unfortunately, the nation began tiring of this generosity as the Cold War wore on, as needs to meet the ill fortune of some of our own population grew and as we saw those we had been helping, such as Germany and Japan, prosper and compete with us in the international economy. When the Cold War ended we essentially gave up the burden and left it to those competitors to pick up, except for a few countries, such as Egypt and Israel, where we have felt a special moral obligation. But the quick response to disasters persists. It lay behind our intervention in the civil wars in Somalia, and we keep reminding ourselves that one reason we are involved in the Balkans is that our involvement helps to prevent genocide.

And so, to summarize: Our nation is, as are all great nations, complex in its outlook and its behavior. It is difficult to characterize briefly and simply. But there are some discernible and persistent attitudes that will condition our behavior on the international scene, and we must recognize them and account for them in providing for our national security or they will lead us to respond, unaware of their effects, in ways that are inimical to our welfare.

We are impatient with restraints on the use of resources, believing that what is there is ours by right and we should be free to take it if we have the means to do so. The clashes over who has this right and the adversarial system on which our laws are built make for an argumentative public life. We are also impatient, period: We want anything we conceive to be achieved almost as soon as the intent is articulated. We do not respect authority and want everything to be proven to our satisfaction, although the proof we accept often tends to be made up more of persuasiveness than of fact. We would rather not know or pay the total cost of many of our enterprises and benefits and are content to let costs be shifted to others who may not perceive that they are being charged. We are more comfortable with an enemy on whom to focus our national security efforts than with the notion of general preparedness to meet unforeseen contingencies.

We know we are right. Our sense of rightness and our determination to have our way feed our leaning toward isolationism. We have a large enough population and economy to feel self-sufficient, even though we aren't, and this feeds the tendency to want to pick up our marbles and go home if we don't get our way. We don't respect secrecy, and we rarely recognize how its denial or violation at critical junctures can work against our national welfare. And whatever the government tells us, it is probably lying or hiding the truth, so that we cannot go along with its proposals. With it all, we are reasonably tolerant of other "tribes" within our country, but we are not prone to learn or accommodate other countries' viewpoints. We are generous, but we may tire of that. We are determined to win in any contest of wills, whether military, political, or diplomatic—if it doesn't take too long.

TRENDS

The United States is, among other things, a technology-based country. We rely heavily on technology to gain and sustain our economic superiority in the world. Maintaining technological superiority over the Soviet Union was one of the main tenets of our Cold War strategy. When we entered World War II, and later during the early years of the Cold War, we were proud of the example of the American boy who could, with ingenuity and simple tools, make cars and farm machines do his bidding. For amusement he played baseball on sandlots and touch football in schoolyards. All that bred the aggressiveness and initiative to take on the world and win.

No longer. A generation of TV-bound couch potatoes has changed the image of American youth. Our youths now play computer games in arcades, drive to school, hang around the shopping malls, and watch football on TV instead of playing it. Or so our pundits have been telling us; it is partly true, but only partly. For the same generation also breeds people who are quick to master the operation of our computer-controlled systems, including military systems; hackers who can win an information war; and women who can run the sensor and communications networks that get the information to where it can be used by military forces faster and to greater effect than the forces of other nations.

The changes in these images, both of them simplistic, track the changes that have brought us from the refinement of industrial technology at mid-century, in which the United States led the world, to the coming dominance of information technology in humanity's economic, social, and political lives as we enter a new century. And in this, too, the United States appears to be leading the world. But we should not deceive ourselves; this leadership is not all a blessing. We are not only leading the world in new, technology-defined directions that are changing lives everywhere; we are being led by that technological evolution. We like to think that we are controlling it, but we are not. We do occasionally call a halt to a technological direction for economic or other reasons. One was the decision not to build a supersonic transport aircraft. Another has been the apparent decision not to pursue further development of nuclear power for generating electricity. But in the free-enterprise system of which we are justifiably proud, the inventions and developments that the enterprise brings to our doorsteps also lead us into ways of living, thinking, and governing ourselves and our relationships with the rest of the world that we might not consciously choose or might value and choose differently from the way it is happening if we thought about it. Let's look at some of these trends.

Technology "Drivers"

Technology at the service of humanity has always derived from humanity's observations of natural phenomena and the applications of the results of the observations to making tools, devices, and processes that have augmented planning ability and given mechanical advantage to mind and muscle. Technology today flows from the implementation of scientific knowledge that is still based on observations of nature. It now uses precise instruments for measurement and the formation of provable inferences about the meaning of the resulting data, both of which are the products of the technology emerging from earlier observations. The process is a bootstrap operation that, so far, has known no limits. Even the purported limits imposed by the physics, chemistry, and biology of real things and beings at any time in the sequence have continued to be redefined and pushed back as scientific knowledge has been gained.

The post–World War II American science program stimulated by Vannevar Bush's famous 1945 report to President Truman, "Science: The Endless Frontier," burgeoned into a huge basic and applied research enterprise that ultimately spread around the world. That enterprise created the knowledge that made the United States the world leader in scientific research and in the application of research results to practical things in all areas of life and its activities. The advance was helped in great measure by the early spur of the Cold War, which offered justification for the large application of resources the enterprise demanded and, more recently, by the spur of international economic competition for the fruits of the advances the scientific knowledge made possible.

Technology in any civilization advances in many areas simultaneously, and in modern times it is almost impossible to summarize the entire set. However, four areas of technology in particular have given the United States very high payoffs, and in consequence we have given high priority, in both government and private investment for research and entrepreneurial purposes, to their advancement. These are information technologies, medical technologies, transportation, and agriculture. A brief word about each in context of their derivation and application in modern America is in order before we look at some ramifications.

Early in the post–World War II years, advance in the information technologies was led by military research and development. Integrated circuits were invented and applied first to intercontinental missile guidance systems. In some areas, such as sensing the environment and things within it, by radar, infrared devices, and other means, the military still leads. But in the areas of information technology that are most prominent today, including computing, communications, and the resulting worldwide networks for transferring and manipulating information of all kinds—financial, scientific, personal, entertainment—the civilian world has picked up the military products and run away with them. There is no need here to describe the powerful impact of these technologies on our society and all its essential and recreational activities; that impact has been the subject of countless contemporary accounts in all imaginable forums, and it has been alluded to repeatedly throughout the previous discussion.

Medical science and technology have benefited from the combined fruits of the need to treat casualties in warfare and to overcome the ravages of disease in civilian life. In our process of saving wounded and disease-ridden soldiers, sailors, and aviators in five major wars through the twentieth century, the imperatives of military applications have advanced some aspects of medical technology tremendously: in the discovery and use of antibiotics; in the rapid recovery and treatment of the injured and wounded; and in understanding and treatment of stress. Civilian basic research, spurred by the quest to understand and overcome disease of all kinds, from bacterial and viral infections to heart disease and cancer, has led to unprecedented understanding of how nature functions in relation to the human body and of how the body itself, with all its subsystems, functions. These advances, bringing us into the age of bioengineering and the mapping of the human genome, have transformed medicine radically. They have brought us to the point where physicians and other clinical and health specialists can approach the treatment and prevention of disease from knowledge rather than guesswork. Not the least impact of this evolution over the past eighty years has been a 40+ percent increase in the average life expectancy of Americans at birth, from 54.1 years in 1920 to 75.8 years in 1995 to more than 76 years now.

Transportation is another area that has benefited greatly from the interaction between military and civilian research, development, and application. The years since 1960 have seen an explosion in air transportation that has almost completely displaced commercial highway and rail transport in intercity travel (providing 90 percent of total passenger miles other than private auto), and that has revolutionized the movement of high-value goods around the world. This expansion was initially spurred by application of jet propulsion and other technology developed for fighter aircraft and long-range bombers to civilian transport aircraft. From there, aviation technology has spread into every other aspect of our public and private transportation system. It is difficult to overstate the impact of that technology on transportation (and much other) performance that we take for granted today. Materials, structures, propulsion, aerodynamics, instrumentation, computing, and computer application to data and control systems and to design and management of large-scale engineering enterprises have all percolated from military aerospace into civilian use. They are seen (but not always recognized) everywhere, from the incomparable American and world airline systems to automobiles, buses, railways, space-based environmental observation and measurement, biology and medicine, communication and navigation satellites, and even recreational land and water vehicles. And just as in information and medicine, civilian applications and manufactures dominate the markets in all of these areas.

Agriculture is another area where special American circumstances have led to revolutionary impacts. Those have emerged from our ability to farm large areas favorable for growth of crops that feed not only people but animals that feed people. The yield from fertile soils in the open spaces of America's cleared eastern forests and the Great Plains encouraged the development of efficient and effective farm machinery, as well as research to find the kinds of crop variants and husbandry practices that would, ultimately, give us the ability to feed not only ourselves but also much of the world. Both the research and the use of machinery and fertilizers that the United States pioneered have spread, directly or indirectly by spurring similar artifacts and methods, around the world. This led to the so-called green revolution, breaking the Malthusian chain so that the world did not go hungry as its population doubled over the past forty years, from 3 billion in 1960 to just more than 6 billion today.

These technological advances, and all others, are not made in isolation from each other. They all interact, and they share the same technical and scientific basis. None of the technology advances described would have been possible without the advances in solid-state physics that led to microcircuits on silicon chips, which in turn led to microprocessors, computers, and instrumentation that are involved in all the communications, transportation, and medical research and applications. Advances in management of the strength, weight, and corrosion resistance of materials that can withstand temperature and corrosion extremes in engines and in all environments from the deep oceans to space have made possible the lightweight, high-strength structures of aircraft, rocket launchers, satellites, improved-mileage automobiles, and skyscrapers. Understanding of the molecular structures of living tissues and living beings is making possible the creation of drought- and disease-resistant strains of basic foodstuffs (whether by bioengineering or natural selective breeding), as well as the creation of new drugs and processes to treat injuries and disease. And these are but a tiny handful of the most obvious interactions.

Taken together, however, these advances have also had powerful effects on how our society is organized and how it operates. New technological capability often demands new social institutions for its effective implementation. Sometimes these institutions are created purposefully, often by adapting existing institutions and changing their missions and sometimes their names: The creation of the National Aeronautics and Space Administration out of the National Advisory Committee for Aeronautics in 1958 is an example. But most often, in recent years, the institutions and organizational forms have grown out of the efforts of private enterprise to manage the new technologies as they appear, for all the reasons of private gain and public good that economists argue about.

Thus, we have seen, over the past century, the growth of large corporations, foundations, and government agencies designed to create and distribute the artifacts and techniques of the twentieth century's technological revolution and to exercise control over its operation and management. This has carried with it large concentrations of both government and private economic power that, had the general populace been asked a priori, it would probably not have voted to create. Yet without those concentrations of power the benefits of the technology would not have been gained.

On the positive side, it takes big corporate organizations that can command huge resources, whether operated by the government or private industry, to create, to acquire and use the necessary machinery, and to manage operations with worldwide reach. And it takes powerful government agencies with much expertise to regulate those organizations so that their efforts are channeled into public good without excessive abuse while preserving the profit incentives for their owners that fuel and lubricate the organizations' operations.

On the negative side, the need to compete in the world economy leads large corporate entities to favor applied research and development that will have a visible payoff in the short term, in the form of products that can be marketed. Also, those entities are coming to have more influence in government, by various processes from lobbying to advertising to influencing elections and to emphasizing the jobs implications of government actions that affect them. In the past, basic research that built the foundation of discovery on which the applied research was based was left to the government. But in a time of government retrenchment, Congress is also pressing for early results from the nation's research investment, so that it, too, wants government funds to buy more application and less of simple exploration for the sake of knowledge. Even when Congress wants to increase support for basic research, it wants to allocate the basic research resources to chosen fields—the antithesis of free inquiry into areas that *may* but are not *known* to offer promise of important discoveries. Congress appropriates money for results, not to support indulgence of curiosity. In the long run, this concatenation of attitudes means that scientific discovery and the technological innovation that builds on it will eventually run down, and when it does it may take another generation to restart the process—if the economic and political power concentrations of the time want to do so. They may not find it in their interest to move in that direction. (You will recognize here one set of implications of this trend that were reflected in the sketch of the future world that opened Chapter 2.)

This view may seem to fly in the face of the currently popular images of computer and software experts in a garage who advance technology by leaps and bounds while working on things that interest them more for their intellectual challenge than for their financial return. After all didn't Steve Jobs and Bill Gates start out working in small quarters on a shoestring? But we might note that Apple Computer, Inc., a corporation with billions of dollars in business, is not viewed as a paragon of success, in large part because it made marketing errors that kept it from growing big enough, whereas Microsoft has been under attack for excessively dominating its branch of industry. And in the areas of pharmaceuticals and bioengineering, the path from a small startup enterprise to acquisition by a corporate giant, or growth into such a giant by agglomeration, have become classic. And the giants buy up the startups so that they can control release of their output better, among other reasons.

The trend toward consolidation of power in large organizations and in the hands of relatively few people is described by economists Robert Frank and Philip Cook in their 1995 book, *The Winner-Take-All Society*. This trend results in large measure from the gradual globalization of economic activity and from the increasing ability to carry the fruits of that activity worldwide in a matter of minutes, hours, or days, depending on the product—not the weeks, months, and years that characterized technological change earlier in the twentieth century. All organizations and activities do not follow the trend, but enough do to characterize the age of bigness at the end of the twentieth century. Important scientific, economic, and entertainment activities that can have broad popular appeal no longer have to be restricted to regions of origin for long periods, nor is such restriction economically desirable or even feasible. This is an unintended consequence of the pressure to use technology, especially in the four areas we have reviewed, to make life better for all people.

Other unintended consequences can be more subtle but just as far-reaching. One is the substitution of capital for labor in almost all endeavors. This substitution has in one aspect been a consequence of the age-old quest for mechanical advantage, safety, and precise control through the use of machines. But the pace of change in this direction in our country and the world accelerated markedly since roughly 1975. It has been driven by the rapid increase in U.S. and other developed countries' labor costs, running ahead of productivity increases that have not fully paid for the labor-cost growth. (Indeed, defining productivity increases while the products themselves are undergoing revolutionary change is no small problem. As Nicholas Negroponte says in his 1995 book, *Being Digital*, it is hard to put a cost on a digit, and much of the new world depends on assembling and manipulating digits.) When combined with rapid communications and shipping that allowed the spread of manufacturing to other parts of the world where labor costs are lower, the high cost of American labor has forced American companies to reduce their labor costs in order to compete in the national and world economies. Having machines do jobs that people used to do is another way to reduce labor costs, and in any case the machines do many things better. Rising to the challenge, U.S. industry has succeeded magnificently in streamlining operations and thereby making them more effective while they are made more efficient.

Systems are designed and managed via computers. We no longer have huge numbers of people operating telephone switchboards; those operations are done automatically by computers. All machine tools are computer-controlled, as are major industrial processes. Ships, airplanes, and buildings are designed in computers such that all their millions of parts fit together the first time they are assembled, with almost no trial and error. Buildings are made of materials that can be produced and assembled by machines, including brick facings affixed to curtain walls that can be put in place in large sections so that the old craft of bricklaying is no longer necessary. The experienced, highly intuitive automobile mechanics of yesteryear have been replaced by factory-trained technicians who diagnose car problems by attaching a computerized instrument to the car's computer and reading the outputs of the hundred or more microprocessors that now control all of the car's functions. Extended lifetimes of all parts, with longer servicing intervals, mean that fewer such technicians are needed than there were mechanics in a shop in the old days.

Scientists, lawyers, and writers do much of their own analytical, secretarial, and illustration work on computers at their desks. They get the work out faster while reducing the need for assistants to help with such work. By consolidating instrumentation on a ship and building in automated control and self-repair capability for many functions, ships' crews can be reduced to ten or twenty people from dozens on commercial freight transports and to a quarter or fewer people in the crew of a twenty-first century cruiser than were in the crew of a ship of comparable size during World War II, fifty years earlier. Packing freight in containers that have electronic tags to tell what is inside, and loading containers instead of items, reduce the need for stevedores while greatly reducing loading time and speeding delivery. As complex a machine as humankind has ever crafted, the Boeing 747 or 777 transport aircraft can be operated by two people in intercontinental flight; the flight engineers who used to be required on an earlier generation of aircraft are no longer needed. The huge American agricultural output is produced by just 1.5 percent of our labor force, down from 3.5 percent in 1960 and about 10 percent in 1950—a very rapid decline while output nearly tripled over the same time.

Enough examples; the idea comes across. The ramifications of this drift are many. Four stand out. One is employment instability attending the change in the nature of work for wages or profit. A second is the reduction of human contact and a sense of community. A third is the drift toward entertainment in many forms as a way for people to fill the time available outside of work hours needed to produce society's necessary outputs. A fourth is distortion of our government processes. Further consequences of these effects on our society are felt in our education system. Increasingly, that system is losing the ability to prepare our citizens to deal with the security problems the nation will face. Let us consider all of these effects in sequence.

Employment Instability

The transformation of industry has transformed the nature and quality of work. Work in all areas has tended to move from the physical to the cerebral. Today, the computer keyboard is ubiquitous in the workplace, from factories to banks to retail outlets to the offices of lawyers, doctors, architects, and engineers. A desktop computer does the work that tens or hundreds of people used to do and much work that any number of people could not do. Increases in income for significant parts of the workforce and the growth of the retired population have increased the leisure time available to about a third of the population and given it money to spend during that time, generating new industries and activities. Part of the transformation has continued the shift from manufacturing to service industries. This evolution has been encouraged by the aging of the population, many of whose retired older members have the health, the time, and the resources to indulge leisure activities, which the service industries support. This development in human activity, which must certainly be viewed as beneficial and even a new stage in the evolution of humankind, accelerated markedly during the second half of the twentieth century.

As in all human activities, however, there has been no free lunch. The gains in our economy's efficiency and performance have imposed their price. The rapid evolution of industry into new areas of endeavor and new institutional forms has created unaccustomed employment instabilities. Jobs that appeared to be secure have been wiped out. There are new kinds of jobs to do, but they are being done by different parts of the population under much changed circumstances. It has happened before—buggy whips went out of production while spark plugs became important, and horseless carriages needed engine mechanics instead of stable hands—but not so rapidly in living memory. It took a generation to make the shift from the horse-and-buggy economy to the automobile economy. It took half a generation to shift from the regionally oriented automobile economy to the nationally oriented aviation economy. Then it took a quarter of a generation to shift into the globally oriented computer economy. The earlier shifts included or were accompanied by much strife—the period of labor unionization and a major depression bracketed by two world wars—but the emerging generation did well. In the latest step, there has been insufficient time for the labor force to adapt. People who have reached the pinnacles of their crafts and professions have been displaced by part-time workers and younger, differently educated, more trainable replacements who require less compensation. The well-known and always sensitive spread of incomes between the very well-off and ordinary workers has increased. The rapid increase in the number of women in the workforce has further distorted both the distribution of income and notions of what is women's and men's work.

In some areas, this instability has been a force for creativity by driving people into businesses of their own. But another, more pernicious effect has been the heightening of tension and restlessness in a society that feels less secure. That effect, together with the substitution of equipment for people and attending budget problems that also have at their root the increased cost of labor, has shaken our acceptance of long-standing ideas about community contact and community responsibility. This is not the place for a treatise on the evolution of the American community, but some illustrations will serve to evoke the changed atmosphere of modern community living.

Loss of Community

A homely illustration can be given by the evolution of morning newspaper delivery, at least as many of us have experienced it over the past half-century. During the 1940s and 1950s, the newspaper was brought to the door by a boy (it was usually a boy) from the neighborhood whom we all knew and could chat with and who was anxious to be helpful. He put the paper inside the storm door when it rained so it would stay dry and we could pick it up without getting wet, and he remembered not to leave one when we were away. During the next two or three decades the paper boy's route expanded as more subscribers were added while the labor force was reduced. The paper boy was often a girl. It was harder to get to know him or her, because we rarely saw the person; he or she didn't have time to put the paper inside the storm door, so that it got soaked when it rained. And there were helpers who were never notified when we were away. Newspapers accumulated to tell the world our house was unoccupied, as the burglary rate was rising. The wet-paper problem was solved by a machine that encased the paper in a plastic bag, but now everyone has to go out in the rain or snow to get it. During the past decade or so the paper route has been taken over by a driver with a car or van full of papers, who could cover a territory that was huge by earlier standards and who could toss the plastic-encased paper out of the van window in the general direction of the front lawn. If you want to let someone know that the paper shouldn't be delivered, or you have any other instructions or complaints, you call a phone number where you can speak to a machine; you never know whether your message has been delivered unless the result appears, and if it is mistaken, there is no further recourse but the same machine. The community has disappeared, at least in that application.

If you think that is simply an isolated instance, think about shopping, whether it be for groceries, clothing, hardware, or exotic artifacts. In three-quarters of a century or so, we have moved from community stores, where we knew the salespeople and they knew us, and specialty stores grouped in districts according to subject matter, to massed stores in malls, where staff and customers are largely disconnected; and from there to shopping from catalogs through a voice on the phone; and now to shopping by computer on the internet. All this has been propelled by economic incentives, with the least costly solutions (for the seller) enabled by the advancing technologies we have reviewed earlier.

The progressive income tax, as another example, had been based on the idea that those who have more could afford to pay a higher fraction of their income for the government's services. In part this was because they made more use of those services, but it was also reasoned that their responsibility to the community of which they were a part demanded that if they could afford more they should contribute more to its welfare. Today, the progressive income tax is under heavy fire. There is strong political pressure for proportional taxation in which everyone would pay the same fraction of income into the tax system regardless of need or available resources—the so-called flat tax—or regressive taxation in which everyone pays the same amount of tax, as in a sales or value-added tax, regardless of income. The notion of a community's responsibility for all its members has been lost in these proposals.

Insurance began in societies formed to afford mutual protection against the effects of accident, illness, and disaster in a community with similar occupations and interests. Now insurance is a profit-making industry with no obligations to anyone except corporate stockholders. The obligation to any community is gone from the insurance industry, having been replaced by economic imperatives with results that are obvious at their most painful in the health care area.

It used to be accepted that the transportation infrastructure should be paid for out of general revenues, since everyone benefited from it in the long run, whether they used parts of it, like the interstate highway system, the air-traffic control system, and the Mississippi River system with its tributary canals, or not. Some elements of it, such as expensive new toll roads and bridges, were traditionally subject to user fees as a means to pay for them. But now there is pressure to finance major parts of the infrastructure, such as the air-traffic control system, with such fees applied to users' tickets. Although arguments can be made that more frequent users of an asset should pay more for the use of it than the less frequent users, the value of the system to the whole community has not appeared as a key factor to be considered in the public discussions of these issues.

Another classic example is the school tax. It used to be fully accepted that since the entire community benefits by educating the younger generation all the adult members of the community should pay taxes to support the school system, whether they have children in schools or not. But objections to paying that tax are on the increase, as school bonds are rejected by an aging population that has fewer children in its midst. The idea of school privatization is undermining public education. Poorer citizens are being given modest rebates on their already low taxes, a meager resource base, to contribute to paying for their children in low-cost private schools, whereas the more affluent members of society, relieved of the burden of supporting public schools at their true cost, will have more resources available to send their children to higher-quality and more expensive private schools. The concept of the school as a community endeavor, expressing and extending the community's values and to be supported by the community for its benefit, is going away.

There are, of course, many reasons for this drift away from community responsibility. The above examples are drawn deliberately to highlight a trend that is difficult to prove with numbers but that reflects a change of outlook on the part of a population whose elements believe they must see to defending themselves against some very subtle threats to their security. Most of these perceived threats arise from population growth, some of whose effects we examined earlier.

As a result of combined internal growth and immigration, the U.S. population has gone from 151 million in 1950, shortly after the end of World War II, to 263 million in 1995 and is projected to be about 335 million in 2025. The comfortably habitable territory of the country has not expanded by much. Total area was increased by the admission of Hawaii and Alaska in 1959. Alaska is huge—it increased the area of the United States by nearly 600,000 square miles, or about 20 percent—but because of its sub-Arctic climate most of the area is not generally available for expansion of habitat by the general population. So even with our modest birthrates we are in the midst of a population growth that will have increased our population by more than 120 percent in three-quarters of a century, whereas the population at the end, continuing to grow, has to fit in much the same area that the smaller population occupied earlier.

The attending stresses are highly noticeable but not usually identified with many of the problems the population faces that appear to threaten its security. They include increased living and traffic congestion; higher crime rates (higher than in the 1950s, even with the gradual reductions of the 1990s); more intense uses of land and water with increasing arguments about everything from transportation noise to environmental conservation; encroachment of industrial activities on residential communities with arguments about the effects of power lines and the disposal of toxic substances on health; and arguments within communities about the very notion of development and expansion of community services for larger populations. Not the least effects are the loss of civility in public discourse and the increasing rates of litigation that social commentators bemoan. These stresses induce a need for increased public expenditure and regulation to mitigate and control their effects, for urban infrastructure, for environmental preservation, for accident and crime control and reduction, for education, and for all the other public services that our population has come to expect. Increased expenditure means increased taxation, explaining in large part why resistance to taxation, the nature of the tax system, and the arguments about who pays for what have come to dominate political discourse.

The Power of Entertainment

The growth of population, the change in the nature of work, and the growth of television as the mass-entertainment medium of choice have converged to make the entertainment industry one of the powerhouses driving our society. According to data in the *U.S. Statistical Abstract* (1997), the average person in the United States watches television about 1,600 hours per year. That is about thirty hours per week and amounts to 75–80 percent of the work year added on to that year. Even allowing for time TV sets are on in public places but not really being watched intently, that is a lot of time spent in front of the tube. The communications industry, which includes radio, direct broadcast and cable television, and print entertainment such as books and magazines as well as transmission of news and public affairs information has revenues of about $180 billion per year; the revenues increased at about $20 billion per year in the 1990s. Personal expenditures for entertainment and recreation of all kinds are on the order of $400 billion per year and have been increasing, on average, by $28 billion per year during the 1990s.

These indicators of the temporal and economic magnitude of popular participation in entertainment and recreation suggest one of the reasons for the merger of the entertainment and communications giants in the ongoing industrial consolidation within our economy. Entertainment, recreation, and communications are closely linked, through advertising, through the use of the communication media to inform and entice people to spend their rising disposable incomes in visiting and enjoying distant places of all kinds, and through the ease of moving about to see sporting events, visit national parks, and travel to foreign lands. It's reminiscent of Willie Sutton, the famous bank robber of the first half of the twentieth century, explaining why he robbed banks: "That's where the money is." It is simply good business to combine the areas. In the process, however, we find that entertainment and the conveyance of public-affairs information in our society are also merging.

The trend has been described by James Fallows in his 1997 book, *Breaking the News*. He shows how the star system has gradually drifted from the entertainment industry into the news media, so that personalities count for more than substance and entertainment counts for more than honesty and accuracy. Television drives this, since television is supported by advertising, and advertisers want to see high viewer ratings before spending the high costs of advertising on television. The quest for high ratings means that even news programs must have high entertainment value to attract audiences, and the amounts of money involved make it worthwhile to pay the most popular "performers" very high compensation.

Some of this admixture of entertainment and the transmission of public-affairs information has always existed, but it has intensified with the spread and increasing prominence of the media and their ability and need to get and hold the public's attention. We see effects of this drift in the increasing popularity of docudramas that have moved from the historical novel to contemporary affairs, in which telling a good story is more important than reporting events truthfully with factual support. We see it in the movement of editorial opinion from the editorial pages to the news pages of high-quality big-city newspapers, where feature stories and the new journalism apply emotional description—instead of just the facts—to current events. This is reflected in the other media, in which all but a few talk-show hosts on radio and television, when they deal with public affairs and matters of government and governance, present a mixture of fact, rumor, and fiction that the public has no way of sorting through. And we see it in the increasing frequency with which television and print programs and articles are faked to support a story that the reporters want to write, such as a fire hazard in car accidents, careless food handling in supermarkets, and the operation of a drug cartel. And we have seen instances in which news stories are made up based on a few shreds of shaky evidence that are found insupportable in the end, as happened with regard to the rumored CIA importation of crack cocaine to support rebellion against a communist regime in Nicaragua and the story about the purported use of nerve gas to kill American defectors at a prison camp in Laos during the Vietnam War. The net result of the rise in power of the entertainment media is that the public is flooded with information that is a mixture of fact, filtered according to its entertainment value as much as for its public affairs importance, entertainment closely linked to public affairs and often presented as purported fact, and pure fiction. All are presented in such a way that the public has little ability to distinguish among them.

The movement toward recreation and entertainment as a major way of filling people's time, combined with employment instability, leads to a population that is misinformed about important public events and is preoccupied elsewhere. The tax revolt and reduced community feeling and responsibility can be seen as reactions to the stresses of increasing population density. Population pressure will overcome those resistances in the long run; the nation's government budgets do keep increasing, faster than inflation, no matter which political party is in power. But in this environment it is hard to work up popular concern about subtle threats to national security, in which effects may not be felt for many years to come. And into this mélange come the effects of instant communications on our very form of government.

Government, California-Style

Attention to polls at all levels of government is not new in our political life. It was an important factor in President Franklin Roosevelt's management of the New Deal's attempts to bring the nation out of the Great Depression and in his management of the country's preparation to participate in the trauma of World War II. He used it to gauge public opinion before he took on fights with Congress and to guide his strategy in those fights, much as a military commander will seek intelligence about opposition morale and preparedness before an engagement. Such polling came into its own as a major tool to guide an election campaign during the 1960 election. John F. Kennedy enlisted the help of political scientist Ithiel de Sola Pool to create a model of popular opinion on the campaign issues, including the issue of how a prospective Catholic presidential candidate could improve his chance to be elected. That model, fed by up-to-the-minute polling data, guided Kennedy through a successful election campaign for the presidency and set the stage for use of fast-response polling as a sensitive instrument to guide election campaigns at all levels in the future.

This has been extended to include the computerized analysis of early election returns in news broadcasting, in combination with analysis of correlations from past national elections, to predict the outcomes of elections. The accuracy of these predictions has gradually increased as experience has been gained and the statistical data and methods have been refined. Despite demonstration that broadcast of the results of such analyses of returns in eastern time zones influences postannouncement votes in western time zones and can therefore influence the ultimate electoral outcomes, the entertainment value of the predictions in holding listeners has overridden the concern about bias, so that this influence has become a permanent feature of our election process. (It doesn't have to be that way. In France, it is forbidden to broadcast poll results within a week before an election. In our country that would be considered a violation of freedom of speech, an issue that we will discuss in due course.)

Then, the pressure toward ensuring one person–one vote fairness in public decisionmaking has combined with rapid processing and communication of election returns to make the referendum process, or direct democracy, even easier to implement. This has encouraged the proliferation of all sorts of ballot issues as a substitute for resolving problems in the legislative arena, so that any local ballot in any community is increasingly filled with questions on which the population is asked to pass judgment.

The process of petition and referendum is, of course, as old as the nation. Laws were passed early in this century, in South Dakota, Utah, and Oregon, that allowed citizens to place issues on the ballot by gathering enough signatures on a petition. Currently, many states and localities have such procedures. The technique has, perhaps, been taken to its ultimate—and certainly the most publicized—refinement in the California votes on propositions. Anyone who can marshal the resources to gather the requisite number of signatures can have some critical issue that would in earlier times have been decided in the legislature, such as the extent and level of property taxation, the distribution of government benefits to immigrants, or the use of billboards for advertising, put on a ballot for the electorate to decide. Then the arguments pro and con take place in the media and on the television screens, bypassing the legislature. This seems on the face of it to be a more democratic way of deciding major government issues, and in various modified forms using polling the approach is being applied at the federal level. We can predict that as issues become more numerous and complex that trend will accelerate.

But the downsides of the trend have yet to be fully felt, and they contain some serious threats to the form of representative government that the Founders built into the Constitution. Rapid transportation and communications have taken us far from the early days of our constitutional government, when a member of Congress would go to Washington and be out of touch with constituents for long periods during a congressional session. Now, representatives and senators are in touch with constituents almost daily; they go home, anywhere in the United States, weekly or monthly to talk with them; and they have the results of polls at any instant to tell them how constituents feel about any public issue. In 1956, Senator John F. Kennedy described in his book *Profiles in Courage* how members of the House and the Senate throughout history took their responsibility to mean that they should represent their state or district according to their best judgment of the issues. In the modern age of rapid transportation and instant communications, this is becoming harder to do. Now, rather than *representing* their constituents—that is, acting as an agent according to one's best on-the-spot knowledge and understanding—members of Congress act more as though they have been sent to Washington simply to vote their constituents' proxies. If government California-style were to take hold nationally and communication of preferences on any issues via computer were to become the popular norm, the members of Congress wouldn't even have to do that. The public wouldn't need someone to vote their proxies; they could vote on the major issues themselves.

"Well," you may ask, "what's wrong with that?" Several problems emerge.

For one thing, the tyranny of the majority could be imposed on the country much more easily. Safeguards the Founders built into the Constitution and into the Republic's government processes to protect minority positions and people and to give them a voice in national governance, whether in the areas of religion, lifestyle, taxation and public expenditure, and education or any other area of modern life, could be overriden by the passions of the moment. The passions tend to be fueled by advocacy in the media that seek to make the best case according to advertising persuasiveness rather than factual logic—the ultimate extension of the legal adversarial system. We can see this pattern of government becoming evident every time California prepares to vote on a new, important proposition. We saw it happen nationally in the 1993 argument about health care reform and the 1998 argument on legislation to ratify the tobacco companies' settlement of state damage lawsuits: The ones who commanded the media carried the day. It bids fair to become a new, twenty-first-century–style of popular government. It will then become much more difficult for a president to guide the country into areas of policy that he or she can foresee that the country must follow but that popular prejudice or ignorance at a moment render difficult to implement.

If that style had existed during the first half of the twentieth century, so that deeply felt and broadly held objections to policy could easily be registered and imposed on policy by popular referendum popularly initiated, it would have been impossible for President Roosevelt to prepare a basically isolationist country as much as he did for the inevitable conflict with German fascism and Japanese imperialism; the length of the war and loss of life would likely have been far greater as a result. It would have been impossible for President Truman to take the steps he did to prevent Soviet imperialism from taking over Western Europe after World War II; the consequences for America's future without the chance for alliance with Europe would have been incalculable. Subsequently, it would have been impossible for a succession of presidents to lead the country to the posture it holds today on civil rights for minority populations; imperfect as that is, it is infinitely better than the posture based on majority prejudice that threatened to tear the country apart before the worst abuses were corrected.

Another problem with government California-style is that in modern, media-mediated voting on all issues money talks. If winning the advertising war usually carries the day, and advertising takes great gobs of money for media access, then those who have the money will win—not always, but more often than not. Thus we see one of the pernicious effects of the trend toward concentration of economic power in fewer megacorporations, especially in the hands of merging communications and entertainment giants, in the national and the global economies. Movement toward greater democracy through popular voting on critical issues without the benefit of argument in the legislature carries with it the perverse effect that the economic power centers can, through their greater access to the media, manipulate the outcomes of disputes on those issues to their own benefit.

Although the outcomes will also benefit significant numbers of voters in many cases, the net result will not necessarily benefit the nation or its long-term future. We may be seeing the ultimate implication of the comment by "Engine Charlie" Wilson, a former chief executive of General Motors Corporation and President Dwight Eisenhower's first Secretary of Defense, at his Senate confirmation hearing, that "what's good for General Motors is good for the nation"; the directions of the nation and of major centers of economic power could become indistinguishable. Since the objectives and the time horizons of the two are not the same—the public welfare over the long term versus return to the stockholders now—this would inevitably distort the governance of the nation away from Abraham Lincoln's government "of the people, by the people, and for the people."

Although arguments and political conflict about life and death issues such as those mentioned just above will continue in the Congress and the nation, as they always have, the continuing trend to higher reliance on instantaneous popular expressions of opinion and voting as the preferred means of resolving large public issues bodes ill for the resolution of those issues based on a broad, long-term view of the public good. When added to the increased chance offered by special interests to amplify their particular points of view and to press those views through media manipulation, the trend can only confuse public understanding and delay essential closure on the issues. Sometimes that lack of closure can work very much to the country's detriment, as events making new kinds of demands overtake behavior in an old style. This capacity to stretch out debate on critical issues indefinitely is a sort of tyranny of the minority, an unhappy counterpoint to the tyranny of the majority that modern technology more readily enables in public affairs. Nowhere is this better illustrated than in the current travails of the country's primary and secondary education system.

The Decline of Public Primary and Secondary Education

The issues in education have been aired at great length in public discourse, and there is no need to repeat them here in exquisite detail. Rather, we need to emphasize a few elements of today's attempts to find an educational path for our young people that will seriously impact our national security.

The education of a country's young people reflects the values and preoccupation of the larger society, and it changes in character as those values change. Throughout the twentieth century the children of all but the wealthiest citizens or those who have a preference for full-time religious schooling were educated in public schools until going to college. This took them through high school, after which most of them went on to work, but some went on to either private or state colleges and universities. The GI Bill led to a great expansion of public-sector higher education, as a greater fraction of the population went on from high school to college.[10] During the 1950s, the K–12 public education system was able to keep up with the demands of preparing people for their participation in the booming postwar economy. But then the accelerated social revolution of the Vietnam War years upset the status quo, and the nation's education system hasn't recovered from the upset yet.

The general trend, not universal by any means but prevalent enough to characterize the education system, has been to place less focus on learning and to direct more attention to broader social matters. This trend is not independent of changes in the work ethic, in values, and in the home environment. Parents who both spend their time working, or single parents supporting themselves, have less time to oversee performance in school. When they have to make day-care arrangements for their young children, they want the school system to assume at least some of the role of babysitter. When adults spend many evening hours watching television, they are not setting an example that helps them enforce rules against television-watching that may interfere with schoolwork. International studies comparing children's school performance in relation to parents' expectations have shown that American parents are less demanding and more satisfied with their children's curricula and performance than are parents in European, Japanese, and Taiwanese schools; if parents demand less, children will produce less. This kind of development is not independent of educational theories and social concerns that pay more or less attention to concerns about levels of stress among younger students in the different societies.

Partying has come to be viewed as a necessary part of socialization in growing up; the class's spring or fall or graduation dance has moved from high school to the fifth and sixth grades in elementary school—from age sixteen or eighteen to age ten or eleven. By the later grades, massive parties covering neighborhoods defined by distances of automobile travel and involving alcohol, drugs, and sex have grown as a popular teen recreation to replace the thrill of the simple senior prom of earlier years. Students are allowed to drive to high school and to spend time and money on automobiles that they are allowed to own from age sixteen in most jurisdictions or that their parents buy and register for them. The net result in a majority of cases is a significant redirection of their attention from academic to social matters. In Maryland and Virginia, only about half of high school students have been able to pass exami-

---

[10]The impact of the GI Bill becomes obvious if we look at the numbers. According to the U.S. Statistical Abstract, in 1940 4.6 percent of the population had achieved four years of college or more. That increased to 7.7 percent in 1960, 11 percent in 1970, and 23.6 percent in 1996. That is, the percentage of the population with a college education had nearly doubled in the decade and a half that followed World War II, and it has continued to increase at about that rate since.

nations confirming their success in meeting planned educational curricula; there is every indication that such performance is typical of that in the entire nation. Attempts to extend the school year as a means to improve declining academic scores are met with resistance by teachers and parents who do not want the interference that would be entailed with their summer plans and with students' working for spending money.

While all this has been happening, the generally standard curricula and pedagogic techniques of the pre–World War II era have gradually given way to more modern and less uniform approaches. The older system was founded on the classics. Children in elementary school had to learn how to read and write, they had to learn basic arithmetic, some facts about American geography, history, and government, mainly centered on the wars we have fought, and this was rounded out with a bit about the rest of the world. The basic curriculum was extended in high school by adding sophistication to learning about American and European literature, how to write coherent essays, some foreign language that could have been Latin or else (usually) French, Spanish, or German, some mathematics and basic science, and a few electives in other subjects. Through school, boys learned shop skills and girls learned about homemaking. Gilbert Highet, a professor of Latin and literature at Columbia University who was well known at the time, stated in his 1950 book, *The Art of Teaching*, that the first essential for a good teacher is knowledge of the subject, and the second is to love the subject and keep learning more about it.

How archaic that all sounds now. Lest you fear it, however, this is not going to turn into another diatribe about the ills of our education system and a plea for going back to basics. But we must recognize what has happened to that simplified model of education if we are to understand the impact of the many external crosscurrents of the second half of the twentieth century on our education system and its influence on our national security. Basically, those crosscurrents shattered the old model, and we have yet to develop a new model to put in its place.

First, as the U.S. population grew and moved into the cities and then the suburbs over the course of the century, elementary and secondary school teaching gradually evolved from an individual occupation or trade into a profession. At the century's beginning, people who were educated in some way settled into teaching as individuals with long tenure and a chance for a modest lifetime living. By mid-century, their calling carried with it specialized education, unionization, and a striving for the same middle-class lifestyle as that enjoyed by their students' parents. Inevitably, as the profession acquired its qualifying characteristics and as the school population acquired a more complicated mix of cultures and behaviors, there was increasing preoccupation with learning the mechanics and techniques of conducting classes and teaching. However, since that material had to be covered in the same four years of college education, it came at the expense of subject matter, although teachers today are, in many school systems, required to continue their education into graduate school and special courses. At the same time, society's larger problems penetrated into the schools to diffuse and disrupt the teaching of knowledge and basic life skills like the arithmetic of keeping a budget and maintaining personal hygiene. Teachers were being asked to take on added responsibilities for discipline and motivation under the pressure of growing, adverse outside influences.

Meantime, the field of what had to be taught—knowledge—expanded exponentially with the post–World War II science explosion and the greater interest in the world outside the United States that the war and the ensuing Cold War had stimulated. This expansion was given a special boost in the schools when the Soviets launched Sputnik, the first artificial satellite, in 1957. After that event, the American public and leadership concluded that we had been failing to teach enough mathematics, science, and technology. That realization started a national soul-searching on how to teach those subjects, and then others, that has not stopped to this day.

The questioning about the effectiveness of our elementary and secondary education system, together with the vast expansion of knowledge that had to be conveyed and the realization that many areas of knowledge overlapped, led to changes in course nomenclature that reflected changes in the way the subject matter was viewed and taught. Reading and writing English and the study of literature were consolidated into language arts. History, geography, and civics became social studies. And the teaching of mathematics and science, especially, were opened to experimentation. It became doctrine that learning by memorization was bad; children had, rather, to learn how to think. "New math" displaced old math as mathematicians theorized about how to teach mathematics in a way that would satisfy this new dictum. So we saw the phenomenon of children learning about sets and infinity lines in early grades but never learning the multiplication tables and long division very well. Later, mathematical fundamentals like how to set up and solve simple equations for things like compound interest and distances traveled also came to be slighted. At the same time, methods of teaching were changed to make learning more fun—perhaps, in part, an attempt to meet the competition from television. Along with this, reflecting trends in industrial management, has come the grouping of children into teams for projects that require them to apply all their acquired skills and knowledge—reading, writing, arithmetic, science, reasoning—in an integrated and cooperative manner to achieve a team objective.

All to the good, you may think, because as adults in our time people can do multiplication and division with electronic calculators, and if work requires it they can have equations solved on computers with the right software. And teamwork is essential in our increasingly complex production facilities. And indeed, many children do learn better when teaching departs from the old-fashioned lecture and drill that characterized much pedagogy before the post-Sputnik ferment began. But there are several problems.

The first is that reliance on machines without effective grounding in the basics tends to erode understanding of fundamentals and leads to errors in both personal and work-related activities—precisely the effect that the new teaching wanted to avoid. Second, when people work in teams there are always individuals who will come to dominate the team while others follow or remain passive. The learning situation for the latter can become worse than individual instruction would be, unless a sensitive teacher can detect the lag in learning and correct it. But teachers, too, fall along a normal (i.e., bell curve) distribution in ability. To expect all of them to perform up to the level of perfection that the theorists assume when new teaching techniques are proposed, in the presence of all the societal distractions, is expecting too much.

Finally, and worst, is the fact that some learning does need conscious memorization. Imagine going to a doctor who "knows where to look up" anatomy or drug effects when he is diagnosing a pain in the abdomen or prescribing for it. The brighter children will remember both facts and techniques in the course of learning by any method. The same issue has appeared in learning language and reading: Advocated teaching technique has traveled from phonics to whole-word recognition and back, with much argument while children learning to read use both techniques. Again, the brighter kids do it better. This also happens in social studies: Surveys have shown that many high school students do not know basic facts that all informed citizens should be expected to know—such as when the U.S. Civil War took place—a natural consequence of social studies from which required memorization of dates has been eliminated as too boring and not entertaining enough.

And these aren't the only things that have happened to the schools in our country. The growth of the suburbs brought with it the consolidation of school districts for economic reasons. This happened while the school year was kept the same length or shortened. As a natural consequence, students came to spend more time traveling and less time in school. Once in school, the students' social values, resulting from the social revolution of the 1960s, influenced their coursework and their behavior. A fundamental quality of the new values was the attitude that "I don't have to do what I don't want to do." This contributed to the general decline of discipline in learning and behavior that was described earlier. It was reflected in more choice of electives at the expense of required coursework, with the result that many students select easy courses as distinct from the ones they might need in later life, which require more mental exercise. Altogether, the time spent in academic learning declined, as more parents spent time away from home left the children on their own more, as more time has been spent in watching television and in social activities, and as more, and more diverse, teachers' duties have taken time away from their attention to students' work.

This downward spiral in learning time and attention has been affected by more than simply attitudes and distractions. It has been accelerated by society's imposition of mandated social change on the primary and secondary school system. Society's move toward emphasis on full equality of treatment and opportunity for all citizens meant that segregation by gender and ability had to cease and more attention had to be given to misbehaving, disabled, and disadvantaged children at the expense of the general child population. That environment has meant less devotion of educational attention and resources to the general population, regardless of what pedagogic theory or data on learning ability say the effect on learning might be. It also resulted in less ability to select and give special education attention to both the very capable children and the slow learners, with the result that the educational attainments of both groups suffered; homogenization has its price.

These effects were reinforced by busing for desegregation and by the flow of immigrants' children into schools in many areas with the attending problems of learning in a different language. For many reasons, the minority black and Hispanic children have tended not to do as well in the schools as the majority children. Observation of this difference led to an attack on the examinations that brought the fact out, accusing them of bias and causing "renorming" of the examinations to account for the downward drift of average scores rather than emphasis on teaching what had to be known to succeed in modern American society. To take a typical case as an example, when Maryland changed its scholastic assessment examinations in 1993 to move away from multiple-choice questions to questions in which students had to write ab initio about what they knew, scores plummeted; as mentioned earlier in a different context, it was found in 1998 that only about half of students, on average, achieved satisfactory grades on the Maryland Scholastic Performance Assessment Program examination. Yet the first complaint was not about the poor overall level of performance but rather that the examinations were biased because minority students fared even worse. In such an environment, social promotions to higher grades became the norm.

These trends reinforced, through de facto acceptance, the lower level of learning, relaxation of standards, and the difficulty of maintaining discipline, all bringing the graduating class to the least common denominator of learning—again, with the exception of the gifted few who would learn well in any circumstances. And the whole trend has been exacerbated by the problem of drugs in the schools, which provides still another distraction for faculty and students away from academic education in addition to destroying the learning process for the students who become captured.

At the same time, many parents' feeling of social responsibility and a desire for local choice that emerged from the Vietnam War attitudes led, in scattered but numerous school districts usually associated with the more affluent suburbs, to more pressure for "participation" by parents in the public schools. This entailed more parent attention to curriculum, and local option carried with it significant variation in what parents wanted their children to learn. Local influence on curriculum worked against any degree of national standardization. Arguments about curriculum could involve matters such as the evolution-creation dichotomy, with the result that much scientific education was diffused in the secondary schools and deferred to the universities. This drift has added to the general trend in universities having to pick up much of the load of basic education in science and technology as the secondary schools have declined in their concentration and ability in those areas. That is also related to a decline in real scientific knowledge among primary and secondary school teachers, which is, in turn, related to what has been happening to the profession more generally.

During the Great Depression of the 1930s and earlier, teachers were reasonably well paid relative to the remainder of society. Afterward, they fell behind. Teaching salaries languished for many years in relation to compensation in other areas of endeavor.[11] As salaries finally began to catch up, the science and technology professions in government, industry, and the university system again offered much more remuneration than did teaching, and potential teachers with technical and scientific educations and training were drained away from the public school systems. As a result, teachers who had a general education, rather than those especially educated in particular areas of science and technology, had to take on the teaching of science, a subject they did not understand very well themselves as the various fields of science and technology expanded in scope and complexity. Harking back to Gilbert Highet's dictum, how could they teach well what they did not understand very well?

Now, the teachers have largely caught up in pay with the general population, but the general education and work assignment pattern has not reverted to that of earlier times. With their additional duties beyond education, with parents working more so that schools are being given more responsibility for inculcating values, with divisions in the community that prevent agreement on what values to inculcate, and with a drift of parent opinion against strict enforcement of honesty codes and long school and homework hours, teachers have been given inordinate responsibility to carry

---

[11]In the early 1960s and 1970s, average public elementary and secondary teachers' salaries lagged behind those of technically oriented workers by about 50 percent. By the 1990s, teachers' salaries were roughly on a par with those of all professional specialty workers, on average.

forward some confused notion of social values that society has trouble defining. In addition, research that compares American education with that in foreign countries, such as Japan and Taiwan, shows that parents in our country expect less of their children academically than parents in those countries. Whereas the latter tend to set high standards and to continually exhort their children to do better, American parents, on the whole, tend to be contented with the performance that is demanded of and produced by their children when they are not in trouble. When the primary or secondary teacher's task is seen in light of all this background, one must wonder that most teachers perform as well as they do.

People do get educated, many in private schools. And there, in the example of the private schools, is the rub. Our governing bodies at state and federal levels recognize the adverse directions our public education system has taken. In the confusion of values that is reflected in public school systems as a result of larger social conflicts in which those very governing bodies are prime movers, they are now espousing policies, such as privatization of schools and granting of tax benefits in the form of school vouchers that would help pay for private schooling, that might, if taken to their limit, eliminate public schools entirely.

The unintended consequence of the loss of an anchoring philosophy and the endless distractions in the public education of our children and teens is the creation of an educated aristocracy of the mind that, for various reasons that lead to better public schools in its communities or use of private schools, is shielded from many of the adverse trends. This group rises to greater heights of achievement while the rest of the population is dumbing down and simply not learning facts and techniques needed for everyday living and the exercise of judgment in public affairs and, especially, international affairs.

This trend is reaching its peak just at the time when, as we have seen, the trend in public affairs is to rely more on citizens' collective judgments. Moreover, a generation whose education has been reduced is a generation passed by. For all but the elite who will achieve success regardless of method and circumstances, or whose affluence will enable them to bypass the increasingly flawed public education system, the current generation's basic education will not catch up. The lack will be reflected in daily living and in public affairs in many ways, from who they select to go to Congress, to how they and their representatives in Congress define and deal with critical public issues, to how vulnerable they may be to new kinds of fraud and the blandishments of misinformation in both political and merchandise advertising.

Ironically, while all this has been going on in the primary and secondary education system, the college and university system has flourished under the initial impetus of the GI Bill and the subsequent support for scientific and technological research that Vannevar Bush's 1945 report started. The research emphasis, and government support from many sources, have created an unsurpassed higher education system that is the envy of the world, one to which much of the world comes to be educated. But even here, we cannot escape reflections of the general trends in society.

A Society Ignorant About Scientific and Technical Matters

If society is infatuated with the products of science and technology, it is not very knowledgeable about what brings them into being. Not only has educational attainment in scientific and technical subjects declined in the primary and secondary schools, those subjects remain relatively unpopular as educational pursuits in the university system as well. Science and engineering degrees (including the life sciences and computer sciences) represented just less than 15 percent of all degrees awarded in 1994, essentially unchanged from 14 percent in 1971. At the same time, degrees in business and law, for example, increased from 13 percent of all degrees in 1971 to nearly 22 percent in 1994. And between 1980 and 1994 the number of foreign students enrolled in science and engineering courses, only some of whom will stay in the United States after their education, has more than doubled, from 67,000 to about 166,000—nearly 70 percent of all graduates in these study areas if all enrollees get degrees! These figures mean that only a small fraction of the American population—less than 5 percent—has any significant knowledge about the scientific and technological foundations of what is a highly technologically driven and oriented civilization.

Beyond that lack lurks the problem of the "two cultures." In a 1959 lecture published as "The Two Cultures," the renowned British scientist and novelist C.P. Snow defined the dichotomy between the cultures of the arts and the humanities, on the one hand, and the sciences on the other, as creating an unbridgeable gulf in British public life at the time. The dichotomy has, since, been seen to apply more broadly in all of Western Europe and North America, at least, and to define a difference in ways of thinking about and understanding society's problems that prevents those raised in one of the cultures from communicating effectively with those raised in the other.

According to the stereotypes, those raised in the scientific culture are trained to think primarily in terms of observation of natural phenomena (including human phenomena) leading to data, testable hypotheses, and conclusions arrived at dispassionately, wherever the data lead. Those raised in the arts and the humanities, whom Snow characterized as "literary intellectuals," are trained to think primarily in terms of human relationships and emotionally oriented expression about those relationships and their derivation. Thus, Snow pointed out, "the non-scientists have a rooted impression that the scientists are . . . unaware of Man's condition. On the other hand, the scientists believe that the . . . intellectuals are . . . in a deep sense anti-intellectual, anxious to restrict art and thought to the existential moment."

Now, we all know that stereotypes exaggerate. There is extensive crossover between the two groups, especially in the United States, so that many trained in the arts, the humanities, and business know a great deal about science and technology, whereas many scientists and engineers are broadly educated in affairs of society and the world. Nevertheless, those from the two basic schools of endeavor—scientific and technical versus nontechnical—are educated and trained to different bodies of knowledge about the world and to different ways of thinking about the world's problems. This shows in many ways, perhaps most fundamentally in their basic understanding of what technology is and how it drives our society.

Think about how scientific progress is presented to the public by the general media and by our governing bodies, which are peopled by and large by nonscientists. They tend to view science as a *thing* rather than as a *process*. Thus, scientists understand that there must be constant argument about any theory that attends the probing for better ways to understand nature, from the size and composition of the universe to evolution to the search for genetic codes. But those not educated in science and its first cousin, technology, view the arguments as discrediting science and scientifically derived knowledge rather than as the means by which knowledge and understanding of nature are advanced. This, in turn, leads to disparagement of the views of the most scientifically and technologically knowledgeable people in the formation of public policy, just at a time when their contribution is essential to the soundness of that policy.

The divergence of technical comprehension within the two cultures is reflected in the very terminology they use. In the broadest sense, *technology* is the application of scientific knowledge to make things happen in nature that would not happen without human intervention. That is a very broad definition. However, current usage in the business and nontechnical worlds talks about technology stocks, technology corporations, and individuals' involvement with technology in their daily lives with statements such as, "He grew up without contact with technology until he started to work in a software company." When one searches the content of these references, one finds that the term "technology" is being used to refer to anything that has a microprocessor chip—chip manufacture, computers, software, networks, cellular phones, and nothing else. That is popular usage and reflects popular understanding by one of the two cultures—the governing one.

And yet if we think about it, technology in our society is reflected in myriad ways that, even though they may use computers or microchips, are far from limited to those applications. People eat food that is processed and packaged by machines. If transported fresh from the fields, the food is imported into cities by means of modern refrigerated transportation after agricultural production that uses scientifically derived, man-made or man-mediated methods, tools, and fertilizers. People live in masonry and wood houses using factory-made furniture and eating and cooking utensils. They have electricity for light and for automatically controlled heating and cooling that may use gas or oil piped in from hundreds of miles away. They have telephones, radios, TVs, paved streets, automobiles, subway trains in many of the larger cities, skyscrapers using all manner of factory-made materials, and magnificent bridges of ever-increasing length. And many people fly in extraordinarily sophisticated machines that are part of a technology-based transportation system, across the country or the oceans for business, schooling, and pleasure. Their medical care depends, among other things, on extremely precise measuring devices and manipulation of natural processes at the molecular and atomic levels. All of these things are products of technology. The current terminology is an indication that those who use it are oblivious to the technological foundations of the civilization in which they live. This may have its good points, but it works to the detriment of effective policymaking.

We can't say that if the scientists and the technologists were in charge they would necessarily do a better job of running things. When faced with the complexities of the world they are just as likely as any other citizen to be puzzled, to have to probe and experiment and flounder, and to antagonize people they need as allies. They do not necessarily make better decisions or govern better in the face of uncertainty and irrational resistance to their ideas and initiatives. The significance of the two-cultures phenomenon is, rather, that it adds a governing body without much appreciation of the basics of science and technology to a scientifically and technologically illiterate population, at a time in our history when almost every matter of public policy has a crucial scientific and technological element that can make for success or failure of public policy. This leads to an even greater tendency toward a country in which a science and technology elite unintentionally becomes the hidden driver of the country's development while the rest of the population, including its leaders, is carried along without appreciating or being able to deal as effectively as they should with the full import of what is happening.

As described in the discussion of the global economy in Chapter 3, technological advance in computing, communications, and transportation has conditioned the U.S. social, political, and economic environments in ways over which we have had very little control. We have been able to ride along, make some changes of a regulatory nature at the margins, and take advantage of the situation presented by adapting to it. But we could not control the main directions of the effects, nor will we be able to in the future. The problem is that without an understanding of the nature of technology and technological change, it is difficult even to adapt to those effects very well by making good policy.

For example, in the environmental area, the Senate declines to ratify a treaty that would reduce greenhouse gas emissions, because we fear the potential impact on our economy that simply reducing energy use would have and because developing countries refuse to inhibit their economic growth by modulating their energy use. In fact, the treaty is a bad idea from the engineering point of view (which includes both devising the necessary technology and the cost of its application), because it sets arbitrary dates for achieving emission reductions and it assumes that energy generation and manufacturing technology will remain static. The policymakers could, instead, recognize that each generation of energy production and of manufacturing processes is more efficient than the last, so that greenhouse gas emissions per unit of production would decline with process renewal. They could then mandate the lower emission levels and the dates for achieving them to accord with both the capabilities that the next generation of technology will offer and the timelines for energy and manufacturing plant write-off and replacement in the developed countries. They could encourage acceleration of those changes through economic and political incentives. And they could entice developing countries to participate with the prospect that those countries will be helped to develop their economies using the latest, most efficient technologies available rather than the older technologies that will not help them develop as fast as they might and that will have more deleterious environmental effects. This technology-based approach would give us a much more viable and lasting position on greenhouse gas emission policy than will the arbitrary approach that has been taken.

That the technology-based approach can pay off if the incentives are right is illustrated by the response of U.S. industry to the oil crunch of the early 1970s. Under pressures of higher cost and reduced availability, U.S. industry drastically reduced the steep rise of oil usage that was projected at the time by renewing its plants with more modern and more efficient energy generation machinery and manufacturing processes, to the point where much power plant construction could be deferred and significant energy conservation was achieved. Where per capita energy consumption had increased by 60 percent between 1950 and 1973, the rise was arrested, and per capita energy consumption actually decreased by 23 percent between 1973 and 1995—all this while gross domestic product was increasing by an average of $1.33 trillion per year and our population increased by nearly 75 percent!

As another illustration, from a completely different field, of the difficulty the country can get into when policymaking is not informed by technological understanding, consider the ongoing argument about national missile defense. The argument was begun, in its modern guise, with President Reagan's March 1983 speech proposing such a defense (dubbed "Star Wars" because of its proposed use of space-based laser weapons to shoot down missiles in the boost phase, i.e., while their rocket engines were still burning, just after launch). The call for a defense against missile attack then, and many succeeding calls for such a defense in Congress continuing until the present, have not recognized two critical technical facts about defense against ballistic missiles that have been demonstrated by decades of research in the area and by earlier attempts to deploy such a system. The first is that no defense can be perfect; whatever defense is deployed will be penetrated by at least some missiles, so that if destruction of even one city by a nuclear missile attack is considered unacceptable we cannot be certain of preventing such a loss by active defense, despite large expenditures on the defense system.[12] The second fact is that it is much less expensive—by a factor of three or four to one, or even more—for the offense to penetrate any defense once that defense is deployed and its characteristics become known than it is for the defense to overcome the penetration tactics and techniques. In the ballistic missile defense area, this was achieved initially by the deployment of multiple warheads on one missile (*m*ultiple, *i*ndependently *t*argetable *r*eentry *v*ehicles, or MIRVs), then by decoys that make it difficult to locate and destroy the true warheads. These steps have been much less expensive to achieve than a defense that will destroy warheads with high probability. These are the reasons why it made sense to have a policy of defense by certain retaliation rather than an active antimissile defense during the strategic standoff with the Soviet Union.

Current calls for a missile defense try to compromise with these truths by considering only a so-called light attack by only a few missiles used by an attacker less sophisticated and massive than the Soviet Union would have been. Even then, they have at their root a potentially very expensive defensive system (on the order of $20 billion or more)[13] to meet an offensive system in which individual missiles would cost less than a quarter of a billion dollars each and in which effective assists to penetrate the defenses would cost only a few million dollars more. Of course in examining the economics of the exchange one would have to take into account the value of the targets being protected—entire cities—but one would also have to account for

---

[12]As an indication of how this phenomenon works, we might hark back to the Japanese kamikaze attacks against the U.S. fleet during World War II. Kamikazes were, in a real sense, guided missiles programmed to impact ships, with human pilots as the guidance systems. There were dense, effective defenses in depth against them, starting with attacks on their bases and including the first use of radar-directed antiaircraft guns on ships. Yet in the Okinawa campaign alone, some 1,900 of these "missiles" were launched against a U.S. invasion fleet of about 587 ships during a three-month period. Although 93 percent of these attackers were either shot down or driven by the defenses to miss their targets, the 7 percent that got through hit 105 of the ships, or 18 percent of the fleet, either sinking them or damaging them badly enough to eliminate them from the battle.

[13]In 1999 a Defense Department estimate for a "light" national missile defense system to be deployed in 2005 came to $11 billion. This was before it was known in detail whether and how the system would work and before all the "unknown unknowns" that plague every new system have run the costs up by the typical 100 percent or more.

the fact that no city could be successfully defended with certainty, even after all that investment is made. And one would have to note that there might be other ways of attacking our cities that do not even involve missiles, for example, storing a nuclear weapon in the hold of a neutrally registered merchant ship that enters one of our ports. In the long run, it might again be decided that even in the post–Cold war strategic situation deterrence by threat of massive retaliation is the best means of defending the country against a missile attack. Then, funds for defense should be spent toward knowing with certainty where such an attack originates—a much simpler and less expensive technical problem. (These arguments do not apply in the same way in the area of defense against tactical or theater-level missiles, where all the parameters are different, as I will note later.)

None of these arguments based on technical fundamentals has been advanced in the recent calls for national missile defense. Rather, the pro argument is based on the emotional appeal that we cannot leave our country defenseless, and the con argument is based on the counter that the threat is not yet imminent enough to warrant the immediate expenditure for deploying a system. Thus, we see another area where the decisions are being argued and made by policymakers who, in the main, do not fully appreciate the technical aspects of the problem. Yet previous generations of deciders such as these were forced to abort two previous attempts to deploy a national missile defense system for reasons similar to those outlined here.

Of course, the technical communities, in the form of the president's science advisers, departmental staffs, and industrial and independent experts, are consulted. And if the public argument becomes heated enough, as it did during the debate over Reagan's Star Wars proposal, the technical arguments are raised, sometimes quite prominently. But we must observe that the ultimate deciders are rarely the technically trained people, and the ultimate arguments for the decision are rarely based on the technical factors that are likely to be the real deciders by affecting success or failure.

Many other examples of government policymaking by nontechnically trained people about things that are essentially science- and technology-driven could be described. They range from the high costs imposed by squeezing the last few percent of emissions from automotive pollution controls to matters of public health and safety, such as how fast to let new drugs come on the market; they touch virtually every aspect of everyday life. But further detailed examples are not necessary here. The two examples elaborated above are enough to illustrate the difficulty the country faces if the educated members of the two cultures cannot work effectively together.

It should be possible to bring the cultures closer together by crosstraining, and, of course, many members of each culture do make an effort to understand the viewpoints of the other. But the barriers are great. There isn't enough time in the university courses to cover one of the branches as well as faculties would like, let alone both. There is great pressure to concentrate on career-oriented education, as distinct from education in the classics that have formed our culture and in the roots of the science and technology that have enabled it. And the negative attitudes toward cross-education formed in the universities persist for lifetimes. For example, the U.S. Foreign Service resists the idea that people educated in science and technology can know enough about foreign affairs to be effective diplomats. This is reflected in the lack of scientific and technical education in the State Department and the overseas diplomatic staff, as well as in failure to involve scientific expertise in many international forums where it would be germane and essential for setting effective national policy.

Beyond this lack of communication at the governing levels of policymaking, few members of the ultimately deciding population—who decide with their votes or lack of votes—have any real appreciation for the technical factors involved in policy decisions where technical matters play a large role. But technical matters are crucial in decisions about almost all defense systems, just as in the one described in the example above. Decisions about our national security made in such an environment are likely to be flawed and costly beyond any good purpose and, as a consequence, to hurt our security in the long run.

We must note that all this refers to technical issues involved in the workability, cost, and effectiveness of government policies, procurements, and actions. It does not refer to ethical questions, such as may arise in connection with the application of technological advances in all areas from weaponry to genetic engineering. In all those cases, of course, the entire population and their representatives must be involved in the decisions. The arts and humanities culture may know more of the historical background underlying the timeless issues of the meaning of life and its philosophies than the members of the scientific and technical culture, but neither group can have a corner on understanding the full human significance of those issues; it is a matter of each participating individual's background, education, and comprehension. The key point to be made here is that we shouldn't be deciding policy matters involving science and technology without deciders who have appropriate scientific and technical education, although we do so frequently at great social and physical cost to the nation.

Where have the trends we have been examining brought us? Let us summarize:

There has been a solidification of the technological revolution of the twentieth century, especially in information-related technology, transportation, medicine, and agriculture, that has brought us to a new stage in the development of world civilization, beyond the industrial revolution that started in the eighteenth century. The technological advances were accelerated by the major wars and the Cold War of the twentieth century, as well as by the need to feed an exponentially growing world population. Many of these advances began with military invention and moved to civilian exploitation, so that now, in all but a few areas, the military is but a minor user of the advanced technological capabilities available to all nations, and it follows rather than leads the civilian world in further development and application.

This is a reversal of the nearly century-long pattern of technological innovation in society to which we became accustomed during the first half of the twentieth century, that is, the military always in the lead and the civilian economy using the products. It will have serious implications for the military parts of our national security in the future. As we shall see, in several critical areas—especially in intelligence and combat information systems—the military will have to depend on universally available civilian technology for its success in battle and in war. That success will then depend more on how the technology is used than on new, secret weapons—a much more chancy prospect.

This technological revolution has enabled and encouraged the consolidation and growth of private and government economic power, because great economic power is needed to exploit the technological advances to the fullest and because their secondary effects need regulation and control. The net result, however, is that ordinary citizens, even though their individual liberties have been increasing, are no longer as free from that great power in the sky as they would like to think they are. Although they feel freer to join groups and press for change in immediate conditions, as they did with vigor during the 1960s, for example, they are being moved along in unforeseen directions without great awareness of the much larger, long-range changes in society being wrought by the combined forces of advancing technology and economic power translated into political clout.

These changes have been accompanied by employment instability attending the substitution of capital for labor for economic reasons driven by the global economy. Our social institutions have not yet caught up with the new situation, making for political and social uncertainty in a search for ill-defined goals of economic stability and social welfare. Technological advances that have enabled economic and social transactions via machines, economic and social trends that have changed the classic family and employment structures, and the pressures of a growing population without the expansion room that characterized the frontier days have caused a loss of the sense of community that supported many public activities in the past. This contributes to what we might call the irritability of modern American society, which in turn leads to much internal conflict that makes it even harder to define and agree on society's long-term goals.

The advance of information-related technology such as television and rapid communications, inexpensive transportation, and increasing leisure time resulting from advancing productivity have together fostered a rise in entertainment of all kinds as a diversion from these problems. The news media and the entertainment media have been joining forces, because the availability of commonly applicable technology enables it and economic competition encourages it. Together with virtually instant communications, this alliance fosters distortions in what the public knows of the world that increasingly affects it while heightening the emotional response to world events. The facts of rapid change and instant communications also encourage a short-term outlook on both domestic and world affairs—to posit a result is to expect it, *now*. When it doesn't materialize, we carp at the agents of government and seek new ones. It is difficult to make and adhere to long-term policy decisions in such an atmosphere.

Government, California-style, based on polls and propositions and bypassing the legislative process, is filtering into the rest of the country. It shifts the weight of public argument on critical issues affecting our domestic welfare and national security into the media. From there, the concentrations of corporate power can have enormous influence on the directions of public policy by driving public opinion that is expressed in polls, in votes, and in figurative signing of proxies over to legislative representatives. The representatives, in turn, are less free to represent their constituents according to their own best judgments rather than simply to vote their proxies. The directions of this influence do not necessarily benefit the public interest in the long run.

All these developments, together with the social revolution that in part created them and that they in part engendered, have led to two undesirable consequences. The first is a muting of patriotism as a force for national unity. If there is only a weak sense of community in the absence of an immediate and severe threat to national survival, and the larger political groupings are under constant criticism and increasingly fractionated, what is there to be patriotic about? This lack of patriotic fervor helps reduce service in the armed forces to the status of just another occupation, with consequences we shall explore later.

The second consequence is a fracturing and corruption of the public education system that, up to about mid-century, was a force for consolidating knowledge and values held in common by most of society. Among the least desirable outcomes of this trend is a society that is, in the main, not literate or well informed about scientific and technical matters even while that advancing technology based on scientific advance is becoming an ever more powerful driver of where society is going. This makes for public policy that, at the least, will be tremendously wasteful of resources and that, at worst, can seriously impair our national security by forcing decisions about technologically involved matters that work against the long-term public interest.

This is not to imply that the policymaking process in our democracy has ever been extremely logical, forward-looking, or economical of resources. Why, then, are our characteristically immoderate, ignorance-driven, conflict-ridden democratic processes, extolled by Winston Churchill as better for humankind than any other despite their many faults, of special concern today and for the future? We have now entered a period of constraints such as we have never seen in our history. We are feeling the confining effects of recently apparent limits to the resources that used to be easily available to us, such as land, clean freshwater, clean air, and material resources for the taking, even as we must accommodate a growing population. The constraints challenge the fundamental attitudes with which we approach the world. We have not yet been able to comprehend where the social and technological trends that have come to the fore during the last quarter-century are leading, even as their pace requires rapid accommodation. We don't know what goals to set, except, in the fullness of our current position of unprecedented world power, to ask that the rest of the world be more like us so that we can live more comfortably in that world.

But we are also bounded by growing power centers and economic forces elsewhere in the world. Those forces inhibit the exercise of our freedom to go where we wish, trade where we wish, exploit the world's resources where and how we wish, and exercise our missionary zeal to spread our values and ideals to make all the rest possible. And as if that were not enough, there are certain conflicts inherent in American democracy that will probably never be resolved but only accommodated to suit the circumstances of the moment. Let's look at some of them.

5

DILEMMAS

Stability is not immobility.
—Prince Klemens von Metternich

Our society, like all societies and civilizations past and present, carries within its institutions and behavioral patterns the seeds of its own fragmentation and destruction, as well as the sources of strength and growth. As we grope for the desired leadership in these turbulent times, our nation must deal with a set of dilemmas that has been with us throughout our history but that takes on new guises in today's circumstances. Those dilemmas can never be resolved definitively; they are built into our system of government and can be resolved only for some sets of circumstances and for certain times. How they have been resolved in particular circumstances and times has determined the nation that came out of those times, the one we are living in today. How we will deal with them over the next few decades will determine the nation that moves through the twenty-first century and meets the century after that. And like all major social change, such as that described at the beginning of Chapter 4, it will take decades, not years, for the particular resolutions to appear and make themselves felt. The kind of nation we are along the way will have as much to do with determining our national security as will the armed forces we build. Let us take note of at least a few of these dilemmas, germane to the topic at hand, before we go on to examine U.S. armed forces in the future.

INSIDE THE UNITED STATES

The Adversarial Process

How far should we let the adversarial process go in settling matters of public policy? By relying on persuasiveness and political and financial clout instead of on facts and thorough analysis to win arguments about matters affecting the public, we invite settlement of disputes based on demagoguery and emotion rather than enlightenment and reason.

We throw matters of deep social concern that are based on physical and biological processes, such as land use, the distribution and disposal of national resources, and public health, into the courts. The courts are bound to have these matters decided according to their adherence to inexact language written into law rather than by the best available scientific and technical information and logic. We set the legal decision processes up so that lawyers who are largely without scientific and technical training attempt to influence juries who are ill prepared and educated to be critical of the lawyers' arguments or to understand the underlying scientific and technical processes. We enlist the advertising industry to use its techniques, designed for influence and persuasion by guileful means, to support all manner of laws that may or may not be in the public interest, regardless of the facts and implied, unintended consequences that may be in store. And we set implicit priorities that tend to predetermine the answers: Jobs must come before conservation of critical resources, even though the full exploitation of the resources may deplete them and eventually eliminate the jobs totally; freedom of the individual comes before the welfare of the community, even to the point of the community's fragmentation and ultimate destruction. In an ideal society, we would fix all those flaws.

And yet. . . . All history has shown that "ideal" societies cannot be established and that when the attempt is made they do not work. It appears to be simply beyond human capacity to be able to get all the details right and to anticipate and know in advance how to deal with all the secondary effects that will emerge from and sometimes come to dominate the outcome of any plan for governing ourselves and for settling disputes. The details and consequences emerge from interactions among so many variables that their number can scarcely be foreseen. Even in this day of the computer and system simulation, the simulations themselves are limited by the scope of human comprehension of the variables that must be entered into the computer programs, as, for example, attempted long-range weather-forecasting has been teaching us for decades. Inevitably, plans to set up the perfect "anything" in government end in tendencies toward inefficiency, corruption, and tyranny in some degree. The golden age of ancient Athens was built on the backs of slave labor—a condition we find abhorrent today—and its organization invited tyranny, which arrived. We have only to look at the fate of the 1917 Russian Revolution and Marxism to know that the establishment of an ideal social system could not happen in our own time, either.

The genius of the U.S. Constitution is that it has persisted for so long and has remained as practically applicable as it has through radically changing conditions during the more than two centuries since its adoption. This is a rarity in all human history, and we are fortunate to have it. This blessing may not be universally recognized. One of the elements of the Constitution's staying power has been the rather broad wording that has allowed it to be adapted to the changing circumstances of the nation and the world. There are signs in today's American political system of impatience with the Constitution and its adaptability to general circumstances. This is reflected in heightened demands to amend it to meet many of the issues of the moment, as well as some continuing efforts to bypass its processes, as with the growing insistence, since Watergate, that any controversy revolving around the president and the Cabinet should be taken out of the constitutional chain of Justice Department and congressional review and handed to an independent counsel accountable to no one. This tendency, which must be considered an intensification of the adversarial process, may become a regretted consequence of the very permissiveness of the Constitution about the details of governing, as distinct from the principles; that is, the principles could become overwhelmed by implementation of the details in our modern idiom.

Fortunately, the very deliberate pace of change that is inherent in the Constitution itself, which leads in part to the current impatience, may prove to be its salvation. It takes so long to amend it, and there are so many voices raised in objection when its processes appear to be corrupted, that the passions of the moment are likely to burn themselves out before any really deep harm can be done, in most cases. And we have found that it is possible to back away from the most egregious errors that may slip through, as with the Eighteenth Amendment instituting Prohibition, and its repeal by the Twenty-first Amendment—but not without social consequences, as this very example so well illustrates.

From all these considerations, it becomes clear that we face the difficult choice between the messy and imperfect adversarial process for settling disputes and better-organized approaches run by some aristocracy that will form for the purpose. The first can ultimately lead to chaotic and harmful social policy and practices. The second poses the risks that the organization itself may turn on us and irrevocably harm the underlying freedoms and democratic processes upon which U.S. society is built. During the Great Depression and World War II, the nation was deeply troubled and in danger of dissolution from within or destruction from without. We took the path of tighter organization to help prevent both, and the patterns and consequences of that approach were encouraged to persist during the Cold War.

Today, having moved out from under those threats and whatever level of discipline they imposed, the nation is objecting to the intrusive presence of government that the approach entailed. In trying to cast that off, we are moving in the directions of contentiousness in and fragmentation of our society. The adversary process built into our legal system encourages that movement. The absence of a severe internal or external threat to our survival suggests that the current tendencies will intensify before they are reined in. How far they go will determine the extent to which we will be able to meet unanticipated and currently ill-defined threats to our national security, from within and without; how long it might take us to do so; and how effective our response will be.

Unfettered Free Speech

The courts appear to be moving toward permitting anyone to say virtually anything they want about anyone or anything, regardless of the consequences. It appears in many respects that the current interpretation of the First Amendment to the Constitution has gone well beyond the original intent of the amendment, which was to protect the freedom to express political opinions without risk of restraint or punishment by the governing authorities. It has been applied in such varied contexts as denying attempts to restrain use of offensive language and odious violence in the public media; denying restraint of public diatribes against minority groups or individuals—diatribes that are intended to encourage discrimination and violence; and permitting the spread of pornography and instructions for do-it-yourself bomb manufacturing on the internet. It has been applied to symbolic actions that do not literally require speech, such as burning the flag and burning crosses on public squares. Attempts to control such verbal or symbolic expressions have consistently been rebuffed by the courts. They have allowed legal recourse for defamation of character, and they have allowed private control of certain communications that affect only the individuals who are communicating, under specified circumstances. They have allowed control of obscenity, according to a definition that looks to prevailing values that have to be defined in every case of objection to some usage. And not much else.

Attempts to constrain real or symbolic expressions of speech, even when it is obvious from the start that they may be harmful to some individuals or groups or may incite antisocial behavior that would have such an effect, are usually rejected in the courts. Further, the courts have looked with disfavor on restraint of product advertising, even when the products are known to be harmful to important groups of the population, such as all those under eighteen years of age. They have refused to constrain political advertising or advocacy advertising in support of or in opposition to proposed government actions, even when net availability of wealth to pay for the advertising strongly favors one side of any argument. Legislative or administrative attempts to control many excesses in the news and entertainment media, such as false or fictional reporting of news events or persistent high levels of violence and "indecent" language and behavior in film, television, and on the internet, are consistently denied. All this in the name of freedom of speech.

It is easy to see where all this can lead and, indeed, is leading. Our society is becoming more fractious. Divisions between groups are widening and becoming more vocal and prone to end in violence. There is a high risk that those who can bring the most wealth to bear will gain the day, in elections and in resolving key public issues such as those arising in health care and environmental conservation. The social revolution we described earlier is being accelerated in the direction of less constrained interpersonal behavior, a direction that interferes with the smooth operation of society's critical functions in maintaining public order and discipline. And the increasing tumult causes many citizens to tune out, so that when important issues do arise for public discussion and decision the public is less informed at the time when a well-informed public is precisely what is needed.

The problem in trying to reverse or moderate this trend toward unfettered free speech and the ills it brings is that no one knows (or perhaps too many people think they know) where to draw the line that separates "enough" from "too much." One person's freedom to speak is another's abuse of the freedom. One person's obscenity is another's beauty or another's political statement (to cover both the cases of provocative nude imagery and the photographic exhibit of an image of Christ on the cross in a bucket of urine). Moreover, the same propensity to degenerate into tyranny that plagues any attempts to better the adversary process operates here.

A personal experience can serve as illustration. During the 1950s, well before the 1960s breakout of mores and behaviors, a movement arose in my community to ensure that obscenity in public media did not reach our children or offend the upright citizens of the neighborhood. At a meeting, pictures of nude foldouts were shown from the new *Playboy* magazine, and lurid, explicitly sexual passages were read. Did we want our children to have free access to such material on the newsstands? Of course not. So the meeting agreed to have the material put away, so that would-be purchasers had to ask for it and it could then be controlled for the age of the purchaser. Having accomplished that, the meeting was then opened for more general discussion. One individual noted that there was also obscene material in our public libraries and proceeded to illustrate with a passage from the Emile Zola novel *Nana*. *Wait a minute*, we thought; many of us had read that book, and in context it was considered great and important literature. The meeting finally concluded that a policy of no restraint would be better than opening the door to outright repression by self-appointed arbiters of public morality.

And there you have it. But in this time of rapidly changing communications technology, the free-speech issues are not limited to the usual attempts, such as the one described, to censor what people can read or see on television.

The issues that may affect the nation's future the most are the new ones, that is, those attending the convergence of politics, money, and the media. The political parties and new entrants in politics, such as presidential aspirants Ross Perot and Steve Forbes, as well as many congressional candidates and major power centers in industries such as insurance, oil, and timber, have shown the risk that those with large funds available can buy and effectively wield political power to the exclusion of the majority population. This is not a new phenomenon in American politics. What *is* new is the joining of money-driven clout with the mass media, which can profoundly influence the weight of opinion in an insufficiently educated public (in fact which in the process distorts the education of the public). This risks corruption of the political system into a de facto oligarchy emplaced, supported, and managed by concentrated economic power. There are indicators of such effects in declining voter interest and turnout and in the decline of politics and news reporting into entertainment. Then we have to decide whether to allow unlimited free speech in the form of political contributions or to mandate free access to the costly media and necessarily keep some marginal contenders out (and who defines "marginal"?). In related areas, we must decide whether to allow advocates of one side in public issues to dominate the arguments because they have the wealth or to require some form of media access for those who have something important to say on public issues but who do not have the resources to buy media access (but who defines which groups should have such a say and on what issues?).

Thus, the dilemma. The nation can follow the path of no inhibition whatever of speech and physical acts that imply speech and accept the attending harm that is done to individuals and the distortions of the governmental processes that are generated. Or it can attempt to temper those ills and dangers by getting on the slippery slope that can lead to arbitrary constraint of behavior and, ultimately, to tyranny. Those are the extremes. Clearly, we will try to find some pathway between the extremes.[1] We will likely go too far in one direction and, realizing and recoiling, go too far in the other. Where we are in that cycle, and how difficult it is to change direction when that is necessary, will determine how we react and behave in times of crisis affecting our security.

---

[1]This may be a good point at which to note that the very same Hayes Office that censored films for about three decades to keep out offensive language and sexually explicit material did not seem to have done the country irreparable harm. In fact, it can be observed that filmmakers had to rely more on good stories about people and adventures to draw audiences rather than on sexually based sensation. You can decide which is preferable. The question is whether more general censorship, once it becomes routine, can remain so benign.

Race, Affirmative Action, and Bilingualism

There is no need to expound on the issues of race in American society here; they are well known to every reader. But those issues will affect our security in ways that are not commonly recognized.

Affirmative action as it has been implemented over the past thirty years has proven to be unfair to the majority population in many respects. Protest as the government will, it has been demonstrated in application that when forced to come to grips with the issue of increasing minority participation in mainstream affairs— whether it be jobs, schooling, or any other activity—the government's efforts devolve into imposition of a quota system. The implementers have not been able to devise any other way to ensure minority participation in society's activities when our notions of fairness insist that participation by minority groups be in rough proportion to their numbers. This realization has begun to cause a serious backlash within much of the majority population. But that backlash has shown early that without some kind of help even the first steps toward a more equitable distribution of national wealth and the benefits of government, such as entry to state-supported colleges and universities, will be denied to large segments of the population. If the race problem is left to natural (and necessarily slow) evolution, it will likely iron out these inequities eventually. At the least, it will bring them to the point where the distribution of benefits and hardships within what is now the minority population is indistinguishable from the distribution for most people. In the meantime, there will remain a resentful minority with festering dissatisfactions that must, at some point, burst into open conflict among elements of a society that will be structured demographically very differently from today's.

Another segment of this problem, which really amounts to a different discrimination issue for a large minority population, is that of bilingualism. As we noted in connection with the fanciful scenario of Chapter 2, language is the matrix that binds the culture together. All groups of immigrants since the beginning of the nation have been able if not eager to adopt English as their working language and adapt to an English-speaking society while preserving their native languages and cultures in social life. But now we see a Spanish-speaking group, one that will become our second largest demographic component, that has many members insisting (often simply by their very presence and the needs it invokes) on bilingual education, bilingual official transactions, and bilingualism in public communications. This risks a loss of overall coherence in the nation and provides another inadvertent mechanism for setting one group against another.

There is no totally equitable way to resolve these issues. The problem facing the nation as a whole is whether to put up with some of the inequities, inconveniences, and risks while the problems sort themselves out by processes of slow evolution, or whether to insist on government action to hasten change in the interest of reducing intergroup conflict, economic efficiency, and elusive ideas about fairness and the exercise of political power. The questions to be decided are complex: Which way does the nation have more to gain or to lose? Which approach will be more divisive and prone to induce conflict? Which will pose the greatest risk of irreparable tears in the political and social fabrics of the nation? Should we insist on uniform solutions for the two major minority groups, or should each one be treated on its merits, even though the resulting solutions appear contradictory? And will each group stand for that appearance, or will that exacerbate the resentments that we were trying to alleviate?

These issues present weaknesses in our society's cohesion that a determined enemy can exploit. Our treatment of them will affect, among other things, the form and underlying discipline of the armed forces and our ability to recruit, train, and sustain an all-volunteer force, representative of the nation, at peak efficiency and effectiveness. This will profoundly affect the ability of the armed forces to meet what are now emerging as new, serious, and unconventional threats to our national security.

Inviting Big Brother In

In the George Orwell novel *1984*, Big Brother kept up with the activities of all individuals and the general population by means of widespread judiciously and secretly placed cameras, microphones, and spies. This was considered to presage a horrible future, modeled on the Soviet system of subjugating the population, and the concern of the novel was that the Western democracies might be moving in that direction. It was a future to be avoided. Now, look about you.

There are closed-circuit TV monitors and cameras in stores to watch for shoplifters and in banks and at automatic teller machines to watch for and photograph bank robbers and street thieves. They watch your transactions, too. There are cameras at highway tollbooths to photograph the license plates of those who run through without paying and to record who should be charged in a legitimate rapid payment plan. The police have for many years used radar to measure how fast we are moving, and now we are putting cameras together with the speed-detection devices along highways to observe speeders and aggressive drivers so that we can fine them without intervention of police officers, who can't be everywhere. Some day-care centers are installing cameras to help keep an eye on the children when the caregivers are otherwise occupied and to watch for child abuse. When we enter major public buildings or travel, our bodies and luggage are searched to guard against terrorist guns and bombs. Our wireless and cellular phones, becoming ubiquitous, are subject to eavesdropping by private citizens and police; equipment for the purpose is sold at consumer electronics outlets.

Every time we make a purchase that requires registration for warranty purposes, we are asked on the registration card for the circumstances of the purchase and our background that led to our interest in that particular product, so that computer profiles of us as customers can be made for future advertising and promotional purposes. Our purchases in grocery markets are recorded on computers, with discount cards acting as the inducement to identify ourselves with the purchases. The stores can then tailor their stocks to induce us to buy more than we would have bought of our own free will. Our routine telephone conversations for business transactions are monitored for accuracy, and the transactions are recorded on computers; indeed, such a record exists for every business transaction in which a computer is used, whether in a store or an office or over the internet, and all retail businesses now use computers for all purposes, from those of the cash register to inventory control. Compiled records of these transactions, as well as the universal credit card transactions that are used in all but the poorest parts of our society, are available to those who want to check our credit history. Our searches on the internet are tagged by so-called cookies that can be used to build a profile of our interests, ostensibly for merchandising or to help the search engines serve us better; but such technology is usable for any other purpose.

Our very genetic makeup will soon appear in our medical records, available for purposes of preserving our health. We have resisted the idea of a national identity card, yet we have one: the social security number and card control all our health, financial, and many other transactions. The banking and health records are also available, for sale or by requisition, to those who need them for business and health reference, law enforcement, and insurance purposes. Many people other than criminals—all those who have had to be checked for one or another kind of security clearance, for example—have fingerprints on record with local police, the FBI, or other national intelligence or law enforcement agencies. We identify ourselves at the polls by the social security number, and we assume that the computer-compiled ballots can't identify who voted which way, although they do keep track of the fact that we voted and of the political party affiliation we claimed if we claimed one. In many transactions our telephone number is recorded, and that, too, becomes an identifier for future reference.

It is possible to compile and analyze all these records by keying them on the social security number and the telephone number, to make a complete record of who a person is, what his or her personal situation is, what a person's interests and political leanings are, and what the person has done in a lifetime. It would appear that Big Brother has arrived, with far more effective machinery than Orwell imagined.

Each one of the applications noted—and the list is far from complete—has a legitimate purpose. Most of the population approves these applications taken one at a
time, because they lead to satisfactory social outcomes. Mainly, we as average citizens
want shoplifters or speeders or toll jumpers or child abusers to get caught. We may
like to receive mail about products and activities the advertisers know we are interested in. We like the convenience of not stopping to pay tolls but being billed for all
our trips at the end of the month. We like not being tied to the wire, to be able to
talk on the phone from random locations. For large parts of the population, using
the internet for information, shopping, and ticketing is becoming an essential convenience. We like the rapid processing of loans and granting of credit that the computerized searches can bring. We want our doctors to know as much as possible
about our genetic background and health history, so that they can better ensure our
current and future health. We certainly want our health insurance to pay for examination and treatment, rapidly and without argument, and if giving our social security number along with our insurance card to the doctor or hospital helps that happen, that's fine. And so on. Indeed, banks, major business concerns and governments
at all levels now cannot function without using computers, all forms of electronic
communications, and the opportunity they afford to consolidate and use widely
scattered information for specific legitimate purposes.

We assume, mainly, that all these uses are benevolent and beneficial. But we are
learning that they may not be, that personal records may be sold for commercial
gain; that our e-mail correspondence and all our business transactions may be requi-
sitioned in lawsuits and analyzed to learn of our daily activities; that health records
and genetic profiles may be used to deny health and life insurance; in fact that anyone who wants to learn enough about us to exploit us as individuals for purposes we
would not agree with can gain access to the records to do so.

We can restrict or prevent such access, but doing so will be a long and painful
process. It will involve trouble on our part, such as locking, encrypting, and taking
other computer security measures to safeguard all computer transactions, thereby
making them less convenient and making it harder for us to obtain access to our
own work and records. It will involve legislation that will be hard to pass (because
much of it will challenge free-speech or crime-prevention principles), and it will involve many subsequent court cases, as the uses of the records and harm from those
uses proliferate. It will involve constitutional arguments at many levels of government and in the courts.

And when all is said and done, it will be impossible to make the safeguards airtight. Any private or government abuser of the easy availability of the behavior observations and the records can keep ahead of steps taken to inhibit them, because
they will have the initiative, and the protectors of our rights will be responding after

the fact. Moreover, just as in combating terrorism, the security measures cannot help but intrude on our daily lives. As we build safeguards against successively invented abuses we will inevitably reduce convenience, functionality, the free exchange of ideas, and freedom of movement until at some point the very convenience that led us to build all the observation and recording means in the first place will have been crippled. And how we resolve the dilemmas posed will determine how we meet the unconventional threats to our national security that were described in Chapter 3.

So there we have it. We can, and likely will, continue to implement the increasingly numerous and difficult-to-counter means of intruding on our privacy, because they bring us huge benefits in convenience and things we could not do in other ways. They make up the very fabric of modern life. We can with reluctance, as experience has shown, build safeguards to prevent abuse of our privacy and safety that those technological advances will make possible, but at the cost of some perhaps significant reduction of the benefits. The conflict between these two directions of modern development will never be resolved; as in the other areas we have examined, local resolutions will oscillate between too much of one direction and too much of the other. Where we happen to be in that cycle when some severe internal or externally induced crisis hits, and how we react to it from that position, could well determine the future of American democracy.

BEYOND OUR BORDERS
Conventional Legality to Fight Unconventional War

A U.S. Navy drug surveillance aircraft over the Caribbean has been tracking a fast boat headed toward the Guatemalan shore just south of the Yucatán Peninsula. The aircraft requests permission to launch a missile that will sink the boat, which intelligence indicates is running cocaine toward the land-smuggling route to the United States. By the time the Southern Command headquarters in Tampa contacts the appropriate authorities in Washington to discuss the question, U.S. authorities contact the authorities in Guatemala, and permission arrives, the boat has entered Guatemala's territorial waters, it has landed, and its cargo of several tons of cocaine has been unloaded and disappeared into the Yucatán rain forest on its way north.

An American passenger airliner is downed by a terrorist bomb over Europe, with the death of several hundred people. It is clearly a reprisal for the accidental downing of a Middle East airliner that inadvertently entered a zone of combat and was thought (because of a mistaken radar identity) to be threatening a U.S. warship. By good fortune, the investigation of the crash by U.S. investigators working with those

of the country where the airliner came down finds incontrovertible evidence showing who the bombers were, where they operated from, and how they did the job.
They are known to be hiding out in the hostile North African state where their mission originated. When pressed, that state refuses to turn them over to American justice. Our intelligence system learns of the culprits' exact hiding place and that they
are in it. The Navy proposes to launch a salvo of precision-guided missiles against
the house to mete out final justice to them and thus resolve the issue once and for
all. A short but intense debate rages fiercely in Washington around the objection that
the action would be illegal according to U.S. jurisprudence; it leaks to the press. The
culprits can read; they flee aboard a neutral airliner headed to another country, a
country that the United States will find inexpedient to attack or even to sanction at
the time. An attempt to force the airliner down to arrest them in a friendly country
along the route is foiled when that country, not wanting to be involved, denies landing permission if the action is taken. The terrorists are home-free.

A cruise ship loaded with Americans off the Alaskan coast, one in the Caribbean,
and one off the coast of Malaysia are severely damaged within a half-hour of each
other by large bombs in their holds. They sink while being abandoned; the loss of
life due to the bombings and subsequent sinkings is in the hundreds. There is a
week of furor in the United States and other parts of the world, in which swift ret-
ribution and all the legal power of the free world are promised to punish the terrorists, and then the furor dies down as the search for the source of the terror goes on.
Word gets out that our intelligence agencies have gained strong evidence that a terrorist group trained and controlled by a hostile Middle East country carried out
what they called the "operation" in retaliation for years of economic hardship that
they blame on the United States. The group had set up cells in several friendly
countries where the ships had ports of call, and the entire action was coordinated
via the internet, using open communications that were carefully crafted not to raise
suspicion. However, the information about the operation has come through clandestine sources; there is no evidence of the kind that would stand up in a court of
law, and we do not want to give away our sources. Cries are raised in Congress and
the media to retaliate against the country named, so that the world will know that
such actions will merit severe punishment, swift and sure. Others argue that if we
did that without firm proof that we could make public (as President John F.
Kennedy did the photos of Russian missiles in Cuba in 1962), we would be putting
ourselves in the class of the pariah nation that purportedly sponsored the operation
and that we would open ourselves to more such lawless operations. While the argument rages, other nations and the United Nations warn the United States against
taking any rash action, and one major power friendly to the presumed guilty party
warns that such retaliatory action without full and open proof can lead to war. The

opportunity to achieve surprise is blown, and the president decides to stand down. The operation is never punished on the basis of what are said to be rumors or on any other basis.

There are three incidents of unexplained regional power blackouts in the United States. Some clever cyber-sleuthing traces the cause to spurious signals entered into the power grid control network by hackers operating out of a hostile country. The United States requests extradition of the hackers, which is refused. We warn of dire consequences if the tampering doesn't stop. But it continues, sporadically, while every software fix we try is overcome in short order. The armed forces propose a strong counterattack to stop the intrusions and to teach a lesson to the world— either a cyber attack or a physical attack on the country's power grid that would put it out of action for years. The attack plan leaks and is brought up in Congress for hearings and public discussion. The opposition argues that such an attack would be illegal and that under international law we are obliged to bring the matter before the United Nations or the World Court. The attacks have ceased as soon as the leaks appeared and are quiescent during the debate; this helps reach the decision not to undertake the counterattack. But after the decision is made, there is a power blackout in the Federal Aviation Administration's Air Route Traffic Control Center for the Northwest, causing havoc in the air-traffic control system for an entire day. No lives are lost, but it takes a week to recover from the flight diversions and the economic dislocations. The source of the failure remains obscure. The country finds itself in the situation where the threat is ambiguous; it cannot attack another country, even if it is considered hostile, every time there is a power failure, because power failures also happen without purposeful human help. Yet the attacks can continue together with random events; the attackers are adept at staying one step ahead of the defense, and they are becoming more adept at hiding the source of the penetrations. The debate continues fruitlessly: Shall it be war or peace, and to decide that, can we be sure the attacks are government-sanctioned?

Every one of these hypothetical scenarios, two of which incorporate elements of real events, poses the issue that our governmental processes are not constituted to act effectively against unconventional attacks on the United States itself. We have built many safeguards against arbitrary arrest and punishment into our legal system to protect our citizens against overzealous or capricious law enforcement that may visit punishment on the innocent. Many of these safeguards, and similar ones, are recognized by democratic nations worldwide. We have extended them to our behavior on the international scene. The system is slow-acting and designed to work in the full light of public scrutiny as long as the rights of the accused are protected until they are proven guilty. And we assign the accused defense attorneys, whose task it is to enforce adherence to the strict standards of evidence imposed in our courts.

The resulting process is made to order for evasion and escape by terrorists, drug runners, hackers, and any others who would attack Americans and the United States from overseas locations. They have only to learn the sequences, time constants, and standards of evidence for bringing cases before U.S. courts to learn how to evade the possibility of apprehension and punishment. In two cases—the planner of the World Trade Center bombing and the terrorist who killed commuters en route to the CIA buildings in northern Virginia—we were able eventually to bring the guilty parties to justice, with the cooperation of the Pakistani government. But in most cases, our system works too slowly. We have tried to circumvent the problem in a few instances, with less than notable success. We don't do it well, the foreign governments don't cooperate, and we earn the world's opprobrium.

During Ronald Reagan's presidential administration, arbitrary military action forced an Egyptian airliner that carried a terrorist leader—Mohammed Abbas of the Popular Front for the Liberation of Palestine, one of the most virulent terrorist groups of the 1980s—to land in Sicily. Capture of the terrorist was foiled, however, when the Italian government released him before we could get the extradition papers in order. He was probably viewed as too hot to handle in their environment, and in any case the Italian government objected to our violation of Italian sovereignty. Our attempt to destroy Libyan leader Muammar Qadaffi by bombing in retaliation for terrorist attacks on Americans in Europe was made difficult and possibly cost us an aircraft and flight crew when France denied overflight rights. Libyan support of terrorist activity stopped for a long time after that attack, but then there was the bombing of Pan-Am Flight 103 over Lockerbie, Scotland, attributed to two Libyan terrorists who could be brought to trial a decade later only after we and the British acceded to Qadaffi's terms for surrendering them. U.S. relations with Mexico have been harmed by kidnappings of Mexicans suspected of being high in the drug-smuggling hierarchy, actions taken because we feared that working through a Mexican government penetrated by the drug cartels would tip them off to pending action. Presumably, Mexican drug operations into the United States have been disrupted to some degree—perhaps an important degree—by the action, but the smuggling has certainly not been stopped. And it took more than a year to repair relations with the Mexican government, and then not perfectly.

In the case of the 1998 bombing of our embassies in Nairobi, Kenya, and Dar es Salaam, Tanzania, we did take early action to attack the Afghanistan terrorist training and support base of Osama bin Laden, the suspected terrorist leader, and a factory in Sudan that we had evidence he had used to manufacture chemical weapons. Although the postbombing damage assessment concluded that we had made his base unusable, at least for a time, the action was carped at both by those who said that we had no right to bomb an innocent country and by those who said we should have attacked the base and its surroundings more heavily. And the government of Sudan started a propaganda offensive, amplified by antiwar groups in our own country, that we had bombed a peaceful, civilian pharmaceuticals plant. The total reaction was not dissimilar to the French, Russian, and Chinese reactions to our punishing series of bombing raids against Iraq when that country expelled the UN Special Commission personnel who had been sniffing out the country's secret weapons programs.

More broadly, the argument can reasonably be made that if we go around the world throwing our military weight around without benefit of due legal processes, for whatever reasons, then we will become little different from other predatory regimes in world history and will be treated little differently. Alliances of expediency with other nations rather than of friendship and affinity would not last long. We would work ourselves into the position of having to sustain ourselves internationally, and protecting our international economic interests, by military force alone, and we would have to pay the price of doing that—a price that could well hasten our decline, as Paul Kennedy argued in his 1987 book, *The Rise and Fall of the Great Powers*. In addition, the habit of evading legal principles can lead to more general corruption of our internal government processes, as was illustrated by the events that led to President Richard Nixon's resignation and to Iran-Contra during President Reagan's second term.

Yet by allowing our cumbersome legal system to constrain our actions to combat the new kinds of attacks that might well become the chief strategic threats against our nation, we will be forcing ourselves into the position of fighting only defensive warfare. We can use intelligence to anticipate where attacks may come, and we will likely foil many of them. But these will be attacks by individuals or what are now called "NGOs"—nongovernmental organizations—not amenable to the traditional rationales for going to war against nations. In the absence of effective legal means, and without legitimate international sanction to strike at the sources of the attacks or to make them painful for the perpetrators by swift retaliation, we will not be able to stave them off in the long run. There has never been a defense in the history of civilization that has not been penetrated after the expenditure of enough effort by a determined attacker.[2] The exploitation of a supremely wealthy drug market and the weakening of American power and will to foil other nations' designs of empire are sufficient motivation for such determination.

---

[2] As an especially germane example of the problem, the history of the U.S. Coast Guard—see *Rum War at Sea*, by Cdr. Malcolm F. Willoughby (Washington, D.C.: U.S. Government Printing Office, 1964)— shows that although the Service made the smugglers work hard for their living, it could not stop the flow of liquor into the United States during Prohibition. Every time the Coast Guard began to work effectively against one popular smuggling scheme, the smugglers devised another. We see the same thing happening in the attempts to stop drug trafficking into the United States today.

Thus, we have the dilemma in trying to protect the country against the new kinds of strategic attack that can weaken it seriously: We can adhere to our internal legal processes for many ethical and practical reasons, giving the attackers almost free license to do harm to our infrastructure and our people; or we can use extralegal means to foil such attacks that will be more effective, at least for a time, but in the process risk making ourselves an international pariah and thereby weaken our security as much or more over the long term. There are few guideposts in our history to indicate how far we can usefully go in trying to resolve this dilemma; the ones that have been established in modern times are not encouraging about either direction. All we can say for certain at this point is that we shall have to feel our way and that we are unlikely to be very successful without very skilled leadership.

Two directives signed in 1998 by President Bill Clinton (Presidential Decision Directives 62 and 63) are designed to come to grips with this problem. PDD-62 reinforces law enforcement agencies' missions to combat terrorism, and it establishes the Office of the National Coordinator for Security, Infrastructure Protection, and Counterterrorism. PDD-63 assigns responsibility for planning to protect various parts of the infrastructure to appropriate agencies, for example, the Department of Commerce for information and communications systems, the Treasury Department for the banking and finance system, the Department of Energy for the electric power system, and so forth. Typically, and perhaps necessarily in our system, the operational responsibility for overall defense against the new kinds of threats is diffused, because even though the defense planning will be done by the assigned agencies, the operational and legal action will be shifted to others: Defense, the FBI, the Coast Guard, and so on, hence the need for a national coordinator. The president's fiscal year 2000 budget requested $2.5 billion to fund these activities. Much of that money will go to state agencies to combat terrorist activities locally and for research into biological warfare agents and how to counter them.

The responsiveness and effectiveness of these arrangements in scenarios such as the ones portrayed remain to be seen. There is no doubt the agencies will make plans, according to their assignments. But as soon as the plans are tested by a serious attack, the country will doubtless have to decide whether it has drawn the line at the right place in trying to resolve the dilemma about how far to go in the direction of either protective legal process or expeditious action. The dilemma won't go away.

Look Inward, Look Outward

George Washington, on leaving office, admonished the country to steer clear of foreign entanglements. He had as a model the ongoing Napoleonic wars and the ease with which the new United States could be drawn into them, to its detriment and perhaps at risk to its survival. It wasn't too many years later that President Thomas Jefferson had to dispatch naval forces to deal with the Barbary pirates off the coast of North Africa. Subsequently, the English-French conflict led the English navy to press American sailors into service and thereby brought us into the War of 1812 with Britain. We were fortunate that the British were preoccupied with Napoleon and so couldn't turn their full attention to this upstart country that had so recently cast their dominion aside. But that war illustrated another point, namely, that if we wanted to be a nation of traders we would have to go out into the world and become engaged with it somehow. The conflict between the desire to be left alone, independent of the world, and to protect and further our interests in that world began early and has only intensified since.

Through much evolution since those early days we have become a great nation and a world power, but the dilemma still plagues us. It has taken on a vastly different form, however. Now, there is little doubt anywhere that we are deeply engaged with the world to keep markets open for American goods; to protect American citizens abroad; to preserve our relations with friendly governments; and to help preserve those governments as part of a combined bulwark against forces of tyranny and destruction. The issues for the United States are associated with how that engagement with the world should be articulated and treated. Some political groups recognize that to sustain our world position we must accommodate to other nations' concerns in many areas, in the interest of our own security and welfare. And we must stay engaged. But other politically important groups would rather not have to accommodate to other nations' needs and desires. They call it "putting American foreign policy in foreign hands." They would rather take advantage of our strength to impose our will on those nations, then go back to our internal pursuits.

The differences appear in the areas of trade and security. In the area of trade, the divergence in policy is articulated in arguments about almost any international trade issue that arises: whether we should join in a North American Free Trade Agreement or the World Trade Organization; whether we should deny trade arrangements on favorable terms with nations that allow large trade deficits with us to build up (Japan) or that do not espouse our concepts of democracy (China); whether we should finance, through the International Monetary Fund or directly, a bailout of a country that hasn't followed prudent economic policies (Mexico; the erstwhile Southeast Asian "Tigers"); whether we should allow some technologies, such as communications satellites, to be launched from potentially hostile countries overseas on their less expensive launch vehicles (China), even while we want to beat economic rival nations (France) in selling and profiting from the services the satellites provide; whether we really need to adopt internationally agreed restrictive policies in favor of reducing environmental contaminants; whether we should buy seafood products from countries that don't follow our environmental laws in protecting endangered sea animals; and many other issues. Some of these arguments made by the opponents of freer and expanding economic engagement with the world are contradictory from case to case, as a few of the examples just noted illustrate. This is an indication that the cause of the argument is deeper than the immediate issue under discussion. Large groups of Americans do not as yet appreciate the extent to which our economy is linked with the rest of the world. When they are exposed to examples of that linkage, such as shifts of manufacturing to foreign countries or an influx of talented immigrants to fill voids in our own technical capabilities, they resent it without noticing the compensatory growth of other areas of endeavor within our own country. The resentment is reflected in heightened argument about our trade policies.

In the security area, manifestations of our internal discord on the matter of foreign undertakings appear in our approach to conflicts in various parts of the world with their frequent underlying need for military action, conflicts that may affect our allies and therefore our own security. We have already examined in Chapter 3 the divergence between our need to work with allies and our desire to go our own way or to have our own way in such matters. We—the nation—continue to be plagued by frustration in relation to these quarrels within and between nations because the inwardness of our views inhibits us from seeing the quarrels from the participants' viewpoints and therefore anticipating how *they* may act—another interpretation of "intelligence failure." We also feel frustrated by our allies' apparent reluctance to become involved many times or even to take the lead in many situations that appear to affect them more than they affect us. We fail to understand that the appearance of our own reluctance to suffer costs and casualties in situations of less than vital interest may lie behind some of their hesitation. We don't recognize that the legacy of ancient rivalries and conditions of modest strength can inhibit nations (in Europe, for example) from joining together on their own to take actions outside their borders, whereas they can willingly band together behind U.S. leadership. We take unilateral actions in imposing sanctions on nations whose forms of government or whose actions we disapprove of, and then we become frustrated when our allies and the rest of the world refuse to follow because they disapprove less than we do.

In matters that do not immediately and obviously affect the nation's survival, there is a strong U.S. tendency to take a shallow view of conflicts, to see them in black or white, as good guys versus bad guys, and therefore to shy away from any involvement that involves more complexity than just flexing our military muscle. For this reason, we do not want long involvements. We don't want to deal with the intricate and unfamiliar politics of a situation, within which the solutions to military conflicts or their prevention often lie. For example, we hesitated to set up an alternative government-in-waiting for an Iraq whose government we wanted overthrown when we had the best chance to do so, or to favor one faction or another in Bosnia, even when taking sides represents the only way out. And when we do take sides, we often tend to do it tentatively and without sufficient force to back up our political action, as in Somalia, or without strong enough political intervention to solve the problems we exercised force against, as in Haiti. We have trouble distinguishing between staying the course (as in Bosnia) and becoming trapped in a quagmire (as in Vietnam). The result of this equivocating makes us an uncertain leader; the internal schism over how deeply to engage with the world detracts from the strength and effectiveness of our leadership when we do become engaged. We did take sides and became strongly engaged in Kosovo, having learned the cost of doing otherwise three years earlier in Bosnia. Even then, however, congressional and public support for the action was grudging, punctuated by calls for an exit strategy before we had entered. None of those calls was tied to an appreciation, specification, or forecast of what should happen on the ground in Kosovo and Serbia before we could depart.

One must observe, in fairness, that those who argue against deeper involvement outside our borders in either the economic or the military spheres to support our ambiguous and uncertain conceptions of national interests in many cases have reasonable logic on their side. We could squander money in bailouts to no good, and we could undertake and perpetuate military occupations in lands where we are either not needed or not welcome, leading to terrorist attacks on our troops or on Americans elsewhere and a drain on our manpower and financial resources. We might bleed our armed forces for small purpose in the short term and reduce our security in the long term. Thus, the arguments against involvement can serve as a useful brake on unwitting commitments that go beyond our capacity to sustain them or beyond the true needs of our economic and physical security. This should properly be the stuff of national debates about international commitments that could drain and weaken the nation if not well considered and judiciously controlled.

Embroilment in warfare in Serbia and Kosovo under NATO aegis, for the highest of purposes, and the subsequent denouement illustrate well all the points that have been raised here. The current fact is that we are there for an indefinite period that depends as much on what, if anything, the Serbian people will do to change their government as it does on U.S. and NATO decisions and actions. Those who called for an apriori expression of conditions under which we could leave can claim they had some justification for their concerns, if they can reconcile the concerns with the humanitarian tragedy that would have been the alternative to entering the fray.

All this having been said, however, we must note that the general trend of events and the pressures of the outside world move us toward more engagement, despite the uncertain and often perverse outcomes of specific instances. The counterarguments usually made, unfortunately, tend to be less about the nature of that engagement than about whether it should exist at all. This is the wrong basis for argument, and its effects can be pernicious. As it is pursued it causes our allies to doubt the seriousness of our commitment and to want to go their own way. It causes our enemies to misread our intentions and the depth of our feeling about issues, leading to miscalculation of our willingness to become involved and our will to succeed. In the long run it makes us more vulnerable to the erosion of our world position under the kind of subtle assault that will be described in Chapter 7, where we will discuss national strategy and others' strategies to counter it.

In trying to come to grips with this dilemma, as with all the others that we have explored, the nation will oscillate between the two positions. Our natural bent, if we could put it that way, is to keep our attention focused inward. We look outward when we are forced to by the impact of the external world. When we do, unless it becomes an issue of national survival—which we haven't seen since World War II and some of the days of the Cold War—or a military or terrorist attack of major proportions, the intensity of feeling about whatever issue we are dealing with tends to have a regional character. Different factions within the nation respond differently to events, depending on the part of the world in which they arise. The East Coast population and businesses feel the pull of Europe and the Middle East. The pull of Japan, China, and the other Pacific Rim countries is stronger for the West Coast. Events in and about Latin America have more poignancy for the southern border states. The great Heartland—the Midwest, the Deep South, the Great Plains, and the Rocky Mountain states—remain less concerned about all those areas beyond our borders. And it is fair to say that Canada tends to be taken for granted everywhere except immediately along our northern border.

These orientations, natural enough in a nation that is continental in extent, are reflected in local media reporting, in the depth of feeling of the population, and therefore in the actions of Congress with respect to taking action or not. The orientations act to restrain strong and immediate action vis-à-vis any specific overseas occurrence, unless the trigger is some violent event like a major terrorist attack or the invasion of an ally or another country in which we have a strong interest. They also act as a constraint on the other end. Those who are less concerned about an event or a situation that we have moved to influence or an obligation that we have taken on in the process exert pressure to end our participation more rapidly, so that they can return to their internally oriented concerns without distraction or expenditure of resources they would rather use for internal purposes. This can lead us to abandon a commitment prematurely; it affects the image and the reality of our staying power.

The pressures against involvement outside our borders beat against the pressures to become involved. How we behave in any given situation will depend on where the nation happens to be between the extremes when the event comes to pass. In critical situations the outcome of our participation will depend on when we entered the events and on the balance between the tugs in either direction at the time. The tensions in resolving the dilemma about whether we should be involved will work against us if the situations are not recognized as critical until events are well along.

PART THREE

THE CORE OF NATIONAL SECURITY

6

THE ARMED FORCES

Covenants without swords are but words.
—*Thomas Hobbes*

Now that we have looked at what is happening in the world and our nation, we are in a position to consider the nation's armed forces. We have to understand something about where they have come from, how they are constituted, and where they are going before we can think about how the country might use them to help preserve its security. To do that, we shall have to range far and wide over their evolution through the twentieth century (and earlier, where necessary). We shall have to examine the progression that they are planning for themselves over the next decade or two, and we shall have to take a broad look at the national strategy the armed forces are being asked to support. Only then can we evaluate the significance of the universal judgment that the United States has the premier armed forces in the world today.

This review will not be a primer on the weapons, the structure, and the operational methods of the armed forces; such matters of technical detail are ably enough presented in many other forums. But we shall have to touch on all those matters because they are, after all, the stuff that makes the armed forces effective and helps them win (and sometimes not win) battles and wars. As we have seen, today's battles and wars will involve more than armed conflict between organized military forces. Another subject of inquiry, then, must be to see how the armed forces can help in those other aspects of protecting our national security.

THE ARMED FORCES AS SOCIETY

The armed forces exist as part of a larger society that spawned them and uses them. Their people have the attitudes, aptitudes, and abilities that are treasured by that society.

If life is held dear by society, the armed forces will be concerned about excessive casualties and will choose tactics and strategy that attempt to minimize casualties. U.S. and Israeli military operations, to take but two examples, follow such doctrine. Conversely, if life is hard and brutish for the average person and considered cheap, soldiers will be fed into battle with little such concern; winning the battle will be the key issue, not how elegantly it is done. We have seen the concern about casualties operate in all our wars in this century,[1] whereas others, such as the Chinese, have used tactics that throw infantry into battle with abandon in "human wave" attacks, trying to drown an enemy in humanity before superior firepower kills all of the attackers.

Similar distinctions apply in treatment of civilian populations caught in the crossfire of battle. Although soldiers who have been shot at and booby-trapped by a hostile enemy population cannot be expected to act as though they care deeply for that population, if the soldiers come from a society that treasures life they will take care not to injure civilians who don't threaten them directly, and they will often make humanitarian gestures to help civilians in distress. Modern U.S. military doctrine, for example, has as one of its tenets the avoidance of what has come to be called "collateral damage" to civilian populations. If, however, soldiers have been taught that the enemy's civilians are less than human, they will likely abuse them mercilessly. We have seen these attitudes, too, operate in all twentieth-century conflicts. The American public was horrified at the deliberate killing of civilians at the village of My Lai during the Vietnam War. However, German forces on the Russian front in World War II perpetrated thousands of My Lais; there were no public outcries and no courts-martial of the officers who ordered them. Bosnia's ethnic cleansing of the Muslim population by the majority Serbs, and the treatment of the ethnic Albanian majority in Kosovo by Yugoslav army and Serb irregular forces, have furnished more recent examples of the latter kind of behavior.

At the technical level, military equipment and modes of operation derive from the technology that the society uses, often extended in the military and then fed back to the civilian arena. Fortifications could not be built that did not use technology available to build houses and castles. The military will have no means of communicating that are not available to the civilian population: telephones, radios, messages carried

---

[1] I limit this observation to this century to avoid argument about the profligate waste of life in some of the campaigns in our own Civil War. But American life was certainly more harsh in that time, so the behavior of our forces and our generals in that war was not necessarily anomalous. There is also the historical fact that all over the world military forces have been trying, from the invention of firearms and artillery until this day, to come to grips with the problems imposed by increasingly deadly firepower on tactics whose fundamentals were developed over hundreds of years previously. Different countries have had different approaches and levels of success in this quest, and this, too, has been a result, in part, of their societal attitudes.

by people using high-speed transportation. There may be some embellishments to help the military communicate secretly, such as encryption of messages, but even those are available to the civilian society in some form. It would not be possible to make rifles and cannons if civilian industry did not have technology for complex metalworking in all its activities. There were no war canoes or warships without ordinary people also being able to travel on the rivers and on the seas, and when wind power gave way to steam power it helped navies and civilian transportation advance together. If the military could observe the ground from the air and travel by air, so could civilians; there would be no air forces if there were no aircraft available in general. Although in all such cases the technological advances might move faster on the military than on the civilian side, or vice versa, over the long sweep of history they have moved essentially in step with each other and with continual mutual feedback. However, as we shall see, there may be significant differences in the way military forces from different societies use the technology available to them.

The way military forces are raised, commanded, and controlled also mirrors the way the society does these things in its everyday life. Authoritarian societies can raise armed forces by dragooning individuals into them. Democratic societies may use the draft in times of stress, but they rely much more on volunteers. In our own case, our populace has had a lot to say about who will serve in the military and why. For example, we reinstituted a draft reluctantly as we could see the probability of our involvement in World War II growing and retained it in some form until we were forced to abandon it and move to an all-volunteer force by popular opposition to the war in Vietnam.

With due allowance for the need to enforce military discipline and adherence to battle plans and tactical and strategic principles, there are marked differences in the way totalitarian and democratic governments exercise command and control of troops in the field. Soviet forces were expected to follow preset battle plans without wavering, whereas U.S. forces have always allowed commanders a high degree of initiative to respond to the exigencies of battle while carrying out a battle plan. The Israeli armed forces, coming from a small country of individualists, have allowed the exercise of commanders' initiative on the battlefield to an extreme, with highly successful results. We must hasten to add, however, that the differences in command and control technique and doctrine do not indicate that soldiers and sailors from the different societies may fight more or less bravely. That depends on their view of the cause they are fighting for and the state of their training and morale in supporting that cause. These things would make for a difference in performance between, say, raw Iraqi conscripts fighting to hold trenches in the Kuwaiti desert and battle-hardened veterans fighting for the survival of their homeland, as Soviet forces did at Stalingrad in World War II.

A society's outlook also affects the way prisoners of war (POWs) are treated. German and Italian POWs, once away from the heat and hatred of battle, were well fed and housed while they were interned in camps in the United States, reflecting the generally humanitarian outlook of this country. Russian and German POWs taken on the eastern front in World War II were treated roughly and died in droves. American POWs in Korea and Vietnam were also abused amid attempts to coerce their thinking and to make them confess to crimes against the society that had captured them, for propaganda purposes, and perhaps for self-justification of the treatment.

An extreme case that illustrates how the mores of a society are reflected in the conduct of warfare is given by the fighting tenacity and treatment of Allied POWs by the Japanese during World War II. It was morally shameful in the Samurai tradition of Japanese society for a soldier to surrender. Japanese soldiers therefore tended to fight to the death even in obviously hopeless situations, making it extremely difficult to overcome them in battles from Guadalcanal to Iwo Jima. Although we honor individual valor, especially when it leads to the sacrifice of life in battle in the higher interest of the individual's unit and the nation's cause, we Americans could not imagine deliberately recruiting and training a corps of suicide pilots to make what amounted to cruise missile guidance systems of themselves, as the kamikaze pilots did in the last, desperate stages of the war; our society would have found it reprehensible, even as theirs found it heroic. And the Japanese attitude toward surrender goes a long way to explaining their extremely brutal treatment of POWs; to them, people who surrendered rather than die fighting were beneath contempt.

These Japanese fighting characteristics, founded in their history and social outlooks, figured strongly in our decision to use the atomic bomb to end the war. And perhaps that decision also reflected other American qualities: We wanted to avoid the American casualties that an all-out invasion would cause; we had this powerful new weapon that emerged from our technological prowess; given that we were in a war with forces who had demonstrated that they would fight to the death, we decided to use our strongest weapon to get on with winning and worry about long-term consequences later.

The American ethos and concern to minimize loss of life lies behind much of our emphasis on technological advance in the armed forces. It is reflected not only in our desire to use superior technology to overcome the enemy's weapons but also in the nature of the technology that is designed to minimize our casualties. We spend a great deal in the design of weapons systems to ensure survival and safe escape of crews in case their tank, aircraft, or ship is hit. We try to minimize exposure of infantry and aviation to enemy fire by increasing the range of our weapons; this is one reason we would prefer to win victory through airpower rather than through combat on the ground. We are starting to use robots—aircraft without people on board, for example[2]—for highly dangerous missions over enemy territory. We espouse attack doctrines involving speed and power that are designed to win quickly, in part so that our own, our enemies', and the civilian populations' casualties can be minimized.

Although it is certainly true that all military forces would prefer to win quickly and decisively and that doctrines for the application of overwhelming force are devised for the purpose, there have been elements in others' doctrines that we would never promulgate or accept. For example, we would not use the Chinese tactic of human-wave attacks in the face of overwhelming firepower in hope of eventually overrunning enemy positions, nor would we use the Soviet tactic of feeding division after division into a battle at the same location regardless of casualties in the expectation that breakthrough will come when the enemy defenses at that point are exhausted by the continuous battle. We would not use women and children as shields for our soldiers; to us doing so seems cowardly. But if they are held in low esteem by a society that also recognizes our reluctance to hurt them, they become a prime protection for military units. We would not shoot down civilian airliners to enforce a blockade over, say, Iraq, but to fanatical Islamic terrorists destroying a civilian airliner with hundreds of people aboard is an ideal way to make their point and to be noticed while doing so. We would not use ten-year-old boys to explode land mines by walking across a battlefield, as the Iranians did in their war with Iraq, but since they believed the boys will go to paradise for their sacrifice they found ample religious justification for this practice.

Enough! The point is made that a country's armed forces reflect the kind of country that builds and fields them. This understanding must be kept in mind when we examine how U.S. armed forces are evolving today. But before we get on with that, we must recognize that the armed forces themselves constitute a society that lives by certain organizational and operational rules that are intimately related to the technology they use.

The elements of the armed forces system include equipment, organization, and doctrine. The *equipment* includes all the weapons, platforms—ships, aircraft, tanks—and supporting systems—from communications and navigation satellites to trucks and forklifts—that the armed forces use to get their jobs done. *Organizations*—varied, enormous in number, and totally confusing to the ordinary person—range from infantry squads and tactical aircraft squadrons through divisions, air

---

[2]UAVs, originally called "Unmanned Aerial Vehicles," and now referred to as "Uninhabited Aerial Vehicles" in a nod to political correctness.

wings, carrier battle groups, and supporting units like engineering battalions. *Doctrine* deals with how the organizations and weapons are used to achieve military objectives.

These three major elements of the armed forces system interact strongly. The nature of equipment dictates much about organization. For example, the Army equips infantry with rifles, machine guns, grenade launchers, and lightweight antitank and antiaircraft weapons that can be used by individual soldiers. It assigns crews to major weapons systems such as tanks, helicopters, cannons, and missile systems. It then aggregates the individuals and the crews into units of various size and organization to use the equipment. The Navy mans ships, and each ship is, itself, a fighting unit. Ships of different kinds, each with a specific capability and mission, are aggregated into battle groups, task forces, and fleets. The Air Force is built around its airplanes and intercontinental missiles, both of which are aggregated into squadrons and wings—the terminology applied to missile units is left over from when the Air Force dealt with aircraft exclusively. The Navy also has combat and support aircraft and organizes its aircraft units in ways similar to those the Air Force uses, although different in detail to be consistent with the way aircraft operate from carriers. The Marines organize generally as the Army does for combat on the ground and the way the air forces do for air combat, and they have devised special organizations and equipment to work with specialized Navy ships in amphibious operations. Then, each of the Services has special units for commando or counterguerrilla types of operations. The sizes of basic units change with their equipment; a tank company may have 100–200 people, depending on its exact composition, whereas an aircraft carrier, which constitutes an aggregation of many subordinate shipboard and aviation units, may have 6,000 people or more. Yet neither of them can operate fully independently; they must be joined with other units to carry out the missions for which they were designed.

Aggregations of basic units such as infantry and tank companies, aircraft squadrons, and individual ships into larger forces such as brigades, divisions, and fleets follows the needs of command and control, as well as the capabilities of the major equipment and the extent of mutual support that different kinds of units can furnish to each other in combat. Organizations to furnish supplies and repair major equipment are added to the combat units in even larger aggregate organizations—corps, armies, air forces, and naval task forces, for example. However, a commander can interact with only so many people, whether he is a squad leader or the commander of an army or a fleet. This leads to pyramidal, or hierarchical, organizations, which have been the norm in military units from time immemorial. However, the depth of the pyramid varies with the technology, the military mission, and the society.

Early armed cavalry, such as constituted the Mongol armies that overran much of Asia and part of Europe during the Middle Ages, or the Plains Indians of the American West, was organized in units made up of warriors from the same tribe. The Plains Indians acted in bands that moved in concert under the general guidance of their chiefs. The Mongol warriors were organized in columns that could range widely but could coalesce for battle at a given location. The "span of control" of these units depended on the distance over which it was easy to communicate in battle. A force that depended on shouted and visual signals would have to be constituted and controlled differently from one that has the capability for over-the-horizon or worldwide observation and communications. The Mongol warriors were able to coordinate widely dispersed forces by virtue of the speed and endurance of the commander's corps of mounted couriers who brought to bear all the speed and hardihood of the steppe cavalry.

As communications and military equipment have entered the modern age, military organization has become more elaborate and formally disciplined. Today, the command and control parameters have evolved with the nature of communications and various technologically based aids to information-gathering and decisionmaking. Units starting from different locations must perform their tasks according to a timetable that allows their actions to mesh for greatest effect. The timetables are, in turn, dictated by technology as much as by desire for surprise and other effects— how fast an army can move, how fast ships can sail, how fast aircraft can fly, how much they can all carry or be supplied in a given time—and also by how long it takes to prepare and promulgate plans and orders and train for an operation.

As ably demonstrated by the historian William McNeill in his books *The Rise of the West* and *The Pursuit of Power*, the pyramidal organization of the military and the hierarchical industrial organizations needed to control large industrial enterprises grew in parallel. That organization reached the peak of its rigidity and complexity sometime during the 1960s and 1970s, both in the military and in industry. Now, as they have grown in the scope of their missions and their geographic reaches, military and industrial organizations are following a trend toward decentralization of command and control (at least in the United States and the NATO alliance). Lower-level civilian corporate officials and military commanders are given more autonomy and more responsibility to use their own ingenuity and initiative. Within the scope of agreed corporate modes of operation and military doctrine, unit leaders and commanders are asked to carry out mission-type orders: "Here is what you are to accomplish, by when, with the following units and resources; the details are left to you."

The purpose of this trend is to shorten the response time of the command structure and increase the efficiency with which it uses the available resources by decreasing the depth of the command pyramid. This applies in civilian corporate competition and in military quest for battlefield success. Every time a command has to be transmitted to a lower-level commander, absorbed and acted on or passed on to others at the next level, a time delay and chance for error are incurred. As layers of command multiply, an organization becomes increasingly unable to respond rapidly to challenges from outside. The stultifying effects of dense organization carried to extremes were felt by our military during the Vietnam War and by our industry during the early years of keen industrial competition with Japan (the 1970s and early 1980s). To avoid the effects, the number of command levels must be reduced. The trend is facilitated today by the availability of computers and rapid, high-capacity communications that allow all the necessary information to be shared by widely dispersed military commanders or industrial managers in a short time. Rapid transportation of key people and needed goods—knowledgeable experts, food, water, ammunition, fuel, replacement parts—is also a facilitator as well as an economic driver. It is no accident that Wal-Mart is a model for both civilian retail distribution and military logistic support. It gets the job done with the least resources, in the fastest time, with the highest payoff.

The interactions among civilian and military social forms, technology, organization, and doctrine are clearly apparent in this evolution. The critical question it poses is whether closed societies can tolerate the greater freedom that must be allowed at lower levels of the pyramid. Answers to this question, which remain to be revealed by history in the making, will determine much about their industrial and military effectiveness and their trend to more democratic governmental forms. At the other end of the scale, terrorist and guerrilla organizations and others who skirt the law, such as smugglers, need little depth; indeed, that is one of their strengths. Small groups can marshal the resources needed for an operation, whereas their small size and dispersal help preserve secrecy and safety. At some point, however, they need inspirational, financial, and technical support from some higher and better-supplied authority. That may be their Achilles' heel in the long run, if we have the will and the patience to exploit it.

U.S. ARMED FORCES IN
THE TWENTIETH CENTURY

Cycles of Support

Until the onset of the Cold War the United States followed a pattern of boom and bust in managing its armed forces. We mobilized the nation and built up the armed forces when we had to fight a war, then demobilized and let them decay. This pattern cost many casualties at the outset of the Korean War in 1950: About 10,000 men were killed, wounded, and missing in battle during the first three months of that war as a woefully unprepared and undersized post–World War II army tried to stand off an assault by a large, well-prepared, well-armed foe that had help from the Soviet Union and China.

The experience of the Korean War, viciously reinforcing the onset of the Cold War, changed the boom-and-bust pattern but not the propensity to fall into it. The armed forces remained at an average strength of about 2 million people through most of the Cold War period, building up to about 3.5 million at the peak of the Vietnam War, and dropping to their current 1.5 million or less after the Berlin Wall came down. In any nonwar period, even during the Cold War, we have argued about the size of the armed forces we need, about how much to spend to keep them ready for battle, about how much the United States must do to carry the burden of the free world's military strength, and about how much to spend for military strength overseas in comparison with defense of the homeland from direct attack. Since the Cold War ended, these arguments have intensified while the armed forces have shrunk.

The United States, unlike traditional European and Asiatic powers, neither wanted nor felt the need for large standing armies. After the wars with Mexico and the fights to wrest the American West from the Indians, we had no enemies on this continent, and until the end of World War II and the Cold War we saw little need to project land-based military power overseas in a time of peace or no-war. Following the post–World War I demobilization, the Army remained a small force of 150,000 men, including the fledgling Air Force that was embedded within it. The Army (including the Air Force) grew to a total of 8 million at the peak of World War II, then dropped to under 600,000 by 1950, when the Korean War started. The Army went up to 1.1 million during Korea, back down to about 900,000 until the Vietnam War buildup, reached more than 1.5 million during that war, held steady at just under 800,000 afterward, and since 1991 has declined to less than 500,000—fewer than its pre–Korean War level. By 1950, the Air Force had been established as a separate military Service, which started at 400,000 people, grew to a peak of 900,000 during the Vietnam War, remained steady at 500,000–600,000 until 1992, and has since declined to 400,000 again.

Our Navy fared better, but not without similar fluctuations. Having let it decay after the Civil War, we were spurred by several late-nineteenth-century and early-twentieth-century developments to rebuild it in more modern form. One of these developments was the appearance of the works of American naval officer Captain Alfred Thayer Mahan, who showed the value of naval power for a nation desiring to reach beyond its shores. Then, at the beginning of the twentieth century, we saw the British creation of the *Dreadnought*-class battleship, the first major ship to incorporate both the inventions of our own Civil War and all the industrial advances of the late nineteenth century; this was followed by subsequent British and German naval buildups. Finally, there was the defeat of the Russian fleet in the war with Japan.

The logic of threat dictated that we would give more attention to the Navy than to the Army: Before the advent of air power, and with friendly nations on our northern and southern borders, any military threat to the United States would have to come from the sea. Naval forces gave America the military capacity to defeat Spain in Cuba and the Philippines, and it thereby became a world power with an overseas empire. Sea power was the "big stick" behind President Theodore Roosevelt's virtual annexation of Panama to build the canal. By the end of World War I, we had enough naval strength under construction to persuade the world's leading naval powers to sign an agreement at the Washington Conference of 1921–1922 limiting the sizes of their fleets and warships. The United States volunteered to stand down on warship construction that would have given us the largest navy in the world. But we were recognized as being one of the world's two leading naval powers, together with Great Britain; both countries were allowed to construct equal numbers of battleships in the following years. (Japan, which had been relegated to a secondary role as a naval power in the agreement, then ignored it and built to parity with the United States and Great Britain.) The Marines, associated with the Navy as a landing force, were a small force until World War II, peaked at nearly half a million men during that war, and have since remained at something under 200,000, with the exception of the buildup to 300,000 at the peak of the Vietnam War.

It is worth noting that although politicians are wont to use support of the armed forces as a bellwether of patriotism and support of the country, the fluctuations in the size of the armed forces have been historically based and event-based, relying on societywide attitudes and world conditions rather than on politics of the moment. Thus, in recent decades, the military buildup under Ronald Reagan actually began during Jimmy Carter's administration, when it was realized that spending on current operations during the Vietnam War had caused us to fall behind in developing advanced military systems to match Soviet progress during that time. Then, the decline in our military forces' size and strength, often attributed to President Bill Clinton's policies by his political opposition, actually began during President Reagan's second term, when the Soviet threat began to recede during the Gorbachev era, and continued during George Bush's presidency. From this perspective, the Iraqi occupation of Kuwait in 1990 couldn't have been timed more badly for them: It caught us with our armed forces still at reasonably high strength; with new equipment, training, and doctrine that needed smaller numbers but could achieve far more powerful effects; and the disappearance of the threat that would, earlier, have kept U.S. forces pinned in Europe. This was an accident of history that is unlikely to be repeated, and that should temper any tendency to hubris deriving from our victory in the Gulf War.

As this history also indicates, numbers of people alone don't tell the whole story about the variation in the armed forces' strength. Through the past century, military technology has advanced at a pace that gave any specific number of people steadily increasing combat power, so that today armed forces smaller than those we fielded during World War I are vastly more powerful than those forces were. Although the advance appears steady in historical perspective it was highly episodic, with the wars spurring technology for military application and civilian markets spurring advances that the military picked up and used, with embellishments, between the wars. This pattern applied even during the Cold War, although the Cold War competition led to many of the nascent technologies that the civilian world picked up and turned to their advantage. Now, with the Cold War over, much of the civilian technology thus derived is dominant.

During this progression that lasted almost a full century, there was another, more subtle evolution. At the time of World War I the U.S. military began by borrowing technology from European allies and, largely as a result of the growth of U.S. economic and industrial strength to world-dominating proportions during World War II, we gradually assumed the lead in originating military technological advances.

Military Technology in the Twentieth Century

It would be impossible in a few paragraphs to recount completely the recent advances in military technology and the effect of the technical advances on how wars have been fought. However, it is worth noting a few of the key milestones to illustrate the foundations on which America's global military power has been built.

We entered World War I with little advanced military technology of our own, except for our Navy. Cannons that featured breech-loaded, rifled barrels (to spin-stabilize projectiles for greater accuracy and range) and exploding shells had begun to emerge from our own Civil War and were advanced during the radical changes in naval ships and the European wars of the late nineteenth century. Advances in the mobility, destructiveness, and rate of fire of artillery on land had been paced by the Europeans, and the U.S. Army adopted their advances as we entered the war. Although the airplane was an American invention, the Europeans had so advanced it during the early years of World War I that we used their combat aircraft in that war.

Artillery and machine guns were the decisive weapons in the land battles of World War I. Another American invention (with the mechanical Gatling gun in 1862 and the recoil-operated Maxim gun, the predecessor of the modern machine gun, in 1884), the machine gun completed the trend toward battlefield carnage that had been initiated centuries earlier with the invention of artillery and enhanced during the nineteenth century with accurate, long-range infantry rifles. It took armies a long time to come to terms with the increased lethality of these weapons. The high casualties in engagements like Pickett's charge at the Battle of Gettysburg during the American Civil War were caused by artillery and breech-loading rifles, which had preceded repeating rifles by a good forty years. The magnitude of infantry losses during the Boer War led to years of British military-board studies on how to reduce the casualties such weapons caused; the result was to exhort the troops to enhance their élan and charge faster so that they would suffer fewer losses before reaching enemy lines. This kind of thinking led to the horrific battlefield slaughters and trench warfare of World War I. It wasn't until World War II, with its armored warfare and dispersed infantry formations, that a measure of control over infantry casualties was introduced, although as that war, Korea, Vietnam, and the Iran-Iraq War of the 1980s showed, infantry-fighting in close quarters will always produce casualties in large numbers on one side, if not both.

The British-German standoff at Jutland showed that surface naval forces needed more than simple gun power to make a strategic difference, unless one side had a large naval force advantage. The added qualities, which the British had failed to provide, especially included targeting at long range to match the longer reach of their naval guns. The Germans advanced submarine warfare as an effective, independent naval arm, showing a decisively different naval capacity by almost isolating the European battlefield. As would happen in World War II as well, they were defeated in this by combined British and American industrial might in building cargo ships and by antisubmarine surface forces and, in World War II, air forces. The pattern of surface naval warfare that used battleships as the main source of powerful naval fire, cruisers as highly maneuverable supporting forces, and destroyers and frigates as screens, scouts, and submarine hunters had evolved from naval warfare in the days of sailing ships and became well established during World War I. The aircraft carrier, invented by the British in 1917, played no significant role in that war.

Aviation was useful during World War I mainly to observe enemy positions on the ground. Combat aviation grew largely from the attempt of each side to shoot down the other's observation aircraft and manned, tethered observation balloons and the other side's response in trying to protect its observation capability. Although aviation played no strategically important role in the war, it had the advantage, still important in gaining the support of civilian populations for the armed forces, of carrying on the romantic tradition of the mounted warrior that the cavalry was losing. Aerial bombing from large aircraft that couldn't go very far and from rigid, steerable airships—dubbed "Zeppelins" after their German inventor—that managed to reach London had mainly nuisance value, since none of the machines could carry enough of a bomb load to make either a strategic or a tactical difference in the war. Thus, civilian populations who were not in the line of fire or advance of ground armies, or in position to be affected by submarine action at sea, were essentially safe from the direct effects of military firepower. As we know, this would change radically during World War II.

Other important technological advances in World War I included the application of telephony to field communications; the use of radio for maritime communications and for long-range strategic communications; the advancement of mathematical cryptography; and the first wholesale application of automotive, motorized mobility for people and cargo transport. Major troop movements still took place on the rails, however. Horse-mounted cavalry was useless on the static battlefields of France, although it hung on in the reaches of Eastern Europe, to the point where the Polish army still tried to use cavalry to meet German tanks in 1939, with the results one would expect. Cavalry's last useful application after that was deep in Russia, where Cossack horsemen were able to maneuver against dispersed German invaders, especially in winter. Tanks, invented by the British as a desperate measure to allow troops to advance while under heavy machine-gun fire, appeared on the battlefields of France, but not in enough numbers to make a strategic difference.

Thus, the dominant technologies of World War I were the firepower that created the stalemated slaughterhouses of the western front in France and the naval forces that contended to isolate or to prevent the isolation of the war zones. But we see the beginnings, in that war, of the technologies that would break the stalemates and would not only restore maneuver to warfare but also extend that maneuver to worldwide scope. The United States had little role in devising and furthering the military technology of World War I. We provided the industrial might that gave the Allies ammunition to keep them fighting, and we provided the critical increment of fresh armed force on the ground that persuaded war-weary German leaders that they had better sue for peace. In the process, however, the United States acquired the knowhow and the interest, embodied in the small professional armed forces that remained, to advance the technology-based military capability that the war had invented. In this advance, we made some important contributions, but we did not yet become the leaders.

Between the wars, key militarily useful technologies were developed, mainly in civilian applications: radio; automobiles and trucks; transport aviation culminating in the first modern transport aircraft, the DC-3 (the Dakota, or the C-47 in military application); and steam turbine–powered passenger ships and advanced cargo ships with increasing displacement and speed. In these areas, the United States excelled. Direct military applications, including military radio, the invention of radar, cryptographic machines, and aerial observation of the battlefield—all contributors to command and control of the forces and to tactics and operations involving maneuver of large and small military units, from battalions to armies—emerged from technological advances begun during World War I. Artillery reached new stages of mobility, range, and accuracy of fire, and tanks were advanced far beyond their beginnings to become small, well-armed, mobile fortresses on the battlefield. The buildup to World War II also saw great advances in fighter and long-range bomber aircraft.

In all these areas except aviation Europe led the way, and even in aviation the United States had not yet assumed the commanding lead that was to emerge from the next war. Although the U.S. aviation industry provided highly serviceable fighters during the 1930s, in the P-36 and the P-40 that helped the Allies fight off German and Japanese air attacks, the fighter field at the beginning of the war was dominated by the British and the Germans. The British Spitfire and Hurricane and the German Messerschmitt 109 and Focke Wulf 190 fighters were the best available until well into the war. Only then did the American P-51 Mustang, P-38 Lightning, and P-47 Thunderbolt, together with American bombers, come to dominate the air battlefield over Western Europe. (The Russian Stormovik was a close air support fighter of first rank on the eastern front late in the war.) Similarly, in naval aviation, the Japanese Zero was the superior fighter at the beginning of the war, to be overtaken later by the U.S. F-6F Hellcat and F-4U Corsair fighters. American bombers seemed also to be outranged and outperformed initially by aircraft such as the British Lancaster, but the American B-17 Flying Fortress, by virtue of its ruggedness and armament, and B-24 Liberator, by virtue of its long range, soon came to dominate the bomber category.

After the British invention of the aircraft carrier in 1917, the Japanese and the American navies followed suit during the 1920s. Carrier aviation was viewed as simply an adjunct to battleship warfare in the United States, whereas the Japanese understood and capitalized on carriers' strategic value as offensive systems. In the United States, the argument was begun, and raged without resolution until the Japanese settled it at Pearl Harbor, about whether aviation put naval ships so much at risk that it would come to dominate naval warfare. Despite the demonstrations, in 1921 to 1923, by General Billy Mitchell that bombers could sink battleships, the nation continued to measure its naval strength by the number of battleships in its Navy. It took the fortuitous circumstance that our carriers survived the Pearl Harbor attack in 1941 simply because they were away from their base to change our outlook; the carriers were most of the capital ships that we had to fight the war in the Pacific through the strategically critical early Battles of the Coral Sea and Midway.

World War II saw the emergence of the U.S. armed forces that make up the popular conception of our military power today, although there would be several additional generations of change. In addition to the transformation of naval warfare with aviation and specialized amphibious landing capability, the war saw the emergence of the kinds of land and air forces that we now take for granted. Mobile armored forces became the determinants of the outcomes of land battles. Aviation developed into a tactical and strategic combat and airlift force that could tip the balance of battles and of wars. The development of radar and sonar vastly augmented human senses for observation of enemy activity in the air, on the surface, and under the sea. The jet aircraft and guided missiles we are familiar with today were conceived and their early prototypes entered service toward the end of the war. The war saw the beginnings of electronic computers. The organization of military formations into integrated land, air, and sea forces that undertook the kinds of joint operations that characterize all our military operations today also began during that period.

The invention of nuclear weapons, to which we shall return several times, brought America and the world into the age of modern warfare that can open all civilization to the risk of ultimate destruction. At the same time, older forms of warfare, such as infantry engagements, and guerrilla and terrorist warfare were augmented by technologically advanced weaponry and communications, including automatic assault rifles, antitank rockets and guided missiles, more powerful explosives, advanced bomb and mine fuzing, and telephones and radios, all of which have allowed small groups of people to wield great destructive power. This led to dispersal of forces on the battlefield, at sea, and in the air.

In the early stages of twentieth-century warfare, ground combat units, ships, and aircraft kept close together to gain the benefit of mutual support by the weapons of adjacent units. As small infantry units, ships, and aircraft became more powerful they could provide that support from greater distances. They spread out to reduce the chance of their becoming casualties, to avoid the effects of concentrated firepower, and because the potential loss of one unit had become more serious than it would be if they had less capacity. At the same time, they could exert more military power from their dispersed positions. As they came to dominate greater areas, however, the individual force units, whether infantry soldiers with their weapons or major ships and aircraft, became more expensive. Smaller forces came to cost as much as or more than the previous, larger ones. These tendencies began their slow movement in World War II. We can see in them the evolutionary basis of today's armed forces, as they accelerated after the war.

Although the warring nations of Europe, as well as Japan, were the innovators in the military preparations and during the early years of World War II, the combination of American industrial capacity and concentrated inventiveness soon brought the United States to the fore as the world's leader in military technology. Among the developments that led to this was the capacity for industrial organization needed to manage very large–scale enterprises. This included the well-organized research-and-development enterprise that was transformed into the peacetime civilian and military scientific and technical establishment that we know today. That establishment has made the United States a leader in all areas of technological and industrial advance during the second half of the twentieth century. This leadership was not easy to maintain, however, as it was challenged both by Soviet hostility and by our allies' rivalry, thus straining our physical and industrial resources, our moral fiber, and our social ingenuity.

The most devastating impact of military technological advance in the twentieth century was the figurative movement of civilian populations to within easy and rapid reach of warmaking forces. In some ways, civilians have been at the mercy of invading armies from the time armies were organized in units that could capture and devastate opponents' farms, villages, towns, castles, and cities and kill or enslave civilians in the process. But that took time, and there was the chance that defending armies could stave off the disaster, perhaps for good. Even in World War I, civilians behind the stalemated front in Europe were essentially safe from attack. World War II aviation and, later, missile technology allowed the attacker to leapfrog over the front to attack the civilians who supported their countries' war efforts, although the capability did not advance to intercontinental range—that came a decade or two later, with long-range aircraft, en route refueling in midair, and intercontinental ballistic missiles (ICBMs).

The invention of nuclear weapons gave those delivery vehicles the capacity to wipe out entire cities and their populations with one or a few explosive devices. The airplanes and ICBMs also had the effect of making the threat immediate: No longer did the attacker have to wait for days or weeks for his armies to overrun and destroy his opponents' population and warmaking potential; it could now be done in hours by airplane or in minutes by missiles. And they made the United States—one of the few great nations whose territory, safeguarded by two oceans east and west and friendly borders north and south, had been essentially unreachable with major military force by its most powerful strategic opponents—vulnerable at last to those opponents' potential attack. This, together with the inevitable spread of nuclear weapons that was discussed in Chapter 3, forever changed the face and the threat of war to the death for the civilian population of the United States.

The evolution of nuclear forces followed its own path, different from that of the conventional forces. We will examine their technological trajectory shortly. Many different kinds of nuclear warheads were developed, intended for various military purposes, but after Hiroshima and Nagasaki these weapons were never used in warfare. It was recognized by all parties that owned them that, in the numbers that the strategic rivalries caused to proliferate, their use in successive escalation to all-out war could wipe out their own countries, civilization, and perhaps humankind as well. But the rivalry for possession of the weapons and the delivery systems, in escalating strength to match the rival's numbers of weapons and systems, became an end in itself under the theory that their holding by one party would deter the initiation of war by the other. [3] And, indeed, the outcome of the Cold War, with its proxy wars and absence of direct military combat between nuclear powers, would seem to bear out this claim.

We must also mention in this context the presence of the other weapons of mass destruction that have emerged in modern form in the aftermath of World War II and the Cold War. These are chemical and biological weapons. Chemical weapons were invented and used on the battle fronts in World War I, but mutual deterrence appeared to have precluded their use in World War II despite the all-out nature of that war. Although they can have devastating effects on civilian populations, against which they can be delivered by any means from ballistic missiles to terrorists' clandestine release (as was demonstrated by the Aum Shinrikyo religious cult in the Tokyo subway in 1995), they cannot threaten total destruction of a population as nuclear weapons can. Biological warfare[4] is much older in concept, having been used, perhaps, by the ancient tribes of Israel against the Egyptians and certainly during the Middle Ages when plague-infected corpses were catapulted over city walls.[5] Whether by deliberation or inadvertence, it figured strongly in the conquest of the Americas by the Europeans. In its modern forms, it can have effects on populations as devastating as nuclear weapons, but with certain differences.

Whereas the destruction wrought by nuclear weapons is instantaneous and impossible to counter except on the fringes of the weapons' effects, biological weapons

---

[3]I haven't discussed this rivalry in specific terms of the U.S.-Soviet nuclear confrontation because there were many complicating factors that spread the strategic standoff beyond those two nations. These included the British, French, and Chinese weapons, each backed by political and strategic doctrine unique to those countries' interests. Those interests did not necessarily coincide with those of the United States and the USSR, but the other countries' alliance commitments could have involved them in nuclear exchanges that neither sought initially. Indeed, it was said that one reason President Charles de Gaulle started the French nuclear deterrent was to give France leverage over the use of the U.S. strategic nuclear forces.

[4]I refer here to biological warfare in which bacteria, such as anthrax, and viruses, such as smallpox, are used to create illness and death. There may be other biological means to attack the health of an opposing force or population. For example, the great rise in heroin use by U.S. troops in Southeast Asia could well have resulted from a biological warfare attack that was not bacteriologically or virus-based. The channels for opium and heroin distribution to U.S. troops in South Vietnam were there; the North Vietnamese had only to ease the flow of the drug from or through territory they controlled to enhance its devastating impact on American troops powerfully.

[5]This is not to mention the inadvertent and unplanned biological warfare that was inflicted by various invaders, in Eurasia and the New World, on populations who had not built natural immunities to the germs that were endemic in the invaders' countries of origin. Smallpox, more than armed conflict, was decisive in decimating the American Indian population.

take time to work, and they do not destroy the warmaking infrastructure of the one who is attacked. They might then be traced to their point of origin, and that point or country might then be counterattacked, perhaps with nuclear weapons. There would also be time to diagnose the nature of the attack disease and to distribute antidotes if they have been prepared. Also, biological weapons are unique in having a built-in deterrent against their use, since backfires caused by such things as adverse winds and unintended contact with infected individuals can inflict high losses on the original user. These diverse qualities of the chemical and biological weapons put them in classes different from nuclear weapons. Each must be treated according to its own potential effects and counters, both in strategy and in direct countermeasures—a fact that tends to be lost when the generic term "weapons of mass destruction" is used indiscriminately.

Post–World War II technological evolution of our military forces was driven by the competition of the Cold War, accentuated by the Korean War and Vietnam War during the strategic standoff with the Soviet Union and the Gulf War at the end of that standoff. The most threatening technological advance during the forty-six years from the end of World War II in 1945 until the collapse of the Soviet Union in 1991 was the elaboration of nuclear weapons, their unique power being noted above. The numbers of weapons designed and built in various sizes for various purposes multiplied in the arsenals of the United States, the Soviet Union, and, later, China, Britain, and France. They ranged over six orders of magnitude in size. The largest have the explosive force of millions of tons of TNT; they are able to destroy cities much larger than Hiroshima and Nagasaki, as well as very deeply buried targets such as strategic command centers. Smaller weapons, ranging down to weapons of as little as a few tons' TNT equivalent, were designed to be fired from cannons or delivered by short-range missiles on the battlefield against tactical targets such as infantry and armor concentrations. In numbers, the United States and the Soviet Union could count thousands in their arsenals—numbers such as 30,000 became current in popular reports—whereas Britain, France, and China were estimated to have added hundreds more to world nuclear weapons stocks.

Initially, piston-engined bombers and then jet bombers were the primary delivery vehicles for such weapons. The strategic standoff of the Cold War spurred the development of ICBMs for nuclear weapons delivery. Application of the principles of nuclear fission to power generation enabled the creation of nuclear-powered submarines, which could stay at sea for months at a time without surfacing—a revolutionary change from diesel-powered submarines. The submarines were then coupled, in the Polaris program, with long-range sea-launched ballistic missiles (SLBMs) that could deliver nuclear warheads to intercontinental distances from under the sea. Thus grew the strategic nuclear triad of bombers, land-based missiles, and submarine-based missiles for delivery of nuclear weapons against U.S. and Soviet homelands that were hemispheres apart on the globe. Each leg of the triad could survive certain kinds of attacks and deliver its weapons in ways that the others could not, so that overall an attacker could not escape devastating retaliation, even though the first strike might have been calculated to destroy the opposing ability to counterattack. As is well known, the Soviet Union, and then the other nuclear powers, followed the United States in fielding all these kinds of weapons and delivery systems, almost always in fewer years than we had predicted; once a technological capability is demonstrated in one part of the globe, it has proven impossible to keep it bottled up at the source.

The development of bombers made them the initial source of technology for the jet transport aircraft that transformed commercial aviation and in the process made possible the rapid transport of people and valuable goods that knit the nation's and then the world's economy into the integrated forms that we see today. The submarines' nuclear power plants were the progenitors of civilian nuclear power production. The invention of the transistor led to integrated circuits on a chip, designed for ICBM and SLBM warhead guidance systems. The integrated circuits were applied in place of bulky, heat-generating vacuum tubes, thus initiating the train of inventions that led to today's computers and the onset of the so-called information age. The missiles led to the design of rocket-propelled launchers for spacecraft, both manned and unmanned, and thereby made possible today's space-based earth observation, communications, navigation, and weather satellites for civilian as well as military purposes. From this flowed exploration of the planets, the Hubble Space Telescope that has vastly extended our knowledge of the cosmos, and the activities of humans in space, from the first visits to the moon in 1969 to today's Space Shuttle and space station activities. Thus, the threats to civilization implicit in the Cold War standoff were also the inspiration and the sources for the spectacular and revolutionary technological advances that have made our closely knit world civilization what it is today.

Significant technological innovations also emerged in the general purpose forces—those that fight the battles on land and at sea against opposing armies, air forces, and fleets. They included the use of satellites for the purposes noted in the previous paragraph; advanced sensors using radar, infrared, and radio as well as visual detection; helicopters; supersonic fighters; guided weapons; nuclear attack submarines; and long-range transport aircraft that could deliver troops and their equipment to battlefields continents away in fractions of a day. Like armored vehicles in World War II, each of these advances changed the face of warfare.

For the first time in history, the controlling factor in the timing of a response to aggression, once decided upon, became the time to gather the forces and prepare their logistic support, rather than the time to march or to be transported to the place where they are needed. Helicopter mobility meant that fighting units could traverse difficult terrain in minutes instead of hours and days. Helicopters became the new mounts for cavalry, and they could also deliver weapons against opposing troops from locations unanticipated by the enemy while working in close proximity to friendly troops. The scope, extent, and complexity of the battlefield expanded enormously as a result of this kind of mobility. Helicopters also changed the nature of amphibious landings, which could now go deep inland through the inevitable holes in opposing defenses, bypassing strong defenses on the beach. And helicopters' application to antisubmarine warfare gave it a new dimension: the ability to dip sonars into the ocean at various widely separated points in a short time to seek, find, and attack lurking undersea ships. Helicopters also figure strongly in minesweeping that must be done in a very short time to clear channels for ship and amphibious movements.

Advanced radar sensors allowed observation of enemy forces in any weather, and infrared sensing opened up the night: Military units on the ground could now move about the battlefield, see, and shoot at their opponents in bad weather and at night while pilots and gunners in helicopters and fixed-wing aircraft could see where to deliver their weapons to support those units. Radar and infrared sensors also became the key components of weapon guidance systems; the latter were extended to be able to home on an opponent's radar and on radio emissions intended to jam the guidance sensors. Sensing of electromagnetic signals at all frequencies from low frequency radio through the radar and infrared spectrums allowed detection and tracking of all broadcasters, or emitters, in any of those frequency ranges. Radars, heat from engines, tank and truck bodies warmed by the sun, and battlefield and strategic communications could all be detected and tracked.

This opened vast new areas of intelligence-gathering, as well as the practice of jamming and other electronic countermeasures, and then countercountermeasures, ad infinitum, initiating an era of intense electronic warfare. It extended into eavesdropping on enemy electronic communications for intelligence purposes and, together with computers, advanced the science and practice of cryptography. Command and control of forces has come to encompass all the means that make it possible for Army, Air Force, and Navy formations to find and maneuver against their opponents. Command, control, communications, computing, intelligence, surveillance, and reconnaissance, known in military shorthand as C4ISR, has become as important a military function as any of those associated with weapons, if not more important. Also, electronic warfare has joined with computers and computer hacking to form the information warfare that is becoming a foundation stone of U.S. doctrine.

While all this was developing, tactical aviation was also proceeding apace. Flying faster than the speed of sound, or breaking the sound barrier, had appeared at the time of World War II to be one of nature's impossible obstacles to overcome. The appearance of rocket and jet propulsion, as well as greater understanding of high-speed aerodynamics that research and development during the war made possible, led to the vaulting of that barrier by Colonel Chuck Yeager in a Bell X-1 aircraft in 1947. A proliferation of advances soon followed. Fighter aircraft moved routinely into the realm of supersonic flight, although a combination of factors deriving from aerodynamic heating and its effect on aircraft structures has limited them to less than 2–2.5 times the speed of sound in all but a few specialized applications. The subsequent directions of advance in tactical combat aviation led to the ability of such aircraft to fly hundreds of miles with large loads of antiaircraft missiles, air-to-surface missiles, or bombs. Then the advances led to design of the aircraft in such a way that they would be difficult to detect by the opponents' radar and infrared sensors that were designed to find them and guide missiles against them. Thus was stealth technology invented and developed.

The first nuclear power plants built for submarines showed the way to development of such power plants for surface ships, leading to the nuclear-powered carriers that, together with the cruisers, destroyers, and attack submarines that accompany them, form the power center of our surface fleet. The aircraft carriers, of a size comparable to that of the Empire State Building lying on its side, constitute floating air bases able to deploy to any part of the world that is accessible by sea and to launch tactical combat aviation from there against targets deep inland. Together with amphibious forces of Marines operating from their own specialized ships, they make up a powerful strike force that can convey American military power where it may be wanted, without the need for bases on land. Nuclear-powered submarines, in the meantime, branched out from their early role as strategic ballistic missile submarines to become an undersea force that can be used to search for opposing undersea forces, attack surface shipping, and attack targets on land with guided missiles like the Tomahawks that were used in the Gulf War and several times since.

Another far-reaching military advance, not commonly thought about in that sense, is the application of computers to modeling and simulation of everything from the operation of systems to the interactions of forces on a battlefield, thereby changing the nature of military as well as civilian planning. Using these techniques, planners can visualize and measure interactions among diverse parts of a system that are too complex to visualize any other way. The system being modeled may be a single aircraft, an intricate network of land forces, ships, and aircraft in dispersed combat formations, aircraft in an air-traffic control system, telephone calls by the million, or a stream of vehicles on a highway complex. It is now possible—indeed mandatory, for economic reasons—to design all major systems on the computer before bending metal or pouring concrete, and the computer programs that make up the simulations often become parts of the system itself. (And, unfortunately, this "software" can be an imperfect part of a system, to the point of causing its failure.)

Just as in the strategic weapon systems area—those with intercontinental reach—these technological developments in the general-purpose forces and their systems also had implications for civilian technology. As we noted for the strategic forces, over the span of the nearly fifty-year Cold War the military forces' technology (including that from both strategic and general-purpose forces, cross-fertilizing each other) and the civilian economy's technology have become essentially inseparable. The most significant evolutionary change over that period has been that, with the exception of specialized areas such as undersea warfare, explosives for weaponry, sensors applied to weapon guidance systems, and stealth in aircraft and ship design, the civilian technology has overtaken the military in the force and vigor of its advance. Once the civilian world adopted advances such as computing, helicopter travel, jet propulsion for large transport aircraft, and satellite communications and navigation, to name but a few, the proliferation of applications and markets for them meant that the resources for military applications would be overwhelmed by those applied to the civilian applications, and the military would have to rely upon the civilian world as a source of basic technological advance.

Technology Shaping the Techniques of Warfare

During the twentieth century (and at other periods of human history) wars have, in addition to their intended political purposes, served both as means to consolidate diverse technological applications for military usage and as sources of innovation for the development of new technologies. The significance of the advances in post–Cold War military technology for the way the armed forces are constituted and fight can be appreciated by a brief look at the applications of the technologies and the techniques they initiated or brought to fruition during the three major wars we have fought since World War II. This will set the stage for a later look at where the armed forces appear to be heading in future decades.

Combat technique and technology on the ground in Korea was largely an extension of trends begun in World War II. However, the Korean War saw the refinement of close air support provided, through continuous radio contact, in close coordination with ground forces to the extent that such support became a key element of total force firepower. (Previously, tactical air support had operated at some distance

from friendly forces, and generally in only coarse time synchrony with their operations.) The first air combat among jet fighter aircraft took place in "MIG Alley" over
the northern reaches of North Korea along the Yalu River boundary with China, in a
contest (which allied forces won) for mastery of the air over the battlefields. And
Korea saw the evacuation of battle casualties by helicopter, the first use of that new
kind of air machine in warfare.

Initially, the possible presence of nuclear weapons on the battlefield caused the
United States and the USSR to redesign their ground forces to use widely dispersed
formations to limit the losses of units hit by nuclear weapons. However, the imperatives of force concentration to break through stalwart defenses limited the degree to
which forces could be dispersed and led to other solutions that had far-reaching effects on the nonnuclear battlefield. First, there was a premium on shielding troops
against radiation effects, which led to heavy armored forces. The heavy armored
forces were to be highly mobile, so that they would be harder to target in the "fog of
war" and so that they could overrun possible sources of battlefield nuclear fire. Their
mobility was gradually augmented by helicopter mobile forces that could put troops
into forward positions rapidly and, in anticipation of the movement of armored
columns, meet them with deadly antitank fire. This led to the "hugging tactic," in
which attacking forces were to close rapidly with their opposition, thereby discouraging the use of nuclear weapons against the enemy since they could severely damage
one's own forces as well. Finally, the use of battlefield missiles to deliver nuclear warheads was invoked to attack opposing nuclear systems before they could fire and before one's own systems could be overrun by the opposition—like getting a forward
pass off before the passing back gets tackled by the opposition line. Thus we see in
the initial concerns about nuclear weapons on the battlefield the genesis of today's
force organizations and high-speed tactics.

Although the French had begun developing attack helicopter tactics in Algeria
years earlier, the U.S. war in Vietnam became the great proving ground for air cavalry. Like horse cavalry in relation to the forces they supported, air cavalry used
transport helicopters to move troops and armed helicopters to support them with
firepower around the landing zones—perhaps the hallmark of the war in the public
mind. The tactics' strengths and vulnerabilities were thoroughly wrung out and became one of the bases for the later development of the U.S. Army's Air-Land Battle
concept that was applied in the Gulf War. Another important kind of military force,
derived from World War II's commandos and rangers and perfected in the new context by British Special Air Service operations in Malaya and Indonesia, was brought
to the fore in Special Forces' operations in and around Vietnam. They ranged from
Army Green Berets training mountain-tribe irregulars to operate against North Viet-

namese forces, to Navy SEALs (Sea, Air, and Land teams) protecting ships in Cam Ranh Bay against swimmers attempting to fasten limpet mines to them, to Army and Marine long-range patrols in Laos to scout the North Vietnamese activity along the Ho Chi Minh Trail (the system of roads and foot trails through the rain forest), to Air Force conversion of transport aircraft into gunships to help defend villages against Vietcong attack and to attack truck movement down the trails.

Vietnam also reinforced understanding of the strengths and limitations of tactical air support designed to stop enemy movement of troops and supplies. In Italy in World War II, Operation Strangle showed that air attacks could not stop German forces from resupplying troops along the battle front. However, they could slow troop movements enough that Field Marshal Albert Kesselring, the German commander, could not move reinforcements to mount effective resistance against Allied assaults on his line of defense south of Rome. The second Operation Strangle, in Korea, did not stop support of Korean and Chinese forces on the battle front as intended, but it did force them to move and furnish supplies only at night at significant cost to their battle effort. In Vietnam, all the bombing of North Vietnamese supply routes through their own country and through Laos did not stop them from moving troops and supplies, but it did slow them enough that they could not capitalize on battlefield successes during a single dry-season campaign, which in effect led to a stalemate on the battlefield. We can appreciate the effect of that use of airpower by noting that when it was removed in 1974 and 1975 the North Vietnamese forces rapidly overran the southern half of South Vietnam to achieve a complete victory.

Vietnam also saw the first extensive tactical use of guided air-to-ground weapons. This usage showed that guided weapons could reduce by an order of magnitude or more the numbers of weapons needed to destroy specific targets, such as key bridges that often couldn't even be hit in aerial bombing with free-fall weapons having accuracies of 200–300 feet. Even so, it took a long time for such weaponry to be adopted unreservedly by conservative military planners. Indeed, the arguments about their value for general application are still ongoing. (Their extensive use in the Kosovo campaign will bring the arguments much closer to resolution, as we shall discuss later.)

Another military milestone passed in Southeast Asia was the first attempt to use what came to be called the "electronic battlefield," a geographically widespread array of electronic sensors, dropped from aircraft to be implanted in the soil, that gave a current picture of traffic along the Ho Chi Minh Trail supply routes through Laos. Again, conservatism in application led the Air Force to distrust the system. It therefore refused to dedicate a force of combat aircraft to strike the trucks moving along those supply trails when they were detected, thereby dissipating the value of the sensor network.[6] A similar network was deployed in and around the battlefield at Khe Sanh, where a greatly outnumbered force of Marines was besieged by the North Vietnamese army in an action reminiscent of the siege of Dien Bien Phu that effectively sealed the French loss of their war in Indochina. Here, the fire-support commanders made effective use of the sensor network to guide the air and artillery fire that contributed strongly to the North Vietnamese defeat in that months-long battle.

Additional consolidation of technological advances in the Vietnam War included the creation of worldwide communications networks that transformed military command and control, as well as transportation networks that greatly increased the responsiveness of the logistic support system. The air transportation network demonstrated the value and power of the tactical and strategic airlift forces that had been built during the period after the Korean War, accelerated by the development of jet transport aircraft. Its development has continued without interruption. The sea transportation network faltered during the Vietnam War, with the 1960s force buildup for our direct intervention stacking ships for months at a time in the harbor at Cam Ranh Bay. Container ships with electronically tracked cargo have become the rule in civilian sea transport, but the military has been slow to move in that direction. The Gulf War buildup still took six months, and it is only now that military logistics is being given enough priority to begin fully modernizing itself.

The communications network, in addition to its effectiveness in supporting the war effort, was available for rapid communications between Washington and the war zone. This facilitated management of the war from the capital and from the president's office. Presaged in President John F. Kennedy's direct contact with a destroyer commander who was intercepting a Russian ship carrying missiles to Cuba during the Cuban missile crisis, this capability can be used for good or ill effect in this period of less than all-out warfare. Like President Lyndon B. Johnson, a Commander in Chief (CINC) who sees that his political position or the fate of the nation—and the two are difficult to separate—may hinge on the outcome of a small or large military action must be sorely tempted to jump command channels and intervene. His military judgment may not always be informed as well as it should be by actual field conditions. Yet the political situation on which congressional support of some military actions will depend is unlikely to be known in detail by the field commander; in our system of civilian control of the military, those in the field should not be ex-

---

[6]The military commander of the sensor system operation told me at one point that he could only bring strikes against about 15 percent of the vehicle targets his sensors found.

pected to worry about it. But as the Gulf War illustrated, the way a war is fought now, in this age of greatly facilitated communications, will depend heavily on how the Commander in Chief and his military commanders work out their day-to-day operating relationships.

In Britain's war with Argentina over the Falkland Islands, overall command was held by Prime Minister Margaret Thatcher in her office, with no joint commander of the separate sea and land forces in the war zone. In the Gulf War, President Bush generally left the field command decisions to General Norman Schwarzkopf, but he intervened at the critical time when the events that could have increased Saddam Hussein's chances of survival or increased the chances of his deposition were unfolding.[7] Thus, we see that the dynamics of wartime command have been changed drastically by the fast-response, worldwide command and control system that emerged from the Vietnam War.

Two additional technological advances that were consolidated during the Vietnam War need mention. The first is the application of radar and infrared sensing to battlefield surveillance, together with the use of electronic navigation systems as a primary means to find and attack targets whose coordinates in a navigation grid are known. The second is the impact of medical and related technology on the human cost of the war.

---

[7] This has been an issue of great controversy. President Bush has argued that the potential loss of American lives, and the reluctance of allies, precluded an attack on the seat of government in Baghdad. From his point of view, those reasons are powerful. However, it may not have been necessary to go that far to achieve much better *political* results from the war than we did. President Bush could have given the field forces the additional day or so they wanted (as described by General Bernard Trainor and Michael Gordon in their book, *The Generals' War*) to finish the destruction of the Iraqi forces retreating from Kuwait, including divisions of the Republican Guard on which Saddam's power depended and still does. That did not require continued killing of the retreating troops, as President Bush has argued in the subsequent memoir he published with General Brent Scowcroft, *A World Transformed*. Cutting off their retreat north of Basra, as General Barry McCaffery's 24th Mechanized Division and General Binford Peay's 101st Airborne Division were poised to do, would have left them no choice but an ignominious surrender. The armed helicopters that were flown to attack rebels in southern Iraq, in defiance of an agreement with General Schwarzkopf to use them for transportation, could have been shot down. As President Bush noted in his book, "In retrospect, since the helicopters were being used offensively, not for communications [as the Iraqis had promised] . . . it might have been salutary to have rapped the Iraqis on the knuckles at their first transgression." The conditions of surrender could have been made much more humiliating for Saddam and his forces by, for example, positioning the American forces to move against Baghdad and a deception campaign that implied that they were about to do so, without actually moving there. There were indications, according to Trainor, that Saddam was prepared to gather up his family and flee to sanctuary outside Iraq as Coalition forces approached, and such a feint could have triggered his flight. All these things would likely have made it much more difficult for him to hold his position, even without an invasion of Baghdad proper.

In addition to sensing moving targets from the air, radar was used to detect incoming mortar and artillery shells and to track them back to their source to guide artillery counterbattery fire. The application of electronic image intensifiers and airborne infrared scanners, the forerunners of the forward looking infrared (FLIR) sensors that opened the battlefield to night observation during the Gulf War, allowed U.S. forces to find and observe many Vietcong and North Vietnamese encampments and troop movements by night as well as by day. That reduced the enemy's operating flexibility but did not end it; one could not observe everywhere, and the geography was of great help for concealment. Electronic navigation to targets whose coordinates were designated by the electronic sensor network was developed and used in the air attacks against the Ho Chi Minh Trail. Both of these techniques continued to advance and were used routinely in the Gulf War.

Finally, the techniques of medical evacuation of battle casualties by helicopter and by air transport to hospitals in Hawaii and the United States, together with advanced fast-response surgery techniques, helped many soldiers survive—and be effectively treated—who would have died or been much more severely crippled in earlier wars. Unfortunately, however, the treatment of disease and other dysfunctions did not fare as well. Tropical diseases, especially drug-resistant strains of malaria, were encouraged to spread. Drug addiction became a destructive illness among a large fraction of our troops. And for all participants in the war, including the hapless civilians around whom it raged, there remained the lingering low-grade but destructive effects of psychological stress; the effects of the use of chemicals such as Agent Orange, designed to defoliate likely ambush locations but severely affecting humans extensively exposed to them as well; and the widespread distribution of land mines and unexploded munitions that exact casualties from the resident civilian population to this day. More than the Korean War, the Vietnam War brought home the human costs of the kind of warfare that the Cold War seemed to spawn. Perhaps this was due to the ubiquitous presence of the news media in places that were neither battle zones nor quiet rear areas, as well as the objection to the war by the American civilian population that was being asked to fight it without believing in it.

The Gulf War saw the advance and effective application of many of the technologies and techniques that were first introduced in Vietnam. Especially important for the war itself and for future armed forces doctrine was the emergence of integrated command and control for joint and combined operations.[8] This was not new, of course; it had begun in World War II and advanced in both the major conflicts in which we had engaged since. What was new in the Gulf War was the degree of inte-

---

[8]Joint: all the U.S. Services operating together, in integrated fashion. Combined: U.S. forces operating with allied army, navy, and air forces.

gration and the speed of response of the entire system that modern technology enabled. The technology included advanced satellite and battlefield communications; the Global Positioning System (GPS) of satellite-based navigation that allowed the pinpointing of forces and of targets with accuracies of a few meters or, in specialized cases, even less; the use of computers to program the movements of forces and coordinate their actions, applied everywhere to activities such as the management of hundreds of air attack and defense sorties in close proximity and in close coordination with each other; and the use of the advanced airborne radar and other sensors to learn about enemy force dispositions and movements so that the maneuver of friendly forces could be planned and adjusted accordingly, feeding the command and control of force maneuvers with great rapidity.

This description should not be taken to imply that there are no imperfections in how the information, command, and control systems operated; there were and still are many. The point is that this war saw the first full application of modern information technology, broadly defined, in a manner whereby its operation changed the quality of warfare and created the model from which all future U.S. military force designs and operations are being planned. It is mainly this system, together with the high state of training, readiness, and esprit of the volunteer forces that emerged from the morale-shaking trauma of our Army, Navy, Marines, and Air Force in Vietnam, that have given our forces their current aura of competence, professionalism, and invincibility.

The combination of these modern means of command and control with long-range transportation for bringing a diverse and widely scattered force—including Special Forces, ships, aircraft, infantry, and supporting arms—rapidly to bear in a zone of conflict from great distances was tested in the 1989 invasion of Panama. The shock and surprise of the attack overcame any major opposition and gained control of the key resistance points within twenty-four hours. This tested the Army's doctrine of Air-Land Battle.[9] The doctrine called for using rapid movement of land forces, including infantry, armor, artillery, and air support (what the military calls "combined arms"), in any necessary and appropriate combination to suit the needs of the immediate battle, together with helicopter movement of troops and devastating firepower by the artillery and air attack, to overwhelm an opponent before he can fight back.

There are many subordinate aspects of the doctrine, which the Gulf War, obviously a far larger, more complex, and dangerous operation than the one in Panama, brought out. As demonstrated during the Gulf War, all of the following must be ac-

---

[9]Now renamed and folded into the larger doctrine for how all the armed forces will fight, as we shall see shortly.

complished in preparation for an attack on the ground and then sustained during the attack:

- To achieve surprise and gain the advantage of a superior battlefield position, our own forces must go where the enemy is weak and doesn't expect them. That was accomplished by General Schwarzkopf's broad westward-flanking movement (his "Hail Mary" maneuver) while some of his forces kept the Iraqi army occupied on its front in Kuwait; it depended critically on the fact that we had information superiority.
- Information superiority must be established. Our forces must know all there is to know about where the enemy and their own (and allied and neutral) forces are in time and space and what they are doing, and the enemy must be kept as much in the dark as possible about any of those things. This was accomplished during the air war and reinforced by continuing electronic warfare, air support to the ground war, and various psychological warfare ploys (leaflets dropped to entrenched Iraqi troops calling on them to surrender, loudspeaker appeals, deceptive maneuvers) while the war was going on.
- The opponent's air defenses have to be destroyed or else too many friendly attack aircraft, helicopters, and close air support fighters will be shot down. That was accomplished at the beginning of the air war, and reinforced as the ground war began, by a combination of Special Forces attacks on accessible early-warning radar installations, air and guided missile attacks against airfields and air control centers, and air combat that drove the Iraqi air force from the sky (using our most modern aircraft, air-to-air guided missiles, and airborne control of the fighters' movements against their opponents).
- The enemy's command and control system, which must be at the heart of its defense against and response to the offensive, must be crippled or destroyed. That was accomplished during the air war that preceded the ground war by the effective use of sea-launched Tomahawk cruise missiles and precision-guided air-to-ground weapons launched by fighter-bombers. These weapons were able to destroy command centers that had been built amid cities without subjecting the civilian population to the levels of death and destruction that such attacks had caused in earlier wars.[10]

---

[10]There was one attack on a building in downtown Baghdad that was said to cover a deeply buried command center, in which many civilians were killed because high-ranking Iraqi officers had misguidedly been sheltering their families there.

- And the enemy's will to resist must be shaken or broken, so that when the attack on the ground comes the defending troops will be more likely to run or surrender than to fight back. This, too, was accomplished during the air war; it included heavy bombardment of fortified Republican Guard positions outside the cities by B-52 bombers based on Diego Garcia, as well as many tactical air attacks on their tanks and dug-in positions.

All of these modes and sequences of attack were brought together powerfully during the Gulf War—again, not without many errors and faults, but enough to achieve many of the war's objectives and to show what would need to be done to perfect the new mode of warfare that the advanced information and weapons guidance technologies have made available. The beginning of the flanking movement was a coordinated helicopter-borne and armored movement to gain positions on the far western flank of the Iraqi army, thereby exposing the entire force to envelopment from the rear and forcing it to retreat before the secondary attack on its front. Such was the force and surprise of the attack that resistance collapsed and a full retreat began within hours of the onset of the offensive (retreat by an army that included battle-hardened divisions, that was one of the largest in the world, and that had fought for eight years in the war with Iran). The night-vision devices that had started to appear in Vietnam had reached the point where they allowed our forces to move and engage the Iraqi army with equal facility at night as well as by day, maintaining the relentless pressure on them that the new doctrine calls for and adding to the surprise and shock of their attack.

The achievement of information superiority before and during the land battle was aided immensely by the destruction of any Iraqi surveillance means. At the same time, we conducted battlefield surveillance using satellite systems, fighter aircraft with reconnaissance pods, and the AWACS and JSTARS[11] radar systems based on jet transport aircraft to carry the crews that operated the equipment. They were able to lay out in great detail where the Iraqi air and ground forces were and what they were doing (in this they were helped, of course, by the lack of any of the vegetation cover that had proven so frustrating in Vietnam). The JSTARS and other radar systems used phased array radars, which, through computer control, steer the radar beam electronically rather than by the familiar rotating dish. This kind of radar, far more effi-

---

[11]AWACS: Airborne Warning and Control System, designed to search for airborne aircraft; JSTARS: Joint Surveillance and Target Attack Radar System, designed to search for combat units moving on the ground. Both incorporate airborne command posts to enable use of the information gathered by the sensors, without delay.

cient and sensitive than the moving dish, had initially been developed by the United States and the Soviet Union for early warning of ICBM attack on their homelands. Like the night-vision sights of the tanks and the FLIRs of the attack aircraft, this represented the first large-scale use of a powerful new technology in combat.

The innovations themselves brought out problems with the capabilities that the technology made available, to be resolved, as usual, by still further technological developments (as in civilian life, the progression that humanity has embarked upon in the industrial age is endless and inescapable). With the tight timing of events and the fast pace that the new way of fighting calls for, coordination of actions by different force elements from the different Services must be what the military calls "seamless" and without errors or delays. This didn't always happen. For example, the Navy was not tied into the communications net on which computerized target information for tactical air operations was passed, so that a day's target information and assignments for naval aviation had to be prepared on paper and flown out to the carriers when they were ready.

The risk of casualties to our own forces caused by those forces' own actions—known to the military as "fratricide," always a serious risk in wartime—had grown. It was driven by the pace of battle and the lesser time available to assess the details of apparent impending confrontations between two force elements. The problem had been well known in air warfare since World War II, where, for example, hundreds of American paratroopers were killed in a mistaken attack on their aircraft formation during the invasion of Sicily and where American fighters often had trouble distinguishing German from Allied aircraft. It was being dealt with by a continuing series of technical developments in what is known as IFFN (identification of friend, foe, or neutral) for aircraft.

IFFN had been neglected for ground forces. The reason was based in reluctance to emit electronic signals that might give away the locations of allied tanks and troops. This reluctance was reinforced by the beliefs that the ground force commander would always know the locations of his forces through radio contact and that individual shooters would be able to recognize their own side's tanks and aircraft. As it turned out, different characteristics of the two sides' armored vehicles were difficult to distinguish from the air, and the ground forces were moving so fast, without taking the time to communicate (and also not wanting to give away their positions to the Iraqis by doing so), that the commanders were often not quite certain of their location at any moment. This had consequences on two levels: Some 17 percent of the American casualties in the Gulf War were caused by friendly fire; and the outcome of the war was changed because maneuvers by several of the major force elements (e.g., the U.S. VII Corps, the British 1st Armored Division, and the U.S. XVIII Airborne Corps) in the flanking attack were slowed because of uncertainty about their locations and fear that they would engage each other or outrun their support.

Lessons learned about the use of accurately guided weapons to attack targets on the ground were also complex. Antitank and antiaircraft guided missiles, which have been in the forces for decades, have always been accepted and were clearly successful in this war. The air-to-ground guided weapons and long-range surface-launched guided missiles like the Tomahawk were clearly of critical importance in defeating Iraqi air defenses and in incapacitating their command and control system—both essential contributors to the stunning successes of allied forces. Such weapons were also instrumental in severely reducing Iraq's ability to sustain a war effort by taking Baghdad's power grid and other key infrastructure elements, such as bridges across the Tigris River, out of action. They also helped destroy the Iraqi air force on the ground and contributed to the destruction of any elements of Iraq's nuclear and other mass destruction weapons facilities that we knew about. And all this was done without creating the levels of mass casualties and random destruction in the civilian population that occurred in previous wars in this century, such as the leveling of Dresden with thousands of civilian casualties in World War II. Despite these successes, which, it was pointed out, were against mainly fixed targets whose locations could be known in advance, the Services have argued that such weapons will not be useful against deployed, maneuvering forces on the battlefield. They have preferred to rely on what they call "level of effort" attacks with unguided weapons against such forces. That means they just keep coming back with so many loads of bombs, hour after hour and day after day, until the battle is over, without specifically keeping track of individual targets destroyed and the effects of their destruction on the battle.

The arguments in favor of that approach are based mainly on the high costs of the guided weapons; whereas a free-fall bomb might cost $2,000–5,000, a guided bomb or air-launched antitank guided missile costs $30,000–100,000 or more, and a long-range missile like the Tomahawk or the Army's ATACMS[12] battlefield ballistic missile costs $750,000–1.2 million. But analyses show that when the total costs of weapons delivery, including the cost of aircraft sorties to deliver the less accurate free-fall weapons in repeat attacks (because they don't destroy the targets the first time) and the cost of aircraft lost in those attacks, are taken into account, the total cost of attacks using guided weapons is less even in battlefield applications. There remain many uncertainties, however, because the potential impact of such weapons on the dynamics of engagements between armies and on logistic support requirements in the theater of operations is not well understood. Impetus to use the weapons more

---

[12]ATACMS: Army Tactical Missile System

in battlefield applications was reinforced, however, by the circumstances of the NATO air strikes in Bosnia in 1995, in Iraq in 1998, and in Serbia and Kosovo in 1999, where the protection of the civilian population from casualties was a paramount consideration. In those cases, large fractions of the weapons used were of the precision-guided variety.[13]

Although those were not true battlefields in the sense of the Gulf War, they highlighted one of the imperatives of future warfare in which the United States may engage, namely, to limit direct harm by the military operations to the civilian populations in a war zone. This has added to the growing doctrine of overwhelmingly forceful and rapid military action to defeat opposing forces. That is viewed as a key means of limiting the destruction, casualties, and costs of war on all sides, in addition to being the best means to defeat an opposing force. Today, the arguments about using precision-guided weapons in ground attack, which started during the Vietnam War, are moving toward resolution. The Services are all acquiring larger inventories of such weapons, and their use is increasingly being incorporated into the developing military doctrine, as we shall see later.

Stealth in aircraft design was another technological advance of proven value during the Gulf War. There were, and continue to be, many arguments about whether stealthy aircraft are worth their significant additional cost. The fact, however, was that the combination of stealthy aircraft that could not be detected by radar, operating at night and delivering precision-guided weapons against well-defended targets, proved extremely effective in achieving the necessary information superiority with no losses and in shattering the Iraqi air defenses and command and control system. This performance was repeated in the bombing of Serbia. (This result is judged independently of other actions in that conflict, air and ground, that affected the strategic outcome; the point is that what was said to be a formidable air-defense system was taken down in short order by stealthy aircraft and missiles. One Stealth fighter was lost due to poor management and execution of the attack tactics.) All new aircraft designs, in the United States, Europe, Russia, and elsewhere, now include stealth characteristics. The United States has made the most serious commitment to the use of the technology, applying it to ships and helicopters as well as to fixed-wing combat aircraft, in the firm belief that it will make the added cost worthwhile by severely reducing opponents' ability to shoot at those systems effectively. We have also, it should be noted, undertaken extensive research and develop-

---

[13]It is worth noting that the individual weapon costs and arguments about the extent of need for them led to levels of purchase that created significant shortages in the intense use demanded by conditions in Kosovo and Serbia in 1999.

ment programs to counter others' use of the technology and to protect our own long lead in applying it.

Finally, we had been, before the Gulf War, watching the proliferation of ballistic missiles for attacking battlefield forces and tactical targets for many years. Such missiles were in American and Soviet inventories through most of the Cold War, reaching increasingly refined states of design and capability. Before the Gulf War, it was well known that the technology was spreading to many other countries, such as Iraq, Iran, Syria, North Korea, India, China, Pakistan, and others—more than fifteen countries all told at that time. And Iran and Iraq had exchanged missile strikes during their war in the 1980s. So their use by Iraq should have come as no surprise. The missiles the Iraqis used were SCUDs of Soviet design, based on early technology and having poor accuracy. The main military threat they posed was their potential use to deliver nuclear, chemical, or biological weapons, and this remains the main concern in our observation of their continued proliferation. It turned out, however, that Iraq's use of the weapons, against both U.S. forces and the Israeli homeland, had large and unanticipated political effects and forced us to face practical technological problems that we have yet to solve.

Simply put, we were unable to defend against them. The Iraqis used a very effective "shoot and scoot" tactic that drained air resources from the main war effort, and our response time was too slow to destroy many of their mobile launchers, if any. The Patriot air-defense missile, adapted to intercept ballistic missiles, was found in postwar analyses to have been only meagerly effective, although it was helpful politically in providing a veneer of defense that helped us feel we were doing something and that helped us persuade Israel not to enter the war against Iraq. The exchanges gave impetus to our current programs to develop defenses against tactical missiles and, by extension, as we observe the increasing range of such missiles that are being developed by countries such as North Korea, Iran, and India, to our concerns about national missile defense. Efforts by all the Services and the Ballistic Missile Defense Organization that was established as a result of President Reagan's Star Wars initiative are included.

Among our concerns in developing defenses against ballistic missiles is the perceived need to provide such protection to allies along the Eurasian periphery, from the NATO countries to Israel (which is developing its own missile defense system, with our help), South Korea, and Japan. Even though the threatening missiles are called "tactical," as distinct from "strategic," these are U.S.-centered definitions.[14] If the missiles can carry weapons of mass destruction, and if they can hit the cities of our allies and their armed forces in their countries, the missiles have strategic purposes and capabilities. Then the only distinguishing characteristics among the differ-

---

[14]For the reasons about to be given, the term "tactical" is giving way to the more descriptive term "theater."

ent kinds of missiles are their range and the speed of their warheads as they reenter the atmosphere from increasingly longer range (this affects the ability and cost to intercept those warheads). The strategic-tactical (or theater) differentiation is being preserved, however, with specific agreed speed boundaries, because it is relevant to Russian adherence to the Anti-Ballistic Missile (ABM) Treaty and other strategic arms control treaties we have with them. We care about that, or should care, because they do have the numerous nuclear warheads that make large inventories of the missiles exceedingly dangerous.

Thus we see that the Gulf War really did usher in a new age of military technology and the kind of warfare it enables or requires between organized armed forces. (We must note that last-mentioned restriction in scope, because, as we saw in Chapter 3, there are now many additional kinds of warfare to be seriously concerned about in addition to warfare between organized armed forces.) With this review of how military technology has progressed and affected military operations since World War II, we are now in a position to explore where our armed forces stand today and where they are headed.

THE ARMED FORCES TODAY AND TOMORROW

Organization and Doctrine

The basic form of the post–World War II military establishment was set by the National Security Act of 1947, which established the Defense Department and the Joint Chiefs of Staff (JCS). The JCS, under a separate Chairman appointed by the president and approved by the Senate, are also the military leaders (distinct from the civilian leaders, the Service Secretaries) of the military Services—the Army, Navy, Air Force, and Marines—who have the responsibility to design, train, and equip the armed forces. The forces actually go into the field under command of regional CINCs of joint forces,[15] a command system that emerged from World War II.

---

[15]The regional joint commands are Joint Forces Command (formerly Atlantic Command), which also oversees joint training and doctrine activities in the United States; Pacific Command; European Command; Central Command, for the Mideast, South Asia and parts of Africa; Southern Command, for the Caribbean and Latin America. The Joint Forces Commander in Chief also functions as the Atlantic Commander for NATO. Commander, European Command is also the Supreme Allied Commander of NATO forces in Europe and the Mediterranean. There are also the Strategic Command, responsible for all the Services' strategic nuclear forces; the Space Command, for defending our spacecraft (such as observation, communication and navigation satellites) against attack, as well as any other warfare that might develop in space; the North American Aerospace Defense Command; Transportation Command for sealift and airlift; and the Special Operations Command that is discussed elsewhere.

This system was put in place to give a degree of centralized focus to the activities of the different Services by having an overall secretary rather than having the military establishment run by the separate and independent Secretaries of War and the Navy who carried us through World War II. It also established the Air Force as a separate service and recognized that the Marines had become more than simply an adjunct to the Navy carried over from sailing days to fight off boarders. The Services were expected to coordinate their activities under the guidance of the JCS Chairman, who was also designated the chief military adviser to the Secretary of Defense and the president. But the organization was deliberately kept rather diffuse as a means of guarding against what was considered a greater danger than its resulting complexity, namely, the danger that a militaristic and runaway general staff in the Prussian model would pose to the safety and security of the nation.

This organizational system was found, through the experiences of the Cold War, to be too loose to make the most effective use of the resources—both physical and human—allocated to defense of the nation. The coordinating function of the JCS also became a means for horse-trading and back-scratching to support each others' favorite systems while they fought each other through the Secretary of Defense and Congress for resources. This led to a roughly even division of the available defense budgets regardless of where the real needs may have been while the ability of the various Service systems to operate with each other in the field lagged. For example, in Vietnam the Navy and Air Force could not track each others' beacons that gave the positions of downed pilots. In another example, until recently the Air Force's AWACS could not send information to the Navy in the appropriate time about attack aircraft that might be crossing a coast to attack a carrier battle group, and the Navy's airborne early-warning system could not see the attackers over land. In several cases the Services could not even use each others' weapons for tactical aviation and artillery, nor could they support each other logistically. In addition, the CINCs were faced with the problem that they had to adapt forces to working with each other in the field while they had little say over how those individual forces would be constituted and equipped to meet the conditions they would face in any CINC's theater of operations. Needless to say, this system was found over the years to have generated many inefficiencies and distortions of effective military operations. The result could be seen in wasteful operations, extended more than necessary, and in needless casualties during those operations.

More importantly, the strategic orientation, the technical capability, and the doctrine of the armed forces were running ahead of the ability of this organizational arrangement to lead and support them. This meant that the highly coordinated and fast-moving operations that were visualized in the air-land battle would be seriously inhibited. The Marines, the Navy, and the Air Force would also have difficulty in working together to effect a landing and establish a base of operations at some location outside the "prepared battlefield" of NATO. The result was evident in the Operation Desert Shield buildup to Operation Desert Storm, a part of the Gulf War less publicized than the spectacular battlefield victories: six months of preparation for four days of combined arms combat (or four months, if one counts the opening air war). A more astute opponent would not have waited for that preparation to take place; if he had attacked the Arabian base area earlier, the outcome could have been very different. In addition, even with its ultimate success, the logistic buildup was terribly wasteful because the machinery to track and position the supplies was not in place, even though the technical capability had long been developed in the civilian world.

In recognition of such growing problems as the Cold War was drawing to a close, Congress passed the Defense Reorganization Act in 1986. By then, the country had become used to the organization, and the memories and fears of the German general staff model had faded. The Defense Reorganization Act gave more authority for reviewing and specifying military requirements and developing military doctrine to the JCS Chairman and provided for a Vice Chairman to work with the Services on these issues. It gave more power to the CINCs, requiring that they review and agree with the expression of requirements for military systems through the JCS command channel before they became operative as Service plans.[16]

General Colin Powell was the first JCS Chairman to attempt to come to grips with the new approach, but as in all matters of government it took time to absorb the significance of the change and, especially, to change ingrained attitudes to the point where it could begin to be implemented. The most recent progress leading to current military doctrine was made under General Powell's successor, General John Shalikashvili, and his vice Chairman, Admiral William Owens. They put in place a system for review of Service-specified military system requirements by the CINCs, the Joint Staff, and the JCS and for specifying how joint forces would be constituted and would operate; this began to form the model for the U.S. armed forces of the future. It linked with the streamlining in the way military requirements had been specified and the systems procured that had been taking place through congressional and executive branch collaboration throughout the 1980s.

---

[16]We must note at this point that the term "requirement" in this context has taken on a highly specialized meaning. It refers to a detailed statement describing a military system, including physical dimensions and specifications, and operational characteristics such as the speed, range, weapon-carrying capacity, and maintenance man-hours per flying hour of airplanes, as well as the accuracy of the system's weapons. These statements are meant to be adhered to rigorously, so that some of the specifications or operational characteristics, if not carefully thought out, can become important cost-drivers without contributing much to overall system performance. For this reason, military system acquisition in recent years has come to include cost targets along with performance as a system requirement, and the acquisition executives have been given the freedom to adjust performance characteristics to meet cost targets and thereby to achieve "adequate" performance without excessively driving cost.

The consolidation and demonstration in the Gulf War of Cold War–derived military technical capabilities, together with the new modes of operation and command and control of forces enabled by modern space-based communications, navigation, observation, and other information technologies—and the evolving military organizations to match—constitute what has come to be called the "revolution in military affairs." Like all but the most violent political revolutions, this one has, as the saying goes, "sneaked up on us." Gradual changes in specific technologies and capabilities for specific purposes in individual areas gradually change how things are done. They interact and consolidate, and the very consolidation engenders further change. Usually, the change is slow enough that we hardly notice. Then one day we look back and realize that the change has been revolutionary in comparison with what went before. And thus it is with the much heralded revolution in military affairs.[17] The stage is thus now set to implement fully the technology-driven change in U.S. military doctrine that has emerged during and after the last years of the Cold War.

The importance of doctrine—the "fundamental principles by which the military forces . . . guide their actions in support of national objectives," in the JCS definition—as a driver of the way the armed forces are used, and therefore of their effectiveness in supporting national strategy, cannot be overstated. The defeat of France in 1940 provides a profound modern example of the impact that doctrine can have when forces on both sides of a conflict have the same technology at their disposal.

Britain invented the tank in 1917. Its importance in defeating the effect of machine guns and carrying a mobile artillery piece across the battlefield was amply demonstrated in the subsequent battles of World War I, although the use of tanks in the war was not extensive enough to have a strategic effect (i.e., they didn't turn the tide in the war). After that war, the British and French armed forces developed the doctrine that tanks would be used in support of infantry, which, in concert with artillery, would still carry the battle. Together with that, their doctrine for the use of tactical aviation relegated it to deep attacks behind enemy lines. In other words, the new technologies were not fully integrated with the other forces in British and French doctrine but were relegated to supporting roles, whereas success in attack would continue to depend on how fast infantry could walk and on how vulnerable they were to artillery and aerial bombardment.

The Germans, in contrast, made armor and aviation integral parts of the advancing forces. They carried the brunt of the initial battle in concert with each other—aviation bombing opposing forces to disrupt them, then attack by armored forma-

---

[17]We must note that the term "revolution in military affairs," currently in common use among American military theorists, was first used in a Soviet military publication in 1973. In Soviet usage, it referred not only to the absorption of modern technology by the armed forces and that technology's implications for how the armed forces operated but also to the integrated use of conventional, chemical, and nuclear weapons to overwhelm battlefield resistance rapidly and decisively.

tions to destroy them—and cleared the way for the infantry to follow and occupy the ground. The result was the blitzkrieg led by armored divisions with close support by tactical air, which changed the nature of ground warfare.

Similarly profound differences drove naval and air warfare. American and British naval warfare doctrine at the beginning of World War II was still based on the use of the battleship, a carryover from the days of sail and the ship of the line. The Japanese based their naval warfare doctrine on the new technology, the airplane, with the result that what we had, again, viewed as a supporting arm became the nucleus of a new way of fighting wars at sea.

In aviation, Britain and Germany relied on a nighttime bombing doctrine to ensure the safety of their lightly armed bomber forces during strategic air attacks, whereas the U.S. armed its bomber force—mainly B-17 Flying Fortresses—heavily and attacked Germany during the day. Not only was the bombing more effective; the bombers, with their six machine gun turrets, helped to defeat the defending fighters of the Luftwaffe more rapidly.

In the tactical aviation branch, the doctrinal argument about whether tactical aviation should be used for close support of troops or to attack the enemy deep in the rear began during World War II and has continued since. Clearly, the U.S. armed forces do both, but even now, though the Air Force has fully accepted the necessity and responsibility for close air support, the preponderance of its effort and expenditure in tactical attack aviation goes to deep attack. This has led the Army to devise close support tactics using armed helicopters, which were needed to escort troop-carrying helicopters in any case. The Marines solved a similar problem with the Navy by acquiring tactical aviation that is specifically designed to provide close support from forward airfields—the AV-8B Harrier, derived from the British design for a fixed-wing aircraft capable of vertical takeoff and landing—and closely integrating their ground-air team (in the Marine Air-Ground Task Force). Thus Marine aviation provides mainly close air support while Naval aviation performs most of the deep attack.

Finally, we should note the pernicious effects of faulty doctrine that helped prolong the Vietnam War, increasing loss of life for all sides and leading ultimately to our defeat there. Seen in retrospect, one major problem was confusion over the idea that a "limited" war for us necessarily entailed limited means within a war's limited objectives. Although it was appropriate to limit the war's objectives to forcing the North Vietnamese to give up their intent to incorporate the South into a single communist Vietnam, we did not make best use of the military means at our disposal to enforce our objective against their powerful will to make unification on their terms happen. For example, we limited our air attacks in strength and in the targets they engaged. It can be speculated that if the North had been subjected to the kind of air campaign that was visited on Iraq, its ability to pursue the war would have been severely hampered. Of course, our ability to do that technically, without vastly increasing the human cost of the campaign in North Vietnamese civilian casualties and suffering, was more limited then than it was in the Gulf War, illustrating again the mutual interdependence of military doctrine and military technology.

Another doctrinal error emerged from a misinterpretation of the significance of the Vietcong's and North Vietnamese use of guerrilla tactics, fighting from ambush and melting away when directly confronted. Our doctrine said that to defeat the supposed guerrillas we had only to inflict heavy casualties on them without holding the territory on which they were defeated in any specific battle. This was based on the premise that as guerrillas they had no territorial base that could be invaded and held; they were assumed to form groups that appeared and disappeared in the general population. This meant that we rarely took them seriously enough as an organized force. That force was indeed building a territorial base, by inducement and coercion, in the villages of South Vietnam, and in combat they used ambush tactics that were ideally suited to their terrain and their numerical and technical inferiority to U.S., allied, and South Vietnamese forces. They were thus able to call the tune on when engagements took place and to manage battle casualties enough to continue engaging us under conditions that were disadvantageous to us. Even though they lost most of the battles, the fact that they kept fighting was, for them, a victory in showing that they were not defeated as the doctrine said they should be. Then the American public, when it realized that many casualties were being suffered to take remote hills and valleys that were subsequently given up to the enemy by our withdrawal under this doctrine was not willing to accept the human cost of the doctrine as an American imperative. The 1969 evacuation of Hamburger Hill in the mountains of central Vietnam after a fierce and costly battle to take it was a prime example. Thus the doctrine contributed to the public's disaffection with the conduct of the war and ultimately led to the defeat of our armed forces—not on the battlefield but on the political front at home.

The consequences for the armed forces were severe. The Army was a demoralized force after Vietnam, with low morale and a widespread drug problem. The Air Force and the Navy found themselves with worn-out equipment and systems and few resources for renewal, yet facing a powerful Soviet opposition in Europe and increasing technological strength on the part of our European allies. At the same time, President Richard Nixon had, finally, to recognize that the draft that had been instituted at a time of national peril had become a liability in the context of a war with limited objectives to which a large fraction of the public had taken exception. The time was therefore ripe for renewal. And renewal took place, slowly and painfully, but inexorably.

The draft was eliminated, and the resulting all-volunteer armed forces were changed from a citizen army into a largely professional fighting force. Attention was given to strategy in the use of the armed forces (discussed below), and the manuals that guide the training and operation of the forces were rewritten to account for the lessons of the war. Specifically, the distinction was made between limitation of a war's objectives and the means by which they are achieved. The criteria for the use of military force in furtherance of national objectives were then reformulated to call for use of overwhelming force to achieve explicitly specified military objectives quickly, in place of the fuzzily stated objectives and the gradualism that had characterized Vietnam (and even Korea before it). Training was enhanced and modernized and revised to include more simulated and actual field exercises for realism ("train as you will fight" became the motto). A new generation of tanks, helicopters, ships, and tactical aircraft was acquired. Systems research and development was increased to fully exploit the new technology that had begun to emerge during the Vietnam War, including especially the improvements in weapon guidance, the acquisition of combat information, and the beginnings of the advances in computers, software, and communications that led to today's information revolution. Reforms in systems acquisition were gradually adopted, to become ratified by the 1986 Defense Reorganization Act. And doctrine was changed to match both the new outlook on the use of the armed forces and the capabilities that new military technology was making available.

Vietnam aside, the primary driver of U.S. military doctrine between 1945 and 1991 was the need to figure out a way for NATO's conventional forces to overcome a possible onslaught by vastly superior conventional forces of a Warsaw Pact led by a militant Soviet Union.[18] Soviet doctrine called for an attack by armored forces organized into several tank and mechanized armies, following a massive air strike to disable NATO's air forces. Their basic doctrine and plan remained unchanged for the length of the Cold War, although many details changed as their own military capability and technology improved and as they saw NATO's responses to their plans. In this they were building on the techniques developed in World War II; indeed, they were believed to have copied their doctrine from Barbarossa, the original Nazi plan for invading eastern Poland and Russia that defeated and captured vast Soviet armies. Such an attack has never been withstood; even the Soviet defense of the

---

[18]The adjective "conventional" is critically important here. NATO's strategy always recognized that the Warsaw Pact armies would likely be significantly larger than NATO's and that in the circumstances of a Soviet (or Warsaw Pact) attack NATO armies might not be able to hold out indefinitely. Strategy called for resort to nuclear weapons when NATO's conventional forces could no longer stem the attack. As it finally evolved under the leadership of General Andrew Goodpaster, NATO's military commander for longer than five years during the 1970s, the nuclear strategy was based on the idea of "selective release," in which weapons might be used sparingly against field forces at critical points to stop their advance. Escalation to more general exchanges of nuclear weapons against warmaking capability and population centers would result only from Soviet response in kind after the first use by NATO (and, of course, NATO would respond in kind to a first use by the Soviet Union). The problem for the conventional forces' defense was to create a battlefield situation in which the possible use of nuclear weapons would be deferred as long as possible, preferably indefinitely. But the sequence of conventional defense, followed by release of nuclear weapons in the theater of war and backed up by the United States' strategic nuclear deterrent, was and remained an inherent part of NATO's deterrent strategy during the entire Cold War.

Kursk Salient in 1943, when they had more powerful forces and perfect intelligence, was penetrated by a relatively weak German attack. And we know about the near-success of greatly weakened German forces in the Battle of the Bulge in France during winter 1944.

In NATO's case the problem was made more difficult by a defensive strategy that gave the initiative for a first strike to the Soviets, as well as by the political impossibility of granting any degree of penetration of NATO territory. Because all of the territory of our German ally was on the frontline, the defense had to work without maneuvering to trade space for time—an unworkable military strategy. In NATO doctrine the fallback in case NATO's forward defenses were significantly penetrated by an attack with conventional forces was to go nuclear against the Soviet armies. Essentially, that was an unacceptable alternative because it would have unleashed a tactical nuclear war within Germany or a strategic nuclear war involving all of NATO, including the United States. The current U.S. doctrine of bringing large ground and tactical air forces to the war zone rapidly over intercontinental distances, followed by fast-paced, overwhelming ground attacks in concert with massive air support—all concentrated at critical points on the battlefield and in the enemy's rear—grew from the need to solve this military dilemma.

Today, the lessons of the Gulf War have been combined with the imperatives of a new international threat structure and new technological capabilities to make up a different set of doctrines of warfare. Without a Cold War threat to our survival, the armed forces have been reduced in size, and they have been turned to protecting our diverse interests on the international scene. With the shrinking of our overseas base structure and constraints on our use of the bases that we do occupy, we are designing the armed forces to undertake expeditionary warfare, that is, warfare in which a base has to be established in the area of conflict and the forces built up from very low initial levels. The Navy and Marines would have the responsibility for establishing a base where one does not exist, by amphibious and airmobile Marine (or Army, as in Haiti) landings from the fleet if necessary. Larger forces would be built up after the amphibious landings or simultaneously with them if the 82nd Airborne Division can be flown in and supported. The people for the Army's heavier forces and Air Force tactical aviation would also be flown in, and the ground forces' heavy equipment would be brought up by sea by the loaded, prepositioned logistic ships stationed at Diego Garcia in the Indian Ocean and possibly at other locations around the world. This approach is derived from the model of the Cold War NATO plan, in which major U.S. equipment was prepositioned in Europe so that American troops and tactical aircraft could be flown in and rapidly equipped for battle. The concept has now been extended to the entire world, or at least the parts of it where we think we may have to undertake military action.

In addition to their reduction in size, the roles and the forms of the Services have changed markedly, both in response to the different strategic needs of the post–Cold War world and in response to the imperative to do what they have to do with much less money at their disposal. In response to this need, the Army is emphasizing lighter divisions and airmobile operations, with heavy armored divisions receiving less emphasis. The general-purpose Air Force is reorganizing around the expeditionary warfare concept. A number of Expeditionary Air Forces, each one able to deploy rapidly and designed to stay in a theater of operations for ninety days, will include aviation units of all kinds from Special Air Forces through tactical fighters and attack aircraft to heavy bombers designed to deliver battlefield weapons. (The reasons for limiting deployment time are connected with personnel problems that we will examine later.)

The Navy has turned its attention from the deep-ocean combat that concerned it during the years of the Soviet threat to warfare along the continental littoral. This encompasses the coastal regions of areas where American forces may have to go into action, stretching from the sea to 100–200 miles inland from the coast for action by the Marines, then as far inland as the Navy's aircraft and missiles can reach. Although retaining its mission of protecting our freedom of the seas and the commerce on them, the Navy is being designed as a force that can establish a lasting presence offshore from an area in crisis, from which the Marines can carry out their broadening mission. The Marines are transforming themselves into a rapid-response strike force that can move deep inland (100–200 miles) while being supported with firepower and logistics from the fleet, without the need to build a big base, including months of supply, on the shore.

Preceding operations by any of the forces just sketched, or operating independently of them in some cases, are the Special Operations Forces. These forces, comprising (in nonofficial terminology) the Army Green Berets, the Air Force Special Air Warriors, and the Navy SEALs, are designed to enter enemy territory stealthily and carry out missions as varied as disrupting transportation and communications, destroying air defenses and other critical installations, and training indigenous guerrilla fighters. They might also operate in the open to train counterguerrilla forces, a mission that has been controversial in places like El Salvador.

All the forces just described are the general-purpose forces, distinct from the strategic forces. The latter include ICBMs, long-range bombers, and SLBM submarines, that still carry out the deterrence mission to prevent or strike back at any attack on the U.S. homeland. Finally, the reserve forces, since they will in general not have the modern equipment and extensive training of the active Army, Navy, and Air Force, are being considered increasingly for supporting roles to free up frontline forces for combat rather than for direct augmentation of those forces at the beginning of a conflict.

All of these forces, when in action, are to be embedded in an information network intended to give them the kind of information superiority that will enable them to know what their potential or actual opposition is doing or is capable of doing while denying that opposition the same kind of information. The information-gathering systems for this network and the communications systems to tie it together will operate under the overall command and control of the regional CINCs, with elements reaching into the individual Service units in the field. The elements may be furnished by space systems fielded and operated by national agencies such as the National Reconnaissance Office, by the Air Force in the form of its AWACS and JSTARS aircraft, by the Navy with its long range maritime patrol aircraft, by any of the Services' tactical surveillance, reconnaissance, and targeting systems, and even by commercial communications systems when they are needed to furnish communications capacity not in the military forces' own equipment. In addition to the CINCs and headquarters in the Pentagon and the civilian agencies, all the military forces, of whatever Service, are expected to have computing equipment and target analysis centers adequate to handle the information and do the planning and the targeting that go with the rapid and far-flung military operations the system implies.

All this evolution has been taking place painfully, through successive cycles of review. There was General Colin Powell's 1991–1992 review leading to a Base Force concept; Secretary of Defense Les Aspin's "Bottom Up Review" undertaken immediately after he became Secretary of Defense in 1993; the subsequent Quadrennial Defense Review required by Congress in 1996, carried out by Secretary William Perry and then Secretary William Cohen and published in 1997; and the 1997 report of the National Defense Panel set up by Congress to review the Quadrennial Defense Review. All this activity, undergirded by the powers granted to the JCS and the CINCs under the 1986 Defense Reorganization Act, culminated in the 1997 issuance by General John Shalikashvili, then Chairman of the JCS, of a document entitled *Joint Vision 2010.* The document describes a new concept of operation for the armed forces based on the new strategic conditions and the new technologies available. The Services have all issued similar related documents.

Under this new concept, even though the armed forces are smaller, they must be ready and able to undertake missions in many more, widely scattered parts of the world than might have been necessary during the Cold War. They will be enabled to do this by the strength-multiplying effects of modern military technology. The technology we have been describing, including especially that having to do with sensors, computers, communications, weapons guidance, aviation, and space, has made it possible for the armed forces to concentrate and use their strength rapidly from widely dispersed locations: The information tells them where and when they and their effects are needed; the weapons guidance and long-range missilery or tactical attack aviation based at sea or on land allow them to concentrate accurate fire on targets from long range; air transportation allows them to concentrate forces rapidly to move against an opponent. Under this concept, the forces' information superiority allows them to choose places and times of battle where the opponent is weak and can be disorganized and routed rapidly by surprise attack and shock action.

The genesis of this kind of operation was apparent in Panama and the Gulf War, and it is practiced routinely in military exercises designed to sustain the readiness of the forces to go into action. It is expressed in *Joint Vision 2010* as giving the forces the capability for what is called "full spectrum dominance," having four components, paraphrased in military parlance as follows:

- *Dominant maneuver.* Mass forces rapidly to outmaneuver the opponent so that he is taken by surprise and can be rapidly overwhelmed by military power where weak and at critical points essential for controlling forces (a modern analogy to Confederate cavalry leader Nathan Bedford Forrest's famous maxim: "getting thar fustest with the mostest").
- *Precision engagement.* Find and attack enemy forces and essential support with accurate firepower, at points where the results will incapacitate them quickly, from a distance or from close-up, to deny from the outset any ability to move armies and air forces in the field and to support them from the rear.
- *Full-dimensional protection.* Use all the means available, from information and electronic warfare to gaining air supremacy to the use of antiaircraft and antitank weapons, tactical ballistic missile defenses, bullet-proof vests, and all other means including information warfare to protect our own forces from attack and injury.
- *Focused logistics.* Get essential materiel and supplies—food, fuel, ammunition, repair parts, replacements for systems fatally damaged in battle—to the forces when they need it, where they need it, and with minimal waste of time and resources.

All of this is to be embedded in and supported by the information network. All of the Service components in the field are to operate together—jointly—as a unified whole and with coalition partners. Underlying it all are to be high-quality, dedicated people; innovative leadership; joint doctrine describing the details of how the forces are to operate together; joint education and training; agile organizations (i.e., organizations that adapt readily to changing conditions and technologies); and improved materiel to keep the forces as modern as possible.

Conceptually and in fact as the military Services continually reorganize and train to conform to the joint vision to which they all contributed, they and the forces in the field can be said to have met the challenge of the postwar conditions. In the Gulf War, the forces had already demonstrated that they were ready to meet these conditions, but they had much homework to do to actually arrive there. If they were to go to war again soon (as they did, on a small scale, in Bosnia, Iraq, and Kosovo), they would show progress in moving in the direction of the joint vision.[19] They are clearly not stuck in the mire of the last war, an accusation often made of military forces. There are, however, some severe problems in moving from the vision to the implementation. They occur in the cold light of reality when trying to consummate the vision in the real world of budgets and domestic politics and in the overarching national strategy that the forces have to support.

Budgets and Politics: Flies in the Ointment

One might think that since the armed forces have been shrinking to match the reduced defense budgets of the post–Cold War era the two would still be roughly in balance. The $250 billion or $270 billion (depending on whether one wants to think about the congressional budget authorization or the actual money appropriated and spent) that is allocated to defense for fiscal year 1999 is, after all, a respectable sum. However, counterintuitive as it may seem, the creation of the new armed forces visualized as *Joint Vision 2010*, or the continued transition of today's armed forces into the new vision, will require more, not less, money, at least in the early years. This occurs because, as in the civilian economy, the concepts embody major substitutions of capital for labor (in areas that we will note directly), as well as a much higher grade of labor to operate the new equipment that will be acquired. If the budget can't be increased to effect the transformation, then money will have to be found within the existing budget. It is in these areas that politics intrudes and creates part of the gap between dream and reality.

Capital Investment.   The simple fact is that much of our military equipment is getting old and out of date and is not well suited to the new kinds of military operations we foresee. This may seem a strange thing to say when the severe Soviet techni-

---

[19]In Kosovo the forces displayed much of the precision of attack called for by *Joint Vision 2010* (except for the unfortunate mistake of bombing the Chinese embassy in Belgrade), but not the speed of maneuver that would have anticipated and crushed Serbia's ability to pursue its own military aims. This failure is more attributable to the slow U.S. and alliance political decisions than to failures in military responsiveness. Political concerns also precluded a preemptive attack on Serbia's forces when they massed on Kosovo's borders before the NATO bombing campaign began, even though the intent of massed forces was obvious.

cal challenge to our security is no longer on our figurative radar screens. However, time passes and the world has not relaxed. With only a few exceptions, our current active-duty ships and aircraft are based on technology that is twenty or more years old, and many of them have been around longer than that. At the same time, new military technology is being brought into being by our friends, more than by any potential enemies, and is spreading around the world to friend and potential foe alike. And new things are needed that weren't conceived of before.

The last generation of Soviet combat aircraft that was brought into being just before the Soviet collapse has been sold in China, South and Southeast Asia, the Middle East, and North Africa. That generation of aircraft was close to ours in performance, and it is being replaced by a new generation of aircraft being designed and built in Europe—for example, the multinational Eurofighter, recently dubbed "Typhoon," and the French Rafale—and offered for sale worldwide. Although we have, as yet, the world's best air-to-air missiles for engagement at long range, there are Russian, French, British, and Israeli short-range missiles that challenge or exceed the performance of even the latest versions of our Sidewinder dogfight missile. Antiship cruise missiles of Russian, French, and Chinese designs are also being widely sold. All the new combat aircraft and antiship missiles incorporate stealth characteristics, making them harder for our antiaircraft systems to shoot down. At the same time, Russian antiaircraft missile systems developed toward the end of the Cold War and also being widely sold have incorporated counterstealth characteristics, thereby negating some of the advantage of the advanced stealth design in our own tactical aircraft. Further, our attack missile guidance systems are coming increasingly to depend on the GPS satellite navigation for accurate guidance. The system is vulnerable to jamming, and others can also make use of it to guide missiles against our own forces, so that safeguards have to be built into the next generation of the system; the safeguards must be incorporated in new GPS satellites as they are built and launched into orbit, and part of the system renewal schedule will depend on countermeasures that can be taken in the interim.

Our warships are manpower-intensive in design, and they are not outfitted for the growing combat information network as effectively as they must. They must therefore be changed. They must be outfitted with extensive instrumentation and automatic machinery to help fewer sailors operate them from the bridge rather than by swarming all over the ship, as well as to help automate damage control, which is now heavily manpower-dependent and is one of the chief obstacles to using shipboard manpower efficiently. New weapons systems will also be needed: for example, extended-range guided shells for modified naval guns, and newly designed land attack missiles and vertical launchers, all to support the Marines from the sea (remember: the Marines are to go deeper inland with lighter forces). The ships will need more up-to-date communications terminals and more elaborate combat direction centers to acquire and integrate combat information from Air Force–operated battlefield surveillance systems; and advanced antiaircraft systems that can engage stealthy attack missiles. The instrumentation and new systems would be incorporated during periodic overhauls. The refitting will be costly. New ship designs will be quite different from the old ones, incorporating the new equipment and combat systems from the start. The new ships and their weapon systems will likely be more expensive to purchase than their older counterparts, although they will be cheaper to operate during service life. However, spending current dollars to achieve future savings is a trade that Congress doesn't like to make.

Although the Army was able to get ahead of the pack in its acquisition of the best tank in the world today (the M-1 Abrams) just as the very effective Soviet tank design and production machine was grinding to a halt, it has many other weapons system and supporting equipment needs. These include lighter-weight artillery (which the Marines are also working on), new combat and support helicopters, new anti-tank weapons to replace the ones that have difficulty overcoming the last Soviet tank to be widely sold, the T-80, new battlefield missiles and targeting systems, and communications systems that accord with the growing, massive information exchange needs of the Joint Vision forces. At the same time, the Marines have just begun to acquire the V-22 Osprey tilt-rotor vertical-lift aircraft and an advanced amphibious assault vehicle, both designed to speed their ability to cross the sea-land boundary and to penetrate deeper into enemy territory on landing.

The Air Force, the Navy, and the Marines are all in process of acquiring a new generation of combat aircraft: the F-22 Raptor air-superiority fighter, which will be the most advanced in the world by a large margin when it goes into service;[20] the Navy's F/A-18 E/F Super Hornet, which will replace three types of carrier-based aircraft (the F-14 Tomcat long-range fighter, the earlier F-18 C/D Hornet multipurpose fighter, and the A-6 Avenger attack aircraft); and the Joint Strike Fighter, which, in various versions, will become the standard multipurpose fighter of the three Services. The Joint Strike Fighter will replace Air Force F-16s, older Navy F-18s, and the Marine Harrier vertical takeoff close air support attack airplanes.

---

[20]At the time of writing, the Defense Appropriations Subcommittee of the House Appropriations Committee has eliminated funding for production of the F-22 just as it was about to begin. This has appeared to be part of the balanced budget–tax reduction contest between a Congress and president of different political parties. The Senate has funded the program fully. It is difficult to imagine that Congress will abandon an investment of fifteen years and $20 billion to bring the aircraft to the production stage and in the process deal a strong blow to the Air Force's ability to sustain its uncontested position of world superiority in combat aviation, but it could happen.

As if that weren't enough, we must meet the threat posed to our forces and to allied forces and cities along the Eurasian periphery by the growing numbers of ballistic missiles capable of delivering nuclear, chemical, and biological warheads in addition to conventional high explosives. These are held and being developed by potentially hostile nations: North Korea, Iran, Syria, and probably Iraq, to mention but a few of about thirty nations undertaking such developments, excluding the United States. The Navy, Army, and Air Force are all working on antitactical (or theater) ballistic missile systems. Their work is largely not duplicative, but some of it is competitive. The different systems being developed are intended to cover different parts of the conflict spectrum in different ways. For example, the Navy system is being designed to cover large areas on land from offshore, as an extension of its AEGIS air defense system; the AEGIS extensions will also enable that system to engage stealthy antiship missiles better. The Army system in parallel development is also designed for both wide area and close-in protection, but it works according to different guidance principles from the Navy system. One missile or the other, depending on which works better, may be adopted by both Services, assuming a successful test for the Army system. The Air Force, in the meantime, is developing a powerful airborne laser weapon intended to shoot down a missile earlier in its flight than either of the other two systems will be able to do (i.e., in boost phase, while the missile is still in powered flight after launch and before it can deploy multiple chemical or biological agent bomblets or decoys to foil later stages of defense). While there will probably be fewer systems in operation after the different designs are thoroughly wrung out, there is still not enough technical information to be able to make the choice; as we noted earlier, the development efforts are expensive.

Finally, the long-range airlift fleet and the sea transport fleet are also becoming obsolete and are in various stages of replacement. The Air Force's C-141 Starlifter transports are wearing out and too small to carry many of today's combat loads. The largest transport, the C-5, is of 1960s vintage. The replacement aircraft are being acquired, in the form of the C-17 transport, but the oceangoing logistic transports are lagging. The Navy is acquiring one new type of amphibious landing ship, but the ships that hold the prepositioned Army and Marine Corps equipment for deployment in emergency are not suited to the rapid off-loading operations that will be required under the new fast-action strategy and doctrine. So far, acquiring new, suitably designed transport and prepositioning ships are beyond military budget capacity, even though the concepts are accepted.

And none of this addresses major augmentations of the information matrix in which all the operating forces are to be embedded. That will require more surveillance systems, on land, on and under the sea, in the air, and in space. It will require more robust communications systems that can mesh with the explosively expanding commercial systems. And it will require vastly increased computing power at all the command levels. Although there are many programs under way to meet these needs, the final information network design has not yet emerged, nor has its total cost been estimated.

Reequipment of the armed forces—"recapitalization" is the word the military uses—will require some $60 billion per year of new systems procurement money, after some $35 billion in research and development to create the systems. Typically, in the 1990s, the procurement budgets have been on the order of $40–50 billion. Other claims on the budget, which have preempted the modernization of the armed forces, include maintaining their readiness to move into combat in case of a crisis and a continuing stream of ongoing operations that, in the absence of specific funding that Congress has shown great reluctance to appropriate, drains funds away from the core business of building the armed forces and keeping them modern enough to meet the exigencies of world events.

"Readiness" is a term much used but little explained. It includes continual training of personnel, individually and then in units, while simulating combat-related activities. It includes field exercises that vary from test-firings of weapons, including tank cannons and expensive missiles, to large-scale exercises that may involve thousands of troops, hundreds of aircraft, and dozens of ships. There must be regular training flights by combat and transport pilots and steaming at sea by ships, to keep crews' proficiency at peak performance if combat is necessary. At least once during every tour of duty, the people in a tank unit should have undertaken a mock combat exercise at the National Training Center in the California desert to learn how units operate in the field under conditions where "Murphy" rules.

Training and exercises take up the time of personnel—from foot soldiers and airmen to top commanders. They use live ammunition, including missiles costing hundreds of thousands of dollars, so that the crews who use them can sharpen their own training and verify the systems' performance and their reliability. In doing so, they avoid having to train under fire and to learn critical system characteristics while their lives are at stake. The flying and steaming and road marches use fuel and impose wear and tear on the machines—artillery, tanks, ships, aircraft—that make up the armed forces' core capability. The ensuing maintenance and overhaul is also an integral part of the cost of maintaining readiness.

Real operations—deployments to Somalia and Bosnia, the Haiti landing, patrolling the air and ground in the former Yugoslavia, standing ready to meet one of Saddam Hussein's threatened breakouts—cannot substitute for the ordered activity that contributes to the readiness of the armed forces. These deployments keep soldiers, sailors, and airmen at duty stations associated with weapons and support systems for extended periods. They don't have a chance for training in all the complex actions involved in multiforce joint combat when they are patrolling a border or no-fly zone or steaming off some shore looking for smugglers. Ideally, units would be assigned to such operations for specified periods, then be replaced by other units so that they could resume their readiness training. However, the armed forces are no longer big enough to be able to function that way. Navy ships, for example, are now deployed on active operations more than half the time, as compared with 40 percent or less during the Cold War years. The costs involved in the deployments, even if there is no combat—soldiers, sailors, and airmen must still be paid; ships, tanks, trucks, and aircraft still use fuel and wear enough to require maintenance—must be taken from other defense expenditures, and those shifts usually reduce the procurement budget. Thus, shrinking armed forces, together with the nonshrinking, or even escalating, demands of current actions and maintaining readiness all work against making and keeping the armed forces as modern as they might be—and as they must be.

People. In addition to being more effective than current machines of war, new military systems are designed to include extensive instrumentation and automation so as to work with fewer people. As in the civilian economy, there are many components to this trend.

One is the fact that automatic machinery, controlled by microprocessors and computers, can work more effectively than people can in many situations. This doesn't mean preempting human decision processes, creating an army of automata, or that computers are smarter than the people in the armed forces. It means that tasks requiring remote sensing, precise measurement, very rapid correlation of extensive data from many sources, and very rapid reaction times can be performed much more effectively by instruments, computers, and microprocessors, with human supervision, than they can be performed by people alone. In other words, the machines help the people do their jobs better, and the peoples' jobs change to incorporate the help that the machines give them.

Second is the desire to expose as few people as possible to the risks of combat. As we have noted previously, this country is extremely sensitive to the level of combat casualties, especially in situations of less than vital interest to the survival of the nation.

Third is the fact that people are costly. About half of the defense budget is used to support people—for pay and allowances, family housing, training activities, medical care, and much else. In addition, if one looks at the distribution of costs over the long term (the so-called life-cycle costs of military systems), one finds that the initial acquisition cost, high as it might seem for many systems, is dwarfed by the operation and maintenance cost of the systems over their lifetime of twenty to forty years. Typically, for major platforms, the life-cycle cost is on the order of two to three times the initial acquisition cost. Most of the excess is made up of personnel costs. This includes personnel costs for periodic overhauling and modernization of systems, as well as costs for operations and maintenance, some 70 percent of which supports the people doing the operating and maintaining. Thus, if the Services need money to pay for recapitalization within an essentially static or decreasing defense budget, a natural place to seek it is in the reduction of personnel costs. It follows that systems requiring fewer people will make up for the decrement by relying more on automation and all its attributes.

Fourth, there is the political issue that Congress, reflecting the popular will, keeps reducing the authorized number of people in the armed forces. Without an immediate threat to national survival, with many other claims on federal funds, and with intense political pressures at all levels to reduce taxes, funding for the armed forces makes an attractive source from which to draw funds needed elsewhere. One way to do that without seeming to short-change the armed forces is to reduce authorized personnel.

All these reasons, in addition to the demands of modern combat machinery, make for the same substitutions of capital for labor that we have been experiencing in the civilian economy. The problem is that the substitutions involve ever more complex machinery that, although rendered easier to use by the associated instrumentation and computer-based controls, requires a greater depth of understanding and skill on the part of the user. Think about it as analogous to using your personal computer. Some people can simply turn it on and type away, or log on, or e-mail. But to take advantage of its full capability you need extensive and varied software programs, you have to understand the complexities of the software, and you have to know how to troubleshoot the system when a glitch causes it to crash. Technical jobs in the civilian world that require the extensive and flexible use of computers and automated machinery require people with a high level of education and training. The same is true for any of the military occupational specialties associated with the operation of the new military systems—and that includes virtually all of them. Even the infantry, usually perceived as grunts with rifles, is being given ever more complex equipment—antitank and antiaircraft missiles, sensors, satellite-connected radios, and rugged laptop computers that contribute to "situational awareness" and the ability to communicate—that conveys a decisive battlefield advantage.

Given such educational and skill requirements, the volunteer armed forces are coming into increasing competition with the civilian economy for the pool of qualified people. Moreover, population projections show that, with an aging population distribution the pool of those eighteen to twenty-four will remain essentially constant over the next fifty years. In the absence of the draft, the essential elements of the civilian-military job competition become career opportunity, job satisfaction, and pay. Basic pay and allowances have to be competitive with the civilian world.

The advantages of long-term job security and continual training for increasingly complex jobs are then offset by concern for family care as soldiers, sailors, and airmen are deployed overseas for extended periods. Military people who must worry about the quality of housing, medical care, and education for their families while overseas for extended periods may not turn in their best dedicated performance in the kind of no-war, no-peace occupations in which most of them are engaged. There is, in addition, the risk to life and limb involved in military action, even in training exercises; families must be prepared for that and cared for if it results in the loss of a breadwinner.

There are two untoward results of all these changes in how military service is viewed and accepted by the civilian population. The first is that military service is viewed as a career opportunity like any other. As we noted earlier, the loss of a sense of community has taken with it a view of the nation as the ultimate community that one wants to defend. In the absence of a mortal threat to the nation, notions of patriotism take a backseat to the economic and training opportunities the career offers. This increases the demand for a civilian-style quality of life. Extended periods away from family and the risk of injury and death are viewed as reasons for dissatisfaction with the career and reasons to change it at the end of a period of enlistment, unless the compensation is deemed adequate. The second problem is that a military career can simply be seen as a stepping-stone to advancement in a civilian career. Many join the military knowing they can use their training to further their fortunes once they leave service. And indeed, education by the military has contributed important technical skills to the civilian economy: aircraft pilots, electronic technicians, and industrial managers, for example.[21] These two characteristics of the modern military career are most evident in the increased movement of Air Force and Navy pilots to civilian jobs in commercial and corporate aviation. The dissatisfactions expressed that lead to these Service separations center around the long deployments; indeed, the Air Force moved to change its entire organization and deployment strategy, in the directions described above, to try to resolve that problem.

---

[21]I talked with a sailor on a carrier who said quite frankly that he had enlisted and sought a job as a photo-interpreter in the Combat Direction Center so that he could qualify to do such work with one of the shoreside intelligence agencies and work his way through college that way. A devious route, but that was just the kind of person the Navy would want to keep. In Contrast, a high-ranking Marine officer commented to me that he would want the ordinary infantrymen in and out after one term; he doesn't favor family entanglements for such infantrymen; he wants them while they retain their fighting spirit with no personal **distractions**. Some of these infantrymen will be selected for promotion, however, starting them on a career track that will provide just such distractions. The personnel issues are far from simple, as these two anecdotes indicate.

The needs to match or even to exceed civilian incomes, to enhance the quality of life for military personnel and families, and to continually train replacements, before the training investment in those who have departed has been fully realized all increase the already high cost of military personnel. This puts increasing pressure on the military budget, reinforcing the trend to substitute capital for labor. But it should be apparent that the cycle cannot go on forever while the defense budget is constant or decreasing. Recent moves to increase the defense budget will go only part of the way toward solving these problems, as we shall see. At some point, the relative costs of equipment and people must reach a new balance.

However, achieving that balance in the most effective and efficient way is inhibited by our political system. In particular, Congress has consistently been reluctant to invest in more expensive machinery now to save money on people and maintenance downstream. At the same time, we see members complain about the escalating costs of military systems even as the costs of personnel go unnoticed and unappreciated. The reason is obvious: Voters can hold members accountable for the tax money spent in this year's budget for expensive military systems, whereas the future savings generated in reduced crew costs may not be realized during a member's time in office. Furthermore, the savings are usually not specifically identified as such because they become lost in the complexities of the huge budgets in question. For example, operations and maintenance costs are not accounted for by types of ships and aircraft but simply as a huge lump sum in a Service budget, not identified with any particular system. This congressional attitude is one of the consequences of the typically American short-term point of view that we called attention to in Chapter 4. It doesn't have to be that way; in many European countries, defense budgets are planned (and adhered to) for periods of fifteen years, more in keeping with the life cycles of military systems. In the United States, Congress has resolutely resisted the idea of even a two-year appropriation for defense to give the Services and their contractors a somewhat longer planning horizon.[22]

Bases.   There are additional constraints on military management that reduce its flexibility in comparison with management of civilian enterprises. These constraints make for waste and inefficiency in defense expenditures.

Civilian corporations can decide to stay in or leave an area, to open and close factories and office complexes, strictly according to the economics of their current situ-

---

[22]In fairness it must be pointed out, however, that the long-range view of Europeans is often accompanied by a degree of inflexibility that precludes budget adaptations to meet unexpected contingencies or to capitalize on newly appearing technological opportunities.

ations. They may try to protect communities for public relations or even humanitarian purposes, but basically the decision whether to grow, shrink, or move is theirs to make. Not so for the military.

Every military unit, of whatever Service, needs a base from which to operate. Bases use expensive real estate; they agglomerate costly services such as maintenance and provisioning for the platforms of the units assigned to them; they house the units' families and services such as food, schooling, and medical care. Because it is less expensive to consolidate bases rather than maintain scattered ones for fleets, air force wings, and ground force divisions, a structure of major bases grew during the Cold War years at strategic and economically useful locations in the United States and overseas. The economic consolidation included military schools and training grounds, and, depending on the Service, they were built close to major installations such as shipyards, airfields, maintenance depots, and the historic forts that are no longer needed to protect citizens on the frontier (the forts were on extensive government landholdings, saving a huge acquisition cost). The geographic distribution and size of the bases must be related to the size and number of units that use them. The many associated activities attract civilians to help serve the support needs—food, medicine, clothing, schools, and so forth—of the military populations, so that over time the bases become major regional economic units.

It must be obvious that when the armed forces are allowed or encouraged by the flow of world events to shrink, their bases must also shrink, in both size and number. Overseas, this has happened rapidly as our armed forces reduced the numbers of units stationed in various countries and as our strategic needs changed; overseas bases now number less than half the number that existed during the Cold War. The base structure in the continental United States is another story. With the regional economic importance of bases spread around the country, providing jobs, income from armed forces' personnel and family expenditures, and imports of materials and facilities associated with the maintenance and support of military systems, the reduction or closure of a major base is of extreme importance to the local population and therefore of importance to their representatives in Congress. Resistance to closing U.S. bases is a political given, regardless of need. And it is subject to untold horse-trading among members of Congress as to who will support whom in keeping some base open against the logic of sound military planning.

To get around this resistance and to eliminate the political horse-trading in rectifying the armed forces' infrastructure as the armed forces shrink and their needs change, Congress set up the Base Realignment and Closure system (BRAC). Under this system, the administration, including the Secretary of Defense and the Services, work out with the Congress the closing schedule of a number of bases that are not needed any longer. Congress then has agreed that the entire package will be voted on, to be accepted or rejected as a whole regardless of pain or gain to any particular congressional district or constituency. The BRAC process had gone through two cycles, with much pain to many communities. For example, the Navy bases at Charleston, South Carolina, and San Francisco, for generations considered among the mainstays of the fleet, were closed. As can be imagined, there is a great deal of background maneuvering associated with deciding which bases will be closed, and the politics, in the form of lobbying by communities and their hired representatives, acts all through the process. It doesn't take much to upset the delicate balance of economic and political forces contending for position in the process. (This is independent of the fact that most communities, when finally pressed to accept the inevitability of closure, have managed to attract or build alternative economic activities to their permanent benefit. As in every other endeavor, communities would rather rest comfortably with the status quo than scramble for uncertain replacements that may take many years to pay off.)

Unfortunately, an incident that upset the political balance occurred during the 1996 presidential campaign, when President Clinton proposed measures to mitigate the impact of planned base closures in Texas and California by promising contracts to local civilian organizations to perform some of the work that was done at the bases. As a consequence, although the last Quadrennial Defense Review and Service program reviews have called for another BRAC round of base closings, Congress has refused on the grounds that the process has been politicized. The consequences are severe. Service infrastructure costs amount to about 25 percent of the defense budget, or some $60 billion per year. A 1996 Defense Science Board study estimated that about $30 billion of that could be saved by a combination of stringent cost-cutting measures associated with new ways to manage the armed forces' procurement and logistic support activities (mainly, eliminating duplicative and inefficient procedures that grew by accretion during the Cold War years), as well as by closing unneeded bases. These are funds that have been counted on to fund the recapitalization of all the armed forces. Thus we are left in a position where the Services have been reduced faster than their infrastructure, with attendant cost-shifting from acquiring the essential "teeth" of the fighting forces to preserving a nonessential "tail" useful only for supporting forces that no longer exist.

Intelligence. Another distortion in the national security system appeared when intelligence was considered as another Cold War expenditure to be eliminated or starkly reduced when the Soviet Union collapsed. Senator Daniel Patrick Moynihan, losing patience with the fumbling that allowed the "mole" Aldrich Ames to provide critical information about our intelligence system to the Soviet Union, even proposed abolishing the Central Intelligence Agency. Although intelligence budgets have been published officially only since 1998, earlier news reports suggested that the nation's intelligence budgets, for both central and military intelligence services, were simply reduced more or less in proportion as the armed forces were reduced.

However, it remained (and remains) important to keep up with developments in Russia, Ukraine, and other former Soviet countries that still had a significant remnant of nuclear weapons capability and materials. The nature of that intelligence need changed, because control over the weapons and the materials has loosened in the collapsed Soviet and Russian economies, so that there are at once less focus and more places to search. In addition, Russia has allowed much military materiel to be sold to other nations. In the case of combat airplanes and sophisticated air defenses, they have offered them for sale; in other cases, weapons may have been sold on the black market or there may simply have been uncontrolled help on a freelance basis, as was rumored to have been the case in the test of a North Korean ballistic missile that overflew Japan. It is therefore more necessary and more difficult than before to trace such flows of military materiel, and our armed forces may run into the consequences of failure to trace them in places like Korea, the Middle East, and the Balkans. Thus, although there was a need to shift the *kind* of effort—for example, from satellite surveillance to human intelligence or old-fashioned secret spying by people on the territory of the spyee—there was no reduction in the need for a significant effort.

In addition, even though there was some intelligence effort devoted to the Third World during the Cold War, the shift in kinds and locations of conflicts affecting our security gave the intelligence agencies much more territory to cover than they had to worry about before and much more detail that they had to look for. They have had to be concerned with such things as the kinds and effectiveness of military capability NATO may meet in the Balkans, whether in antiaircraft defenses or weapons on the ground or both, and whether Serbian forces are adhering to the promises made by their leader, Slobodan Milosevic; with how the Iraqis are concealing their ballistic missile, chemical, biological, and nuclear weapons programs; with the progress of India and Pakistan in their nuclear and missile programs; whether North Korea really is able to maintain armed forces at high readiness to attack the South while their civilians are starving; whether the North Koreans are really standing down on their nuclear program, as promised, or just hiding it better; whether China really means to invade Taiwan and has the capability to do so if Taiwan does declare its independence; whether there is a chance Laurent Kabila can be overthrown by the rebellion in the Democratic Republic of the Congo, so that we can prepare our position vis-à-vis any successor government; whether Yassir Arafat can really control Hamas and the other militant Palestinian organizations that can destroy the Middle East peace we have been striving to broker, or even whether Arafat may be overthrown by one of those groups; whether Iran has really backed off from supporting terrorists, as it has claimed; and the progress of Iran's missile and possibly nuclear weapons program (and its connection with Russian help); whether Indonesia's military will stage a coup or let the country drift toward democracy; and on and on. All these questions, and more, must now be high on the agenda of the intelligence agencies, in a much more fractionated and conflict-ridden world than existed during the Cold War.

Additional information for which we must look to those agencies has to do with simple knowledge about areas of the world that our military forces may have to enter under conditions of no war, no peace. Examples have occurred in Somalia, Haiti, Liberia, and Rwanda, among others. It is the intelligence agencies who must compile information about the physical conditions in cities and countrysides, about matters of culture that can ease the way for our troops if they know how to appeal to local leaders and populations or that can generate hostility, and about local politics so that we don't get involved in losing propositions like the attempt to depose and capture local warlord Mohammed Farah Aideed in Somalia. Although the national agencies and the Services have done such intelligence-gathering for years, the effort has been small. The importance of smooth and rapidly successful operations when we enter a country, the need to keep our own casualties and local civilian casualties down, and the large political consequences of even minor failures, such as occurred in Mogadishu when a company of Army Rangers was trapped in a close-in firefight, have become so great that the intelligence-gathering and analysis must now improve greatly in quality.

It should have been obvious at the start of the new post–Cold War era that these much more diffuse and difficult intelligence tasks might require more rather than less effort and budget. There is no indication in the public record that any consideration was given to that possibility or the changed needs during the appropriation process. Yet when a surprise appears somewhere in the world, the first cry, in the media and in Congress, is to ask why there was a failure of intelligence. It is certainly true that many failures of intelligence can be traced to a mind-set that excludes the possibility of an event. For example, Stalin in 1940 did not react to ample warning of a German attack; we did not build our defenses against the very kind of attack that many of our military people thought was possible at Pearl Harbor; we did not think the Soviets could ever beat us into space; we thought Saddam Hussein would

be warned off from invading Kuwait by our ambiguous cautions; and so forth. However, there should be no excuse for not having all the facts available on which sound
intelligence judgments can be made. Denying our agencies the resources needed to
gather those facts is a consequence of the reduced intelligence budgets. Rectifying
the situation means still another increase in the resources needed for national security, just as the nation is trying to reduce those resources.

And budget isn't all, as far as the intelligence agencies are concerned. The intelligence community was severely battered during the days when Congress and the
news media were castigating it for its roles in the wars in Vietnam and then in setting
up or deposing governments in Central America and Chile, as well as in covert operations generally. The Ames affair built on the general disillusionment and disaffection with the intelligence community. The heroes of novels and movies in battling
the KGB in the early part of the Cold War became the media's and Congress's vil-
lains in its tailing-off, even as secrecy in espionage became harder to preserve. The
intelligence agencies, too, followed the trend of substituting capital for labor, as
satellites and other technical means gradually displaced intelligence-gathering by
human agents. Further blows were dealt by occasional true intelligence failures, such
as the failure to anticipate the onset of the Iranian revolution and the Indian nuclear
tests (some of which failures were brought on by the very trends, in budget and environment, that we have just described). Regardless of the politics of it all, this has not
only degraded the quality of intelligence at a time when its quality must be first-rate
in the national interest; it has made it more difficult to increase the intelligence budgets and activities as they are needed.

More Budget Politics. It is an unfortunate by-product of our political system that
when a congressman or senator accumulates enough seniority he or she, and especially his or her staff, can insert or remove or change any budget request, and can influence the vote that accepts or rejects it, regardless of the merits of the change. This
derives from the constitutional provision that legislators are supposed to raise armies
and navies. The Constitution is silent about congressional staffs, but the staffs would
probably argue that they are only bringing issues and possibilities to the attention of
their principals, who do the actual proposing and voting.

The consequences of having large congressional committee staffs steeped in the details of defense systems and their procurement are large swings in budget authority
that, for as much as 10–15 percent of the defense budget, do not reflect the expressed
needs of our military planners. This phenomenon, too, has its positive and negative
aspects. On the plus side, it allows for correction of a strategic mind-set among the
military that an outside view detects as wrongly directed. During the Cold War, for

example, Congress decided that a growing propensity to undertake covert operations as a combined enterprise of the intelligence agencies and the military Special Forces—a propensity that emerged as a response to Soviet and Chinese war-of-national-liberation strategy—had to be controlled carefully or it would get the country involved without civilian supervision in conflicts peripheral to the main contest with the Soviet Union. It also allows Congress to intervene to break up military-industrial cabals established to make profit for the industrial giants and to give the military more and exciting equipment and people to control. This is the very activity that made Senator Harry Truman a hero and a preferred candidate for vice president after he exposed such a profiteering cabal in hearings during the early days of World War II and that President Dwight Eisenhower warned against on his departure from office.

The negative side of Congress's ability to free-wheel on defense occurs when senators, congressmen, and their staffs join the military-industrial complex. They could not long remain unpunished by public opinion, the voters, and the law by being so crass as to join profiteering cabals openly. The operation of the system is much more subtle than that, and it has several components.

First is the simple combination of prejudice and the unfettered exercise of power that the responsibility to assemble several hundred billion dollars' worth of industrial effort engenders. It is difficult to describe in a short space the powerful impact that a single knowledgeable staffer can have on military systems acquisition. As a single example, one staffer came to a congressional committee from a Service laboratory and immediately questioned why a weapon that laboratory was experimenting with was not being purchased. It took extensive study (at a cost to the Defense Department), repeating work that had been done earlier, to make an airtight case that the weapon was not worth buying. This staffer, however, continued on to review the defense budget every year for more than a decade, making changes in funding and direction of development that imposed his opinions on countless defense programs and overriding all military and civilian judgments in the Defense Department that had gone into preparing the budget. He was supported by his committee, since he clearly had more precise knowledge of defense program details than they had. At times, other congressional committees complained (obliquely, in their reports) about his actions and moved to undo those they found irksome. This particular twist on congressional oversight of the defense program made it even more difficult than usual to plan and carry out that program in an orderly way.

This was sheer exercise of personal power by a nonelected official. More subtle and more widespread is the simple issue of what has come, sometimes with justification and sometimes not, to be called pork: making sure that some of the money being spent is spent in your district and your state. Companies fall right in with this and use it as a protective measure. Contention over whether to procure systems is then colored by the fact that major companies acting as prime contractors for the systems have subcontractors and suppliers in a large number of states, giving all the state delegations to Congress an electoral stake in preserving the system.

For example, the two major military aircraft contractors, Lockheed Martin and Boeing, and the two manufacturers of the engines that power their military aircraft, General Electric and Pratt and Whitney, have major installations of their own in nine states. The next tier of major subcontractors that provides aircraft parts and equipment has plants in twenty states, with only partial overlap with the prime contractors. Additional suppliers of parts and equipment are even more widely spread. There are especially large concentrations of this industry in California, Washington, New York, New England, Pennsylvania, Georgia, Kansas, and Texas, all large and influential states or regions in many ways. In addition, there is work for U.S. military aircraft in six countries abroad. This is not to say that the subcontract work is distributed deliberately to create the constituencies. That happens in the United States simply as an accident of where industries that can furnish defense materiel happen to be located. It is common practice to put work in foreign countries as specific offsets to the countries' purchase of aircraft from U.S. companies.

More obvious than the general concern with preserving the widespread distribution of jobs is the simple addition of procurements to assure continuation of production in one's own congressional district or state. In the fiscal year 1999 defense budget passed by Congress there were, for example, eight more Sikorsky CH-60 Army utility helicopters, at a cost of $66 million, and six C-130 transport aircraft in various versions (cargo, tanker, electronic warfare), at a cost of $400 million, provided than the defense budget asked for. Senator John McCain estimated that the budget included $5 billion of what he called "defense pork"—expenditures that the military did not ask for and that various senators and congressmen inserted in the budget to help their constituents. And this does not include such things as shipbuilding contracts that help sustain the shipyards in a senator's state and similar actions that can be viewed as having been steered in the direction they took by those with the power to do so.

Of course, in all such areas, which can appear on the surface to be bald moves to distribute the defense dollar to local, private, and electoral benefit, the arguments are murky. No one will admit that an item was inserted in the budget solely to sustain employment in his or her district or state. There are legitimate arguments about needing to preserve the industrial base, that is, the capacity to produce complex defense systems and components in case increased procurement is needed. And it can be argued that specific procurements help do that. Also, there may be legitimate arguments that the military really needed the systems that were added but that it had to hold back asking for them in favor of other priorities in a budget-constrained atmosphere. Thus, pork can be viewed as Congress adding the systems as a favor to a military that could not break discipline with the decisions of the Secretary of Defense. These kinds of arguments make it difficult to sustain the charge that all additions to or changes in the defense budget are made for selfish reasons. Each of hundreds of cases (line items in the budget) would have to be looked at and judged separately, and this is an almost impossible task for any but the most dedicated and well-informed citizens.[23]

The bottom line, however, is that if there is, say, $5 billion in the defense budget that is being spent for possibly frivolous or selfish reasons that will not enhance the nation's defense, there is an opportunity cost to be paid, in weapons or intelligence systems not acquired or people not well taken care of because that $5 billion is not available. And we may note in this context that in addition to all the other needs we have outlined, the JCS has informed Congress that with the current pattern of expenditure readiness is on the ragged edge of decline.

And this isn't all. There are times when some segments of Congress simply run away with an idea, against all advice and ignoring all suggestions that it might not be in the national interest to do so, creating a juggernaut that is impossible to stop and that imposes other such opportunity costs. One such area current today is officially known as National Missile Defense (NMD). Ever since the signing of the ABM Treaty with the Soviet Union in 1972, in which both countries agreed to forego deployment of extensive, nationwide defenses against land- or sea-launched intercontinental ballistic missiles in the interest of maintaining the stability of the Cold War system of mutual nuclear deterrence, there have been objections that the United States should be able to defend itself against incoming missiles. This view was given much support by President Reagan's March 1983 speech, which led to the establishment of the Ballistic Missile Defense Organization and led to renewed calls by many influential members of Congress and the defense community to rethink the ABM Treaty.

Since the end of the Cold War the dynamics of the situation changed markedly. The ballistic missile defense research and development program changed emphasis. It had been emphasizing a multilayered defense designed to meet a massive Soviet attack. Included were space-based weapons systems to destroy Soviet ICBMs during

---

[23]All this discussion deliberately avoids the question of whether campaign contributions influence the actions that determine the distribution of defense dollars. Although the area is fraught with presumption and innuendo, one would be hard put to point to cases where deliberate actions by members of Congress (or the executive branch) in return for industry campaign support have been proven.

their powered flight (boost-phase intercept); complex space- and surface-based systems designed to overcome a wide array of known and anticipated Soviet aids for penetrating the defenses during the missiles' flight through space and just after reentering the atmosphere; and terminal defense systems to make last-ditch efforts close to the attacker's targets. It is now concentrating on simpler, mainly surface-based defense systems designed to overcome the shorter range ("tactical," or theater-level) ballistic missiles proliferating around the world. At the same time, many members of Congress joined together to call with increasing insistence for deployment of a missile defense system to protect the U.S. homeland from an attack by a state with smaller missile holdings than the Soviets had, such as China or one of the rogue states. They make the argument that even though the risk of an attack by Russia has subsided to virtually zero,[24] the risk of an attack by a single or a few missiles from one of these other sources has grown immensely and that we must meet the risk. This argument would appear, also, to recognize implicitly that in the current climate of compassion for oppressed populations as distinct from their evil governments, and with our total national survival not at stake, we might not want to respond to such an attack with a devastating counterblow that would essentially destroy the launching country and its population. It argues that the dynamics of the Cold War have given way to a different world balance of destructive power in which the Cold War deterrence equations no longer hold. The proponents of this view argue that with the Soviet Union gone the ABM Treaty is no longer a valid treaty to be respected by the United States.

The counterarguments are many. We have reviewed some of their technical aspects earlier. Those who wish to preserve the ABM Treaty as a treaty that remains with Russia point out that Russia still deploys a formidable intercontinental nuclear missile force on land and at sea. Russian conventional defenses have shrunk to the point where they must rely much more on their nuclear missile forces for national defense, and it is avowedly doing so at a time when control over those forces is less secure and is said to be becoming shakier by the day. Then, if we want to agree with Russia and take offensive systems off alert, we should not create a situation in which we can defend against an attack while Russia cannot afford to defend itself. That would make Russia even more skittish and *increase* the chance of an accidental or deliberate launch—the opposite of the result we want. Thus, this would not appear to be a propitious time to abrogate the ABM Treaty and thereby enter a destabilizing

---

[24]And this may actually not be so, since reports indicate that centralized control of the Russian strategic missile forces has declined while the criteria for launch have not been changed. This leads to increased risk of accidental launch of a Russian attack, as was believed to be near happening when word of a Norwegian research rocket launch did not get through to Russian central command authorities.

impulse into the strategic nuclear weapons balance. Also, Russia has said that if the United States violates or abrogates the ABM Treaty Russia will not ratify the START II Treaty reducing the levels of nuclear weapons in their arsenal and ours.[25] This agitates our allies in Europe, where nuclear missile holdings have stabilized under the influence of the START levels. In addition, it is argued, it would further weaken our counterproliferation efforts elsewhere in the world.

None of this means that we cannot deploy a missile defense at all. One can be deployed within the constraints of the ABM Treaty, but it would have to be limited to defense of the national capital area and one ICBM field at least 1,300 kilometers (800 miles) away, each with 100 defense missiles and specified numbers and kinds of radars. However, this kind of system could not defend the entire United States, including Hawaii and Alaska, or even the conterminous forty-eight states, from either a small or large attack originating anywhere in the world, without violating the understanding with Russia on the boundaries—missile range less than 3,500 kilometers (2,170 miles) and speed on reentering the atmosphere of less than 5 kilometers per second—between tactical or theater and national missile defense.

In addition to all these arguments, questions arise as to whether the technology is ready, even if the somewhat arcane judgmental and political arguments can be overcome and we are willing to bear the high cost of a missile defense system. The Clinton administration argued that it is not; the administration policy concentrated on building tactical or theater missile defense while advancing the technology to be able to intercept missiles arriving at higher speeds from farther away, as well as to be ready to deploy a national missile defense system quickly if the threat reaches a point of danger. That point is predicted to be as far off as 2005 to 2010, depending on which intelligence estimate one wants to accept.

The advocates of deploying a national missile defense predict that the threat will become real much more quickly, citing the Korean, Iranian, and Indian missile tests as indicators that an intercontinental missile capability beyond the stable Cold War standoff is imminent. In fact, they argue that the most recent Korean tests show that a missile capability can be built in secret, in underground factories, and sprung upon us full-blown without all-up system tests to prove that the missiles work (an achievement no nation, including ours, has ever been able to demonstrate).[26] They there-

---

[25]They are finding many reasons to delay such ratification. This would give them another one, possibly stronger because they could argue that we could not be relied upon to adhere to the treaty even if it were ratified.

[26]It is true that the rapidity of many technological advances by others, such as the Soviet testing of nuclear weapons and their entry into space, have not been anticipated by our intelligence services. In this case, however, unless there is a wholesale transfer of proven Russian technology that obviates the need, the

fore want to move rapidly to cover what they believe is a large and dangerous national vulnerability. All this comes despite a report by a technical panel that several Defense Department agencies together established in 1997–1998 to review the situation, a panel chaired by General Larry Welch, a highly respected former Air Force chief of staff. The panel reported that the technology and a plan for developing it were not ready and that pressure by Congress to develop and deploy a system without adequate time and resources to remedy the technical shortfalls greatly increases the risk of failure and of wasting large amounts of money in the process. As noted earlier, we are talking about costs on the order of $10–20 billion for even the "light" defense that the current advocates favor; the costs can go much higher if in the future it is found that a more dense defense is needed (costs on the order of $50–100 billion were mentioned in various quarters during the height of the debate about President Reagan's Strategic Defense Initiative).

Such arguments notwithstanding, those in Congress who have determined that we need such a system have refused to relax the pressure to move forward rapidly with a national missile defense system. Under pressure from Congress the Clinton administration has added money to its budget requests, which already included extensive funds for tactical missile defense and for developmental aspects of national missile defense, to move much more rapidly toward deployment. In early 1999 Secretary of Defense William Cohen inched the administration closer to committing to such a system, with $10 billion dedicated to it in the six-year defense plan beginning with the fiscal year 2000 budget. The Russians have been approached about modifying the ABM Treaty to accommodate our perceived need to meet a worldwide threat of a light attack. Whatever Russian leaders may say in private, the public response has been what would be expected; indeed, the timing is unfortunate, coming as it does simultaneously with the Kosovo crisis to affect Russian attitudes toward any cooperation with the United States and the West at all. On June 29, 1999, President Clinton, acceding to the congressional pressure, signed the National Missile Defense Act, which makes it U.S. policy to deploy an NMD system as soon as technologically feasible. The prospects for technical success remain uncertain, however, and the costs to the nation and to our other defense efforts will become increasingly apparent.

All these, then, are some of the practical problems of implementation faced by the military forces as they move to make real the new military doctrine envisioned in

---

intermediate engineering steps could not be bypassed, and they could be detected. The potential of Russian help cannot be discounted. If it does lead to intercontinental missile capability in a hostile nation before a national missile defense is in place, we would still have the massive deterrent to counter it, and we would have developed theater missile defenses to protect our allies.

Joint Vision 2010. Basically, they are trying to draw on modern technology to craft armed forces able to use that technology to do things that no armed forces have ever been able to do before, with fewer people and a smaller proportion of the national wealth with which to do it. And now we must face the fact that those armed forces, even if they could be built just as the JCS has specified and as the Services desire, might still have some critical vulnerabilities that, if not accounted for as the forces are built, can lead to their defeat in spite of the unparalleled capability they will be able to bring to bear against any opposition.

Chinks in the Wall

Despite all the obstacles—foreseen and unforeseen, self-imposed by a set of military institutions given to conservatism and self-protection and imposed by outside forces bent on using resources that would be allocated to them for many purposes other than national security—history shows that when the U.S. military makes a commitment to change as profound as that embodied in *Joint Vision 2010* it does move in that direction. In this case, much of that movement has already taken place, spurred first by the Cold War, then by the testing ground of the Gulf War, as well as by the constant pressure on the budget. It can be assumed that over the next decade or two the armed forces will take on the shape and capabilities described in the new joint doctrine.

Because of the constraints and the nibbling away at the edges that we have described, the forces won't be quite as efficient and effective as they would like to be, and their strategic readiness will be lower than it needs to be. Yet they will have something close to the form and operating characteristics the joint doctrine and the individual Service plans describe. What could be in store when they go into action? This depends partly on the national strategy for using them; we will examine that in Chapter 7. But it will also depend on the forces' inherent strengths and weaknesses. The Joint Vision doctrine sketched above describes their strengths; now let us explore some of the weaknesses.

Lean Forces Can Be Fragile.   First, the forces and their modes of operation will be lean and their operations will be finely tuned. Being "lean" means that duplicative organizations will have been eliminated in the press toward jointness. Each Service's tasks will be laid out so that only that Service can perform them, on behalf of the entire force under a CINC's command. For example, the Navy may be able to undertake tactical air attacks before other tactical air forces arrive, but it may have to depend on the Air Force's Special Operations and bomber forces to prepare the way by taking out opposing air defenses. Or the Air Force may have to depend on Navy Special Operations to prepare the way for the bomber force by neutralizing an accessible defense command center in advance of a bomber attack. The Marines may be the first force ashore, but they may have to depend on the Army for armored combat units and for units able to deal with issues of psychological warfare and civil government.

Each Service, and national organizations like the National Reconnaissance Office, will provide part of the information network. There will be enough information within each Service's part for it to operate independently up to a point. However, to achieve the "dominant maneuver" and "precision engagement" the doctrine calls for will require all the information all of them have, as well as the national information provided by the national intelligence agencies—integrated, accessible, and disseminated to all of them in a form any of them can use. It follows that if any part of the force from any Service is unavailable for some reason during a joint operation, then the entire operation will be penalized. The most likely reasons a force will be unavailable are lack of readiness, some critical equipment incompatibility that keeps it from operating with the other forces, or that it has been disabled or destroyed by enemy action.

"Finely tuned operations" mean that every element of a total, joint force must be able to do its tasks according to a tight timetable, in such a way that all the Service tasks come together *when* they must and *where* they must. This includes joining up forces to engage the enemy, defeating the enemy, and exploiting the victory. But everyone in the military, and every student of military history, knows that this happens rarely in warfare. Aside from surprises by a clever and skilled enemy, the fog and friction of warfare get in the way.

What has been called the "fog of war" means that when forces actually join in fast-moving combat the commander rarely knows in detail what is going on until one side or the other is overrun or some other decisive outcome appears. Some critical bit of information appears always to be missing. As an example, an Israeli commander told me of an incident in which he was in radio contact with two of his units as they were engaging what was supposed to be the enemy during the 1967 Israeli-Arab war. He had realized to his horror from chance remarks they made that they were engaging each other. He was able to stop the action before they hurt each other. Twenty-five years later, in the Gulf War, much of the actual Desert Storm timetable for the ground war was driven by some of the force commanders' concerns to ensure that the separate columns in the broad sweep around the Iraqi forces in the desert did not engage each other.

What Carl von Clausewitz called the "friction of war" means that there is almost always some unforeseen, chance event that keeps one or more units from meeting their timetables or appearing at an appointed place at the designated time: The terrain is harder to negotiate than was anticipated; the weather closes in before it was predicted; an essential airstrip is hit by a shell and is unusable for a time; a critical load is lost when a transport aircraft is downed; a soldier at an observation post falls asleep and a threatening enemy movement is completed without his observing it, causing a local change in plans that keeps the soldier's unit from its rendezvous. The possibilities are infinite (it is no accident that Murphy's law was first articulated by a military man). Remember that Desert One, the 1979 attempt to rescue the American hostages being held by Iran, had to be aborted when one of the aircraft on the ground in Iran crashed into another during maneuvers on the deserted airstrip the rescue force had occupied, creating a situation in which the planned rescue attempt could not proceed.

In many military operations, an alert and resourceful commander can adapt quickly to the unanticipated situations fed to him by the fog and friction of war. Indeed, it is such responses and the successes they bring that create military heroes and lead to advances to top command. But the leaner the forces and the more finely tuned their operations, the more likely that they will be brittle under actual wartime conditions—that the battle plans and force elements could "break" and fail irretrievably. Finely tuned operations are likely to be more susceptible to the friction of war, whereas leanness means that there will be few reserves on which to draw if things go wrong, for example, if force elements become bogged down and need help to resume their maneuvers, if unanticipated openings in enemy defenses appear that should be exploited, or if casualties are higher than expected.

Under the new doctrine the information network is supposed to, and is being designed to, minimize the effects of the fog of war, and the maneuver capabilities of air and sea mobile forces are designed to minimize the effects of the friction of war. The various air and naval forces, and diverse maneuvering elements of the ground forces that use air mobility—helicopters and battlefield transport aircraft and precision parachute drops of people and equipment—are designed to act as reserve forces in support of each other, as well as being primary strike forces in their own elements. Thus, the new mode of warfare embodied in *Joint Vision 2010* is being crafted with the idea of minimizing the brittleness of lean and finely tuned forces.

Reading *Joint Vision 2010* also makes it clear that our military forces are being designed to achieve rapid successes by offensive action. That is, if our military units move first to achieve surprise and apply overwhelming force at critical locations to cause the opposing forces to collapse, as occurred during the 1967 Israeli-Arab war and during the Gulf War, they are more likely to be able to call the tune on the battlefield and not to be defeated by the fog and friction of war. This can also work for defensive conflict, under the principle that the best defense is a good offense.

But how far off from the plans would events have to take the forces before their designed modes of operation fail? Harking back to the scenarios with which this book opened, we can anticipate that the world will surely ante up situations for our forces that will hardly ever, or never, be the ones on which their planning was based.

Our military leaders are aware of this. Therefore, the forces are also being designed to be adaptable enough to sustain the offensive in the face of any unexpected eventualities. But a resourceful enemy, having seen the potential effects of the doctrine in the Persian Gulf, and even in the relatively smaller actions in Iraq and the former Yugoslavia, will now have models against which to work to learn how to take advantage of the weaknesses of lean and finely tuned forces.

Weapons of Mass Destruction Can Destroy a Campaign. Lean and finely tuned forces will be especially vulnerable to an opponent's use of nuclear, chemical, or biological weapons. A nuclear weapon taking out a major logistic depot like the one built up in the early days of Operation Desert Shield to support the pending attack on the Iraqi forces in Kuwait, or one or more of the logistic support ships visualized in the new Navy and Marine doctrines for expeditionary warfare, can essentially destroy the military campaign. Used against a major battlefield thrust, it can delay or stop that thrust and raise with utmost poignancy the issue of whether the gain for continuing in furtherance of an "interest" is worth the losses.

Of course, we hope to deter such use of nuclear weapons by being ready to retaliate in kind. This is where opposing strategies based on other value systems that were discussed in Chapter 3 can come into play. If opposition forces hug their population centers and put their weapons storage and missile launch pads within them to use them as shields against retaliation (as indeed the Iraqis have done), and we are reluctant to kill what we deem to be innocent civilians who are distinct from their nefarious leaders, then the high value we assign to human life can act as a deterrent to our retaliation. We might overcome this problem by being able to retaliate with small weapons against enemy forces in the field, but we have essentially decommissioned and are destroying all our smaller tactical nuclear weapons and will have no such capability. Another possible defense is to have our forces well shielded from nuclear effects. We can also train our forces to be able to operate in a nuclear environment; this has been low on the priority list of an already overloaded and underfunded training schedule. Both of these steps would in any case make the forces heavier, when we want them to be lighter. The only way out of this dilemma is to deter the use of nuclear weapons. We shall have to visibly overcome our scruples about human life on the opponent's side to do this credibly.

Chemical and biological weapons present other problems. Resistance to penetration of the agents can be built into equipment and platforms, and we are doing that in our new military systems. Troops can be vaccinated against known and anticipated agents. We have started to do this with anthrax. There are preadministered medications that can protect troops against some chemical agents, and some of these were said to have been used in the Gulf War. But they may have been implicated in

Gulf War syndrome, the complex of illnesses that has proven to be so vexing to many veterans of that conflict. Troops on the spot can wear protective gear, but that significantly degrades their performance just when it must be at its peak for the fast operations foreseen in *Joint Vision 2010*.

Again, as with nuclear weapons, the best defense is to deter the use of these weapons as well. But how? We cannot threaten to respond in kind, because we have given up chemical and biological weapons. We can threaten to respond with nuclear weapons (as Secretary of State James Baker hinted—with apparent success—we would do if Saddam used chemical or biological weapons in the Gulf War), but that brings us into the same realm of difficulty and uncertainty as we saw above for the response to nuclear weapons. There is no easy way out of these difficulties. The preferred but uncertain defense is to pursue the nonproliferation regime, as we have been doing assiduously but with accompanying controversy and uncertain success. It has also been argued that our possession of very precise conventional weapons can substitute for the use of nuclear weapons. To some extent that may be true, but the effects are different. They are more discriminating, which is a plus, but also more time-consuming to eliminate a complete array of threatening targets, which can give an opponent time for more devastating action.

All of this gets us into the esoteric realm of deterrence theory, which is well beyond the scope of discussion here. It simply reinforces the growing difficulty and complexity of modern warfare in its totality. Perhaps prior information warfare, or the rapid and focused action visualized in *Joint Vision 2010*, can help solve some of the problems if military action is required where nuclear, chemical, or biological weapons can be used. More likely, we will count on mutual deterrence to operate, creating the difficult political situations of compromise with evil that runs so against the grain in American politics (as in the reaction to the deal with North Korea to get it to give up its nuclear weapons program—maybe).

Not Designed for Extended Defense.   One way to defeat lean forces that operate on tight timetables is to extend the conflict and to frustrate the value of their maneuvers. Lean forces are not designed for sustained operations. They are likely not to have much staying power if they are bogged down in overcoming a staunch defense, or if the other side can somehow turn the offensive against them and force them either to undertake a siege against a strong and critical defensive position or to have to defend themselves in place. A sustained drain of casualties, even at a fairly low level, as well as the need to build a fixed logistics tail to sustain static operations, can keep the forces from exercising their freedom of maneuver and achieving surprise breakthroughs to overcome the defense. An enemy, even a low-tech enemy, who retreats, gives up key territory, and then turns to guerrilla warfare can accomplish this. Another variant can be the preparation of strong points rooted in one or more cities where there are many civilians for an occupier to protect and to feed while the opposing forces keep the cities from being safely occupied and governed by the attackers. For example, such a situation could have faced the Coalition forces in Operation Desert Storm if they had tried to take Baghdad as a way of deposing Saddam Hussein's regime. The choice was then to take this risk or to let him stay in power and try to depose him by other means. We chose the latter, and he was then successful in remaining in power to frustrate many of the Desert Storm objectives.

The armed forces' doctrine for the future is being designed to reduce the chances of becoming bogged down in long wars of attrition and long, static, and indecisive campaigns—both descriptive of the war in Vietnam. But it must be recognized that the very features of the forces that suit them to the decisive kind of offensive action they are being designed for makes them vulnerable to an opponent who is adept at creating the situations they are designed to avoid. An opponent who can move in unexpected directions, create unexpected alliances, and otherwise frustrate our plans to counter his anticipated moves will cause confusion and stretch out the time to respond with and to complete decisive military action.

We are designing our military forces to achieve quick victories. If an opponent can find means and resources to frustrate those quick victories, our forces are likely not to be well suited to handle the military situations that will result. Nor will the nation be in a good position to manage the resulting strategic situations. We will likely not have built up the needed strong background of reserve military strength, the capacity for rapid industrial mobilization, and the national determination to want to fight a long war that is not a war of survival. We will continue to fear future Vietnams. Reducing this vulnerability is a matter of will. We can search through the attitudes and trends reviewed earlier to try to answer the question whether the will might be there, but ultimately only history in the making will tell.

The Information Connections Are Crucial.   None of the operations planned for our forces can succeed unless the called-for information superiority is achieved and maintained. There is no doubt that needed information at many tactical and strategic levels, from troops in the field to the JCS and the president, can be gathered. There are and will be many means to do so, from many points of view and many sensors. There will be satellites and airplanes and unmanned aircraft and ships and submarines and troops in the field and Special Forces scouts and many forms of direct observation from human spies to eavesdropping on radio communications. There may be missed information, and any information will be subject to interpretation that may be right or wrong. But all the means added together, from all the sources, will mean that copious information needed to establish the information superiority specified in the new doctrine will be available, in some form, somewhere in the warmaking system. We can even stipulate that, although it is not an easy task, all the civilian and military research and development in the area will eventually give us search engines and computer algorithms to be able to find, in timely fashion, the information needed by everyone from the most isolated soldiers to top commanders. We will even be able to sort the wheat from the chaff and discard false signals and planted data, at least some of it.

In the end, however, all that information will be useless if it doesn't get to the ones who need it when they need it. For this purpose, the forces in the field, whatever Service they are attached to or wherever they are operating, will have to be immersed in an unbreakable communications network through which the information can flow, without interruption and without the ability of the opponents to listen in and learn what is on the network. All the forces, at all levels, will need such "connectivity," as the military calls it, to know where to move; when to move; when their air support and supplies will arrive; what danger of attack they are in, at what time, and what defensive or offensive measures to take; who will be coordinating their own attack or defense actions with them; what weapons to launch, at what time, at what targets, at what locations—in other words, all the data and information that must flow to make certain that the forces at all levels from infantry squads and fighter pilots to division and ship commanders can do what they need to do at the appointed times and places. (This doesn't mention the top commanders, from the theater CINC to the president, who will also need up-to-the-minute information to deal with the evolving strategic situation as a conflict proceeds.) The entire concept of operation of the future forces, including rapid maneuver, precision attack, effective defense, and supply when needed, depends on sustaining secure connectivity.

If you were an opponent facing forces with such a doctrine and dependency, what would you do? Obviously, you would try to break the information connections. You would also try to feed false information into the system to deceive your opponent and lead the attackers into a trap or cause them to maneuver against inconsequential objectives and get out of position while you prepare to counterattack. Such steps are often iffy, and the one who undertakes them cannot be certain whether or when they are working. But at the very least breaking the information connectivity among forces that are as totally dependent on it as our forces will be would be a prime objective of any astute opponent. The attempt would be made by jamming, by physically destroying key communications nodes like fiber-optic cable terminals (subject to bombing, even by terrorists), by attacking satellites that are subject to damage and destruction by high-powered laser weapons on the ground, and by any other means at hand. A resourceful enemy would not lack for ways to attempt the break, and it would not be necessary to know if each one is successful.

The philosophy could be, "If you throw enough stuff at them, their system will break somewhere; just keep at it."

To avoid losing this critical connectivity, our forces will have to build many redundant and sturdy communications links, using both military and civilian channels. To avoid the loss of information and time, the information will have to be able to flow over many channels, and the flow will have to switch automatically and instantly from a broken to an alternate channel. All this is aside from the struggle to gather information, to know how reliable it is, and to use all means possible to keep one's opponent from doing the same. And it is added to the task of detecting and excluding deceptive information and preventing mischief within one's information systems through computer hacking and any of the other means that will be available to undertake information warfare. The ability to maintain connectivity and information integrity will determine whether the new design of the armed forces can succeed.

The danger for the future forces (aside from any posed by current or future enemies) is that budgeters, from Congress to the armed forces' own planners, may not remain fully aware of the criticality of providing unbreakable connectivity. It will be expensive. It will require additional fiber-optic lines and wireless frequency bands (bands that we are auctioning off to commercial interests at a high rate for short-term income), extra satellites, extra security and priority arrangements for the military to be able to rely on commercial communications, electronic components designed to withstand electromagnetic pulses from nuclear weapons or microwave weapons aimed at them, and complex jamming–resistant circuits. All those things will increase the costs of the communications networks to unaccustomed levels. We are used to spending money first on the airplanes, ships, tanks, weapons, missiles, and other direct combat systems of war before money is spent on things as mundane as communications: telephone links, fiber-optic cables, communications satellites, terminals, and servers for routing and managing the information, and especially all the expensive safeguards for keeping the information secure and the connections unbreakable. So it will be easy to short-change the essential connectivity among the forces and thereby unwittingly make the forces more vulnerable to the obvious countermeasures that can most jeopardize their success in the field.

Other "Show-stoppers." Prospective opponents can interrupt the movement of forces and their supplies by many means, not all of them high-tech. All shipping is in danger of disruption by near-shore mine warfare. Mines stopped the Marines from landing in Kuwait during the Gulf War; we put the best face on it, after two ships were hit, by saying the landing force tied up many Iraqi forces to guard against the landing. But even World War II–vintage mines can still be effective; indeed, mines left over from the 1904–1905 Russo-Japanese War were used to disrupt traffic in the Persian Gulf during the Iran-Iraq War of the 1980s. Mines can be used to make it difficult for the fleet and a Marine landing force to approach the area where a landing is necessary. Similarly, simple shoulder-fired antiaircraft missiles can make the area around an airfield untenable for transport aircraft. They are difficult to suppress because the ones who fire them can run, hide, appear out of nowhere to shoot, and then disappear. In other situations, they can seriously interfere with combat operations; the Army Ranger company that was so badly hurt in Mogadishu was pinned down when two of its helicopters were brought down by shoulder-fired antitank rockets used in the antiaircraft mode.

The armed forces are taking some halting steps to counter mines and cheap antiaircraft weapons. But this is another area where the work isn't glamorous and there are more exciting things to do with increasingly scarce dollars. All those who share responsibility for the defense budget—the Services, their civilian Defense Department overseers, the Congress—can easily let the funding decline and the work slide as they allocate priorities to bigger and more visible programs like new aircraft or national missile defense, until the countermeasures are not available when needed. Then it will be too late, and the price in casualties and disrupted and delayed operations will be high.

Antisubmarine warfare is another area that has been allowed to languish since the Cold War. When our Navy faced a large and highly competent Soviet Navy, we knew we had to give attention to antisubmarine warfare or our carriers and other naval forces would be in mortal danger. In addition, such warfare was needed to guard against Soviet strategic ballistic missile submarines. Now, although the latter threat still exists, we have let our guard down. Our antisubmarine forces have greatly reduced their practice in the open ocean, and the antisubmarine warfare research and development program has been severely reduced. Yet we are undertaking a strategy of expeditionary warfare that puts our military shipping into areas along the world's coastlines where antisubmarine warfare in the shallower waters of the continental shelves is much more difficult than in the deep oceans. While troops and combat aircraft may fly to a potential war zone, all major force deployments will depend on shipping to carry and deliver their heavy equipment, major weapons, and continuing supplies of fuel and ammunition. The shipping, whether from the United States or the prepositioned ships at Diego Garcia or elsewhere, will have to use existing ports or land heavy equipment over the beach or in improvised port facilities. Without effective antisubmarine warfare capability, the flow of shipping will be easily interruptable by hostile submarines, with obvious consequences for "dominant maneuver."

Where will the hostile submarines come from? Modern, quiet, conventionally powered submarines capable of staying submerged for long periods are being sold by

Russia, Sweden, and Germany to Iran and North Korea, among other nations. China is building a submarine force that includes conventional, diesel-powered submarines as well as nuclear-powered submarines. India and Pakistan are acquiring advanced submarines. The undersea craft can show up in Iraqi or Libyan hands through third-party sales. Russia retains and operates a large nuclear- and diesel-powered submarine force. Many other countries, allied and neutral, have them; most of these countries do not currently constitute a threat to U.S. military shipping. But the future is obscure. Who would have predicted, for example, that Britain would have to divert large resources to fend off a threatening Argentine submarine while recapturing the Falkland Islands? And many of the nations operating submarines are not neutral or friendly, even now. The disruption that a submarine can cause to lean forces' "dominant maneuver" and "precision engagement" by sinking even one major military cargo ship, or even landing a torpedo on a major warship, should cause us to take notice. This is another area where complacency can easily—indeed, already has—set in, in the interest of reducing the defense budget while sustaining a degree of readiness and pursuing projects that create more jobs or that are more visible, like ships and aircraft.

There are additional risks. An Iraq or an Iran or a North Korea may actually acquire nuclear weapons and use them in a desperate attempt to defeat a vitally threatening military action. Or they or some other nation in the distant future, after the lean and mean forces have been configured and used, could attack them with chemical or biological weapons, in a strategic calculation that the circumstances of the time will preclude a response in kind. The critical danger would not be so much the casualties caused, although they would be horrendous, but that the forces would not be constituted to sustain their offensive unless they were prepared to meet the situation. Preparation would include having appropriate radiation, chemical, and biological warfare protective gear for personnel that would not hobble their effectiveness; protections built into the ventilating systems of all major platforms like tanks, aircraft, and ships; and training in continued operations under the circumstances of use. It would also have to include the deterrent doctrines, announced and unannounced, that lay out the circumstances and natures of response and retaliation. Few of these things have been finalized yet, nor are they very visibly in work. In the absence of adequate preparation, we are less able to deter such attacks, and our response may face the unhappy choice of retaliating in such a way that large civilian populations may be hurt or calling off an operation under circumstances that would invite further such attacks in the future.

Finally, we must recognize an element of risk in the very steps we are taking to make the armed forces less expensive to build and sustain in an uneasy but essentially peacetime world. Part of the defense savings we seek come from cost-cutting procedures being undertaken to streamline systems acquisition and the management and support of the armed forces. These procedures involve the civilian world heavily in furnishing key services such as base operations, transportation, and maintenance of military equipment, including ships and aircraft. Congress and the Office of Management and Budget are gradually easing the restrictions on farming out such activities to the civilian economy. Indeed, they are encouraging such movement in the interest of cost-cutting competition. There is also increased emphasis on using commercial off-the-shelf equipment for many applications such as communications, navigation, and even weapon guidance. Logistic support is being changed to follow the civilian practice of providing parts and supplies as needed from the factory rather than tying up large inventories in transportation pipelines and supply depots. The Navstar/GPS satellite navigation system, originally designed for military use, has become so tied into civilian applications for air-traffic control and surface navigation that the military will have difficulty denying it so that opposing forces cannot use it in times of conflict, because friendly and neutral nations and our own civilian commerce will be so heavily dependent on it.

All these civilian dependencies increase the risk that the military forces can be hobbled by what are euphemistically called "job actions" and other civilian constraints at critical times when they must move fast and sustain a high tempo of operations. One has only to think about the 1990s experiences of General Motors, when strikes at one or two carefully targeted parts plants were able to bring the entire company's production to a halt. Such an action on the part of, say, workers at key manufacturing plants, at an aircraft maintenance depot, or on the part of merchant mariners whose ships are needed to deliver supplies to an expeditionary force could change the ability of the country to meet a challenge requiring rapid military action. Indeed, the prospect opens the possibility of subversive agitation on the part of an opponent to cause such strikes as a defense against U.S. military action. And labor might not be the only offender; there were instances in World War II when management of large companies involved in war production were accused of holding back that production in order to build reserve postwar civilian production capacity.

Such disruptive actions were met in World War II by congressional action (the Smith-Connally Act of 1943 made strikes in government-owned facilities illegal) and by executive action, such as having the government take over plants to force workers back to work and to force labor-management settlements. But that was a time of all-out war for national survival, not of military action in support of regional interests. Even then, the strike-prevention actions came hard, beset by conflict and recrimination on all sides. How much less likely might such actions be in cases of lesser but nevertheless real national peril? At the same time, how much more disruptive might the attending delays and turmoil be when our military strategy calls for fast action that is decisive early and that can easily fail under a few days of disruption?

Perhaps an example is given by the air-traffic controllers' strike in 1981, soon after President Reagan's inauguration. The strike threatened the welfare of the national economy. President Reagan fired the striking air-traffic controllers as soon as they walked out. The air-traffic system continued to function, operated by the few non-striking controllers and supervisory employees. Safety did not suffer (that is, there were no accidents attributable to the change), but air traffic flew at markedly reduced rates for some months. It was years before the system recovered its full capacity, and indeed residual effects of Reagan's draconian action are being felt in some areas to this day.

From all this it is clear that current trends in organization and management of the armed forces are increasing the vulnerability of the armed forces to civilian rear-area disruption of forward-area military operations at critical times. Such disruptions could severely impact the country's ability to succeed in favorable resolution of overseas crises. Although it would be politically difficult when there is no pressing immediate problem to pass laws prohibiting labor and management from interrupting the flow of goods and services to the military in times of crisis, the pain and losses if we wait for the crises to happen before taking remedial action can be much worse than any difficulty in dealing with the problem prospectively. This is a difficult national choice to be made, going far beyond the capacity and reach of the armed forces to remedy. But it is one that could profoundly affect the success of the new military organization and operational doctrine.

Another such profound effect, transcending all the uncertainties we have reviewed thus far, is the issue of what we want to design the armed forces to do. Armed forces must have a purpose rooted in a national strategy. We have seen what they are being designed *to be able* to do, in terms of pure military mission. But we have also seen that as yet there is no outstanding enemy force that they must be specifically designed to meet and defeat. Is there a strategy that they fit into? And how well do they fit? We explore these questions next.

7

A NATIONAL
STRATEGY?

The history of the world is the record of a man in quest of his daily bread and butter.

—*Hendrik Willem van Loon*

In Chapter 6 we reviewed the technology that is and will be available to the armed forces, as well as the evolving form and function of the armed forces that the technology will enable. In form, the armed forces organize around the technology. Obviously, then, military organizations evolve and are created as the technology evolves; horse cavalry went away when armies became mechanized, and aviation units were created when the airplane joined the armed forces.

Generally, doctrine, which says how the armed forces are to be used, tends to follow the changes in technology and organization. The process is usually slow, although it can be speeded drastically if necessary. Whereas it took decades to phase out horses as primary transport, and it took a war to make the carrier supreme over the battleship and to bring aviation into the forefront of all the combat forces, we brought nuclear-powered ballistic missile submarines into being in the space of a decade. That was because we saw, in the invention of long-range missiles and nuclear-powered submarines, the opportunity to fill a strategic need for an invulnerable force able to strike at the heart of the Soviet Union.

This is a prime example of something we alluded to in the discussion of doctrine in Chapter 6: Armed forces need a purpose rooted in a national strategy. The adaptation of technology to carry out that purpose, the organization of the forces around that technology, and the doctrine for using those forces all flow from the strategy. Yet today it appears from the behavior of the political parties and the various relevant branches of government, and from the arguments among them, that with the Cold War and the Soviet threat gone we are building and sustaining armed forces in the absence of clear strategic objectives. If we listen carefully to the cacophony, we could at alternate times believe that we want armed forces for any of a diversity of purposes. We want them to convey American presence and military might for keeping peace in the world and to convey humanitarian relief to locations of huge natural disasters. We want them to protect U.S. interests "there," wherever "there" is, and to punish transgressors against those interests. We want them to protect the U.S. homeland against missile attack as well as terrorists and drug smugglers. And although we never state it that way, we want them to provide jobs and sustain the national economic welfare.

Actually, we have been using the armed forces for all of these purposes. And good reasons can be given for all of them. But many of those reasons are in conflict with each other. We are told by Senator John Warner, Chairman of the Senate Armed Services Committee, that we are dissipating our military strength in "operations other than war" in places like Somalia, Haiti, and Bosnia when we should be preserving that strength for "real" military engagements. Indeed, the long and unpredictable humanitarian and peacekeeping deployments are contributing to the difficulty of keeping skilled soldiers, sailors, and aviators in the armed forces and having them practice their combat skills in military exercises. The costs of these operations also detract from the speed with which the armed forces can capitalize on technological advances, simply by reducing the resources available for research and to develop new systems and equipment.

As we noted earlier, the strength and readiness of the armed forces are in fact being eroded thereby (although it can be argued that ship and aircraft crews certainly gain combat training in operations against Serbian forces and against Iraqi defenses that threaten them while they are on patrol). The Secretary of State questions what the armed forces are for if they cannot be used to support U.S. policy overseas. Congress insists that the armed forces be used for drug surveillance in the Caribbean and along our Mexican border, which are ordinarily tasks for the Coast Guard and the Border Patrol. And Congress resists closing unneeded bases that furnish jobs and sustain local economies. It appears that unless some overarching strategy can be articulated the armed forces' strength and the resources to sustain it will be diffused or dissipated in such tugging and hauling. The uncertainty can negate all the fine work the armed forces themselves are doing to adapt to the new age of world politics that we have entered.

A STRATEGY EMERGING

General Andrew Goodpaster, former Supreme Allied Commander of NATO forces in Europe, has elegantly defined a strategy as stating what the nation wants to accomplish, how it wants to accomplish it, and with what resources. The characteristic American outlooks on the world that we described in Chapter 4—short-term, self-centered—almost preclude our country from consciously crafting and then following a long-term strategy expressed in such terms, looking years and decades in advance.

Big ideas that are rooted in our history do take hold, however, sometimes very quickly. The notion of a manifest destiny to create a nation that stretched from the Atlantic to the Pacific started with Thomas Jefferson and dominated our national strategic thinking until it finally came into being in the first half of the nineteenth century. A few such ideas dominated our strategic thinking during most of the twentieth century: War to spread democracy and freedom is worth fighting; Nazism and fascism were evil and must be destroyed; we would not fight to preserve the European empires; communism threatened all that we stand for and had to be resisted and defeated.

Only rarely, however, did we articulate explicit strategies to realize these grand ideas when they emerged. Rather, the ideas were embedded in what might be called our collective unconscious. The strategies to support them emerged as an agglomeration of responses to events, conditioned by the ideas, held tacitly as often as they were clearly articulated. Then, as the accumulation of responses was perceived and tested against the awareness of what we basically believe as a nation, they were sorted into some logical context related to the ideas and subsequently expressed and examined in extensive discussion by the media, government, and scholars. Out of this sometimes painful process a generally agreed and ratified strategy emerged—a product of revealed behavior, if one will, rather than of conscious planning. The U.S. tendency to build a strategy this way is illustrated by many historical examples from the twentieth century.

Our acceptance of the need to fight German imperialism early in the twentieth century was triggered by such events as Germany's unrestricted submarine warfare, which led to the sinking of the liner *Lusitania* with many Americans on board. An additional push was given by the secret Zimmermann telegram that was intercepted and decoded by the British and brought to President Woodrow Wilson's attention. That telegram, sent by the German foreign minister to their ambassador in Tokyo, showed that Germany was trying to induce Japan to invade Mexico as a way of keeping the United States busy in its own backyard, thereby keeping us out of the war in Europe. The idea of promoting democracy in the world—"making the world safe for democracy," in President Wilson's phrase, which would underlie most of our national strategy until the present day—was devised to justify our entry into the war to our people and to give us a stronger voice in the postwar peace conference.

Later, even though we recognized the intent of Nazi Germany to dominate Europe and then the world, many Americans argued, through the America First movement and other contemporary organized resistance to the notion that we would have to fight Germany, that entering the war would be an act to help preserve the British Empire, an idea to which we had a total antipathy as a nation. Those arguments delayed our preparations for war, at some unknown cost in casualties later. The policy of unconditional surrender profoundly affected the prosecution of the war by forcing Germany and Japan to fight to the bitter end. Their surrenders then created the conditions for the emergence of the political configuration of the postwar world. But this powerful idea was put forward without preplanning and accepted ad hoc at the Casablanca Conference of 1943.

The opposition to the spread of communism by force or subversion that was the bedrock of our Cold War strategy built up over the years from the end of World War II, in 1945, until it became apparent, in 1949, that the Soviet Union was bent on dominating much or all of Europe and spreading communism to the world. It began at the end of World War II when we realized that Stalin had established communist governments in the countries occupied by the Red Army in its sweep toward Berlin, in defiance of understandings we thought had been reached at the Yalta Conference of 1945. It continued with aid to Greece and Turkey in 1947, when those countries were in danger of falling under Soviet sway as a result of Soviet-supported internal communist rebellions. From this beginning grew economic aid to Europe under the Marshall Plan, the organization of NATO, and the folding of West Germany into the community of democratic nations. All this happened under the spur of three causative events: the Soviet clampdown of strict communist dictatorship on the Soviet-occupied areas of Europe after the war; Stalin's prediction that war between the capitalist and communist worlds was inevitable; and the Berlin blockade in 1948 and 1949.

Our resistance to the North Korean invasion of the South in 1950 was a spot decision related to the local situation. During President Harry Truman's deliberations about how to respond to this invasion the idea that the spread of communism by conquest had to be resisted by armed force was articulated, and that grew into the policy of not tolerating the spread of *any* dictatorship by conquest across any nation's borders if that had implications for American national security. The policy was followed in many instances, including support to Israel during the 1973 war when it was attacked by neighboring Arab states, and support to Afghanistan when it was invaded by Soviet forces in 1979. It was last articulated when Iraq invaded Kuwait and in subsequent deterrence actions when Iraq has again acted threateningly against Kuwait and Saudi Arabia.

The developing Cold War and Russia's explosion of an atomic bomb in 1949 initiated a long period of trying to fit nuclear weapons into American strategy. We went from massive retaliation to limited conventional war with nuclear deterrence, then through many gyrations, including the strategies of mutual assured destruction (dubbed "MAD" by those who were horrified by the idea) with antiballistic missile (ABM) limitations, and "selective release" of nuclear weapons in case of an invasion of Europe by Soviet conventional forces. All of these policy gyrations tried, never totally satisfactorily, to come to grips with the role of nuclear weapons and their horrific destructive potential in defense of Europe, the United States, and the free world.

In similar fashion, a policy of resisting Chinese expansion grew as the People's Republic of China was declared after the communists' defeat of Chiang Kai Shek's Nationalist forces. Conditioning events were China's entry into the Korean War, development of its own nuclear forces, and its echoing of the Soviet Union in declaring the strategy of supporting "wars of national liberation" from domination by the colonial powers (which included the United States in their lexicon). China did help to instigate and then supported such wars in the Philippines, Malaya, and Indochina, impelling the United States and Britain to enter those conflicts. Close relations with Japan, and early support for the rebuilding of the Japanese economy after the war, became bulwarks of our strategy to contain the spread of Soviet and Chinese communist power. Our entry into the war in Vietnam emerged from our concern about that spread, as well as from President Truman's concern that if we did not support France in the war against Ho Chi Minh France would leave the NATO alliance.[1] One might argue about the wisdom and efficacy of America's way of pursuing that war, but by the time we entered it the counter-Soviet, anticommunist strategy was well rooted and gave the rationale for supporting an independent government in South Vietnam against what was known (to the intelligence services but not widely believed by the public) to be an attack supported by Communist North Vietnam. Although the "domino theory," first articulated by Secretary of State John Foster Dulles and then used by President John F. Kennedy in support of our intervention—that if South Vietnam fell to communism all of Southeast Asia would follow—has been much disparaged, it is indeed not known what the sequel to an early

---

[1]In one of the great ironies of history after Truman's decision, President Charles de Gaulle of France used U.S. intervention in Indochina as the reason to withdraw France from the NATO military command in 1966. He argued that our policy in Vietnam showed that we would pursue our own world agenda in disregard of the strategic needs and desires of our European allies.

communist takeover of South Vietnam would have been if we had not resisted it at such high cost to both sides.

All of this strategic evolution developed in response to Soviet and other communist nations' actions, within the broad notion that we would use all possible means to resist the spread of communism in the world. As it happened, once that notion took hold it provided a steady, long-term framework for a strategy of engagement with the world. Through half a century of severe strategic stresses we have remained staunchly loyal to the NATO alliance and to our security arrangements with Japan, as they have remained to us. Today, we all maintain those loyalties as a strategic anchor in an international climate that has become murky and uncertain for all involved.

But there are stresses in the alliances, which will become worse as regional events push nations in directions that affect each differently. We are currently in the painful process of crafting a new national and international strategy to meet the new world conditions. We are not there yet. But some outlines of another "big idea" are emerging. Then, when it is fully understood and articulated, we shall have to craft a strategy to support it.

That new, grand idea is rooted in the observations made earlier, in Chapter 3, about the gradual evolution and significance of the global economy. The Gulf War grew out of President George Bush's determination that a hostile Iraq bent on regional hegemony could not be allowed to dominate a large fraction of the world's oil supply (i.e., its energy supply). President Bill Clinton, after the heat of current political conflicts and unhappiness with his personal foibles have cooled, may be understood in history to be the first post–Cold War president and to have set the strategic tone for the future. The nugget of the new strategy was contained in his first Inaugural Address. There, he said: "We earn our livelihood today in peaceful competition with people all across the earth. Powerful forces are shaking and remaking our world. . . . We must invest more in our own people, in their jobs, in their future. . . . [And] we must meet challenges abroad as well as at home. There is no longer a clear division between what is foreign and what is domestic. The world economy, the world environment, the world AIDS crisis, the world arms race: they affect us all." Since then, the world economy has had a prominent place in U.S. thinking about its place and role in the world.

The preface to the "National Security Strategy of the United States," a document mandated by Congress and published by the president, states that "nations with growing economies and strong trade ties are more likely to feel secure and to work toward freedom. And democratic states are less likely to threaten our interests and more likely to cooperate with the U.S. to meet security threats and promote sustainable development." Later, the document states that "our national security strategy is based on enlarging the community of market democracies while deterring and containing a range of threats to our nation, our allies and our interests. The more that democracy and political and economic liberalization take hold in the world, particularly in countries of geostrategic importance to us, the safer our nation is likely to be and the more our people are likely to prosper." The document enlarges at length on how the armed forces are being planned, kept ready, and used to meet any threats to this strategy and the interests involved in it.

Indeed, there is empirical support for the general idea behind the strategy expressed in this document[2] that democracies are less likely to engage in deadly conflicts with each other. With the exception of the ongoing conflicts attending the breakup of Britain's empire on the Indian subcontinent, there has been no war between democratically governed states since the U.S. Civil War ended in 1865.

The Clinton administration's policies have to be seen in context of these strategic expressions. The president pursued the North American Free Trade Agreement (NAFTA) in conflict with his own party and at the expense of attention to what might be called his "first policy love"—reform of medical care—at what may have been the critical time for that policy. He pursued the idea, for which there is a nugget of support in the political system, of extending NAFTA farther into Latin America, starting with Chile. He made certain that the General Agreement on Tariffs and Trade spawned the World Trade Organization, which we view as our prime mechanism for encouraging and enforcing the free world trade that is at the heart of all our trade policy and that has been pursued assiduously since the end of World War II, regardless of the party in power in the United States. He established the Organization for Asian Pacific Economic Cooperation, intended to stretch the free trade idea to the Pacific region, where roughly a third of our national economic activity was oriented before the Asian recession and will likely be oriented again and grow. Much of our policy arguments with France, Japan, and China have centered on those nations' restraints on free trade. The beginnings of U.S. proposals are emerging, in response to the Asian economic collapse of the late 1990s, to refashion the international financial system that was crafted at Bretton Woods in 1944 to govern post–World War II reconstruction and subsequent economic development activity. The need is to gain a measure of control within the world economy over the capricious and destabilizing short-term international flows of capital, roughly analogous to the kinds of controls that were imposed on our internal trading after the

---

[2]I distinguish this expression of strategy from the need for a national strategy deeply rooted in some "big idea" almost universally accepted by the public. The strategy outlined in the published document is as yet hardly recognized or widely accepted, and we still hear calls for a true "national strategy." That may have to grow out of events, as did the other strategies outlined above.

stock market crash of 1929. We don't know how to go about doing that yet without excessively interfering in the free market, but the issue has been posed by serious economic commentators—an essential first step.

And, we must note, these policies of the Clinton administration did not originate with that administration. They actually represent a continuation of the traditional trading economy that the new United States developed and nourished throughout the nineteenth and twentieth centuries. They were being pursued by the Bush administration before Clinton came to power, and even that pursuit was rooted in the earlier post–World War II economic policy trends. These policy trends tended to be submerged by the physical and military threats of the Cold War. With the evaporation of the Soviet threat, they have resurfaced.

Another aspect of this economic orientation has been our pursuit of technological advance and advantage in the world. The technology tends to be taken for granted as we grapple with matters of individual and collective human behavior. However, neither the American nor the world economy can function today, in the world that technology has wrought, without the advances in transportation, information, and communications technologies that created that world. The increasing life span of humanity, and its improving but as yet incomplete mastery over disease, could not have been brought about without the advances in medical and biotechnical sciences and technologies that the search for those improvements has engendered. The world could not sustain its current and growing population levels without the advances in agriculture and the transportation, processing, and packaging technologies to get the food to hungry peoples. The ones just mentioned are not, of course, the only aspects of technology and its underlying science that have brought the economic progress and improved health of the industrial nations to their current stage and that are beginning to percolate into the developing nations. But in their visible manifestations they encompass most of it. And, of course, excellence in scientific achievement underlies excellence in technological achievement.

We should remind ourselves, also, that a large part of our successes in World War II and the Cold War lay in our strong scientific establishment and our application of its products to the technology of war. This included weapons, ships, airplanes, rockets, sensing and guidance systems, electronic warfare, and electronic navigation and communications systems and exploitation of many of the applications of these systems in space and the oceans. As indicated in Chapter 6, the technology of war led to the technology that both spurred and enabled the global economic revolution, until the civil technology attending the latter has come to dominate its military forebears in many areas.

Thus, the "big idea" emerging after the Cold War is that we will preserve America's security by crafting, then nurturing and, in effect, leading the development of the world free-market economy on the assumption that democracy and peace will follow free development of that economy. Within that broad conception, we might articulate our national security strategy in the terms given above, as follows:

- *What do we want to do?* We want to play a primary role in the growing global economy as a means of assuring life, liberty, and the pursuit of happiness for the American people. We believe that by encouraging economic development everywhere in the world we will also help the advance of democracy and human rights, which will lead in turn to a more benign world less plagued by armed conflict.
- *How do we want to do it?* By encouraging and setting up the mechanisms to enable free trade and using our armed forces to protect our economic interests and related political interests worldwide and to prevent threats to those interests from getting out of hand. This includes forming alliances with nations who are similarly oriented. The countries in the alliances, including ourselves, will have a common interest in protecting against military and quasimilitary threats to their economic well-being and to democratic processes that can affect that well-being while they engage in peaceful economic competition with each other and with those on the outside.
- *With what do we want to accomplish this?* With technology: civilian technology to ensure our competitiveness in the world (both within and outside the security alliances); and armed forces technology to ensure their ability to move rapidly and decisively to protect our interests (together with our allies, but alone if necessary) and to ensure their supremacy in any armed conflict.

This is not a strategy that has been articulated this way in any of our public forums, and indeed many would object to the crass commercialism that it seems to convey. But it describes a strategic direction in which the nation seems to be moving without much planning, as we moved to the past strategies I have sketched above. And as I have stated, its scope is broad enough to accommodate any of the moral and humanitarian responsibilities we believe we must accept as the world's most powerful democracy.

The purpose of the armed forces, then, should be to meet threats to this strategy and to the nation and our citizens as they go about implementing the strategy, anywhere in the world. Threats can be expressed as threats to our interests if they impinge on aspects of this free development. The interests will become more vital as the threats come closer to U.S. and our allies' economic prosperity and physical survival in the world. And the fundamental importance of technology in the strategy, and therefore the underlying science that fosters it, must be accepted. Without it, we would have no hope of achieving or sustaining our strategic objective on a global scale.

It is in connection with this strategy that we are trying to revise our policies relative to nuclear, chemical, and biological weapons. Although it is clear that we no longer need the large Cold War arsenal of nuclear weapons that grew to oppose the Soviet arsenal, it is not clear that we need no such weapons at all. Arguments, by people such as Admiral Noel Gayler, a former commander of forces in the Pacific, General Lee Butler, a former commander of the Strategic Air Command, and General Andrew Goodpaster, a former NATO commander, have been made that we can dispense with such weapons. The proposed circumstances under which this should happen depend on the arguments being made and by whom. Arguments and counterarguments revolve around the residual size of the Russian arsenal, should Russia turn hostile again; around the risks of proliferation of nuclear weapons to dangerous rogue states that would not hesitate to use them to spread regional hegemony against U.S. military resistance to such spread; and around issues such as whether conventional precision-guided weapons can substitute for nuclear weapons and whether we might need nuclear weapons to deter and perhaps retaliate against the use of nonnuclear weapons of mass destruction (i.e., chemical and biological).

Ideas are emerging that nuclear weapons will be useful only to deter the use of nuclear weapons against the United States and its allies by others and that we are prepared to give them up altogether as soon as the rest of the world is ready to give them up, in verifiable fashion, at some indefinite time in the future. The number of weapons we need to implement this strategy is yet to be determined by a combination of military planning and public debate. Numbers as low as 200 have been proposed as adequate—far below the Cold War holdings and well below the numbers agreed in the START agreements with Russia. Altogether, however, the nuclear threat has receded into the background of public consciousness and is not a subject of extended public argument, except in connection with the arguments about national missile defense and in the indirect context of our nonproliferation policies and the unsavory bargains they sometimes lead to overseas. Warnings have been issued by the government against the threats of chemical and biological attacks, and some halting steps are being made to meet those threats; the public does not appear to be exercised over the threats.

The anticipation that democratic government will follow economic progression must not be minimized as an important corollary to the main strategic thrust of ensuring our national security by essentially dominating the world economy; it is a fundamental part of the "big idea." But we must be careful not to insist, in our characteristic missionary zeal, that democratic forms in other countries, like China, must be expressed exactly like ours. As suggested by the discussion in Chapter 3, we shall have to learn to be satisfied to see an absence of tyranny in China and a reasonable modicum of respect for basic human rights, or else we shall jeopardize the success of the entire strategy. It is a curious but all too human fact that we tolerate ideological diversity among our friends better than we do among others. For example, Britain's Official Secrets Act limiting what the news media can publish would never pass our free-speech screen; the absence of habeas corpus in several NATO countries, and the ability of the Belgian and French gendarmerie to make arbitrary arrests and hold people indefinitely on suspicion of illegal activities, would never pass our courts. Yet we have never accused these allies of falling short as democracies.

In some cases, our ideological orientation will determine policy actions from the reverse direction, with concerns about government abuses and human rights origi-nating the actions, but the economic implications will never be far behind. For ex-ample, we support Israel first because it is a democracy, and our support of that democracy is seen as fulfilling our obligation to a nation that we helped bring into being in part because of its roots in our Judeo-Christian heritage. But we press for a peaceful resolution of Israel's quarrels with the Arabs because that will enhance our own and our allies' economic security. We have supported peaceful resolution of the ethnic and religious quarrels in the former Yugoslavia (unsuccessfully, it turned out) in part because there is a humanitarian component to the conflict resolution. But we have also been aware that if those quarrels can be resolved in ways that promote de-mocratic evolution and reduce the threats of expanding war in the region, with im-plications for Europe's peace and prosperity, then our own peace and prosperity will be enhanced. We sustain friendly relationships with nations that are not democra-cies, such as China and Saudi Arabia, when that is in our economic interest, even as we try to coax them in the direction of democratic reforms. In China's case, we as-sume that democratic reforms will follow economic development. This policy orien-tation has, perhaps, had its greatest successes in Latin America, and those successes encourage us to continue in that direction everywhere.

In a real sense, economic issues underlay all issues of national strength and power anywhere, and they always have. Conquest has always had an economic component as well as components of religion, ideology, and national honor and pride (whatever the last are taken to mean at the time). The European conflict that began in 1914 had as one underlying element the competition for colonies in Africa that were im-portant to the economic welfare of European nations at the time. Germany's drive for world domination in the 1930s and 1940s had as one component the desire to capture Russia's resources for Germany's use in sustaining its military power. Japan's primary motive for the attack at Pearl Harbor was to neutralize the U.S. Navy's abil-ity to interfere in the conquest of Southeast Asia, which Japan wanted to secure for the natural resources needed to feed the growing Japanese economy.

Until now, U.S. armed forces have not been crafted with support of economic interests as their primary purpose. Nor do we admit that that is their primary current purpose. To do so would put off our allies, who would not want to be seen as being protected to be instruments of U.S. economic domination in the world; indeed, France has always resisted American leadership, precisely on the basis that they fear such economic domination is our strategy. And as shown by the negative domestic reaction to the prospect of going to war in the Persian Gulf in 1991 mainly over oil, the idea would not be popular in the United States, either. Thus, although the idea of protecting America's preeminent role in the world economy, from which all the other benefits are expected to flow, may be foremost in our strategic thinking, we embed the idea—legitimately—in a collection of other purposes of higher moral value that justify our military and its presence in the world.

Would it make a difference if we crafted the armed forces explicitly to support our economic position in the world? Partly it would and partly it would not. The motives for which armed forces are built are reflected in the intensity with which they are pursued and the ingenuity with which they are designed. As we noted earlier, the armed forces of Nazi Germany were designed for rapid conquest in a continental environment, whereas those of imperial Japan were designed to do the same in a largely maritime environment. In our case, we may have the strategic initiative economically, but we are on the strategic defensive militarily. Almost all the of the strategic *initiatives* sketched in the previous paragraphs are economic, yet we talk of military actions for *defense* of our country and our people and *protection* of our interests.

As we saw in Chapter 3, the threats to our interests may come from many directions and in many forms at different times. Without a simple purpose like outright conquest of areas that we can clearly target, as Germany and Japan had in the 1930s and 1940s, how can we build armed forces with focus and power such as they were able to achieve? The way we implement and use the forces of *Joint Vision 2010* will test whether that kind of focus and power can be reached by an economy-driven, defensive military strategy.

To make it even more difficult we have, in addition to the apparent diffusion of focus, the internal economic constraint that we wish to minimize the cost of the armed forces to the nation. Whereas those bent on conquest were willing to give first priority to building their armed forces, we give first priority to building our economy and caring for our population. We want only enough armed forces to protect the aspects of our economy that depend on our overseas connections—allies, resources, and transportation—and to protect against attacks on our homeland that may be stimulated by the trials and progress of the overseas connections. Can we devise a strategic focus that will allow us to build armed forces in the circumstances thus visualized? Let's examine that question next. Then we shall look at some of the additional hard questions that must be resolved to proceed with the armed forces themselves. Finally, we must look at what could be done by those who wish us ill to defeat our emerging strategic thrust.

IMPLEMENTING THE STRATEGY

In the face of all the overseas developments described in Chapter 3, which will make America's international life much more complex and confused in the future than it has been in the past, the country's attention is flagging. Much interest in foreign affairs went away with the end of the Cold War. One doesn't have to be attuned to the nuances of popular attitudes to sense, in the attention given in news broadcasts and media commentary to domestic mayhem, atrocities, and disasters relative to foreign affairs, or to the budget wars, or to campaign financing irregularities, or to the president's extracurricular misbehavior, and on and on, that the country generally does not want to pay much attention to what happens beyond our borders. That seems to be true even though such events may affect our security profoundly (unless it be the drug trade or illegal immigration, and then the focus is why we don't stop it *at* the border).

After the Berlin Wall fell, U.S. public interest in events overseas flared up, at the time of the Gulf War and again during the worst of the killing in Bosnia and yet again over the renewed Serbian war to save its writ in Kosovo Province. It arose periodically when Saddam Hussein tweaked our nose over weapons-site inspections. It rises to some modest level of interest over events such as the Irish or Israeli-Palestinian struggles for peace, a major terrorist attack against Americans, as happened in Kenya and Tanzania, and the Indian and Pakistani nuclear weapons tests. But each time it has subsided rapidly. There is great interest in economic developments such as the meltdown in Asia, but these are mainly of the kind that ask when the Asian economic woes will affect the U.S. stock market or interest rates or business.

America's impatience with the behavior of the rest of the world tends to be reflected in rampant "go-it-aloneism." The general tenor of opinion, reflected in the media's person-on-the-street interviews and in congressional commentary about conflicts overseas that affect us, has been "this isn't worth American casualties," or "why don't our allies do it?" or "do more," or "let's move in there and get it over with fast," or "what's our exit strategy?" or "why do we spend defense dollars on extraneous missions like peacekeeping?" and similar attitudes. There is an impatience with the complexities of foreign affairs, of working with coalitions, of understanding other cultures and points of view on the international scene, and of having to work on resolution of adverse situations over periods measured in years or decades rather than days, weeks, and months. Or once an issue is joined, as it was over

Kosovo, there is an immediate drumbeat of criticism on how it is being handled, with the implication that whatever you've done it could have been done better and it should have worked immediately.

And yet even though Congress's first reaction is to want to avoid direct military intervention in any crisis (indeed, that was the attitude expressed when Serbs were attacking Kosovar Albanians in a relatively covert way before the crisis was blown up by NATO's ultimatum to stop and its subsequent intervention), Congress starves our diplomatic corps of resources it could use to do its important jobs of creating friends or staving off enemies before crises occur. Those resources must include the cost of the important work of the military in sustaining contact with the world through its forward-presence, peacekeeping, and other such activities. There appears to be an unwillingness on the part of our media and lawmakers to recognize that involvement with allies to keep them as allies, or with potential allies to convince them to become definite allies, or with potential opponents to help stave off their challenges requires hands-on engagement with them in the problems that are bothering them, rather than advice and cheerleading from the sidelines. Thus it was, for example, that ethnic cleansing and atrocities by the Serbs in Bosnia went on for many months while the United States was deciding to put ground forces in alongside those of France, Britain, and other countries that had been bearing the brunt of the peacekeeping effort. And we decided in advance that we would not put ground forces into Kosovo. In both cases, we made it a condition of our intervention on the ground that the forces would not have to fight to get where they were needed. By our use of airpower as the preferred instrument and these conditions, we convey that we are looking for immaculate intervention. There is a tendency to forget that if we wish to lead we must do it by saying "follow me" rather than "here's what you should do."

Part of our problem in coming to grips with the welter of international issues that has come to face us since the Cold War, and perhaps a reason that the general populace and therefore the national attention becomes jaded and inattentive to the things that will affect our long-term security the most, is that we have lost the presence and value of a big and worthy enemy to focus our attention and our energies. At the same time, the view and the flow of events has become so disjointed in this world of instant communications around the planet that we simply become saturated with what amounts to trying to assemble a giant jigsaw puzzle that has no end. With all this happening at essentially the same time, and no strong focus, how do we deal with it all at once?

It is true that he who defends everywhere defends nowhere. And it is also true that today's convolutions in world events make it difficult to know where our attention and effort ought to be focused. A July 1996 report of the Commission on America's National Interests[3] undertook to sort through these complexities and described a structure of importance and priorities. Without repeating the entire structure here, it is worth showing its general outlines to demonstrate that it is possible to find a path through the apparent swamp.

The commission divided America's national interests into four major categories: Vital (blue chips); Extremely Important (red chips); Just Important (white chips); and Less Important or Secondary (translucent chips). The following kinds of security threats or overseas events are included in each category (this is not a complete list, and it is paraphrased). In reviewing the list, we must keep in mind that where our own or our allies' physical security is not directly at stake the issues reduce to economic, humanitarian, or ethical dimensions; as we shall see later, these dimensions also threaten our physical security but only indirectly and over a longer time period.

- *Blue chips* require attention to eventualities that would threaten the United States directly (paraphrased in my own words): minimizing the risk of attacks on the United States by nuclear, chemical, and biological weapons; preventing the emergence of a hostile hegemon—a dominant power—in Europe or Asia, or the emergence of a hostile major power on U.S. borders; preventing the catastrophic collapse of major global systems for managing trade, finance, energy, and environmental matters; and ensuring the survival of our allies (since they help assure our own survival).
- *Red chips* are less important only in that they deal with matters outside the United States that can have serious impacts on our security rather than those that would impact our country directly. Examples include preventing the proliferation or use of weapons of mass destruction anywhere; preventing the emergence of a hostile regional hegemon in areas important for our national well-being or that of our allies, such as the Persian Gulf; protecting our allies from significant external aggression; suppressing, containing, and combating terrorism, transnational crime, and drugs; and preventing genocide.
- *White chips* cover a host of activities that make up the substance of America's day-to-day dealings with other nations. They include such things as discouraging massive human rights violations in other countries; promoting freedom, democracy, and stability in strategically important states; preventing nationaliza-

---

[3]Established with support from Harvard's Center for Science and International Affairs, the Nixon Center for Peace and Freedom, the Rand Corporation, and the Hauser Foundation; cochaired by Robert Ellsworth, Andrew Goodpaster, and Rita Hauser. For information, call the Harvard Center at (617) 496–6099.

tion of U.S. assets abroad and protecting U.S. citizens from terrorist attacks and kidnappings; promoting beneficial international environmental policies; and maximizing U.S. economic growth from international trade and investment.

- Finally, the *translucent chips* cover many more items and activities perpetually in the news, such as balancing bilateral trade deficits, enlarging democracy elsewhere for its own sake (in places like Congo, Haiti, and Cuba), and helping other states who are not allies preserve their territorial integrity.

One doesn't have to like this particular division of our national interests and the allocation of world events to the different categories or accept it without reservation; there is room in such a listing for argument. Also, it will be found that in real life these divisions are often not pure. For example, we have no alliances in the remnants of Yugoslavia, but the conflicts there verge on involving our close allies in ways that could bring them into conflict with Russia or with each other, in the cases of Greece and Turkey. In addition, the issue of genocide arises as Serbia attempts to extend its territorial writ to all places where there are Serbs and to push other inhabitants out or destroy them. So even as the strict criteria of direct importance to the United States might make Yugoslavia a white chip, these apparently extraneous factors make it an important red chip. Other such areas are Haiti and Cuba, where we have policies of promoting democracy as a matter of principle but where nationalization of property, growing drug connections, and periodic floods of refugees to the United States can change their status in a matter of days, from translucent to red. Yet such ordering of our national interests lends perspective and a means of assigning priorities to what must otherwise seem to be chaotic and irrational activity from day to day, hard to get a handle on and hard to maintain in the focus of attention. We should also note that these interests can be defended in many ways—economic, political, diplomatic, as well as military. The possibility of using those other means often affects what we decide to do militarily.

CRAFTING ARMED FORCES TO MATCH

The armed forces visualized in *Joint Vision 2010*, if they could be brought into being as they are being designed, would have the moxie and the operational flexibility to support the national strategy that is emerging. They could move fast to end crises by rapidly decisive military action, then return home to be ready for the next action in another place. But like all other things in life, their development will be beset by adverse intrusions of the real world. Those intrusions include many disparate factors: the need for institutional evolution that will come hard for dedicated proponents of traditional Service points of view; the budget constraints and distortions that we have already explored in some detail; the resulting lack of resources in critical areas where they may be needed the most; and lingering misconceptions based on past history about the way the armed forces must be used in this new and complex world. The last, especially, will affect the size and design of the armed forces in ways the country has, as yet, shown no signs of accepting. Let's explore these real-world constraints in more depth.

Changing Organizations for Changing Missions

There are two important strategic reasons to change the emphasis in our military force planning. Think about the shape of the world that the new armed forces must interact with. First, there will be few overseas bases. Second, operations from bases that we do have available will always be subject to limitation if the host country doesn't like the use we plan. Thus, we will always be in the position of having to craft a coalition that includes the host country for a purpose we want to serve. If we are fortunate, we will already have an appropriate alliance in place, but we can't count on it. For example, France is almost always at odds with us over the prospect of armed conflict with an Arab country, as was the case with the 1986 air strike against Libya and as has been the case in almost every confrontation with Saddam Hussein since the Gulf War. The Arab countries around the Persian Gulf may or may not allow operations from their territory. Japan might or might not be happy to provide a base of operations against North Korea in some future faceoff, say, over the North Korean desire to develop nuclear weapons. Manned aircraft operations instead of missile strikes against a terrorist base in the depths of Afghanistan may depend on whether Pakistan is willing to give us overflight rights. And so on.

One way to overcome much of this kind of constraint is to have a force that incorporates the base within itself and that can launch military operations without being constrained to follow the preferences of host countries. That force is, of course, the combination of Navy and Marines, what are technically called the "naval forces." The Navy can be used for a variety of purposes, from making port visits to promote international friendship, to training with friendly navies, to undertaking military actions that do not depend on other nations' sovereign decisions and permission for their origin and destination. The Navy can contribute to deterrence by sustaining a forward and noticeable presence for extended periods without impinging on the sovereign territory of any nearby nation. The Marines can work with friendly ground forces in similar ways. If it becomes necessary for combat operations, the Marines can land from the sea, and in the new combat modes they are devising they can either move rapidly against objectives like airfields, ports, capital cities, and command centers to end a military issue decisively, or they can simply establish landing zones that can become base areas for follow-on Air Force and Army units if such bases are unavailable initially for whatever reason.

If we think about the political shape of the future world that was sketched in Chapter 3, we can see the other reason for a military strategy that gives the naval forces a significantly larger role than they have had as the forward force. When the Soviet Union was the main threat to our security, whatever its intentions, it was poised to invade Western Europe with land armies. This was the main threat that we had to meet, and to do so we had to have a forward force on the ground in Europe, including the Army and the general-purpose part of the Air Force, to meet such an invasion. Today there is little threat of major war in Europe, although we keep a smaller number of troops and aircraft there to guard against lesser threats arising in the European region and also as an indication of our continued involvement in European security. Those forces are providing a base for friendly engagement with the newly freed nations of Eastern Europe by U.S. military units. Starting with the major school at the George C. Marshall European Center for Security Studies in the Bavarian Alps, American education and training units, including personnel from all the Services, are making contact with and helping reorient the Eastern European armed forces from Soviet to NATO doctrine and operational techniques through the Partnership for Peace program. Obviously, a program like this, connected to NATO and involving all NATO nations in one way or another, is a major element of the peacetime engagement that helps stave off war and that builds coalitions if war threatens; it will be continued as long as the nations in Europe, inside or outside NATO, want it to continue.

While we use the NATO presence to help consolidate peace in Europe, we can anticipate that, short of a hostile Russian resurgence in the short term, the focus of threats to our security will shift to the Middle East and the Pacific. There is no place in those regions (outside of Korea, currently) to keep large standing armies or tactical air forces. Although current hot spots that threaten to blow up include the Persian Gulf region and Korea, we noted in Chapter 3 that reunification of Korea, distant as it may seem now, would likely require us to withdraw our Army and Air Force units from the peninsula. And at some point we shall have to give more attention than we have been giving to Iran, India, and Pakistan, and our interest in Southeast Asia is likely to revive with their economies. We should, and are in some measure trying to, build and sustain friendly relations with all these countries. And we hope and expect that our close relationship with Japan will continue despite the frequent clashes over economic policy. But all these countries' interests often diverge from ours and from each others', and it is possible for friendly relations to break down when interests vital to one party or the other appear threatened. Even if future confrontations requiring military action should arise in the Asia-Pacific region, it is difficult to imagine that they would involve major land campaigns deep into the Asian interior for any reason. Most likely confrontations over regional interests outside the NATO arena, such as were illustrated in Chapter 1, would involve mainly naval force actions, at least at first. Even in the Mediterranean, it has not been unusual for the president to ask "Where are the carriers?" when a crisis breaks or to quickly move them into place when one wells up. Thus, for reasons of both ready accessibility to likely conflict areas and the nature of the military actions the geography would impose, the Navy and Marine Corps are highly likely to be the first force involved. The most effective force planning would recognize this.

A number of difficult institutional adjustments would be required to orient the forces this way. (Actually, they *are* oriented and used this way much of the time; the issue is to formalize it so that the forces can be crafted and trained in the most efficient and effective way). The Air Force, shortly after the Cold War ended, issued a doctrinal claim—"Global Reach, Global Power"—that said it could be first on scene with military power and could launch precision strikes by B-1, B-2, and B-52 bombers from the United States without needing overseas bases. This by itself would pose no great issues, had it not been coupled with the suggestion that the bomber force could thus fill the deterrent role much less expensively than could Navy carriers. Of course, that claim can't hold up.

The Air Force cannot sustain an overseas presence indefinitely in the absence of bases, so that its global reach from the United States with the bomber force is useful for striking but not for lying in wait or for making sustained local contacts without a complex presence on land. Also, detailed analysis of the military capability of the forces in being shows that the bombers could launch one flight every day or two by each bomber that is in flyable condition. The time is a combination of turnaround time for the aircraft and crews and long flight times to their targets. Running the arithmetic would show that this can't sustain the weight of attack that local tactical aviation squadrons, whether Air Force from land bases or Navy from carriers, could. Both carrier-based attack aviation and land-based tactical air force aircraft can fly several combat sorties[4] per day, and the bombers' extra load-carrying capacity can't make up the difference in sortie capability. Thus, in the absence of tactical air bases ashore or permission to use the bases that we do occupy, the Navy is the logical first-strike-from-on-the-spot force.

But the Navy has problems, too. With the safe standoff that the carriers need from possible shore-based attack, their reach inland may be more limited than a successful

---

[4]A "sortie" is a combat flight, from takeoff to landing, including any attack and defense activities in between or none but flyout and return.

tactical air strike would require. For example, Tomahawk cruise missiles with rather light warheads could reach into Afghanistan to strike a terrorist camp or could reach into northern Iraq or Iran from the Mediterranean Sea or the Arabian Sea. But a tactical air strike that had to go several hundred miles inland from a carrier would likely be so loaded with extra fuel that it could not fully benefit from the much larger attack payloads that the aircraft could carry in close-in attacks. The standard practice of using attack aircraft to fly as tankers within the attack formations for midair refueling part way to the target would also reduce the attack capability of the available strike force. The way around this, of course, would be to use the bomber force for such deep penetration. Extension of this kind of argument suggests that the Navy and Air Force should split the mission: The Navy would strike within a relatively close distance of shore (e.g., not more than 100–200 miles inland) when the heavy tactical aircraft payloads are needed while the long-range bomber force (and the Air Force's F-15E Strike Eagles when shore bases are available) would be responsible for deeper strikes.

However, the Navy has sought ever more complex strike aircraft with ever greater range at ever greater cost on the rationale that it must be prepared to carry out the entire mission by itself, whereas the Air Force has prepared to perform the long-range strike mission with only minimal coordination with the Navy's strike forces. The allocations of responsibility are resolved when the area Commander in Chief (CINC) plans the action, but by the time the forces reach that point they have suffered the inefficiencies of uncoordinated planning and expenditure to bring them into being.

Additional changes should be in the offing when we plan to send the Marines ashore from the sea. They have (embedded within the Navy) their own very specialized amphibious fleet with heavy lift helicopters and the new Osprey tilt-rotor vertical-takeoff-and-landing airplane. With these, they now plan, under a developing doctrine—operational maneuver from the sea—to move ashore very rapidly against critical military objectives that may be as deep as 200 miles from shore. Their logistic base would remain in ships at sea, avoiding the need to build up a large supply base on land and thereby give an enemy much warning and defense-preparation time before our own offensive action is undertaken. That warning, and the vulnerability of the large supply base, could make the difference between success and failure of the Joint Vision's "dominant maneuver"–"precision engagement" approach.

Full implementation of the new mode of operation poses some further, excruciatingly difficult institutional problems. If the Marines are to go rapidly far inland over a broad front they must be light and mobile. If they are to be supported logistically from the sea, that support will have to be largely by air until a land connection to a home base is secured sometime after the initial stages of the action succeed. The tonnage that can be delivered by an air line of supply is much smaller than the tonnage that can be delivered over land. One of the Marines' greatest logistic burdens is imposed by the need to take artillery batteries ashore and keep them supplied with ammunition. If that weren't necessary, three-fourths or more of their logistic load could be avoided. But they need the firepower: How to provide it? It is becoming technologically possible for the Navy to launch precision-guided missiles from multitube vertical launchers on ships to ranges as deep as the Marines' air mobility will carry them. Calculations show that such missiles from shipboard, together with close air support based on the Marines' amphibious carriers, could supply a higher rate of sustained, accurate firepower where it is needed and when it is needed than the Marines' own artillery ashore could, without the need to continually carry heavy ammunition resupply loads ashore. But to achieve this a number of problems, falling somewhere between force design and trust, would have to be solved.

The Marines would have to be convinced that they would get the firepower from the sea as quickly and reliably as though it were from their own cannons on land in their immediate rear. The only way to do that for certain might be for the Marines to command the ships that deliver the firepower. But these ships would be cruisers and destroyers that are also needed to protect the fleet, or to deliver firepower themselves in the absence of carriers, perhaps at different locations from the action ashore. If it continued to command the ships carrying the firepower, the Navy would have to commit them to staying offshore in position to support the Marines as long as they were needed. This would preclude them from moving off to other missions when timing may be critical both for the Marines and for the other missions. The Marines would be under pressure to finish their missions quickly, in case enemy action made the other claims on the supporting ships too strong to resist. To do that, they might have to rely on early entry of Army forces, which poses additional issues that we will examine directly. Thus, to get the most out of smaller and more mobile forces each Service—Navy and Marines—would have to change the way it is constituted and the way it operates to enable the two Services together to capitalize to the fullest on the synergistic capabilities of both. This means changing things that are deeply ingrained in tradition as well as in valid rationale—not easy to do.

Next, think about the Army, together with the Marines. Some part of the Army will have to remain a heavy armored force. Such a force is essential for powerful offensive actions on land, such as the ones that were undertaken against Iraqi forces in Operation Desert Storm. Often, too, maneuvering armored forces furnish the best way to defend against an attack by such forces. And despite the fact that Soviet armored armies are no longer a threat, there remain large armored forces in nations that may turn hostile. The Marines also must retain some strong armored units for times when they are fully established on land and must strike out against a well-armed enemy. Many such instances occurred in World War II; the Marines dealt Chinese Communist forces one of their bloodiest defeats at the Battle of Chosin Reservoir in Korea; and they constituted a key part of the offensive thrust in Kuwait. But the Marines' armored equipment is inferior to that of the Army; they have older and less capable tanks, and their artillery support, when it is landed, is not as powerful or as mobile. When heavy Marine forces are needed, usually they are landed from the fleet in either a classic amphibious operation or at a port. The Army could do that as well; indeed, it has. But to be part of the heavier forward force that lands with the fleet, it would need training in the amphibious parts of the operation, and that would make it look more like the Marines. Interestingly, the Army's heliborne combat units demonstrated that they could operate from the sea when they landed at Port au Prince, Haiti, from a carrier in 1994.

At the other end of the force-design scale, the early-entry Army and Marine forces are coming to look very similar in equipment and technique. Although the Army airborne forces are trained and specialized to parachute into operational areas or to land from transport aircraft, the Marines are planning to land from their own aircraft based on amphibious carriers. Both types of training and capability are needed. But once ashore, both Services face similar mobility, combat, and logistic support needs. Both forces are designed to be light but to carry a powerful punch by being able to move fast and to call in high firepower from a distance. Both could benefit by having fire support from the sea so that they would not, early in an operation, have to carry and supply a constant flow of tons of ammunition for artillery ashore. Both will need some lightweight vehicles to provide local mobility once they enter enemy territory. Both will need some lightweight antitank and antiaircraft weapons as parts of their force to afford themselves local protection against counterattack while the supporting aviation and ship-based fire support are brought in. Both depend on helicopters to deliver local fire support, as well as on transport helicopters to facilitate force maneuvers. Both are devising and training in small-unit tactics, especially for urban environments, that are similar to the tactics that the Special Operations Forces (SOF) have devised for land operations. Both could be resupplied by precision airdrop techniques that the Army and Air Force are developing together. Both are planning special capabilities in battlefield psychological warfare and to engage local governments in cooperative activities to maintain civic order in war zones and captured areas. Both need the same kinds of connections to the overall information system to be able to perform their missions successfully.

Thus, the two forces appear to be converging. The main differences occur in the specialized landing techniques that the two are equipped and trained to use: Army parachute assaults and Marine amphibious assaults. The two forces also have different doctrines and tactics for land combat that emerge from their different histories.

They would have to reconcile them, but as the two forces look to the future combat tactics of their lighter combat elements, they are tending to converge. There would appear to be much room for consolidation of the two forces and crosstraining in their specialized landing and operational techniques. Although parachute and amphibious assault require different training and equipment, much of the other operational gear, at both the light and heavy ends of the force spectrum, are similar. All the operational capabilities described above would be available if forces were merged.

This possibility is not raised as another in the perennial string of proposals to phase out the Marine Corps in favor of the Army. More to the point, since the Navy and the Marines are best suited to be the nation's forward force outside of the NATO context and Korea currently, the light assault parts of the Army could more properly be merged into the Marines. The Army would bring their parachute assault capabilities and much of their helicopter assault capability with them as the Navy provides firepower and logistic support from the sea. At the same time, the heavy armored combat parts of the Army and the Marines could become a single ground combat force to be landed as soon as there is a secure area in which to land them. Similarly, the units trained in civil government and psychological operations could operate as part of the Marines, or vice versa, depending on when they are landed. The key point is that it may be possible to create a different force design that is both more efficient in using resources and more effective in operation. None of this change would preclude the participation of people from either of the Services in the training and other exercises that would be involved in peacetime engagement; the people involved would be chosen for their military knowledge and skills, as they are today.

If the institutional issues between the Navy and the Marines appear to be difficult to resolve, they pale in comparison with the ones such a rearrangement of the ground forces would pose. The key question for the nation is whether to seek the gains in efficiency and effectiveness at the cost of years of conflict and turmoil over the process, both in Congress and in the defense establishment, or to accept the inefficiencies and losses of potential effectiveness of our shrinking forces in order to avoid such derangement of the existing order.

You may wonder why, in the midst of all this speculation on radical restructuring of the sea and land forces, I have not raised the issue of merging what have been called the four separate tactical air forces of each of the Services. It has been pointed out many times since the Air Force was established as a separate Service after World War II that each of the Services appears to have its own air force, at great apparent waste of resources. The famed Key West agreement crafted by Secretary of Defense Charles E. Wilson in 1956 assigned fixed-wing aircraft responsibility to the Air Force and rotary-wing responsibility to the Army (there are some exceptions in detail, but that is the essence of the agreement). From this beginning, the Air Force has (aside from the bomber force, which was never in the same field of contention as the tactical forces) built its tactical air combat force, including fighters, interceptors, and attack bombers, while the Army has built its helicopter-borne assault units and an armed helicopter combat force that provides close support to ground combat units. At the same time, the Navy also has carrier-borne fighters, interceptors, and attack bombers, whereas the Marines have their vertical-lift transports and combat helicopters and fighter-bombers that operate in close coordination with ground forces. It is these air forces that have periodically come under attack as the four separate tactical air forces that defense accountants want to merge in the interest of saving money.

However, even the nominal description of these separate aviation forces in the previous paragraph already conveys what more detailed examination would show to negate the claim that these four air forces duplicate each other's capabilities and missions and can be reduced to one:

- The Air Force tactical aircraft are designed to operate from fixed airfields, allowing them to maximize their range and weapon load.
- The Navy fighters and attack aircraft are specialized to operate from carriers. That makes them heavier than comparable Air Force fighters and attack aircraft, to withstand the catapult and arresting-gear loads that operations from a carrier deck impose. Since the added weight for carrier operations comes at the expense of combat range and weapon load, Navy tactical aviation gives that up to capitalize on the fact that it carries its air base in its pocket, so to speak. Also, the Navy pilots must be trained extensively for such operations; such training is not necessary for Air Force pilots.
- The Marines' tactical combat aviation is designed around vertical-lift fighter-bombers that can operate from the Marines' amphibious carriers or from very small fields near Marine units ashore, neither of which the Navy's or the Air Force's aircraft can do.
- The Army's (and the Marines') helicopters can operate out of the terrain that the ground forces occupy. The transport helicopters can move troops from one part of that terrain to another, and the armed helicopters are closely integrated with the maneuver units. They are able to provide very close-in armed escort as they move, they can clear landing zones of opposing forces from close quarters, and they can hover in clearings or just above the treetops to engage enemy tanks and combat units that are immediately threatening troops on the ground.

Each of these different types of tactical aviation units is sufficiently specialized that, if there were only one air force, the different specialized units would have to be provided and trained within it. None of the kinds of combat performance the different units provide can be foregone; all are needed, often at the same time. By the time the separate units were equipped and trained and then assigned to the command of the force commander needing them (e.g., an air wing commander, a carrier battle group commander, an Army division commander, or a Marine landing force commander), the units would have taken on their current specialized complexion and command structure. Thus, it does not make sense to think about merging all the tactical air forces into one. The only exceptions may exist in the areas of close air support for the Army and fighter cover for the Marines. However, even here, appearances can be deceiving.

The Air Force's fixed-wing close air support aircraft would seem at first glance to carry out the same functions as the Army's armed helicopters: attacking threatening enemy forces and installations in close proximity to ground forces. However, a detailed review shows that the two kinds of aircraft carry out different functions even at that detailed level. The fixed-wing aircraft can deliver much larger weapon loads against threatening targets; the weapons may be specialized to destroy artillery or to counter attacks by soldiers spread out on a battlefield. The aircraft can circle over a combat area to be on call for a time, if opposing air defenses do not drive them off; such loitering aircraft can be called in for an attack, and they can be replaced when their fuel and weapons run low. Mainly, however, they are specialized for fast, heavy attacks—get there, deliver the weapons on targets the ground controller designates, and get out of there before the antiaircraft gets you. The helicopters, in contrast, can move together with the troops on the ground, they can rest on the ground immediately in the troops' rear, and they can fight in a way that is much more closely integrated with the ground force operations than the fixed-wing aircraft can. In this case, the forces are complementary; it is not a matter of either-or; it is a matter of needing both.

The Marines' case is somewhat different. They also have armed helicopters, and their own fixed-wing aircraft provide close air support of the kind the Air Force provides for the Army. The fact that their vertical-takeoff-and-landing fixed-wing aircraft can operate from small clearings near the ground units and from relatively small amphibious support carriers gives them a special advantage; they have operational capability somewhat near that of the Army's heavy assault helicopters as well as that of the Air Force's fixed-wing fighter-bombers. And since air and ground forces are under the same commander, one very important layer of potential delay in transmitting attack orders or chance of force diversion is eliminated. The Marines also have fighters to protect their forces from air attack and to attack enemy forces far beyond the areas of ground force contact. Those fighters could be provided by the Navy (and they often are). Here the issue is the same one of trust that is involved in the possibility of substituting ship-based supporting firepower for Marine artillery on the ground: Will the Navy fighters be there when they are needed? Thus far, the argument has been resolved in favor of the Marines and their closely integrated command system that enfolds all the aircraft together under a single ground force commander. The same kind of problem exists between the Army and the Air Force in the close air support mission area. Merging the ground forces as described above would make both the Marines' fixed-wing close air support force and the Army's heavy attack helicopter force available to the new ground force. Some consolidation and streamlining of the forces might then be possible.

Interestingly, in all this the Special Operations Forces appear to be the best organized and adapted to their missions. In part as a result of the lessons from the Vietnam War and in part because they have been seen as an important force for assignment to many of the military tasks that were foreseen in the post–Cold War world, they were consolidated under a separate command in 1989. Congress also established an Assistant Secretary of Defense to oversee SOF affairs. That move was intended to give the SOF a more important and visible role in the developing strategy of military engagement with the rest of the world to suit them better to the developing conflict environment that could already be foreseen in the 1980s. The SOF can thus be said to have anticipated many of the institutional changes that the other Services are currently grappling with. (It is noteworthy in this context that General Henry H. Shelton, Chairman of the Joint Chiefs of Staff beginning in 1997, was commander of these forces on his promotion to the Chairmanship.)

This has been a long and involved discussion of possible changes in the military forces that must be considered to suit them better to the emerging military strategy: defending our interests in many venues and circumstances while consolidating the claims on resources so that the forces will be supportable under the implicit rules the country seems to be imposing. It is important to understand the underlying structures and issues if we are to understand the restructuring that must take place to use the available defense resources to greatest advantage over the long term. Let us summarize:

- Strategy calls for rapid maneuver and entry into a crisis area, marshaling powerful forces from a distance at the right places and the right times for fast and precise military action to settle the military phases of a crisis or conflict quickly and decisively. Evolving world circumstances will require that this be done without an elaborate forward base structure.
- The naval forces—the Navy and Marines—are the logical forces to represent the nation's forward military presence, outside the NATO context and the current arrangements in Korea, to carry out that strategy. They have been and are

designed for the traditional mission of protecting the lines of transport over the oceans. They are best positioned and constituted to sustain a forward military presence from a minimal forward base structure for purposes of peaceful engagement with friend as well as possible foe, and for deterrence of military adventures by the latter. Indeed, in their ship-borne strength they substitute for the bases on shore that we have had to give up in many areas. They are best specialized to establish a lodgment ashore when there are no bases for the Air Force and the Army to occupy and depart from should extended combat be anticipated or needed.

- The Air Force's bomber force based in the United States and at forward bases in the Pacific and Indian Oceans is a logical complement to the Navy when a strike force is needed. Acceptance of this alliance would allow the Navy to avoid the cost of manned aircraft for deep strikes into enemy territory and would allow it to concentrate better on expeditionary warfare and theater missile defense along the continental peripheries.

- The light forces of the Marines and the Army are similar in many respects, but each has some unique qualities for early entry into crisis areas and for establishing and maintaining order in civilian areas that they enter. It would make sense to merge the light Army forces into the Marine light early-entry forces while maintaining the unique qualities of airborne and amphibious assault, psychological warfare, and civil government that each can bring to the combined force.

- The early-entry forces can avoid substantial cost and weight—translating into longer reach and faster movement—by relying on the Navy for heavy firepower support rather than carrying their own artillery with them. They can avoid substantial delay in landing and maneuver against critical enemy objectives by relying on Navy-furnished and -protected logistic support from a base resting on ships at sea instead of the traditional practice of building a huge logistic base on shore before undertaking offensive action. This, too, would require the Navy to orient many of its operations and systems shoreward, in effect subordinating them to the Marines for the expeditionary mission. That requires a significant reorientation from the traditional deep-ocean outlook that dominated their thinking for a century or more; the Navy is moving in that direction, but very slowly.

- The Army's heavy forces are better suited to offensive land warfare against strong armored forces than are those of the Marines. The Army can take over that mission, but then it would have to change to be able to operate better in coordination with the Navy for landing and for logistic support. That would allow the Marines to concentrate on the early-entry mission, it would take better advantage of the Navy's forward presence, and it would help eliminate the duplication of large Army and Marine equipment prepositioning fleets. The ships of those fleets must be redesigned in any case because they are not well suited to the fast movement and streamlined support visualized by *Joint Vision 2010*.

- The tactical air forces of the respective Services are the targets of much of the pressure for Service consolidation by congressional and outside experts because they are very expensive forces to equip. In fact, however, each is well specialized for its task, and changes are possible only at the margins. Given the magnitude of the other institutional changes involved in the above steps, the gains that could be achieved in tinkering with the tactical air forces, beyond those noted just above, are probably not worth the accompanying pain. Similarly, the evolution of tactical or theater missile defense, which we discussed earlier, also seems to be moving in directions that will give each of the Services a distinct role to fulfill and that will avoid unwarranted duplication of effort and cost.

- Last, but far from least, we should note from earlier discussion that we can significantly reduce the strategic nuclear deterrent forces and somewhat reorient their mission. But in view of continuing world conditions, we will not be able to eliminate them altogether at any time in the foreseeable future.

Finally, we must remind ourselves of other institutional problems that were hinted at earlier. If all the military forces in the field are to be increasingly and heavily dependent on what can be called the "infosphere" in which they are embedded, then we must give priority to that infosphere in allocating the budget. That means spending money first on the surveillance and observation systems, the accurate navigation, weather and ocean conditions forecasting, the computers, the information search and interpretation software, and the communications systems that will make up the infosphere. It means additional spending to make the information system especially responsive to the needs of military forces in rapidly moving situations, since information that is not timely will be useless or even treacherous to ongoing military operations. It means extensive, expensive attention to information security to prevent penetration and disruption of any part of the information system. It also means developing a corps of specialized and highly trained information warriors, analogous to the specialized infantry, artillery, and aviation warriors in organizational conception. And the information organization must be adapted to the need for tight coordination with the other specialized parts of the Services.

In addition, we have noted the very difficult problems of attracting, training, and keeping the highly capable, well-educated people that the new armed forces will need in all military occupational specialties. We cannot forget that such personnel will require more resources than we have been accustomed to spending for people in the armed forces; we are finding that the cost of competing with the civilian economy for them will be much higher than anyone thought would be the case.

If we get our priorities right for the new kinds of warfare, then *after* the information and personnel issues are in hand we can turn the remaining resources for defense to the acquisition of the new kinds of ships, aircraft, tanks, and weapons that make up the combat strength of the armed forces. Of course, it is never either-or. Money must be spent on both, but priorities in the expenditure of funds at the margin have to be reversed. That means a significant institutional wrench. Weapons, and such things as ships and aircraft, have come first in building armed forces since time immemorial. Many of the largest defense contractors, with all their local economic dependencies that are of interest to Congress, are centered in those areas. It is not at all obvious that, despite the catchiness of such phrases as the Navy's "network centric warfare" or the Army's "digital battlefield," the entire collection of defense planners, administration budgeters, and congressional authorizers and appropriators is willing or able to make such a shift in fundamental thinking, attitudes, and constituencies.

More Budget Woes

We have already discussed many of the problems in assembling and focusing a defense budget to craft the armed forces we will need. The problems include the need to resolve the issues of priority just discussed. They include the many political uses of the budget that were discussed earlier. They include the budgetary implications attending the outcomes of arguments about broader defense priorities, such as the resolution, one way or the other, of the national missile defense issue. And they include the question of reducing the defense infrastructure—eliminating the unneeded bases and excess manufacturing capacity—and being able to use the resulting savings to build and support the fighting forces. One or two additional budget problems that we have not yet reviewed must be added to these already extremely difficult ones.

First, we should note that the arrangement of Service missions and rearrangements of force capabilities that we have discussed mean rearrangement of funding allocations to the Services. Notoriously, the tugging and hauling among the Services in our political system have tended to lead to an approximately equal allocation of defense budget shares to each of the Services. Within broad limits, and allowing for such things as the Marines having their budget embedded in the Navy budget, it has been easiest for the many managers and congressional advocates of all stripes who must pass on the budget to arrive at an approximately equal share of the defense budget pie for each of the Military Departments. (This is aside from the defense agencies, such as the Defense Advanced Research Projects Agency, the Defense Information Systems Agency, the Defense Logistics Agency, and others, which claim an additional share of the budget that comes from the resources that would otherwise be available to the Services.)

But if national military strategy were to call explicitly for relying more on the Navy and Marines as the nation's main forward military presence, those forces must be larger than they are now, and they will therefore claim a larger share of the available resources. Economies and further budget rearrangements would be found in consolidation of Marine and Army units and missions, but some unknown amounts would have to be spent to adapt each force to the modes of operation that have been characteristic of the other. Similarly, the enlargement and strengthening of the information system, as well as necessary changes in the logistic support system—for example, suiting logistic support ships to act as elements of a continuous supply base[5] that remains at sea in a war zone rather than simply landing supplies ashore and then going back for more—will require different budget allocations from the ones the entire budgeting system has been accustomed to.

All of these changes will require different budget categories as well. This accords with the recognition among management theorists that the accounting categories an organization uses must reflect how it views its mission and how it does business.

Yet even with the budget reforms that Secretary of Defense Robert McNamara imposed on the system in the 1960s, which established budget categories more closely associated with the purposes of different force elements (e.g., strategic forces, general purpose forces, and the like), Congress and the Office of Management and Budget still budget according to the older budget categories: for example, the Army, Navy, and Air Force separately, regardless of joint missions or system sharing; military construction–Army, for barracks or field installations regardless of purpose; missile procurement–Navy, regardless of whether the missiles are part of a larger weapon system; and so on for dozens of budget categories. There are no budget categories to cover major systems as a whole, such as fleet or ground force air defense systems or tactical air force strike systems. Also, there is no single budget category for an integrated information system used by all the forces in the field under a single CINC's command.

---

[5]Since the early 1990s some consideration has been given to the possibility of a floating platform that can be moved by sea to one war zone or another. It would be some 300–500 feet wide and 3,000–5,000 feet long, to act as an offshore supply base and runway for transport airplanes. It would be assembled from modules similar to offshore oil platforms. Many engineering problems, military problems in moving, using, and defending such a base, and its costs and practicality have yet to be resolved. We may or may not see it in the years ahead. If we do, its function would be the same as the fleet of logistic ships we have been describing.

It is difficult for military planners and congressional staffs to get a clear view of what capabilities are really being supported by a budget with thousands of line items allocated in this fragmentary way. Until and unless that can be changed, the tendency toward equal divisions of the pie, and acquisition of individual system components (whether major ships or small-arms ammunition) in quantities determined by traditional levels of expenditure in a budget category instead of by military need, will continue. It's rather like having medical treatment determined by cost accountants rather than by doctors. The "system" awaits, perhaps, another confluence of people and events such as existed when President John F. Kennedy was elected in 1960 to impose a different budget system and discipline suited to future rather than past military needs. That change took place at the focused height of the Cold War. In today's confused and diffused international security environment, such a confluence is not yet in sight.

If all that has been reviewed weren't enough, we must also remember that the intelligence budget is also being short-changed. As discussed earlier, instead of adding resources to be able to anticipate events in a more complex and disorderly world with many more flash points to watch, we have decreased the resources available for intelligence. At the same time, smaller armed forces have to cover more of the world, and they are being planned to do so on shorter timetables. We've thus put ourselves in the position of a city that has become more prone to fires and has responded by reducing the size of its fire department and the number and accuracy of the fire alarms spread around that city.

But even if we as a nation come to realize we have done that and want to change it, we can't just react by throwing money at the armed forces. We must first know where money is required, then know how much will be required after we make all the changes in the system—the alarms and the fire department, if you will—that are necessary to suit it to the new world situation. We will almost certainly find that we need more money to build and support our armed forces and the intelligence and information structures that they need to function in the new strategic environment. The issue is, How much more, and where should it be put?

To get at that, we need to decide, first, which of the changes in their structure that we examined above (or others that will surely arise when the issues are joined seriously) can and should be made. That should lead to savings in the budget needed for armed forces of a particular size.

Next, we need to decide how much must be added to satisfy the intelligence, other information-gathering and -processing, and connectivity needs that the term "information superiority" implies. Then, we should decide how big the resulting armed forces need to be. Included in that consideration would be the question of keeping the number and duration of deployments down to levels the personnel of the armed forces can tolerate. If people are to be kept at their home bases longer and for more predictable periods, the armed forces will have to be bigger. Or, perhaps, they need only more people; there may be enough ships and airplanes, but if they are to be deployed overseas for long periods new crews can be flown out to them periodically—an idea that has surfaced in Service deliberations but that needs to be analyzed and tested in practice. Finally, we need to set a schedule for the recapitalization of all the forces that we talked about in the previous chapter—all the renewal of equipment needed to enable them to operate in the modes visualized in *Joint Vision 2010*.

Although most of these questions remain to be answered, we can make some rough guesses at how large a budget increase might be needed. A round number for military spending in the 1990s and early 2000s might be taken as $250 billion per year. Let's start with that as a base planning number.

The forces now spend on the order of 50–55 percent of their time in deployed operations—peacekeeping, deterrence, and other operations other than war. That is generally considered too high. It is a confirmed factor in the Services' difficulty in keeping experienced personnel. That number was more like 40 percent during the Cold War, and then there were more overseas bases where soldiers, sailors, and airmen had their families, so that the deployments were neither as far from home nor as long as they have become since. These numbers suggest that to follow the readiness scheme that was described previously we would need armed forces about 15 percent larger than the current forces just to do what our forces are doing today. The forces could then have more rotating elements so that time away from home for individual Service members is reduced, with a total force of current size remaining ready for combat action while additional units are deployed in the noncombat missions. Let us postulate that that would increase the defense budget by 15 percent, or $37 billion. This is high, since operational forces use only about two-thirds of the budget, but it can account for additional equipment. (Although some major systems such as ships, tanks, and airplanes could simply stay in the field while crews rotate, the crews in training at home will need some additional equipment to train with. Also, maintenance of the fielded systems will be higher because they are used more, requiring more equipment so that the needed amount is available while more of the total set is in the shop.) And it can also account for additional time and effort occasioned by the availability of fewer bases overseas, which will make everything take longer and add to the logistic load of supporting deployed forces farther from their bases in the United States.

Then, we know that each of the Services needs about $5 billion per year more than is now available for continual modernization—buying new generations of ships, aircraft, weapon systems, and the critically important information systems that the new forms of the armed forces require to keep ahead of evolving opposition.

This adds, say, $18 billion to the above, incorporating the Marines' needs into the Navy's total and assuming the Special Operations Forces will be equipped out of the Services' budgets. (This is consistent with the estimated increase from about $45 billion to $60 billion for annual procurement needed to recapitalize the forces that was mentioned.) This will bring the additional funds needed to $55 billion. If we are to pay for all of the personnel problems that are leading to loss of military personnel in competition with the civilian economy, that should be rounded up to $60 billion, at least. And this doesn't yet account for many "unknown unknowns" that will be encountered along the way to the new armed forces in their new modes of operation. Thus, we can estimate, in very round numbers, that annual defense expenditures would have to increase by about 25 percent over today's, just to remain where we are today but more firmly and comfortably in place.

There have been rough estimates made in various studies, such as one by the Defense Science Board in 1997, that about $30 billion per year that is now spent on supporting the forces through our currently overlarge base and support system could be shifted to the other needs if that base and support system were brought into line with modern business practices and sized and organized to support the smaller, post–Cold War military force. This, if it could be done, would thus gain about half of what might be needed. More could be captured if the Service reforms described above could be implemented; how much couldn't be said without careful planning of the new organizations. Reduction of the strategic nuclear forces would also make some money available, but since those forces consume only about 6 percent of the nominal $250 billion in defense expenditures (about $15 billion per year), the savings from that quarter will be less than many would hope for. They would be added to any savings from reorganizing the general-purpose forces.

All that wouldn't yet account for the needs of other agencies, such as the intelligence agencies and the other civilian agencies that would be involved in meeting the threats that cross national borders and that have to be countered by more than just military force. For example, the president asked for $10 billion in the fiscal year 2000 budget to counter terrorism. This adds to the $6–$7 billion already devoted to that area for such things as enhanced protection of the civilian population against chemical and biological warfare attack and protection against cyberwar. (There is some overlap with Defense Department programs, but how much has not been described.) Nor does it account for the expenditures needed to suit commercial communications, navigation, and weather systems, on which the military will increasingly rely, to the military uses. This includes things such as ensuring that the capacity is there to handle a sudden surge in military communications without cutting off civilian communications, or vice versa, and making certain that protections are in place against hostile penetration or jamming under conditions of war or near-war. It would be impossible to guess what the overall needs are without a thorough, government- and industry-wide study of the entire national security problem. That would go well beyond looking at the armed forces alone, which the congressionally mandated Quadrennial Defense Review is focused on. Overall, however, we can see that far more resources than are now devoted to or even contemplated for expenditure on national security, broadly defined, are needed.

Even after all this, we won't quite be there. In addition to resolving some of the critical arguments that we have looked at about allocating defense resources between defending America at home and projecting its power overseas, we need to think more deeply about some critical issues in using the forces overseas.

USING THE ARMED FORCES

When national survival is not immediately at stake, there is always a question about when and how military power should be applied. Moving military forces into place as a matter of deterrence and to be ready to act in a crisis is not a controversial step most of the time, although it could certainly be viewed by a prospective opponent as provocative and in some circumstances might even provoke a preemptive attack. Starting to shoot is another issue. Loss of life on our side and on the opponent's side then become matters of concern: whether we value the potential results of the action enough to be willing to spend American lives to achieve them; whether we want to put allied lives at risk (aside from what the allies may think about that); whether the lives of the opponent's general population are to be thought about separately from those of their evil leaders and their armed forces; whether by saving lives now we risk greater loss of life in some action that our failure to act now may encourage in the future.

Generally, in post–Cold War actions to protect our interests (and even in Cold War actions, such as the Cuban missile crisis), we have tended to try other remedies before initiating a military conflict. Those actions run the gamut of possible things that can be done to change a situation, from diplomacy to economic action that may vary from attaching an offending country's bank holdings to economic sanctions that amount to a blockade. A blockade, whatever it is called, involves interfering with shipping and flows of money into and out of a country. When it is undertaken through means like halting U.S. exports to a country or seizing bank assets, military forces will be in the background. Allies, the United Nations, and neutral countries may be involved and affected, however. If it becomes a matter of intercepting and interfering with shipping, then the naval forces and perhaps the air forces become involved, and the sanctions become military acts of war. If the interceptee fights back, then it is indeed a shooting war.

The boundary between the initial economic response (with attempts to gain diplomatic support) and the ultimate military response is thus seen to be fuzzy. It can be crossed gradually, as when we stopped Soviet ships when Soviet missiles were discovered in Cuba or when we denied wheat exports to the Soviet Union after it invaded Afghanistan. Or it can be crossed rapidly, as when we responded to the invasion of South Korea. An additional step may involve giving military assistance to a country we want to help. Such assistance may involve only shipment of materiel and some training in its use, as happened in El Salvador and Afghanistan, or it may involve the participation of American forces, as happened in the early stages of our involvement in South Vietnam before the conflict there was extended to become essentially an American war.

Depending on the stakes for both sides, the sanctions and military assistance may work or they may not; then we have to decide whether we want to go farther. Sanctions did not encourage the Soviet Union to desist from its war in Afghanistan, but the military help to the defenders—especially the Stinger antiaircraft missiles that we gave them—helped the defenders make the war untenable for the Soviets. Sanctions did not persuade Saddam Hussein to evacuate Kuwait; we had to defeat him in war to pry his forces loose from there, and sanctions have not persuaded him to give up his major weapons programs since. They took nearly a decade to persuade Qadaffi to give up his intelligence agents for trial in the Lockerbie bombing of Pan-Am Flight 103, and then we had to accede to his conditions to obtain their release for trial in the Netherlands. They have not visibly helped move Iran toward a less antagonistic policy vis-à-vis the United States. Military assistance was very successful in helping Greece, Turkey, and the Philippines ward off communist-supported insurgencies after World War II. That encouraged us to think that the same might happen in Vietnam. There, the military assistance did not work, and we concluded the stakes were high enough that we had to take direct military action, with extremely painful results for all concerned. When we came to loggerheads with North Korea about its hidden nuclear program in 1994, it said that application of sanctions would be an act of war. Knowing that the regime was xenophobic and unstable, we chose not to accept the implied risk that the North would invade the South if we applied sanctions. At the same time, the North evidently decided that it had more to lose than it wanted to by pursuing that challenge, and so it acceded to a deal to control its pursuit of nuclear weapons, a deal that it may or may not be adhering to.

These few examples, too sketchy to be called a history, illustrate that the region between political response to a challenge to our interests and war to defend them is fraught with uncertainty and has a checkered record. Out of this record has come the current pattern of using military forces as instruments of foreign policy in broader application than simply fighting or not fighting. We have always used them to support U.S. interests by their presence and engagement in areas where policy may be in danger. There has been a critical change in our strategic posture, however, in the gradual evaporation of our overseas base structure. We must deploy much more often from the United States, and the reason to deploy is often open to argument, even by our closes allies. Taking all the other possible actions before actual military conflict can be an extended process that can easily come across as (and might actually signify) vacillation, uncertainty, and lack of will.

Be that as it may, to the extent that they can deter actions inimical to our interests by their presence and military buildups to reinforce the potential of that presence, the military forces will not have to be used in war. To the extent that they can use their special characteristics to assist civilian agencies in diplomatic and humanitarian actions, they can engender goodwill and also help get things done quickly that the agencies would have difficulty doing by themselves. Those characteristics are discipline; trained and available personnel; organization for fast action; ability to marshal vast resources and move them rapidly to where they are needed; and engineering know-how. Few, if any, civilian agencies have all of them in combination.

These kinds of activities, together with relatively modest military actions such as escorting tankers in the Persian Gulf and patrolling no-fly zones over Iraq and the Balkans, constitute what the military have called "military operations other than war," known also by the horrible acronym MOOTW. MOOTW has come to be one of the most contentious post–Cold War issues in the structuring and funding of the armed forces. The dilemma has been posed most succinctly by Senator Warner, who was quoted in the September 30, 1998, issue of *USA Today* as having said (as we noted earlier) that the president's decisions to send troops into crisis points such as Bosnia, Haiti, and perhaps Kosovo add up "in my judgment to too many missions, too few troops and too little equipment." Implicitly, the statement argues for fewer missions rather than for more troops and equipment. The real issue is, Should military operations other than war be folded into the military mission under our current national strategy and the armed forces be sized and structured to match?

As we have already noted, there is no question that using troops for various humanitarian and peacekeeping missions, using them to supplement civilian missions such as guarding our borders against drug-smuggling and illegal immigration, and keeping them on station for deterrence purposes detracts from their availability and readiness for military combat missions. It detracts from time they would be in training for the combat missions, which are the most demanding thing that the armed forces have to do. If they don't do that well, they will suffer needless casualties and they will lose battles. Yet as we have seen, the uses of military force for the purposes other than combat are many, and those uses have come to be an essential part of our post–Cold War strategy.

In fact the uses of the armed forces in missions other than war occur with far greater frequency than engagements in warfare. At the same time that we have engaged in the Gulf War, the bombing of Serb forces in Bosnia and Kosovo, and the few cruise missile launches over the decade or so that the Cold War has been over, there have been several military operations for all the other purposes each year—many of them called for by the Congress as well as by action of the administration. Although there have been arguments against specific noncombat military actions, no one has made a persuasive case that none of them should have been undertaken. And military plans and doctrine recognize and include their necessity. Nor can we attribute that direction in strategy to misguided policies of the Clinton administration, as a Republican Congress has often done. The deployment into Somalia for a mix of humanitarian and peacekeeping purposes was ordered by President Bush. He also had the Army and the Air Force undertake humanitarian and protection missions in northern and southern Iraq; the Navy intercept refugee boats from Haiti; and the Navy involved in drug surveillance in the Caribbean after the Panama invasion. The last was, itself, undertaken mainly to suppress the drug flow through that country. (Whether it succeeded or not is another question, part of the checkered record mentioned above.)

If the use of military forces is to include deployments for friendly engagement, deterrence, peacekeeping, border-watching, humanitarian relief, and all the other purposes for which we need them in the post–Cold War world, the forces have to be trained, equipped, and allocated for those purposes as well as for their primary combat missions. The two are not independent. As we saw in Bosnia and as we have been seeing in the Persian Gulf and Yugoslavia, the combat capability and readiness of the forces are what suit them for deterrence and peacekeeping. The ability and skill of the military to undertake drug surveillance or humanitarian relief operations derives from their combat skills and training. Indeed, as we saw in Somalia, it was the perceived combat capability that enabled the forces to land without opposition and convey the humanitarian relief in the first place. But their essential and finely honed combat skills deteriorate without exercise and practice on training grounds and at sea. As we noted in Chapter 6, the solution is obvious. The forces need to be divided according to their current assignments. When one part of the military is deployed for other than combat reasons, the other part can be in preparation and training for its combat missions.

We noted earlier that this apparently simple means of enfolding all of the military's post–Cold War uses into one universe of missions poses the need for larger forces than we have in being. We must plan for large enough forces to be ready to undertake the combat missions we anticipate for them while military forces are used for all the other purposes for which they are required most of the time. Such planning is included in the budget estimates presented above. At this point we run into one of the bedrocks of our strategy since at least 1990, one that begs for but has not received critical examination outside the military planning forums. That is the two-war strategy: the expressed need for our forces to be able to fight two major regional wars at one time.

Think about what that means, in historic terms.

The concern derives from the Korean War, when we feared that the Soviets would take advantage of our involvement there to start a military crisis in another place where we simply wouldn't have the military strength to respond promptly. It didn't happen, but the specter has haunted us ever since. The prospect would be that while, for example, we were deeply involved in a war like that in Korea, Saddam Hussein would decide to take advantage of our preoccupation to invade Kuwait or Saudi Arabia, and we would have to respond with the massive force that we used in Desert Storm. Or while we were committed to and involved in a major conflict in the Persian Gulf, North Korea would decide to attack the South with all the force at its disposal. Or we would have had to be able to respond to either the Kuwait or the Korean attack while deeply involved in the Vietnam War. In each of the major wars we engaged in after World War II, we committed a substantial part of our available military force; indeed, often the forces were enlarged by calling up reserves. In the future armed forces, the reserves are likely to be useful in supporting roles, but they wouldn't have a priori enough of the specialized training or equipment to engage in the kinds of operations visualized in *Joint Vision 2010* without extensive training after callup.

Thought about in these terms, if the feared but unlikely situation of a major attack against our vital interests in one part of the globe were to follow soon after a deep involvement in meeting such an attack in another place, our ability to respond with the forces in being that are visualized now, and the reserve forces likely to be available, would be marginal at best.

By perpetuating the fiction that we could do so, we are requiring the active forces in being to be ready to engage in two major conflicts (the Major Regional Conflicts or Major Regional Contingencies, or MRCs, of the military plans) at once. From this flows the concern that with every moment the forces are off on a peacekeeping, deployment, or another mission other than war they are detracting from their readiness to respond to the first and then the second MRC. In other words, the two-MRC strategy with the forces we have been willing to support says that all of the available military forces have to be on a hair trigger and therefore cannot be used for the normal and out-of-routine day-to-day purposes that our "national security strategy of engagement and enlargement"[6] calls for. It is like saying that the fire department is too busy training and waiting for the five-alarm blaze they may some day have to handle to be able to

[6]The title of the congressionally mandated presidential national security strategy.

deal with smoking stoves, or car fires, or cats caught in trees—all contingencies that the community expects them to be able to deal with.

The way out of the dilemma is to discard the fiction. We can have enough forces in being to hold a large fraction of them ready to be able to respond to a single MRC while responding to the everyday strategic needs of the nation. This may require more force than we have available now, but it would recognize the dual peacetime-wartime nature of the need for military force in today's and tomorrow's anticipated world. The size of the forces would be based on the criteria we examined earlier. Part of the available forces would include the ones that can deliver vast and sudden destruction: the bomber force, submarines armed with long-range missiles, even ICBMs that could be armed with large numbers of conventional warheads able to seriously damage an attacker's vital underground command and control centers and other critical installations. We could have an announced strategy that says, "If you attack our vital interests while we are occupied with a conflict elsewhere we will deliver upon you a rain of destruction that will cripple your nation until we can get around to dealing with you more thoroughly." That would more realistically fit our capabilities, and it should act as a sufficient deterrent against such an attack. Indeed, it is likely to be a more credible posture because it will visibly match our observable military capabilities better.[7] If the second attack does come, we would face a situation requiring national mobilization in any case, and we would be in what amounted to a worldwide conflict. The strategy would not be all that different from our strategy in World War II, at least insofar as the allocation of resources is concerned.[8]

There has been some fear in military circles that if we abandon the two-MRC fiction Congress would react by reducing the defense budget even further on the theory that with less conflict to be concerned about we can get by with a smaller defense budget. The strategy was retained by the 1997 Quadrennial Defense Review. However, the National Defense Panel that Congress established to act as a sort of reviewing and second-opinion body judged its retention to be counterproductive. The panel said that even though it might have been useful as a force-sizing concept, it has

---

[7]There is enough information around in trade journals, the congressional record, and the popular media that, together with direct observation at our many bases, can give a would-be aggressor a fairly accurate picture of the size of our military forces and their readiness.

[8]During World War II, our strategy was to defeat Germany while holding the Japanese at bay and making whatever gains we could against them with limited resources, then to turn our attention to the Pacific afterward. In the event, we always had about half as many men (or less) in the Pacific as in the European theater. By the time the major buildup against Japan was well under way after Germany's surrender, the war had essentially been won by the march up the islands to position ourselves to invade Japan and by aerial bombardment. The Hiroshima and Nagasaki bombings applied the coup de grâce.

outlived its usefulness. The panel thought it has come to be an inhibiting factor in preparing the forces for all the challenges we foresee in the coming decades. This idea was brought forward and exposed to Congress and the public with scarcely a ripple. The sizes of the defense budget and of the military forces remain in contention, but not for that reason. The issues we have been discussing throughout this and the previous chapter dominate the discussion.

COUNTERSTRATEGIES

Our national strategy and the role and structure of the armed forces within it are obviously becoming known to the world as they unfold in many mostly public forums at home. Those in the world who wish to defeat that strategy and avoid tangling with what are, and we hope will continue to be, formidable military forces in the process will continually be able to tune in to our defense debates and observe the outcomes as they try to develop their own counterstrategies. What might the latter be? We have already examined some of the vulnerabilities the new armed forces themselves may present to those out to defeat them. Those vulnerabilities can be dealt with, if we want to spend the money, by the design and support mechanisms of the forces themselves. But the fundamental national strategy for the use of the forces will also have vulnerabilities that opponents will seek and try to exploit.

We hear a lot, in the media and in the councils of government, about "postmodern warfare" and "asymmetric threats." These ideas were especially emphasized in the National Defense Panel report. Their implications are that as we prepare armed forces for conventional warfare with armies, ships, and aircraft the world is preparing to attack us through chips, germs, and terror. The implicit advice seems to be that we should stop giving so much attention to the more conventional kinds of warfare and get on with meeting the new threats the hostile world out there is generating. This kind of reasoning is in many ways naive and also dangerous because it can cause us to narrow our focus when we should actually be broadening it.

There have always been "asymmetric threats," because any adversary force will play up its own strengths with intent to exploit its opponents' weaknesses. Thus, for example, the Germans devised blitzkrieg warfare to overcome the Maginot Line, a formidable defensive line built (but not extended far enough along the Belgian border to the sea) by the French. The Soviets prepared to counter our powerful carrier-based Navy with submarines and missile-armed long-range land-based bombers. And, as we noted in Chapter 3, terrorists (including infoterrorists) and guerrillas plan their clandestine tactics to overcome the far stronger forces that they cannot face in the open. A classic example of an asymmetric response to the West's conventional and nuclear military strength at the strategic level was the Soviet and Chinese support for "wars of national liberation" that started, at least, as terrorist and guerrilla actions. This approach pulled us and our allies in various ways into conflicts in Greece, Turkey, Africa, the Philippines, Malaya, Indochina, and Central America and led us into our own war in Vietnam, one of the most difficult in U.S. history.

Contrary to the implications of the emphasis on postmodern warfare and asymmetric threats, in today's and tomorrow's world of U.S. international security concerns these threats to our welfare come *in addition to*, not *instead of*, the threats posed by so-called conventional armed forces. We should remember that although the wars in Vietnam started as guerrilla wars, both France and the United States found they were fighting organized North Vietnamese divisions that demanded action by our full conventional military capability. Let us ask ourselves why nations are pressing to build modern forces with tanks, advanced combat aircraft, ships, submarines, and long-range missiles with nuclear warheads (or even conventional ones) that can reach far into an opposing country's war-supporting civilian rear areas. Or let us note the proliferation of weapons designed explicitly to sink our ships and shoot down our aircraft. Then we must realize that the earlier kinds of warfare between organized military forces have not gone away. They have been added to, and if one wants a good planning definition of "postmodern warfare" one must account for all of the above. It is not a matter of one kind of problem replacing another; it is a matter of all the perpetual kinds of problems in modern guise cascading to face us with a far more complex military and paramilitary world than we have been accustomed to thinking about.

It is clear from all that we discussed in Chapter 3 that we don't know what kinds of military or quasimilitary operations may be in store for us as the twenty-first century unfolds. They can range from classic military conflicts to conflicts in the recesses of our perception, having a character that we will learn only as the events happen and that we are not prepared for psychologically, organizationally, or politically. We must shift our viewpoint to understand how we may be attacked in all the possible dimensions.

The United States, with its enormous economic and military power, does not perceive in today's world an immediate threat to its own survival and that of its close allies, as during the Cold War. Rather, as we have noted repeatedly, we see threats to diverse interests of varying degrees of seriousness distributed around the world. These threats wax and wane according to actions by local entities over whose activities, with motivations driven by their own internal concerns, we appear to have little control. In our open society the meaning of the ensuing events and the appropriate response to them, or even deterrence actions that might be taken to forestall them, are subject to extensive public argument and, consequently, delayed response. We argue about whether to commit armed forces, and if the actions needed do not involve "countries" as such on the other side, we argue about whether we should intervene at all and, if so, which agencies are responsible for the action. Foreign misinterpretation of both the delay and the response are to be expected and do occur. Wars are built on misinterpretation of intent as well as of capability.

The current perception, both at home and abroad, is that when we finally commit military forces in an international crisis our objectives are to minimize casualties, minimize costs, succeed rapidly in achieving some limited objectives according to timetables that may be prompted by domestic political considerations rather than situational needs, and bring our forces home as soon as possible. Although these perceptions may not always be accurate, as aggressors in the past century have found to their sorrow, the perception leads to a developing strategy toward us on the part of our challengers, of all stripes, that is inimical to the interests we are trying to protect and to our long-term security. The developing counterstrategy can best be summed up in Nikita Khruschev's famous "salami tactics": small slices, none of which will stimulate a powerful response by itself, but which in the aggregate will weaken and defeat us.

Unlike the United States, opponents in international activities that may require U.S. commitment of military force, be they national or transnational, are concerned with matters of survival or dominance in their areas and their endeavors, not simply with protecting interests. Their response to possible U.S. use of military force plays on the perceived limitations of our commitment, leading them to plan on longer staying power and on being able to exact more casualties than they believe we will be willing to tolerate. They use elusiveness, surprise, and deception and face us with the new kinds of warfare—irregular warfare, terrorism, drugs, economic and social disruption—that their reading of our open media tell them we are not well equipped to handle or that we will handle according to processes that give them much time for evasion and deception. If committed militarily, they will use their pockets of sophisticated military capability, such as mines, antiaircraft weapons, and antiship missiles, to subject us to the "tyranny of the single hit" on major platforms. By downing an aircraft or seriously damaging a major combat ship they can stimulate our news media and then our Congress to search for blame and thereby discourage further presence in an area. They will further exploit our media by continually posing the question for the American public whether the price in casualties, costs, and damage, even civilian damage to our opponents, is worth paying for the situation and the gains at hand. This was, for example, the basis of the public argument that preceded our 1990 decision to liberate Kuwait, as well as in the later decisions to intervene with military forces in successive conflicts in the former Yugoslavia.

Over the long term, the emerging strategy of major challengers in various regions of the world will be to enforce their own regional dominance while holding U.S.

power at bay. If the challengers' domains transcend national or state boundaries, they will attempt to hold us outside the domains they wish to dominate or they will evade our attempts at interference while pursuing their particular objectives. Those objectives may be running guns (i.e., in today's idiom, building weapons of mass destruction) or pushing dope or manipulating currency. Such a drive for dominance would involve countries intimidating regional neighbors or transnational groups intimidating the countries that furnish the bases for their operations. The victim countries, who may indeed want our protection, may not want it to be highly visible for fear of punishment by those right on their doorsteps or inside their borders. We have only to look at how Saudi Arabia equivocated about supporting a punishing strike at Iraq when UN inspectors were denied access to sensitive weapons sites, and the alacrity with which Italy released the Palestinian terrorist leader Mohammed Abbas when he was captured by American Special Forces on Italian soil after the *Achille Lauro* hijacking, to see the effect of fear of punishment in action.

At the same time, rising national powers will build or acquire what must now be viewed as today's decisive strategic weapons: economic power; long-range ballistic missiles with nuclear warheads; modern, quiet submarines; aviation armed with antiship missiles to threaten our naval forces; chemical and biological weapons; and the capacity for massive but covert disruption of the information systems on which both our civilian economy and military forces depend. These weapons, and the new kinds of warfare with which the world enters the twenty-first century, will ultimately threaten the United States at home—not by invasion but by disruption and destruction.

Thus, at some point what might have been threats to U.S. interests abroad can turn into threats to the survival of U.S. global power, with all the implications of such a development for the welfare and prosperity of our nation. These challenges will arise differently in different parts of the globe at different times according to different plays of events. All of the rising regional powers and the hostile transnational organizations will have greatly differing political and military styles rooted in their histories and current circumstances, leading them to emphasize and to use various elements of the "decisive" weapons in different ways. We can expect any or all of these challenges to arise during the twenty-first century—indeed, early in that century.

None of this need imply that our relationships with emerging national power centers, such as China or Iran or a new Russia, will *necessarily* be hostile, although the potential for hostility certainly does now and will in the future exist in varying degrees. And it will always be hostile vis-à-vis the mafias of the world. But we must heed the lessons of the twentieth century, which tell us that we must be one of the "big guys on the block," to quote former Secretary of Defense William Perry, and preferably the biggest. We can do that by making certain that our armed forces can meet any of the threats that can be posed to them, including but not limited to the "asymmetric threats." We must also display the will to use the armed forces and other appropriate government instruments of power effectively when that use is called for, at the appropriate level and, especially, in the appropriate time. Only that way can we be certain of our ability to hold our place at the table of international decisionmaking that will affect our future, to deter threats and conflicts, to encourage friendly or at least civil relationships with potentially antagonistic powers, and to achieve our strategic objectives of preserving American security in a confused and often violent world, regardless of whether the interaction with the other power centers is friendly or hostile. Can we bring this off? We consider that question next.

8

THE REAL WORLD

The future is hidden even from the men who made it.

—Anatole France

It is now time to draw together all the diverse threads we have been following to see if they can, collectively, give us some clues as to how we might actually manage our national security future. We may not like the result of the fabric they will be woven into, but we had better be aware of it. Indeed, awareness could cause us to change it to be more to our liking and more suitable to our future needs.

After the turbulent twentieth century, the major industrial powers recognize that settling their affairs by warfare, as they and their predecessors have done for 5,000 and more years, is no longer a viable option. Does this mean that war that might reach world-shaking scale is a past phenomenon? Not by a long shot!

There are many possible flash points, sudden or festering or still latent, involving our vital or near-vital interests, entailing special risk and requiring special awareness. We reviewed many of them in Chapter 3. They include China and Taiwan in the Far East; a Japan that needs reassurance about availability of resources essential for its prosperity and survival; Algeria, Iran, Iraq, and Afghanistan all contributing to the spread of militant Islam; the struggles for domination and capture of energy and water resources in North Africa, the Middle East, and along Russia's southern border as far into Central Asia as western China and Mongolia; Israel and the Arabs in their religion-based quarrel that apparently allows no compromise; the evolution of Korea; Russia, NATO, and the Baltic states; India, Pakistan, and Kashmir and the prospect of a war that may go nuclear; residual quarrels in Western Europe involving the former Yugoslavia's Balkan tar babies, Greece and Turkey, the neo-NATO na-

tions of Central Europe, and their neighbors; Africa, a constant drain on world attention and resources, finding its place in the twenty-first century; any number of
surprises that may be in store from the major countries of Latin America as they
sneak up on America's consciousness; and the increasing reach of world criminal organizations centered around the drug trade and their penetration into national entities and our own economic and social welfare. And those are only some of them.

We thought we could relax into a "new world order" after the Berlin Wall came
down and we subsequently defeated the Iraqi army. Instead, there is uncertainty, instability, and potential menace from many quarters, as far into the future as the
mind's eye can see. We don't know which of the possible flash points will flare up or
when. As Korea in 1950, Kuwait in 1990, and Kosovo in 1999 showed, things on
the back burner can come front and center very quickly.

The international environment we are moving into thus proves to be a tangled one.
Our old and comfortable alliances are groping for new intellectual and spiritual an-
chors in a world that threatens them, less with the obvious monstrosities of fascist or
communist dictatorship and nuclear holocaust and more with obscure and insinuated
dangers dimly perceived in the depths of human misery and venality. New power centers are growing. Some have the force of nations and groups of nations whose moral
appeal or repulsion and potential for greatness or mischief are yet to be revealed.
Some reach beyond national borders with known malevolence but hidden lines of attack. The two kinds of power centers and their different kinds of activities are often
interwoven. Our physical future will depend in large measure on the strength of our
economy and its ability to support the armed forces and the other measures we must
take to keep our nation strong. But increasingly, our economy is tied to a global economy, which American business helped greatly to build and in which it plays a strong
role. But the global economy is becoming a force that can influence our security profoundly while not being fully subject to our own or any one's control.

Our physical future will also depend on our moral fiber, as well as the outlook of
our population as it perceives and interprets or misinterprets the rest of the world in
the decades ahead and reacts to what it perceives. In Chapter 4 we explored where
that moral fiber and outlook have gone during the twentieth century, through two
world wars and especially during the decades of the Cold War. Through all that
trauma, building on our constitutional and frontier heritages, attitudes have grown
and evolved that condition how we respond to events in the outside world. We have
touched on many trends that the evolving attitudes, the march of technology, and
the flow of events have set in motion, and we have explored some of these trends in
some depth. All of them are part of our future.

The beginning of this book set the stage for thinking about the future with some
scenarios describing how the world of the early twenty-first century might bear in on

us in ways that require (or that may cause us to avoid) military action. The scenarios examined how we might respond to drifts of events within our country and on our continent that might be shaping up, ever so imperceptibly, even today to take place in the coming years and decades.

These scenarios were built on some additional speculations about the shape of the future. Even though they are fanciful, they bring out some of the dangers inherent in the world developments and our attitude-conditioned responses to them. They were presented first to grab your attention and start the juices of concern and curiosity going. The subsequent descriptions of the state of the world and of the nation can be taken to have exposed some of the anatomy of the scenarios—the reasons why the actors on the international scene might behave as predicted to bring them about, as well as how our national makeup and outlook might lead us to react to the resulting events. It should be possible, in that light, to judge how plausible the scenarios might be. Although they were billed at the beginning as fiction, many of their perverse and intractable qualities, and the impact of national and international attitudes and trends discussed in later chapters, have been illustrated in the chilling reality of Kosovo. We cannot continue without reviewing those events.

First, as to strategy: The crisis did not involve U.S. security interests directly, and the nations that emerged from the breakup of Yugoslavia, considered dispassionately, are not critical to us economically or geopolitically. But the crisis emerged from the very ethnic and religious quarrels that the end of the Cold War has brought to the fore in world events. There was the prospect of genocide, close by the site and conscience of the earlier twentieth-century Holocaust. That generated a need for the United States to act to hold the North Atlantic alliance together for its own welfare. We had to lead, as the European part of that alliance is too recently away from its own sharp divisions, and insufficiently united as yet, to be able to act on its own. As part of that, we wanted to ensure that the alliance's two members in the vicinity of the Yugoslavian conflicts (Greece and Turkey) did not become embroiled on opposite sides of the religious and ethnic quarrels next door. All that conspired to turn what might have been a "white chip" (in the strategic language we reviewed in Chapter 7) into a "red chip." In deciding to act, we did not fully appreciate the depth of tribal and religious feeling of the perpetrators of the horrors we wanted to stop; mere threats of violence had to give way to applied violence. Congress and the public demurred initially, then agreed because there was no alternative course to follow.

Then, the implementation: In the interest of saving casualties (itself an implicit judgment on the measure of importance the crisis had for us and our NATO allies) and because there was no fast and easy point of entry for forces of the size that would be needed, we decided at the start against a ground war. This put the ultimate ability of airpower to affect events and decisions on the ground to the test. It was successful but not unqualifiedly so. The outcome was conditioned by several factors. By nature, the U.S. and coalition decision processes are slow. We had to build up the air offensive in methodical sequence by destroying the Serbian air-defense network, destroying their ability to support their forces in Kosovo, and finally attacking those forces. This deliberate approach was necessary because in the absence of a mortal threat it does no good to risk losing a large fraction of an air force in the opening stages of a campaign. In the end, a surrender on the ground was forced by airpower alone, for the first time in history. However, given the pace these circumstances of the campaign set, the cruel dictator who stimulated his people to perpetrate the horrors we were trying to prevent was able to do what he had set out to do on an accelerated timetable. His forces were able to move inside the coalition's effective response time to devastate a population and destroy a community of nearly 2 million people. The people were used as human shields; they were abused and robbed and herded like animals in a scorched earth, to be turned into refugees who died or, if they survived, had no place to go. The community's males of military age and any intellectual leaders who could be captured were summarily shot, the bodies burned or buried to hide them from observation. And much of the worst part of this—the suffering of the refugees—was shown on the world's television screens. The horror of the images, combined with frustration at not being able to act fast enough and on the ground, led in this country to recrimination and calls to become engaged to a level that had been opposed earlier—too late to change the result.

Finally, the aftermath: Serbia's military capacity and much of its civilian infrastructure were left in smoking ruins, with a defiant population that will doubtless act in hostility again, in unpredictable ways. This accomplished what we said was our objective in using our airpower: to destroy Serbia's ability to make war, at least for a time. But given the destruction of Kosovo as a community, it was a Pyrrhic victory. Russia stood by making helpless noises while all this was going on, and Russia's budding orientation toward the West has been set back to some undefinable, uncomfortable degree. The mistaken bombing of the Chinese embassy in Belgrade at the height of the air campaign raised tensions and hostility between the United States and China just when revelations about Chinese espionage had brought U.S.-China relations to a high level of irritability.

The ethnic Albanian population of Kosovo, almost all of whom had become refugees either inside or outside of Kosovo, streamed back to their villages, towns, and cities while most of the formerly resident Serbs departed in fear of retaliation and revenge. The European Union, together with Russia, has begun the process of trying to reconstruct the war damage throughout the former Yugoslavia. The intent is to fold that area into a peaceful and economically vital community that encompasses all of Southeastern Europe. But Serbia has been excluded while Slobodan Milosevic remains in power. He may be gone as these words are printed, but the deep Serb feeling of paranoia that Warren Zimmerman describes in his book *The Origins of a Catastrophe* will surely linger as a result of all these events. However the local political dynamics play out, containing future Serbian aggressive behavior and others' reprisals will continue to be a nagging nuisance in Europe's peaceful development, and the Balkans, together with Greece and Turkey, will remain a potential tinderbox.

Our air forces demonstrated magnificently the power and precision of their attack capability. The degree and focus of the destruction they wrought would, in World War II or even Vietnam, have been accompanied by thousands of civilian casualties; in this case, there were relatively few (and the Serbian media told us every time there was even one). That demonstration of effectiveness has been lost against the backdrop of criticism and disillusion that we couldn't or wouldn't do more to help the Kosovo civilians survive this latest example of ethnic cleansing. That by itself demonstrated the power of moral and ethical concerns, and of will and its limits, in relation to the armed forces and their utilization in helping to resolve our international affairs.

Could we have written a fictional scenario that would better illustrate all the concerns this book has tried to highlight? All these events fit right together, in unpredictability, horror, and intransigence, with the fictional ones that opened the book.

Despite all the frustrations that the scenarios and real life pose for us in using military power, we cannot give our armed forces short shrift. We have, in this work, examined our armed forces, second to none in the world and the only ones today with the ability to project military power to any region on earth where U.S. and our allies' interests may be threatened. We have examined some of what makes them tick, in addition to the national strategy that seems to be developing that they are designed to support. And we have thought about what any of the world actors who may wish us ill now or in the future, because we interfere with their own designs, might do to defeat both the armed forces and our national strategy.

From this basis, let us now think about what might actually happen in the years ahead. It is trite to say that we cannot predict the future. Of course we can't. But we can consider the directions in which the tracks to the future run because of the internal and external constraints and enticements that our own situation and that of the world will impose.

LINKAGES: IMPLEMENTING OUR STRATEGY

As we have noted, our national security strategy, slowly emerging from revealed behavior rather than from any logically articulated long-range rationale and plan, is appearing as a fundamentally economic one. Underlying it are certain assumptions, derived from our historic moral imperatives and with some strong support in history, about the growth of democracy and its implications for a secure world without war.

The nature of the strategy is coming to be recognized nationally and has been a subject of debate. The issue has been whether America's historic moral foundation is consistent with a strategy that looks initially to our economic welfare or, put more bluntly, whether we will compromise our moral values for trade and money. We shall return to that issue in a moment.

First, we must note one of the important influences of technology on our way of dealing with strategic matters. Technological advance of the kind we have seen developing in the twentieth century fosters big projects and big organizations. The United States excels in this ability to marshal economic power, and it conditions our approach to government and how we organize our society. Examples abound, and mention of just a few will illustrate how pervasive they are.

Perhaps it started with the military. The story of the creation of the nuclear submarine and the Polaris sea-launched ballistic missile is taken by technology aficionados both to describe the post–World War II beginning and to illustrate the nature of this American-developed ability to build vast, technology-driven system structures. But this was preceded by our organization for the war itself, as well as the way both military and civilian enterprises were drawn together to fight it successfully. That approach has been reflected in civilian enterprise since, which takes off from and extends the way the military systems are brought into being.

Think about the applications of modern technology to the interstate highway system; or to the building of the air transportation system with its complex of aircraft, highly automated airports, and air-traffic control; or to the integrated fiber-optic, wireless, and satellite communications systems that are proliferating around the world; or to the medical care system that, although it is the subject of much controversy at home, is also viewed as the best in the world. In these few civilian examples we see both the evidence of our scientific and technological prowess and one of the aspects of our ability to organize large projects and systems that has impacted our society in subtle but important ways.

For not only have we been learning to pull together the technical and financial resources to implement systems of huge scope and diversity; we have learned to carry them out through many jurisdictions and many forms of social reaction and regulation in our hyperdemocratic society. And indeed that is true even of the military systems, when one thinks of the planning and the congressional authorization and appropriation processes that must be traversed to start and carry through the technical aspects of any major system's creation.[1]

---

[1]This multijurisdictional aspect of our management of large enterprises has been pointed out explicitly by Thomas P. Hughes, emeritus professor of the history and sociology of science at the University of Pennsylvania.

An important management concept and practice emerging from our agglomeration of enterprises into entities of global scope and power has been the decentralization of management: Policy is established at the top or at the center of any enterprise, but implementation is delegated downward and the responsibility is assigned to action organizations. The "action organizations" might be military-industrial project teams, or perhaps contractors carrying out major integration of civilian systems or furnishing major components for such systems. The implementation is observed, and its success is measured by any means, from amount of usage to economic outputs to effective operation. The center can intervene if it must to change performance and even to change the action organizations when it doesn't like the output measures of any component. As we noted in Chapter 6, our military command and control system follows the same general pattern of decentralization.

This is, actually, consistent with our organization for governing ourselves, which includes governing bodies for localities and cities, states, and the nation. In the case of government, the voters are the center of the enterprise, the body that sets policy and is the ultimate arbiter of whether and how it is being implemented.

Our hopes for growth of democracy out of free-market economies lie in this parallel between large military and industrial enterprises and government. We see this enterprise model spreading to the rest of the world, and we hope and expect that the decentralization of decisionmaking authority will carry with it the transformation from authoritarian to democratic forms of government.

In crafting our strategy we are still groping for ways to adapt our loosely organized peacetime industrial and governmental mechanisms to meet the new kinds of attack on our security that are short of mortal but that can affect us seriously. And because the attacks *are* short of mortal, and the strategy is economically based, the tensions it generates are seen to create a dilemma in dealing with the rest of the world that is more fundamental and more profound than those we reviewed in Chapter 5. That is the dilemma between tolerance and evangelism. As we saw in Chapter 4, both are inherent in the American psyche, and the tension between them vastly complicates the development and implementation of our strategy.

For if we are to concentrate on advancing our economic interests, we shall have to be tolerant of other forms of government and of other nations' means of managing their affairs. This means confining our concerns only to making certain that those foreign institutions and behaviors are not detrimental to our civil pursuits and our relationships with the rest of the world. This could certainly include expressions of concern about abuses of human rights by more authoritarian governments, at least when those abuses begin to get in the way of the other concerns. Yet the threshold of abuses that would demand our condemnation and withdrawal from trade relationships would probably be set rather high. In the other direction, if we want to impress our moral values on the rest of the world as we extend our contacts with them, simply because of our confidence in the rightness of our beliefs, we are highly likely to antagonize much of the world in the process. This will inevitably have adverse consequences for our economic strategy, because it will cause us to forego trade relationships with regimes of which we disapprove, and other nations will readily move into the gap created in order to gain the economic advantage over us. In the long run, this policy could increase the likelihood of armed conflict because of the heightened international antagonisms it creates.

It is safe to predict that the arguments within our country that are generated by these tensions will, short of an immediate and deadly threat to the nation's survival, never be fully resolved. Even in the case of an egregiously offensive insult to our moral sensibilities, we will argue about whether it is in our interest to become involved, and we will temper our decision about the moral values with concern about other consequences. Think about how long it took to rise to the Nazi threat during the 1930s, or more recent actions in the cases of Cambodia, Rwanda, and Yugoslavia's components, Bosnia and Kosovo. When our survival is not at stake, our concern about human life applies first to the avoidance of American war casualties and only later to worry about other peoples' lives being lost in unjust conflicts and genocide. The arguments will add further to institutional delays in taking actions that we need to take in our own interest. They will divide our society. They will, in the long run, be detrimental to our security. But unless a huge and direct threat to that security arises we will have to live with them and accept their consequences as an essential element in the way we deal with the world of the twenty-first century.

This highlights a downside that is not commonly acknowledged in our ability to structure large enterprises through large industrial and government organizations. We live with it and have essentially come to accept it as part of the normal course of doing business to the point where we scarcely recognize it for what it is. That is inertia; it is hard to start new things and hard to change their direction once started. Major enterprises associated with economic or security concerns become vested interests with constituencies of their own. They demand resources and resist changing an enterprise once it is under way. It is hard to tell the difference between persistence toward a commendable goal against all difficulties (as our pursuit of the international space station might be) and persistence in a foolish enterprise that ought to be abandoned (as our pursuit of the international space station might also be).

Despite the parallels noted above, there is an important difference between the military and industrial decentralization, on the one hand, and governmental decentralization on the other. When we don't recognize it, it often deceives us into thinking that we have only to follow the effective industrial model to get socially and politically sensitive things done in government—like contracting out school-system management or managing health care.

The difference is that in military operations or industrial enterprises there come to be defined, eventually, a job to be done and objectives to reach that focus the decentralized organization. The mission, goals, and implementation methods are guided by the policy that governs the organization and the enterprise and that is set by the top governing body (in that sense, maximizing income for a corporation can be thought of as a mission). In decentralized government, however, the strong mission focus is usually hard to find or doesn't exist. Rather, arguments over mission, policy, and methods are central to the government organizations' functions. Thus, all questions about what goals really are and those about approaches to achieving any goals that are agreed upon, and allocation of resources to do so, can be raised again at any time and repeatedly, even after it appears they have been decided.

All these characteristics of the way we do things reduce flexibility, which we will need to meet rapidly evolving world conditions. The layering of government, which is highly desired under our constitutional system, also makes possible the growth of what I have called "government, California-style." That can add a random element to federal policymaking that can defeat rational planning and the effective joining of government, industry, and social organizations to carry out strategy effectively. It may not appear in propositions (ballot issues) to be voted on, but it will certainly appear in government as its elected members seek guidance in polls, as well as in the arguments of myriad special interest groups, before they vote on the issues.

Beyond the delays and uncertainties in setting and pursuing goals in the government sector, our unwillingness to recognize limits to resources and to accept limits on behavior when the need presents itself, our sense of the rightness of our views, and our impatience to move on create a certain belligerence in the face we present to the world. Reluctance to accept limits on behavior means that special interest groups or small segments of the population can try to disrupt government and convey disunity to an opponent when effective implementation of strategy would call for strong shows of unity. It also leads our media to publish any information they can gain about military plans or operations, which can be of great help to an opponent and usually denies the option of surprise. These qualities allowed the North Vietnamese to exploit our media and our social organization very effectively and have led other opponents like Saddam Hussein to use our media as vehicles for their own propaganda. We convey, also, that we are impatient with the differing objectives of potential coalition partners and with the international organizations, such as the United Nations, that we helped to create to deal with international issues. We have vocal and influential factions who continually insist that we go it alone rather than reconcile our viewpoints with those of others who may be involved. None of this makes it easy to hold coalitions together. All these results may be necessary consequences and elements of our democratic system, but we have to be aware that they are often not helpful and might be harmful in times of stress over international events.

Our belligerent words often pose the issue, which we rarely articulate clearly in our public arguments, that if we were to follow through on our utterances we are inviting armed conflict—that is, war. At the same time, our reluctance to sustain casualties and the tangible and intangible costs of war hold us back from actually going to war in the places where our words bring it closer, places such as Iraq, Iran, and North Korea. The combination of belligerent utterings with a display of caution in action turns Theodore Roosevelt's advice to "speak softly and carry a big stick" on its head. It decreases our credibility and makes us easy targets for the "salami tactics" described earlier, and it makes deterrence of others' actions that are inimical to our interests and those of our allies more difficult because the promised punishments rarely appear to be forthcoming. The behavior must also encourage independent action by our allies and weaken our alliances in the long run.

Our short-term view of events combines with our show-me attitude to make it exceedingly difficult to sustain policies that try to anticipate and deflect or transform long-term threats to our security. In particular, we don't fully fund the armed forces far enough in advance to enable them to prepare for their part in meeting the threats. We tend to look for the threats to materialize on time scales of months when they may take years to develop fully. When the months don't bring perceptible change we tend to turn our attention and resources to other uses. Thus, we have shifted the allocation of resources in the federal budget from a mix in which more than 27 percent of the budget went to defense and 50 percent to development and support of human resources (including social security, health and Medicare, education, housing, and veterans' affairs) in 1985 (the peak year of the Reagan buildup) to 16 percent and 67 percent, respectively, in those areas today. In other words, over a fifteen-year period some 10 percent of the federal budget was shifted from defense to human resources. In addition, a good deal of the growth in the budget was put into human resources rather than into national security expenditures.

We also play the zero-sum game with the budget. Our lawmakers and administrators resist admitting that we can raise more in taxes if that is necessary to see to our security and other needs. They do that because they haven't been shown with certainty that our security will be threatened or that we can deflect the threats better if we act early rather than late—when they are a cloud on the horizon no bigger than a man's hand, as it were, rather than when they are fully developed and strong. Or if taxes bring more money than is needed to meet current expenses, as began to be the case in 1998 and appeared very definitively in 1999, the areas that claim significant amounts of the surplus do not include defense. Rather they include human resources, mainly, and foment the clamor for tax refunds by the political system. These tendencies on the part of our body politic make it easier to understand the apparent need for an identified and powerful enemy to focus our attention and encourage the actions and expenditures needed to meet the long-term threats to our security that such an enemy would pose.

The growing trend toward employment instability exacerbates the difficulty of re-acting early to threats when they are at a low level and haven't reached the stage where chaos and social turmoil can degenerate into war. At that stage, many of the actions taken will tend to be economic or to require money in our own national budget (for example, to support the International Monetary Fund) to be spent against ill-defined international concerns. It becomes difficult to persuade Americans whose own jobs are insecure that taxpayer money should be spent to make the jobs of workers overseas more secure. The argument that money should be spent for eco-nomic assistance now to make it less likely that we will have to spend money and lives for military action at some future time is not accepted when the aid money must be appropriated now but the prospect of military action is distant and specula-tive. When such military action becomes imminent, the alternatives are to sustain the costs of war, including the human costs, or to retreat again, for then it is too late to take the long-term preventive steps that would have deflected the crisis, whatever it is, before it began.

The power of the news and entertainment media to condition and influence na-tional attitudes is an important contributor to this response. We have already noted at several points how their attention to human interest–oriented peripherals instead of underlying substance in reporting of international events conditions our national attitudes toward those events. Their emphasis in presentation of national and inter-national news determines what the bulk of our population knows about critical in-ternational issues; it conditions our emotional response and how prepared we may be to take action.

Think, for example, of the international situation at the time of the impeachment hearings regarding President Bill Clinton's behavior over an irresponsible but private dalliance in his office. The Asian economic crisis was failing to recover despite inter-national measures to assist it, and we were beginning to feel its effects more severely in the United States; Russia was falling farther into economic and social chaos; Israel and the Palestinians were approaching closer to a renewal of the open conflict that characterized the Palestinians' Intifada of the late 1980s and early 1990s; Iraq was more openly flouting the terms of its Gulf War surrender, daring us to take action (which, finally, we did amid accusations it was a diversion by the U.S. president to take attention away from his private troubles); North Korea appeared to have renewed its pursuit of nuclear weapons; Iran was more openly displaying its military strength in the Persian Gulf while ultrareligious factions seemed to be gaining in their fight with the more moderate secular Iranian president; and Serbia was gradually edging toward renewed ethnic warfare in the former Yugoslavia. Yet all this turmoil receded into the background in the media that, true to the behavior of the congressional-media axis, were riveting the nation's attention on the president's problems and paying attention to the world problems only minimally (if, for example, the president's activities, such as his trips abroad, connected with them or some latent crisis blew up into major proportions). Any crisis beyond the chronic Iraqi and Balkan imbroglios that required immediate attention and drastic action, especially military action, would essentially spring upon the American people full-blown. The news and entertainment media would have done little to prepare and educate the public to understand the development of events and thus better judge them. The public could not be blamed for reluctance to support severe government measures to meet the crisis, even if the president could have devoted the necessary attention to it amid the impeachment furor to determine wisely what those actions should be.

The condition of the U.S. education system only serves to reinforce the difficulties in arriving at and supporting foreign policy actions that will ensure the success of our basic strategy, if that is the strategy we want to follow, or to devise an alternate strategy if we don't like the one that is developing. More education on matters affecting our national security is done in the entertainment media than in the schools. This, again, plays up matters evoking an emotional response to immediate events and ignores such basic information as current geography and government, as well as such deeper knowledge as the influence of their history and tenets of religion on other nations' policies and actions. This, too, makes for the absence of an informed public opinion at a time when the international issues are more immediate, complex, and difficult to understand and evaluate than they have ever been in our history.

This lack, added to the dearth of education in science and technology, makes it more difficult to implement a strategy based on achieving and sustaining economic superiority. That is so because economic strength now and in the future depends on a scientific and technological base. Indeed, lack of scientific and technological understanding encourages resentment of technology of the kind that began to grow during the Vietnam War. It can reinforce resistance to change and even to taking measures to safeguard the nation's health and well-being, as we are seeing with nuclear power and storage of nuclear waste in the energy area and with the use of genetic engineering to extend the resistance of crops to pests and disease. It also draws public attention from matters that might affect the public in the long run to those of which it is most aware in the short run. Thus, our research budgets are becoming increasingly skewed in the direction of direct application to health and disease while they are being shifted away from things such as research into the energy sector, the atmospheric and ocean sciences, and fundamentals of physics, chemistry, and materials, where more knowledge could have a profound impact on the nation's future. These allocations tend to be more emotional than rational responses to planning for the future. By preempting the available resources, such allocations vastly increase the difficulty of tailoring the armed forces to the world scene the nation is entering.

LINKAGES: THE ARMED FORCES

We have noted at several points that the technology and the operational forms of the armed forces must, of necessity, pattern themselves after the society of which they are a part. This quality has, indeed, appeared in many areas. Let us recap.

The armed forces' expenditure patterns are conditioned by the need for competition-based cost reduction because they are indeed in competition with many other parts of society for the resources to build and sustain themselves. To succeed, they are substituting computer-enabled capital investment for labor, that is, ever more complex and capable machines are taking on jobs that people used to do, thereby enabling the remaining people to do much more than larger numbers of people were able to do earlier. As a consequence, and in keeping with the dispersed nature of the resulting physical plant, they are planning on the use of communications and rapid transportation to assemble their components and fighting power from many widely separated locations. The assembled forces can then carry out military tasks at critical locations, positions that they are able to pinpoint with precision using advanced surveillance and navigation systems with computer support. The resulting operations are lean, in having just what is needed to do a job with few redundant parts (i.e., military units) and not much more. And the operations of all these units must be closely timed so that they come together and perform their component tasks as elements of a complete military system.

These characteristics exactly parallel the way major industry is developing, with widespread component suppliers using air and surface transportation to feed central assembly and distribution points on just-in-time schedules. In both cases, the plans and movements are designed, tracked, and controlled by computers, and in both cases communications connectivity is critically important to ensure that the end results are achieved. The lean and closely timed operations make the organizations and missions highly vulnerable to interruption. The interruptions may be due to chance variables, such as adverse weather and breakdowns in machinery and personnel, or they may be due to malevolence, such as labor strikes in the case of industry or enemy counteraction in the case of the military. In both cases, the vulnerabilities can be mitigated, but the mitigation will cost money, which both stockholders (in the case of industry) and the taxpayers (in the case of the military) often begrudge because threats are indirect and the results of the expenditures are not immediately obvious. In short, anticipated success in reducing the effects of a hypothetical strike or of possible jamming of a communications or navigation satellite at some future time are not as apparent as shipping a new car or delivering a new combat aircraft.

The organization, discipline, and ability to marshal resources that characterize the military suit them ideally to engage in what have been called "military operations other than war." The military forces could, if assigned to do so, fully take on the missions of meeting the threats that cross national boundaries that we have reviewed, including terrorism, drug-trafficking and other smuggling, and many forms of information warfare. However, we argue about even the partial assignment of responsibility to the military in these areas because our civilian society is, itself, not certain about how it wants to organize to handle them. In addition, these activities do take the assigned military units' time and effort away from training and preparation for combat operations. This impact of the use of military forces for other-than-war missions that are necessary to support the security-related aspects of our foreign policy can be remedied by having larger forces. But that takes us right back to the availability of resources in the competition with civilian needs for the resources that our society is willing to spend, through the tax system and budget process, for the functions of government.

We have seen how we can reorganize the forces to make them more efficient in order to keep their cost down as much as possible. In the process they would be streamlined and made more effective for the new modes in which they will be used, even with the added strength that would be needed to mitigate the vulnerabilities brought on by the streamlining. All of the changes we talked about would severely challenge the existing order of things in our government and even more broadly in our society. They would involve everyone from Congress to the people in the military at all levels, from the soldiers, sailors, and airmen who do the work and the fighting to the commanders who lead them and plan what they will do and how they will do it. These connections reflect back into civilian life in all areas, from career planning to our understanding of what the armed forces are all about and what they do, as conveyed by our news and entertainment media and in our education system. That affects peoples' views on whether to use the armed forces in specific situations that will arise. Everyone's attitude toward what makes for national security and the armed forces' role in it would have to change along the way. The so-called revolution in military affairs is thus seen to be but one aspect of a revolution in the nation's views about national security and how to deal with it.

The employment instability that will undoubtedly characterize our society for some time to come will also affect the armed forces. On the face of it, one might expect that it would encourage people to join the armed forces for the steady jobs they represent. However, the kinds of people who will face the employment instability problem most severely are not the ones who would normally be candidates for the armed forces. The people who will feel the effects of employment instability the most are those who have passed the age where they can easily adapt to the physical training rigors that youth can undertake. They are settled, with families, and not eager for the interruptions of that life that unexpected (or even planned but sustained) deployments will require. Some of them would be able to lend the skills and knowledge that attend increasing maturity to assist in areas of military endeavor that do not require physical exertion, in areas such as information management, computing, and complex fixed systems like missile defense systems. But the military needs flexibility, since the person who mainly has to watch a radar or sonar screen or work at a computer keyboard may often have to do it under rigorous conditions in the desert, at sea, or in an austere winter landscape. The settled older people will have more trouble in this respect. All these considerations suggest that the main effect of unemployment instability may be to deflect attention away from the national security problems that the armed forces have to deal with, and from the armed forces themselves, toward peoples' personal problems in civilian life. That can only increase the separation between the civilian population and the armed forces.

The outlook of the country on military careers has also changed in a subtle way, because with the volunteer force and the passing of the World War II and Korea generations the emotional connections between the population and the armed forces have become more tenuous. During the Vietnam War there came to be a distinct class separation between most of the people in the armed forces and those who did not go. Mainly, the military was made up of troops from the less affluent parts of society, together with career officers. The children of the affluent were exempted from the draft or found ways to avoid it. Today, although there are, of course, still military veterans in politics (including such people as Vice President Al Gore, Senator Robert Kerrey, Senator John McCain, and others), it has been pointed out by former Navy Secretary James H. Webb Jr. that we have a unique situation in which the president, the Secretaries of State and Defense, the president's national security adviser, and key leaders in both houses of Congress have not seen military service. In addition, the media, not fully understanding how the armed forces operate, tend increasingly to misrepresent what the armed forces do and how they do it, at critical times.[2] All this can account in an important way for the loss of patriotism as a motivator to join the armed forces. To the opinion-forming elite of our society, the armed forces are increasingly outside their ken as an honored and sought-after career or as a commitment they had to make to the security of the nation.

This trend away from participation in the armed forces by the movers and shakers joins with the reduction of bases at our population centers to continue to remove the armed forces from the center of society's consciousness. All kinds of undesirable consequences flow from this separation. With the armed forces as a professional force in being rather than a rotating force of the people via the draft (with a core of professional commissioned and noncommissioned officers), the risk will increase that the armed forces will no longer be as responsive to civilian authority as our constitutional government demands. Although there is no sign of it yet, we could approach closer to the situation in which the armed forces become simply another political interest group. As such they might be reluctant to undertake expeditions with which they are not sympathetic, or perhaps they might press for actions that the nation does not sympathize with, rather than follow the civilian government's conceptions of where the national interest lies. This, in turn, could cause them to start exercising political clout with Congress and the administration in furtherance of their own interests—careers and power in the body politic—rather than the interests of the nation. We had just the barest hint of the potential consequences of such a drift in Iran-Contra, during President Ronald Reagan's second term in office.

If such circumstances develop, the professional armed forces can come to be viewed by the mainstream as simply mercenaries, and they would then be treated as mercenaries. They wouldn't be able to enlist the high-quality people needed to populate and run the armed forces of *Joint Vision 2010*. They would be looked down on as somehow inferior, as mere servants who somehow couldn't make it in the larger economy and took the armed forces as a way out. These "mainstream outsiders" would then resent any political influence the armed forces might have. The armed forces would, in turn, sense and resent that antagonism and the resulting image, their treatment under it, and the accompanying lack of understanding of their ethos and their work. They

---

[2]A good description of how this phenomenon operates and how it can affect the national will and national policy is given in Peter Braestrup's book, *Big Story*, an account of how the media reported the Tet Offensive in Vietnam in 1968. That the phenomenon persists can be gathered from President Bush's and General Brent Scowcroft's remarks about the media in Iraq, in their memoir on the ending of the Cold War.

would again become an object of division in the country, as they were during the Vietnam years, instead of a force that helps ensure the country's security.

There are voices in our country that are sensitive to this issue. They raise the possibility of reinstituting the draft in the interest of fairness by spreading the risks and the experiences among all levels of society. However, the issue has not been treated as a significant one among the opinionmakers—the media, Congress, and the entertainment world.

THE REAL WORLD

The real world is perverse and refuses to follow theoretical or even desirable constructs in politics and matters of state. George Washington, in the Farewell Address we referred to in Chapter 5, cautioned against the "insidious wiles of foreign influence." Rather than succumb to them, he admonished, "the great rule of conduct for us, in regard to foreign nations is in extending our commercial relations to have with them as little *political* connection as possible. . . . Europe has a set of primary interests, which to us have none, or a very remote relation. . . . Our detached and distant situation invites and enables us to pursue a different course." Washington then posed this query: "Why quit our own to stand upon foreign ground? Why, by interweaving our destiny with that of any part of Europe, entangle our peace and prosperity in the toils of European ambition, rivalship, humor or caprice?"

This injunction has become thoroughly embedded in the American soul, reinforced since the founding of the United States of America by more than a century of isolation, ensured by two oceans and neighboring countries that posed no threat on our borders. Now, however, "Europe" has become "the rest of the world," and our situation is no longer "detached and distant." Moreover, because attacks against us can now easily cross those oceans, we have no choice but to "stand on foreign ground" to fend them off or to nip them in the bud. And our commerce with the rest of the world, having become essential to our prosperity and even our survival as a great power, now forces us to become entangled in their politics to exert our influence for our own strategic ends. It is extraordinarily difficult to root out deeply embedded attitudes that have the force of religion, so that we as a nation tend to drift back into the "detached and distant" mode with primary attention to our pursuits of commerce and other internal interests whenever the rest of the world is relatively quiescent.

This is another tendency that plays directly into the nibbling challenges of the hostile parts of the rest of the world's counterstrategies. They will keep presenting us with problems for which there are no easy solutions, such as smuggling of drugs, money, people, and arms to terrorists, and threats to create, and use nuclear, chemi-

cal and biological weapons, and genocidal actions that will demand our moral involvement but that we will want to avoid because we will not want to incur the
human and economic costs of intervention. Edward Tenner, in his 1996 book, *Why
Things Bite Back: Technology and the Revenge of Unintended Consequences,* has pointed
out that often when we solve an acute problem we are left with a chronic one that is
much harder to deal with. For example, after we eliminated most acute bacterial diseases that caused early death we have been left with the chronic diseases of old age—
arthritis, diabetes, Parkinson's, cancer, and others for which a complete cure or certain prevention remain far distant. So, too, in national security affairs we have
overcome the threats to our survival posed by Nazi Germany and Soviet-led communist imperialism, only to be left with a running battle against those who resent and
wish to check the strength we built in the process. A reading of the significance of
the prevailing attitudes and trends in our society does not lend encouragement that
we will meet this kind of nibbling, nationally debilitating, chronic challenge in the
most effective manner.

We'll doubtless survive the challenge as a nation (although a plausible scenario
like that presented in Chapter 2 can even put that proposition in question), but
quite possibly we might find ourselves in a weakened state, not the triumphant superpower sitting astride the world that we wish for ourselves. As we noted in Chapter 1, the ancient Chinese philosopher on the art of war, Sun-tzu, observed that it is
better to overcome one's opposition without fighting battles than to have to fight
and win many battles in the contest. It can be argued that the strategy of economic
dominance that we appear to be developing is the appropriate one to achieve that.
However, for it to work we would have to display a high degree of national unity
about that strategy—or any other strategy we seek to develop in its place. We would
also have to accept, as a nation, the necessity—which will accompany any strategy—
to build effective military force and to use it, for friendly pursuits mainly but in
anger on occasion. Since the end of the Gulf War, neither the necessary degree of national unity nor the essential attention and resources allocated to the armed forces
have been easily detectable. (Indeed, the unity and the allocation of resources often
faltered even during previous periods of more immediate national peril before World
War II and during the Cold War.)

It is probably safe to predict that even though we will make efforts to sustain some
semblance of military power in the armed forces, we will not go deeply enough to
ensure the robustness and readiness of the armed forces for all the peacetime activities and military challenges that can be foreseen. We will see to obvious perceived
needs like missile defense and the retention of some basic numbers of carrier battle
groups, bomber and tactical aircraft wings, and Army and Marine divisions. We
will—with protracted argument over the need—sustain our military research and

development efforts and the acquisition of a modest number of major new ships, aircraft, and weapon systems, because the needs for those things are obvious at least to some in our government and because their acquisition will help sustain jobs in defense industries that would evaporate otherwise.

However, there is no reason to predict that the drift downward of the fraction of our gross domestic product (GDP) devoted to the armed forces will stop. That reached above 6 percent of GDP during the mid–1980s at the peak of the Reagan buildup, but today it is roughly 3 percent and still trending downward. The armed forces are, after all, in competition with the inexorable rise of resources needed for the health and retirement care of an aging population and for continual civilian infrastructure renewal, both of which demand ever increasing fractions of the national budget. But we have drawn a line at a fraction of the national wealth we will devote to all these things in the form of taxes at all levels—about 26–27 percent of GDP, it turns out. As productivity raises national income, the constant urge is to put the gains into private investment and personal consumption by reducing taxes proportionately.

However often the lesson was repeated in the twentieth century, our nation has steadfastly refused to devote all the resources to our armed forces in peacetime that would ensure their ability to protect our security with powerful and effective action early in a developing crisis. We have done better at it in recent years, but the voices against it are always there, and they are insistent. Thus, history suggests that we will probably not go beyond the expenditures needed to keep some modest level of armed forces and their readiness in being. We are unlikely to spend the additional money that it will take to make the armed forces robust against the vulnerabilities to which their direction of evolution will increasingly expose them. Likewise, we are unlikely to fully resolve the interference between readiness and the operations other than war in their assignment.

We noted in Chapter 7 that to do so, and to suit the armed forces to the style of operation visualized under *Joint Vision 2010*, would likely require about a 25 percent defense budget increase, in addition to security-related increases elsewhere in the national budget. Even in 1999, when it was decided to increase the defense budget rather than hold it steady or let it decline, only as much as an 8–10 percent increase was proposed by the most ardent advocates, and more like 5 percent will come out of the political process. And one rarely or never hears about the other departments that are involved in our national security in that context. Moreover, increases like this take place in good economic times. If the economy goes into recession, the military will share the pain of reduced resources along with the rest of the country. Recruiting will pick up, but the resources to prepare and fit the recruits into first-rate forces will decline.

We also noted that it might be possible to capture half or more of the needed additional resources (beyond what we spend today for these things) by modernizing the military's operational base and business practices. But those very steps of modernization would challenge long-held, comfortable positions in the national economy and the political lineup; they would require significant departures from the classic business as usual that planners in Congress, the military, and the industrial economy have become used to inveighing against during the last quarter of the twentieth century. Experience has shown that the changes would be painful and difficult to achieve even under ideal circumstances. And, as we know, circumstances short of a national emergency are rarely ideal for such change.

In addition, we know from history how powerful tradition can be, especially the tradition of loyalty to and fighting for one's Service in the armed forces. In many ways, that is one of their strengths, and it doubtless helps to ensure that the armed forces do not go out of balance in any one direction. By the same token, however, the institutional constraints within the armed forces will work against their full adaptation to the new concepts laid out in *Joint Vision 2010*, thereby making them more costly and less flexible and responsive than they might be. This is likely to be especially true in the way they meet the pervasive but subtle demands for jointness, as well as in the critical intelligence, information, and communications connectivity that will be essential to battlefield success in new modes of operation. There has been every indication since the Gulf War that this will be the pattern as long as the short-run level of threat to our survival appears as low and subject to interpretation and argument as it does now.

What does this mean for the way our armed forces will perform in the future? The experience of Korea in 1950, long forgotten by most of our population, can give us a hint. We had let the armed forces' readiness and the modernity of the equipment decline. When the North Koreans attacked, our infantry on the peninsula, among other lacks, did not have antitank weapons that could stop their armor. They and their South Korean allies were pushed back into the small Pusan perimeter at the southeastern tip of the peninsula, and they were almost driven off the peninsula before they built enough strength to hold until General Douglas MacArthur's brilliantly conceived landing in the North Korean rear at Inchon caused the North Koreans to retreat headlong. U.S. forces suffered about 10,000 casualties during the first three months' retreat and holding action.

By contrast, when Iraq invaded Kuwait our armed forces were at peak readiness driven by the Cold War, and we were able to defeat the Iraqi veterans of their war with Iran with a ground campaign that lasted four days, after a thorough softening-up by airpower, with fewer than 200 soldiers killed in action. Even then, however, the story could have been different had the Iraqi invaders simply moved through

Kuwait and into Saudi Arabia. We had not anticipated their move into Kuwait, and we had no alert forces in the area. Then, if they had moved beyond Kuwait and if we had decided to respond militarily, we would have faced the problem of trying to slow them without the long preparation time while we built strength in the area. U.S. forces committed piecemeal in that circumstance could have suffered much more severe losses, and the war to follow could have been much longer. The lesson in these data and speculations is that our armed forces can prevail when pressed hard but that if the nation is not readied to commit them by strong leadership and good prior intelligence, properly interpreted, and if the armed forces are not ready for combat against the kind of enemy they may meet when they are committed, then the price in casualties and cost can be high indeed.

Our newly crafted, lean, powerful armed forces are being designed and will be poised for quick victories against many kinds of opposition. They will be formidable if we have the foresight and the will to use them in the circumstances for which they are being designed. Then they will succeed, just as they did in the Gulf War. But the nation's probable reluctance to support them to the fullest extent needed to create the depth for use in peace while maintaining adequate readiness for war, and to build into them the needed robustness against countermeasures together with staying power in war, will leave them only half-ready to meet challenges of unanticipated severity. The biggest risk the forces and the nation face is that we will commit to what we think will be a short conflict against an opponent who surprises us by turning it into a long one. It is easy to mount a tiger, not even recognizing the beast for what it is, but very hard to get off, as we learned to our sorrow in Vietnam.

Our earlier view of the prevailing attitudes and preoccupations in the nation, the trends in our economy and our society, and the sometimes paralyzing dilemmas we face suggest that we will be slow to recognize and respond to the drift of events that will threaten us in the long run in any region or globally. This may be an unduly pessimistic view. The American people shouldn't be sold short. When they do respond, as they did in World War II and its aftermath—which included the need to rescue a devastated Europe and form an alliance against a fearful threat that led to the forty-odd years of the Cold War—the power they bring to bear is awesome indeed. That is what brought us to our current position as the premier world power.

But this isn't the same nation that came through the last half-century of hot and cold conflicts. We have been jaded by two hurtful hot wars in two decades, in Korea and Vietnam, without clear victory in one and with a defeat in the other. Our victory in the Cold War has left us with a chaotic Russia that may pose more of a threat to us and the world in defeat than it ever did at the height of its power. Our victory in the subsequent Gulf War has, perversely, left us a chronic problem with a nasty dictator who threatens our access to a key resource and the unity of our alliances and who, unless he is somehow overthrown or dies suddenly of natural causes, we neither know how to live with nor how to defeat at a price we are willing to pay. Similar considerations apply in that cauldron of past wars—the Balkan Peninsula. The world is changing into forms and behaviors that we have yet to learn how to deal with, and our reaction is to argue to the point of bluster but then to respond conditionally or withdraw. We have a shifting mix of population that is slow to want to pay attention to the threats to its well-being from outside our borders that are distant in time and place. The population is turned inward, trying to resolve the economic and social dislocations that the century of recurring warfare, the recent technical and economic revolutions, and that very growing and diverse population itself have brought about.

In the long run, the nation has demonstrated that it will respond to threats to its welfare and its security with the formidable power that it has displayed in the past. But as far as we can see ahead now, it will likely respond late, with high human and monetary costs to ourselves and to the rest of the world. Our Civil War, two world wars, four decades of conflict with additional wars embedded, and our responses to sundry smaller crises in the Balkans, Africa, the Middle East, and Southeast Asia make it clear that we don't usually respond promptly and elegantly unless the threat becomes sharp and immediate.

It may take a crisis of major proportions to cause us to pay attention to the long-term needs of our national security and our survival: a resurgence of a hostile and "Nazified" Russia; or a major and obvious loss of geopolitical position or a critical source of resources to a competing nation like China in the Far East or even Iran in the Middle East; or the breakup of our alliances over some cause we cannot now foresee, with some of their major members, like France and Japan, moving independently in directions that harm us; or a drift into war in unforeseen circumstances of the kind illustrated in Chapter 1; or loss of such a war. And it may take the fortuitous rise of an inspiring national leader, either out of such a crisis or in anticipation of one, with deep understanding of the new circumstances and a transcendent long-term vision, to help us find our way through the maze to a new kind of security.

There have been a few instances where farsighted national leaders have seen a long-term national goal and encouraged, coaxed, cajoled, or pushed the country in the direction of that goal. One thinks of the giants of American history who led the country to and through each of its major milestones: the Founders, of course, who started the country and began its expansion westward; Andrew Jackson, who brought to it a new level of democracy; James K. Polk, who, with methods that we would condemn today, led America to fulfill its manifest destiny, realizing Jefferson's dream of a nation stretching from the Atlantic to the Pacific; Abraham Lincoln, who kept the country from tearing itself apart; Theodore Roosevelt, who began what we would today call the environmental movement; Woodrow Wilson, Franklin Roo-

sevelt, and Harry Truman, who successively brought the United States out of its isolation and into the world community. Each of these steps toward the preeminent position the United States holds in the world today was accompanied by turmoil,
messy and wasteful of resources. The steps toward a new kind of security in the future world are likely to be no different.

What might be the dimensions of our new kind of security in that future world?
In Chapter 3 we noted that from about the year 1500 A.D. on the West spread its
civilization to the rest of the world and that the rest of the world has now absorbed
the artifacts of that civilization and has begun to reflect its power to use those artifacts back onto the West. During the preceding period of balance among the major
civilizations and power centers of the Eurasian world, from about 500 B.C. to 1500
A.D., there was a great ebb and flow of the influence and the areas of physical control
of each of them. However, none was strong enough to overcome and fully dominate
any of the others in all of its territory. The four civilizations thus maintained a rough
world balance of power and cultural influence for two millennia, until the rise of
Western technology and culture upset that balance by doing what couldn't be done
before by any of them—invading and imposing its culture on the others. Western
technology, including the technology of war, was part of that transfer.

Although the imposition of Western culture wasn't complete, as the four original
major groupings—Western, Middle Eastern, Indian, Chinese—still retain many of
their distinguishing characteristics, the adoption of Western technology, including
the technology of war, was more thorough. And though the other regional cultures
have yet to match the American and European (including Russian, before the Soviet
collapse) synthesis of technological, economic, and military strengths, they are moving in that direction. Japan has essentially arrived there in economic and technological power; China is fast approaching. At the same time, the joining of the technology
to the different cultures is creating new forms of economic expansion and of waging
war with which the West, and the United States as the strongest exponent of the
West, has yet to come to terms.

There have been additions to the four civilizations, vying for a place in the world
order, whatever it may come to be. They include the African nations, still searching
for connections to the modern world in their complex heritage and reaching for participation in the world economy. And they include all the "illicit" ones—the international criminal organizations. Historically, the possession and use of advanced military technology and the technique that goes with it have been a decisive element in
deciding how and whether one of the major power centers can overcome another, at
least from the time of Alexander, through the conquests of Rome, the cavalry of the
Eurasian steppes, and the European expansion. Because modern technology by its
very nature has now become globally available, and technology-based economic

strength has also diffused around the world, it appears unlikely that any one of the major regional or even global powers will be strong enough to dominate the others at any foreseeable future time.

This is the reason for anticipating the onset of a new period of balance in world affairs and relationships, as suggested in Chapter 3. There will be regional power centers, and some of them may follow the earlier example of the West to reach across the world and change it, as Japan has done economically in the second half of the twentieth century, and as we have done economically, politically, and militarily through most of that century. But America won't be able to dominate that world as, for example, the European colonial powers did in the nineteenth century. We will find ourselves able to exert influence, sometimes through economics, sometimes through cultural artifacts like music and fast food, sometimes through military force, and perhaps subtly but continuously by the moral example of our democratic freedoms with their good as well as their unhappy aspects.

Our security will depend on how effectively we can exert that influence without bringing the rest of the world down on us in those same domains—economic, military, moral. And that, in turn, will depend on all the factors, internal and external, that we have reviewed in this book, combining in ways that we cannot fully anticipate. Without a strong unifying force, it will take extraordinary leadership to see the nation through this new and baffling prospect. Even with such leadership, the adaptation process will probably be so diffuse that the results may be recognized only by a future generation of historians, as was, for example, the case with Harry Truman and the beginnings of the ultimately successful Cold War with the USSR. The leaders who can undertake the new strategic advance may or may not be among us as we enter the new century and millennium.

BIBLIOGRAPHY

Following are some of the books and papers that have contributed in some way to this work. To have listed all the books that helped shape the thoughts and the work, I would have had to list my entire library and much more. The books and the few other publications listed are all those to which the text refers in some way, as well as a few that are closely related and that I believe can shed additional light on some of the important topics I have discussed and opinions I have expressed in the book.

Acheson, Dean. 1969. *Present at the Creation*. New York: W.W. Norton.

Allen, Frederick Lewis. 1931. *Only Yesterday: The Fabulous Twenties*. New York: Harper and Brothers.

Braestrup, Peter. 1978. *Big Story: How the American Press and Television Reported and Interpreted the Crisis of Tet 1968 in Vietnam and Washington*. Garden City, New York: Anchor Press/Doubleday.

Bureau of the Census. 1974 and 1997. *Statistical Abstract of the United States*. Washington, D.C.: U.S. Government Printing Office. (For data continuity, years 1974 and 1997 were used).

Burrows, William E. 1986. *Deep Black: Space Espionage and National Security*. New York: Random House.

Bush, George, and Brent Scowcroft. 1998. *A World Transformed*. New York: Alfred A. Knopf.

Caidin, Martin. 1974. *The Tigers Are Burning: The Story of the Battle of Kursk*. New York: Hawthorn Books.

Campbell, Paul R. 1996. *Population Projections by Age, Sex, Race, and Hispanic Origin, 1995 to 2025*. Washington, D.C.: U.S. Bureau of the Census.

Chairman of the Joint Chiefs of Staff. 1997. *Joint Vision 2010*. Washington, D.C.: Office of the Joint Chiefs of Staff, The Pentagon.

Clausewitz, Carl von. 1832. *On War*. Transl. and with an Introduction by Anatol Rapoport, 1968. Great Britain: Penguin Books.

Cohen, William S., Secretary of Defense. 1997. *Report of the Quadrennial Defense Review*. Washington, D.C.: Department of Defense.

The Commission on America's National Interests. 1996. *America's National Interests*. Cambridge: Center for Science and International Affairs.

Cooper, Chester L. 1970. *The Lost Crusade: America in Vietnam*. New York: Dodd, Mead.

Conrad, Joseph. 1953 (orig. publ. 1907). *The Secret Agent*. New York: Doubleday Anchor Books.

de Solla Price, Derek J. 1963. *Little Science, Big Science*. New York: Columbia University Press. (Regarding social and economic phenomena and the logistics curve).

Defense Science Board. 1996. *Defense Outsourcing and Privatization*. Washington, D.C.: Office of the Secretary of Defense.

Deitchman, Seymour J. 1964. *Limited War and American Defense Policy*. Cambridge: The MIT Press.

_____. 1976. *The Best-Laid Schemes: A Tale of Social Research and Bureaucracy*. Cambridge: The MIT Press. (Esp. chaps. 11 and 14, on the press and Congress.)

_____. 1983. *Military Power and the Advance of Technology: General Purpose Military Forces for the 1980s and Beyond*. Boulder: Westview Press.

_____. 1991.*Beyond the Thaw: A New National Strategy*. Boulder: Westview Press.

Department of Defense. 1998. *Report of the Panel on Reducing Risk in Ballistic Missile Defense Flight Test Programs*. Washington, D.C.: Department of Defense.

DeVoto, Bernard. 1942. *The Year of Decision: 1846*. Boston: Houghton Mifflin.

Diamond, Jared. 1997. *Guns, Germs, and Steel: The Fates of Human Societies*. New York: W.W. Norton.

Fallows, James. 1996. *Breaking the News: How the Media Undermine American Democracy.* New York: Vintage Books.

Frank, Robert H., and Philip J. Cook. 1995. *The Winner-Take-All Society: How More and More Americans Compete for Ever Fewer and Bigger Prizes, Encouraging Economic Waste, Income Inequality, and an Impoverished Cultural Life*. New York: Free Press.

Goodpaster, Andrew J. 1993. *Further Reins on Nuclear Arms: Next Steps for the Major Nuclear Powers*. Washington, D.C.: The Atlantic Council of the United States.

Goodrich, L. Carrington. 1959. *A Short History of the Chinese People*. 3d ed. New York: Harper and Row.

Goodwin, Doris Kearns. 1995. *No Ordinary Time: Franklin and Eleanor Roosevelt—The Home Front in World War II*. New York: Simon and Schuster.

Gordon, Michael R., and General Bernard E. Trainor. 1995. *The Generals' War*. Boston: Little, Brown.

Greene, Graham. 1978. *The Human Factor*. New York: Simon and Schuster.

Guderian, Heinz. 1957. Abridged ed. *Panzer Leader*. New York: Ballantine Books.

Hardin, Garrett. 1985. *Managing the Commons*. New York: W.H. Freeman.

Heclo, Hugo. 1999. "Hyperdemocracy." *Wilson Quarterly* 23, no. 1 (Winter): 62–71.

Highet, Gilbert. 1950. *The Art of Teaching*. New York: Alfred A. Knopf.

Hughes, Thomas P. 1999. "The Secret Triumph of American Engineering." *Invention and Technology* 14, no. 3 (Winter): 56–63. (An Interview by Frederick Smoler).

Huxley, Aldous. 1932. *Brave New World*. New York: Doubleday.

Ikenberry, John G. 1999. "Why Export Democracy?" *Wilson Quarterly* 23, no. 2 (Spring): 56–65.

Jewkes, John, David Sawers, and Richard Stillerman. 1969. *The Sources of Invention*. New York: W.W. Norton.

Joint Chiefs of Staff. 1989. *Department of Defense Dictionary of Military and Associated Terms*. Joint Pub. 1-02. Washington, D.C.: U.S. Government Printing Office.

Keegan, John. 1982. *Six Armies in Normandy: From D-Day to the Liberation of Paris*. New York: The Viking Press.

_____. 1993. *A History of Warfare*. New York: Vintage Books.

Kennedy, Senator John F. 1955. *Profiles in Courage*. New York: Harper and Brothers.

Kennedy, Paul. 1987. *The Rise and Fall of the Great Powers*. New York: Random House.

Leckie, Robert. 1963. *Conflict: The History of the Korean War*. New York: G.P. Putnam's Sons.

Lomov, Col. Gen. M.A., ed. 1973. *The Revolution in Military Affairs*. Moscow: Transl. and publ. in the United States under the auspices of the U.S. Air Force.

Maddison, Angus. 1998. *Chinese Economic Performance in the Long Run*. Paris: Development Centre, Organization for Economic Cooperation and Development.

Mahan, Alfred Thayer. 1890. *The Influence of Sea Power Upon History, 1660–1783*. Boston: Little, Brown.

McCullough, David. 1992. *Truman*. New York: Simon and Schuster.

McNeill, William H. 1963. *The Rise of the West: A History of the Human Community*. Chicago: University of Chicago Press.

_____. 1982. *The Pursuit of Power: Technology, Armed Force, and Society Since A.D. 1000*. Chicago: University of Chicago Press.

_____. 1992. *The Global Condition: Conquerors, Catastrophe, and Community*. Princeton: Princeton University Press.

Moore, Lt. Gen. Harold G. (Ret.), and Joseph L. Galloway. 1992. *We Were Soldiers Once . . . and Young: Ia Drang Valley—The Battle That Changed the War in Vietnam*. New York: Random House.

Morison, Elting E. 1966. *Men, Machines, and Modern Times*. Cambridge: The MIT Press.

_____. 1974. *From Know-How to Nowhere: The Development of American Technology*. New York: Basic Books. (Esp. chap. 8, on the U.S. Navy.)

Morison, Samuel Elliot. 1963. *The Two Ocean War: A Short History of the United States Navy in the Second World War*. Boston: Little, Brown.

National Defense Panel. 1997. *Transforming Defense: National Security in the 21st Century*. Washington, D.C.: U.S. Government Printing Office.

Naval Studies Board, National Research Council. 1997. *Post–Cold War Conflict Deterrence*. Washington, D.C.: National Academy Press.

_____. 1997. *Technology for the United States Navy and Marine Corps, 2000–2035: Becoming a 21st-Century Force. Volume 1: Overview*. Washington, D.C.: National Academy Press.

Negroponte, Nicholas. 1996. *being digital*. New York: Vintage Books.

Orwell, George. 1949. *1984*. New York: Harcourt, Brace.

Pacey, Arnold. 1990. *Technology in the Western World*. Cambridge: The MIT Press.

Prange, Gordon W. 1981. *At Dawn We Slept: The Untold Story of Pearl Harbor*. New York: McGraw-Hill.

Richardson, Lewis F. 1960. *Statistics of Deadly Quarrels*. Ed. Quincy Wright and C.C. Lienau. Pittsburgh: The Boxwood Press; and Chicago: Quadrangle Books.

Sheehan, Neil. 1988. *A Bright Shining Lie: John Paul Vann and America in Vietnam*. New York: Vintage Books.

Snow, C. P. 1993 (orig. publ. 1959). *The Two Cultures*. Canto ed. with an Introduction by Stefan Collini. Cambridge: Cambridge University Press.

Sterling, Claire. 1981. *The Terror Network.* New York: Holt, Rinehart, and Winston, and Readers' Digest Press.

———. 1994. *Thieves' World.* New York: Simon and Schuster.

Stevenson, Harold W. 1992. "Learning From Asian Schools." *Scientific American* 267, no. 6 (December): 70–76.

Sun-tzu. *The Art of War.* 1963 (orig. ca. 500 B.C.). Trans. and with an Introduction by Samuel B. Griffith. Oxford: Clarendon Press.

Tenner, Edward. 1996. *Why Things Bite Back: Technology and the Revenge of Unintended Consequences.* New York: Alfred A. Knopf.

Toffler, Alvin, and Heidi Toffler. 1993. *War and Anti-War: Survival at the Dawn of the 21st Century.* Boston: Little, Brown.

Tuchman, Barbara W. 1958. *The Zimmermann Telegram.* New York: McMillan.

Turley, William S. 1986. *The Second Indochina War: A Short Political and Military History, 1954–1975.* Boulder: Westview Press.

The White House. 1994. *A National Security Strategy of Engagement and Enlargement.* Washington, D.C.: U.S. Government Printing Office.

Willoughby, Malcolm F. 1964. *Rum War at Sea.* Washington, D.C.: Treasury Department, U.S. Coast Guard, U.S. Government Printing Office.

Womac, James P., Daniel T. Jones, and Daniel Roos. 1990. *The Machine That Changed the World: The Story of Lean Production.* New York. Rawson Associates.

Wright, Gavin. 1986. *Old South, New South: Revolutions in the Southern Economy Since the Civil War.* New York: Basic Books.

Zimmerman, Warren. 1999 (rev. ed.; orig. publ. 1996). *Origins of a Catastrophe: Yugoslavia and Its Destroyers.* New York: Time Books/Random House.

INDEX

supersonic flight, 211
Sweden, 265

tactical air forces, 295
tactical aviation, 211, 226, 228, 229, 232,
    286, 291–293
Taiwan, 156
    and China, 5, 33, 71, 247
tanks, 203, 210, 220, 221, 228, 238, 265,
    289
    and military doctrine, 228
technological advances, scientific basis,
    136
technological innovation, 137
technological revolution of the 20th
    Century, 163
technology, 65, 69, 73, 133, 194, 231, 275,
    313
    and concentration of economic power,
        137–138
    education, 155, 163
    and environmental policy, 159
    and ethics, 163
    impact of, 65, 86, 102, 134–140, 159,
        164, 165, 317, 334
    mafias' use of, 100
    military-civilian transfer, 209, 212, 275
    and military timetables, 197
    and national missile defense, 160, 254
    and strategy, 276
    and terrorism, 95
terrorism, 93–95
    and conventional legality, 177
terrorist groups, 94
terrorist threat, 95
terrorists, 94
    fighting against, 96–98
theater missile defense. See ballistic missiles,
    defense against
tolerance
    in US attitudes, 130
Tomahawk, 211, 219, 222, 287

"tragedy of the commons," 119
transportation
    and economic power, 70
    impact of, 83
    technology, 95, 107, 134, 135, 317
    technology and criminal activity, 100
    technology, future use of, 324
    technology, impact of, 147, 158, 198
transportation networks, and logistic
    support, 215
Truman, President Harry, 82, 114, 134,
    148, 250, 271, 272, 334, 335
    Korean war constraint, 13
Turkey, 76, 82, 84, 124, 271, 283, 302,
    308, 312, 314
"two cultures," 157
    implications, 158–159
    joining to govern, 162
two-war strategy, 305–307
"tyranny of the single hit," 309

U.S. Air Force, 196, 199, 213, 218, 226,
    229, 230, 233, 234, 238, 239, 243,
    256, 290, 304
    and U.S. Army, 290
    and U.S. Navy, 286–287, 294
U.S. and Canada, implications of union,
    55
U.S. Army, 196, 199, 201, 213, 218, 229,
    230, 233, 238, 239, 290, 292, 294,
    304
    and U.S. Air Force, 290
    and U.S. Marine Corps, 290
U.S. Coast Guard, 269
U.S. Marine Corps, 196, 200, 215, 218,
    230, 237, 256, 289, 292
    and firepower from the sea, 288
    and U.S. Army, 290
    and U.S. Navy, 226, 233, 284, 287–288,
        293
U.S. military forces, designed for quick
    victories, 261